GOVERNANCE AND PUBLIC POLICY IN THE UNITED KINGDOM

GOVERNANCE AND PUBLIC POLICY IN THE UNITED KINGDOM

David Richards and
Martin J. Smith

OXFORD

UNIVERSITY PRESS

Great Clarendon Street, Oxford OX2 6DP

Oxford University Press is a department of the University of Oxford.
It furthers the University's objective of excellence in research, scholarship,
and education by publishing worldwide in

Oxford New York

Auckland Cape Town Dar es Salaam Hong Kong Karachi
Kuala Lumpur Madrid Melbourne Mexico City Nairobi
New Delhi Shanghai Taipei Toronto

With offices in

Argentina Austria Brazil Chile Czech Republic France Greece
Guatemala Hungary Italy Japan Poland Portugal Singapore
South Korea Switzerland Thailand Turkey Ukraine Vietnam

Oxford is a registered trade mark of Oxford University Press
in the UK and in certain other countries

Published in the United States
by Oxford University Press Inc., New York

© David Richards and Martin J. Smith 2002

The moral rights of the authors have been asserted

Database right Oxford University Press (maker)

First published 2002
Reprinted 2003, 2005, 2007

British Library Cataloguing in Publication Data

Data available

Library of Congress Cataloging in Publication Data

Data available

ISBN 978–0–19–924392–1

5 7 9 10 8 6 4

Typeset in Minion and Stone Sans
by RefineCatch Limited, Bungay, Suffolk
Printed in Great Britain by
Antony Rowe Ltd., Chippenham, Wiltshire

For our parents –
John and Ruth Richards
and Phil Smith

PREFACE

The origins of this project lie in our shared frustration at the absence of a textbook which manages to address the issue of the changing nature of the British state, its impact on the nature of power and how change, in the form of governance, has affected public policy-making in Britain. Both of us teach courses on governance at our respective universities, Liverpool and Sheffield, and we felt that, for the sake of our students or, to be truly honest, in order to make life easier for ourselves when teaching our students, we would collaborate to produce this textbook.

In the course of this project, we would first like to thank David Marsh (Birmingham) with whom, for the last five years, we have worked on two ESRC projects (award numbers L124251023 and R00022657) examining the changing nature of central government under both the last Conservative Administration and the present Labour Government. Dave will recognize his imprint on this book, although we refrained from revealing its content to him until it was finished, for fear that he would have told us: 'You don't want to do it like that, you want to do it like this'. We must also thank the numerous ministers, civil servants, pressure group representatives and various other individuals we have interviewed in the last few years. Their views have helped shape our understanding of the nature of policy-making in Britain today. We must also thank Rod Rhodes (Newcastle). He taught both of us when we were undergraduates at Essex University and, in his classes, he always challenged us to question his own views. Rod is one of the leading international authors in the field of governance and we hope that the views we have expressed here will bring a smile to his face – even though we know he will fiercely disagree with many of our arguments. We must also thank Dilys Hill (Southampton) who read through numerous manuscripts of the text and whose comments were always insightful and her attention to detail knew no bounds. We also appreciate the four anonymous referees for their helpful comments. Elsewhere, we would like to thank Ian Bache, Jim Buller, Matt Flinders, Francesca Gains, Andrew Geddes, Robert Geyer, Colin Hay, Dennis Kavanagh, Neil McGarvey and Matt Watson. Angela Griffin at Oxford University Press proved to be a first-rate, sympathetic and astute editor and we would like to acknowledge the effort both she and her support staff have provided at different stages throughout the writing process.

David Richards would like to thank Liverpool University for allowing him a sabbatical in 2000, which he spent as a Fellow at the Department of Politics, University of Sydney and in particular, Rod Tiffen and Martin Painter for being so welcoming and helpful. It was in this most conducive of environments that this book first took shape, despite the slight distraction of the Olympics. He would also like to thank the numerous friends in the Sydney suburb of Mosman, most notably: Willie Docherty, Nick Marlow, Nikki Reid, Travis, the Frosties, George and

Jane Heywood, Bubbles Grant and Jago Atkinson. He will never forget all those revealing moments shared together, when moored at Cobblers beach on board the good ship *Adele*!

Finally, our greatest debt of gratitude goes to both Emma and Jean for their continual support and tolerance during the course of writing this book.

David Richards
Martin J. Smith

December 2001

Contents

Detailed Contents

Boxes

TABLES

FIGURES

ABBREVIATIONS

ACAS	Advisory Conciliation and Arbitration Service
ACPO	Association of Chief Police Officers
APEC	Asia Pacific Economic Cooperation
ASEAN	Association of South East Asian Nations
BMA	British Medical Association
CAP	Common Agricultural Policy
CBI	Confederation of British Industry
COREPER	Committee of Permanent Representatives
CSR	comprehensive spending review
DEn	Department of Energy
DEFRA	Department of the Environment, Food and Rural Affairs
DETR	Department of the Environment, Transport and the Regions
DG	directorate-general (EU)
DoE	Department of the Environment
DSS	Department of Social Security
DTI	Department of Trade and Industry
ECB	European Central Bank
ECHR	European Convention on Human Rights
ECJ	European Court of Justice
EMU	Economic and Monetary Union
EP	European Parliament
ERM	Exchange Rate Mechanism
ESC	Economic and Social Committee (EU)
FCO	Foreign and Commonwealth Office
FDI	foreign direct investment
FMI	Financial Management Initiative
FOI	Freedom of Information
FPP	first-past-the-post
GATT	General Agreement on Tariffs and Trade
GDP	Gross Domestic Product
GMO	genetically modified organism
IEA	Institute of Economic Affairs
IGO	international governmental organization
IGR	inter-governmental relations
INGO	international non-governmental organization
IMF	International Monetary Fund

JAC	Joint Advisory Committee
JMU	Joint Management Unit
LEC	Local Employment Company
MAFF	Ministry of Agriculture, Fisheries and Food
MCA	Monetary Compensation Amounts
MINIS	Management Information System for Ministers
MLG	multi-level governance
MNC	Multi-national Corporation
MPC	Monetary Policy Committee
NAFTA	North American Free Trade Association
NDPB	non-departmental public bodies
NEB	National Enterprise Board
NEDC	National Economic Development Council
NFU	National Farmers' Union
NPM	New Public Management
NSM	new social movement
OECD	Organization for Economic Cooperation and Development
OPD(E)	Overseas and Defence Committee
OPEC	Organization of Petroleum Exporting Countries
OPS	Office of Public Service
PAR	Programme Analysis and Review
PESC	Public Expenditure Survey Committee
PFI	private finance initiative
PR	proportional representation
PWC	postwar consensus
QMV	qualified majority voting
SEA	Single European Act
SEM	Single European Market
SMR	senior management review
TEC	Training and Enterprise Council
TUC	Trades Union Congress
TGWU	Transport and General Workers Union
UKREP	United Kingdom Permanent Representation to the European Union
WTO	World Trade Organization

1   Introduction: Public Policy in a Changing World

Public policy in an era of change

In the last thirty years, the environment in which politics in the UK is conducted has undergone substantial change. Eighteen years of Conservative governments committed to reducing the role of the state, an increasing involvement in supranational organizations such as the European Union and the World Trade Organization (WTO) and, most recently, a Labour Government that has fundamentally altered the contours of the state through the devolving of powers away from Westminster to Edinburgh, Belfast, Cardiff, and a London Assembly have affected the nature of political power in Britain. The aim of this book is to explore this impact, and the effect these changes have had on the making of public policy in the UK.

But what is public policy? The word 'policy' is a general term used to describe a formal decision or plan of action adopted by an actor, be it an individual, organization, business, government, etc., in order to achieve a particular goal. 'Public policy' is a more specific term applied to a formal decision or a plan of action that has been taken by, or has involved, a state organization. Public policy can be analysed in a number of different ways. For example, one approach would be to analyse the link between aims, actions, and outcomes. Another would be to explore the inputs in the making of public policy, which may include the actors, resources and structures involved. Alternatively, one could explore the outputs of public policy and the impact on society, for example in the area of health, transport, or education policy. John (1998: 1) observes that in democratic states such as Britain, 'a multitude of public actions affect what governments do, and a host of public- and private-sector bodies seek to shape public decisions, much of which passes unnoticed by the media and the general public'. What we have set out to analyse in this book is how the nature of the state and the actors involved in the making of public policy have changed in recent times. In particular, we have set ourselves the task of considering whether or not forces in the shape of, for example, globalization and state fragmentation have undermined the ability of governments such as the Thatcher or Blair administrations to control and determine the making of public policy.

Public policy and governance

Any student who wishes to understand the way in which public policy in Britain is made today will soon discover that a term which constantly surfaces in the literature is 'governance'. Indeed, although relatively new, it is a term which has gained great currency in political science over the last decade. Part of its popularity stems from the multiplicity of definitions attached to it. Unfortunately, the diversity of the meaning of the term does little to help comprehension as to the nature of governance. So let us start with a formal definition:

> 'Governance' is a descriptive label that is used to highlight the changing nature of the policy process in recent decades. In particular, it sensitizes us to the ever-increasing variety of terrains and actors involved in the making of public policy. Thus, it demands that we consider all the actors and locations beyond the 'core executive' involved in the policy-making process.

As with any definition, unless applied to a real-world setting its meaning remains clouded in obscurity. So perhaps the easiest way of introducing governance to those unfamiliar with the term is to tell a story. Of course, as with all stories, the narrative is conditioned by what the authors believe is relevant to the plot. Thus, this is our story of 'governance'. It is certainly not the definitive or the only version. There are others. But we hope our version at least allows you to reflect on a key question in contemporary political science: to what extent has governance undermined the ability of central government, in particular ministers and civil servants, to make policy and control the policy arena?

We feel this is a significant question, as it is a crucial element of a larger theme which other authors writing on public policy frequently gloss over—the issue of power. Much of the literature on public policy has a tendency to address specific micro-themes concerning, for example, accountability, policy tools, actor relations, or the structure and nature of organizations. These issues are important, yet the attention they receive tends to lead to an oversight in addressing the important macro-theme of the nature of power in any political system. For us, questions relating to power are some of the most fundamental questions that a student of political science can address.

It is therefore our intention throughout this book not to ignore large macro-themes concerning the nature of power in the British political system. A fundamental challenge that the issue of governance presents to the making of public policy in the UK is to understand the extent to which traditional ideas concerning the power of government to control the policy-making arena have been undermined by a whole range of pressures, including globalization, internationalization, Europeanization, privatization, and agencification. By telling our story of governance, we hope to shed some light on the debate concerning the extent to which policy-making today is a result of forces beyond the control of the core executive.

A story of governance

An era of government

This story of governance can be told through a series of images of the British political system throughout the second half of the twentieth century. The first snapshot of the British polity is taken during the late 1940s and 1950s. It reveals that the then democratically elected governments of the day, be it Conservative or Labour, were seen as being in charge of the policy process. At the time, politics was regarded as being a relatively uncomplicated activity:

- A Government with a working majority in the House of Commons would decide on a particular policy, for example in the area of health, education, commerce, foreign affairs, defence, law and order.
- It would utilize the Civil Service in drafting a legislative bill.
- The Government would then ensure the safe passage of that bill through Parliament.
- It would then aim to ensure that the legislation was subsequently implemented.

As part of the process of preparing the bill, during the formative stages, the Government along with its civil servants would consult with a select number of key pressure groups with an interest in the proposed legislation. This picture broadly reflects what is referred to as the Westminster model (see Box 1.1).

The main point here is that the Government is regarded as the key, dominant actor in the policy arena. More broadly, this reflects values associated with what is often referred to as the 'modern state' (see Chapter 3)—this suggested that governments governed for the good of society, that they knew what they were doing, and that they knew how to do it and what the outcome of their actions would be. Governing was essentially a process of one-way traffic from those governing (the Government) to those being governed (society) (Kooiman 2000: 142). We can refer to this period after 1945 as an era of 'government' (see Fig. 1.1)

Box 1.1 **The Westminster model**

First, it is important to point out that there is no single definitive version of the Westminster model (see Birch 1964, Rhodes 1997, Smith 1999, Marsh et al. 2001). However, a number of key characteristics are agreed:

- parliamentary sovereignty
- accountability through free and fair elections
- majority party control over the executive
- strong cabinet government
- central government dominance
- doctrine of ministerial responsibility
- non-political civil servants

The model then suggests that, while the doctrine of parliamentary sovereignty underpins the institutions and processes of British politics, the way the system operates is based upon two linked characteristics of the British political system: (1) a first-past-the-post electoral system, which, while it holds the executive accountable at periodic free and fair elections, almost inevitably gives one party an overall majority; and (2) fairly tight party discipline, which together with the electoral system produces majority government, strong Cabinet government, and executive dominance of the legislature.

Implicit within this model is a particular view of the nature of power in the British political system. Power is regarded as sealed within the domain of Westminster. It is an elitist, hierarchical, top-down view, in which politics is a zero-sum game with the Prime Minister dominating ministers, ministers dominating civil servants, or central government dominating local government. It is intended to encapsulate the notion that it is the Government that governs in the interests of the nation and that power rests with the Government (see Chapter 3).

From an era of government to governance

However, if we take another snapshot of the British polity, some time in the mid-1980s, the picture we now look at is less clear. The focus is different and the image we have of the British political system has become more blurred. The policy arena has become visibly more crowded. There are more actors involved, the boundaries between the public and the private sphere are less precise, and the Government's command over the policy process is seen to have receded. Indeed, what we are now looking at we can refer to as a picture of 'governance'. Here, the images reflect the changing contours that the state has undergone in the latter half of the twentieth century. It is a picture which depicts a model of governance, in which the Government is only one actor (although a crucial one) among many others in the policy arena. Thus, it is argued that a shift has occurred from an era of government, in which governing was a top-down, hierarchical process, to an era of governance, in which governing has become a shared process of exchange and negotiation

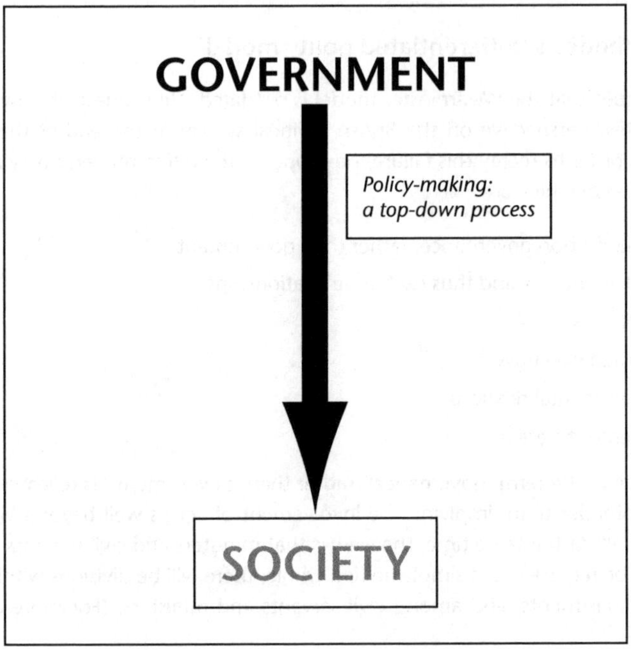

GOVERNMENT

Policy-making:
a top-down process

SOCIETY

Figure 1.1 Snapshot 1: the 1950s, an era of 'government'

involving a range of actors. In the same way that the Westminster model was seen to reflect an era of government, so Rhodes's (1997) 'differentiated polity model' is an attempt to reflect the era of governance (see Box 1.2).

Whereas the Westminster model implicitly suggests that the nature of power in the British political system is essentially top-down and elitist, the same is not true for the differentiated polity model. This model portrays an environment in which the Government is no longer dominant, but only one of many actors operating in the policy arena. The implicit view of power that this model presents is more pluralistic in nature. In particular, power is no longer always seen as a zero-sum game, but rather should be understood as an exchange relationship between the actors within the policy process. For example: ministers need civil servants to win resources for the department; civil servants need ministers to successfully defend the departmental line in Cabinet; a department might rely on a particular pressure group in order to ensure policy legitimation; a Government may rely on particular allies in Brussels, in order to further its own European interests. Power for Rhodes is much more appropriately understood as (often) a positive-sum game between those involved in the policy process.

In an era of governance, our snapshot of the British political system is markedly different to that of the previous era of government. The characteristics associated with the modern state have been eroded, leading a number of commentators to speak of a 'postmodern state' (see Chapter 2). The notion here is that, where before Government knew what it was doing and had the capacity to achieve its

> ## Box 1.2 Rhodes's 'differentiated polity model'
>
> Rhodes argues that the Westminster model is outdated. He suggests it provides a mis-representative perspective on the British political system at the end of the twentieth century. In order to rectify this failure, he proposes the differentiated polity model, the main features of which are:
>
> - an emphasis upon governance, rather than government
> - power dependence, and thus exchange relationships
> - policy networks
> - a segmented executive
> - intergovernmental relations
> - a hollowed-out state
>
> The very use of the term 'governance', rather than 'government', is revealing: 'govern-ance' is a broader term, implying the involvement of actors well beyond Westminster and Whitehall. At the same time, the view is that ministers and civil servants should not necessarily be regarded as a simple unified whole; there will be divisions within Cabinet, between departments, and among civil servants and ministers. (For more details, see Chapter 2)

specified goals, now there is uncertainty and a recognition that Government has lost the ability to control and shape both policy and society. Instead, Governments have to operate in a diverse, fragmented, complex, and decentralized environment. There now exist many different types of policy network within the policy arena, competing discourses on what constitutes the 'public good', and a need for reflex-ivity on the part of the numerous actors involved in the policy process, in order to make a semblance of sense in an ever-changing world (see Fig. 1.2).

From an era of governance to joined-up government?

Finally, we look at a third snapshot, taken after the re-election of the Labour Government in June 2001. The tentative label we attach to this snapshot is 'joined-up government'. Here, the image being depicted is that of the Labour Government attempting to resolve one of the key challenges presented by governance: the inability of elected governments to control and coordinate policy across all of Whitehall. The notion is that as the policy arena has become a more crowded environment with numerous actors competing for political space, so the Govern-ment's ability to maintain some semblance of control has been curtailed. The argument is that the policy process has evolved in such a way that policy is developed in a more isolated, segmented manner. This can be referred to as the 'pathology of departmentalism'. For example, policy may be developed in one area

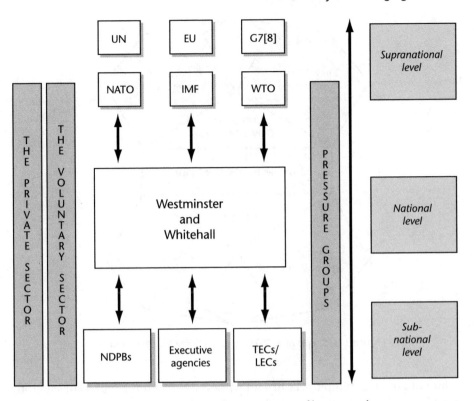

Figure 1.2 Snapshot 2: the 1980s, an era of 'governance'

without taking account of the unintended or unforeseen impact such a policy may have in other parts of the policy-making arena. In opposition, New Labour recognized that at a general level, government was seen as having lost the ability to operate in a single, unified, coordinated manner across the whole policy spectrum (see Mandelson and Liddell 1996). Since 1997, the response of the Labour Government has been to try and wire the system back up. This is an attempt to bring together the many, often disparate elements that constitute the policy arena. Thus, the present Labour Government's antidote to departmentalism is 'joined-up government', based on a model of strong central control from Number 10 and the Cabinet Office (see Fig. 1.3).

The story of joined-up government remains unfinished, as it is a process that will take a number of years to complete. Indeed, one possible conclusion may be that joined-up or holistic government is impossible to achieve within the context of the existing parliamentary system. As the example in Box 1.3 demonstrates, political reality can render the delivery of joined-up government an almost impossible task.

However, the notion of joined-up government does present a number of interesting challenges. If this programme of reform is intended to ensure that ministers once again regain control of the policy process, what are the implications for the

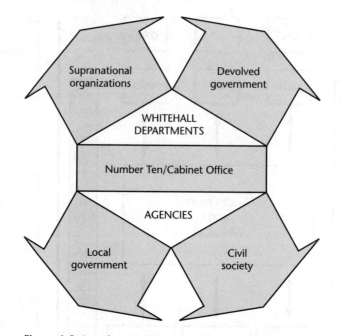

Figure 1.3 Snapshot 3: 2001, an era of 'joined-up government'?

nature of power in future? Will Britain witness a shift from a pluralistic environment, as portrayed by the era of governance, to one in which the core executive once more controls the policy arena in a top-down, elitist manner? Alternatively, are the forces of governance such that joined-up government is simply an unattainable goal?

The story of governance: a summary

Part I: The story starts by arguing that there was a time when governing was a relatively straightforward and clear-cut process. Government made policy and was by far the most dominant actor in the policy arena.

Part II contends that over time, the arena in which policy was made became increasingly cluttered, as more actors became involved and new pressures such as globalization altered the environment in which governments operated. As a result, there occurred a shift from government to governance, where the Government was only one among a multitude of actors involved in the policy process.

Part III: The key problem stemming from this new era of governance was that governments were seen to have less control or, *in extremis*, to have lost control over the policy process. Thus, the response from the Labour Government after 1997 has been to attempt to re-establish control in the policy arena by wiring the disparate parts of the policy process back together. The label attached to their approach is 'joined-up government'.

Box 1.3 **New Labour, foot-and-mouth, and the failure of joined-up government**

On 19 February 2001, the Ministry of Agriculture, Fisheries, and Food was informed that a single case of foot-and-mouth had been detected, a disease feared by generations of British farmers. The lesson of the last outbreak of foot-and-mouth in 1967 was that an instant response was essential to stop the spread of the disease. But, the Labour Government failed to react for three days, after which it introduced a ban on the movement of livestock within Britain. By this point, further cases had been identified, from Northumberland to Devon. The policy options facing the Government came down to two broad choices: culling—a policy for eradicating the virus pursued by Whitehall since the 1920s—or vaccination—the policy option which had been successfully adopted by the Dutch Government, in order swiftly to eradicate a recent outbreak of the disease in Holland. The power of the farming lobby, voiced through the National Farmers' Union, who for decades had enjoyed insider status within MAFF, prompted the Government to adopt the culling option. This was the preferred option of the NFU, in order to ensure that the powerful agribusiness farmers in their union could maintain 'disease-free' status and so protect their highly profitable meat export market.

Agriculture was not the only industry to be seriously affected by the spread of foot-and-mouth. Tourism, an industry that annually generates twenty times the income of agriculture was also severely hit, as were (to a lesser extent) parts of the food, road haulage, sports, and retail industries. The outbreak coincided with the lead-up to the impending general election, which meant, initially, that neither Number Ten nor the Cabinet Office gave the issue the attention it warranted. Furthermore, the clashes between the interests of the farming lobby, represented in Government by MAFF and the more diffuse and disparate interests of the tourism lobby, as represented by the cumbersome Department of Environment, Transport, and the Regions, ensured that a battle royal commenced within Whitehall. Each department automatically slipped into the role of defending its own sector's interests, rather than considering the larger picture. The pathology of departmentalism was undermining any possibility of a coordinated response to the foot-and-mouth crisis from Whitehall. To compound the issue, MAFF failed to draw on the experience of the 1967 outbreak, in which the subsequent report had recommended that the army should be called in immediately to provide logistical support. As Rawnsley (2001: 468) perceptively observes: 'The Ministry of Defence was wary of getting involved; the Ministry of Agriculture didn't ask for assistance, fearing what civil servants characterized as "military occupation". This mocked New Labour's promises of joined-up-government.'

Although our story of governance appears relatively straightforward, as with all stories there is more to it than meets the eye. First, it is important to acknowledge that although the governance narrative presented here is set out in three clear parts, the reality is that there is no distinct temporal break between each of our three snapshots—government, governance and joined-up government. The reality is there is a great deal of fuzziness and overlap. Elsewhere, our simple series of snapshots of the British polity over time leave many questions unanswered:

- Is it actually the case that policy-making was a simple, uncomplicated, top-down, hierarchical process during the 1950s?
- How and why did the policy arena become much more complex by the 1980s?
- To what extent has central government actually lost the ability to control policy-making during the era of 'governance'?
- Will 'joined-up government' be an effective solution to the pressures brought about by governance, or will it further exacerbate the existing tensions in the British political system?

The structure of the book

The key concept underpinning this book is governance. In Chapter 2 we examine the concept of governance as a new framework for understanding the operations of the policy process. Here, we highlight how governance is a description of a new state form. We evaluate the different definitions of governance and demonstrate how it can be used as an alternative organizng perspective to the Westminster model. The central discussion of the chapter is the way in which the state has been hollowed out from above and within, leading to multi-level governance. It concludes by asking whether this has created a postmodern state, and whether governance provides a better model for understanding the policy process.

If governance has become the new, dominant theme permeating contemporary thinking on public policy, it can only be understood in relation to what went before. Chapter 3 therefore looks at the traditional, orthodox accounts of the modern state, examining how it developed, its key features particularly the role of bureaucracy, attempts at state planning, and the importance of territoriality. The main questions of the chapter will be: have these themes ever accurately reflected the true nature of the state, and what were the implications for the analysis of public policy?

Having established two competing perspectives of the British state, Chapter 4 examines the rise and fall of the Keynesian welfare state as a 'modernist' project during the three decades after 1945. It will look at the extent to which this per-ceived era of collectivist government broke down from the late 1950s onwards and ask why. It will examine the idea that by the 1970s, the notion of ungovernability had gained currency and led to a debate concerning the functioning of the state—commonly referred to as the 'overload thesis'. The chapter will conclude by analys-ing the effectiveness of this thesis in delegitimizing the Keynesian welfare state as a political project and in so doing creating a political vacuum which an alternative project, subsequently referred to as 'Thatcherism', came to fill.

Chapter 5 looks at how the perceived crisis of the state during the 1970s led to the development of a New Right critique of the status quo. This chapter will examine the growth of the New Right and its success in filling the political vacuum left by the loss of faith in the Keynesian welfare model. It will examine New Right theoretical accounts of the nature of bureaucracy. The chapter will then look at how the New Right influenced the Conservative Administration on state reform after 1979, and the subsequent programme of reform which was labelled the 'New Public Management' (NPM); assess the actual impact of NPM on the making of public policy; and conclude by asking whether NPM led to an internal 'hollowing-out' of the state and a paradigmatic shift in public administration.

Having looked at the internal challenges to the modern state, we now turn to the external challenges. In Chapter 6 we analyse the impact of globalization on the domestic policy process. We outline the various elements of this process—economic, cultural, and political—and then examine the debate on globalization between the hyper-globalists and the sceptics. The chapter evaluates the changing pattern of global economics and the development of transnational political organizations. It looks at the way in which transnational forces penetrated the state and the impact that this has had on the policy-making process. The main focus of the chapter will be the way that the state has become involved in transnational policy-making and how the state has reacted to the pressures of globalization.

In Chapter 7 we go on to examine the notion of Europeanization and regionalism. We suggest that the EU is the most advanced form of regionalism in the world. The main focus of the chapter will be on the Europeanization of the domestic policy process. The chapter will use three case studies—agriculture, regional policy, and industrial policy—to highlight the varying levels of Europeanization and the differing patterns of governance that have developed.

In Chapter 8 we focus on the actors within civil society. Increasingly, government is seen to be relying on civil society to deliver public goods. This development changes the relationship between non-governmental organizations (NGOs) and the various tiers of government. Following the Conservative Administration's rejection of corporatism after 1979, this chapter questions the extent to which NGOs, often referred to as pressure groups, were frozen out of the policy process, and assesses whether the reality of government ensured that NGOs maintained a key role. It then questions whether Labour's vision of civil society has led to greater pluralism in the policy process. In particular, we ask whether, under New Labour, the perceived greater involvement of civil society in the policy-making process may result in pluralistic stagnation.

Chapter 9 examines the potential impact of governance on ministers and civil servants. We argue that, traditionally, ministers have been regarded as the central site of political authority and perceived as the key actors in determining policy outcomes. This chapter assesses the extent to which internal and external challenges have affected their decision-making autonomy and forced them to develop alternative networks in order to achieve their policy goals. Similarly, notions of governance suggest that the role of civil servants in both developing and delivering policy and services has diminished. In particular, it has been argued that ministers now use alternative sources of advice, such as think tanks, consultants, and special advisers, for developing policy. We assess the extent to which the reforms of government have undermined the traditional role of the Civil Service and altered its constitutional position. It concludes by asking whether the Whitehall paradigm is now simply a myth.

In Chapter 10, our attention turns to the most recent changes in the nature of the state, in particular the moves under New Labour towards constitutional reform, the reshaping of the state, and attempts to achieve joined-up government. We analyse the way in which Labour's reform programme has resulted in a transfer of power of some decision-making to a local and regional level. This chapter examines the explosion in non-national state organizations and the effect of devolution and regionalism, and assesses the impact this has had on policy outcomes both locally and nationally. Finally, we focus on Labour's attempts to wire the system back up as a response to the problems associated with governance. Here, we will suggest that, paradoxically, Labour's record in office has accelerated the process of state fragmentation rather than enhancing any notion of greater 'joined-upness'.

In Chapter 11 we look at public policy in a changing world and assess the nature of the modern state in Britain. In particular, we consider whether new modes of governance have developed which mean that the central state 'steers rather than rows' and is thus just one actor among many in determining policy and delivering public goods. The chapter reviews the various forms of delivery that exist, and examines how often contradictory forms coexist. It will also evaluate the degree to which state control has declined, and look at the various new forms of state control that have developed. We suggest that the state is increasingly intervening indirectly through surveillance and incentive structures, rather than directly, through state administrative machinery. Finally, the book concludes by challenging the idea that fragmentation and hollowing-out has led to a postmodern state.

2

INTERPRETING GOVERNANCE

INTRODUCTION

Less than forty years ago, it was widely accepted that government possessed the political power to control or provide direction to society where and when it so chose. Indeed, this notion was reflected in a key normative, though rarely stated, element of the Westminster model: that the loci of political power in Britain centred on Westminster and Whitehall. Within this context, the British model of government implicitly espoused the view that 'government knows best'. This in turn reinforced the notion of Britain as a strong, unitary state in which the power invested in its governments remained largely unfettered.

In the last thirty years, the capacity of the state to control or direct society and the extent to which the institutions of central government retain a monopoly on political power have become a much more contested issue. Changing relationships between the state and society have brought into question the extent to which Britain is, or ever was, a strong unitary state. In response, governance has become the established concept within political science which is used to portray the changing nature of the state in recent times. Pierre and Peters (2000: 1) argue that the popularity of the concept of governance stems from 'its capacity—unlike that of the narrower term "government"—to cover the whole range of institutions and relationships involved in the process of governing'. Elsewhere, Heywood (2000: 19) defines governance as: 'a broader term than "government". It refers, in its widest sense, to the various ways through which social life is coordinated'.

This chapter examines the concept of governance. It considers the theoretical context in which governance is used, examines a number of definitions of the term, and then looks more specifically at the application of the concept of governance to the British state. The chapter then focuses on Rhodes's (1997) idea of a 'differentiated polity model', as a way of understanding the changes in the nature of governance. Finally, we address one of the key theoretical debates surrounding the issue of governance: whether or not the changes identified by the concept of governance imply that Britain should now be regarded as a postmodern state.

What is governance?

The term 'governance' is not new. Weller (2000) points out that the first Lancastrian king of England, Henry IV, used the term in justifying his usurpation of the throne in 1399, declaring that 'Default of governance and undoying of the gode lawes' (Myers 1952: 21; cf. Weller 2000: 1) was the failing of his predecessors. As Weller (2000: 1) observes: 'The demand for good governance has a long history.' Pierre and Peters (2000: 1) also note that the word was used in fourteenth-century France to refer to officers of the royal court. More recently, the former Labour Prime Minister Harold Wilson provided an insider's view of the craft of governing in *The Governance of Britain* (1976). In none of these cases was the term invested with the same meaning as is currently attached to it. Governance today is a concept which tries to make sense of the changing nature of the state in the last thirty years. The term stems from the notion that we now live in a 'centreless society'. It is a reaction against those who continue to conceive of the state as being monocentric or based on unitary government. The main contention associated with the concept of governance is the recognition that there is not one but many centres of power which link together a whole variety of state actors, be they at the local, regional, national, or supranational level.

In broadest terms, governance has been suggested as a way of conceptualizing the many new forms of government embraced not just by Britain, but by many other liberal democratic states, such as Australia, Sweden, Denmark, Holland, the USA, New Zealand, and Canada. Governance is often portrayed as the combination of New Right reforms, aimed at rolling back the state, with globalization, internationalization, managerialism in the public sector, and privatization. It is argued that a product of these changes has been the loss of sovereignty for central government and the breakdown of the nation-state. So the term 'governance' refers to a change in understanding of what the process of governing is and refers to a new way in which society is now governed. This has led to a whole series of questions surrounding the legitimacy and accountability of present day governing structures. As Pierre (2000: 2) observes:

[T]he overarching question is what significance or meaning remains of the liberal-democratic notion of the state as the undisputed centre of political power and its self-evident monopoly of articulating and pursuing the collective interest in an era of 'economic' globalization, a hollowing out of the state, decreasing legitimacy for collective solutions, and a marketisation of the state itself. Is it the decline of the state we are witnessing, or is it the transformation of the state to the new types of challenges it is facing at the turn of the millennium?

Unfortunately, one of the problems in trying to address these fundamental questions is that governance has become a much-contested concept. Both academics and practitioners employ a variety of interpretations when using the term. Even within the more limited confines of political science, academics have applied the concept of governance to a whole range of sub-fields within the discipline—comparative, economic, societal and regional politics, public administration, and democracy (see Pierre 2000). In the process, the term has had a diverse range of meanings attached to it. For students acquainting themselves with the concept of governance for the first time, this can often lead to a degree of incomprehension and misunderstanding.

In order to make sense of this confusion, we would argue that at a primary level the term should be understood as a concept that reflects the shifting patterns of the state over the last thirty years, from an era of 'government' to a new era of 'governance'. 'Government' is seen to reflect an epoch when, in Kooiman's (2000: 142) terms, 'Governing was basically regarded as one-way traffic from those governing to those governed.' In recent times, as the number of actors in the policy arena have multiplied, the boundaries between the public and the private sector have become more blurred and central government's command over a more complex policy process has receded. Weller (2000) avers that governance centres on the issue of power, and so advocates the definition proposed by the World Bank: 'Governance is the exercise of political power to manage a nation's affairs' (Weller 2000: 3, World Bank 1992). Although helpful, this definition does not fully capture the different levels in which governance should be understood. For example, it can be argued that a 'two-way model' of governance has developed. This leads us to our formal definition, set out in Chapter 1:

> 'Governance' is a descriptive label that is used to highlight the changing nature of the policy process in recent decades. In particular, it sensitizes us to the ever-increasing variety of terrains and actors involved in the making of public policy. Thus, governance demands that we consider all the actors and locations beyond the 'core executive' involved in the policy-making process.

One of the fundamental questions we address throughout this book is whether or not there has been a shift from government to governance or, alternatively, whether governance is a discursive construction, adopted by those wishing to advocate the primacy of markets and extol the virtues of a minimum state. In order to address this question, it is helpful to refer to two different approaches to governance observed by Peters (2000) and Pierre and Peters (2000). The first, labelled 'old' or 'traditional' governance, refers to a state-centric approach concerned with 'identifying the capacity of the centre of government to exert control over the rest of government and over the economy and society'. 'New' or 'modern' governance, on the other hand, questions 'how the centre of government interacts with society to reach mutually acceptable decisions, or whether society actually does more self-steering rather than depending upon guidance from government, especially government' (Peters 2000: 36).

Of course, traditional and modern governance, and the questions they each pose, are not mutually exclusive. Throughout this book we will implicitly address both approaches. However, we have chosen to adopt a predominantly state-centric focus which emphasizes a traditional governance approach. This is because, as political scientists, our main concern is to explore the nature of power, in this case within the British political system. Here, we are interested in assessing the extent to which central government retains the capacity (power) to either (i) 'steer' or (ii) control society and the economy through 'political brokerage and by defining goals and making priorities' (Pierre 2000: 3).

Governance and the British state

A number of political scientists have set about addressing the impact that governance has had on the British state and the extent to which governance has incapacitated central government (see Pollitt 1990, Campbell and Wilson 1995, Foster and Plowden 1996, Rhodes 1997). One of the more influential writers in this area, Rhodes (1997), argues that governance can take seven different forms, while Stoker (1998) claims that there are five forms. We have already seen that Pierre and Peters (2000) have distinguished two different forms of governance. It is this very multiplicity in defining the concept of governance that has led to confusion, misunderstanding, and inappropriate application of the term. The definition we have provided above aims to encapsulate the broad sentiments of what most authors mean by governance, while at the same time providing an easy, comprehensible, and accessible explanation of the term. Box. 2.1 provides a summary of the various definitions of governance by some of the key political scientists working in this field.

Despite the multiplicity of definitions attached to the term 'governance', Rhodes (1997: 15, 2000: 55) correctly points out that the concept sensitizes us to 'a new process of governing; or a changed condition of ordered rule; or the new method by which society is governed' (cf. Finer, 1970: 3-4). This is a useful starting point for understanding what is meant by the concept of governance. Similarly, Pierre and Peters (2000: 1) claim that 'the recent popularity of this concept is its capacity—unlike that of the narrower term of "government"—to cover the whole range of institutions and relationships involved in the process of governing'.

What all the authors in Box 2.1 touch upon is the complexity involved in the many new forms of government, as a result of the fragmentation in recent years of traditional, centralized state apparatus. This trend is not confined to Britain alone. As Weller (2000: 1) observes, 'While western democracy is seen to have triumphed over communism and state socialism, the Australian state, along with similar OECD nations, has experienced some loss of confidence and authority since the reputed "golden age" of the 1950s and 1960s.' The point here is that nowadays governing is not confined to the nation-state, but can involve a range of institutions, both public and private, from the supranational to the national and local levels. Here, the suggestion is that governance is no longer about command, a key characteristic of the Weberian bureaucratic state (see Chapter 3), but is instead concerned with control. This is derived from an analogy offered by two influential

Box 2.1 Definitions of governance

Rhodes (1997)

One of the leading authors in this field, Rhodes argues that governance refers to a 'new process of governing'. He then notes that the multiplicity of meanings attached to governance is problematic, before suggesting that in the British case, 'Governance refers to self-organising, interorganisational networks characterised by interdependence, resource exchange, rules of the game and significant autonomy from the state' (p. 15). Rhodes then identifies six separate uses of governance: the minimal state; corporate governance; new public management; 'good governance'; a socio-cybernetic system; and a self-organizing network.

Pierre (2000: 3)

Another leading author on governance, the Swedish political scientist Jon Pierre argues that the concept has a dual meaning: 'On the one hand it refers to the empirical manifestations of the state's adaptation to its external environment as it emerges in the late twentieth century. On the other hand, governance also denotes a conceptual or theoretical representation of co-ordination of social systems and, for the most part, the role of the state in that process.'

Pierre and Peters (2000)

Elsewhere, Pierre has collaborated with the eminent US political scientist Guy Peters. In their work on governance, they suggest that historically, four common governance arrangements have existed: hierarchies, markets, networks and communities. They then suggest that governance concerns the process of steering and coordination, but make a distinction between the use of the term in Europe, in which it refers to 'new governance' ideas of the involvement of society in the process of governing, and in the USA, where it refers much more to the concept of steering.

Rosenau (1992, 2000: 171)

Another US political scientist, Rosenau's specialism is international relations. He therefore focuses on what he refers to as global governance, and adopts a perspective that 'allows for governance occurring apart from what governments do, here governance is conceived as systems of rules, as the purposive activities of any collectivity that sustain mechanisms designed to insure its safety, prosperity, coherence, stability, and continuance'.

Gamble (2000b, 2000c, 111)

The British political scientist Andrew Gamble has predominantly concentrated on the relationship between governance and the economy. One of his arguments is that many of the governance mechanisms on which global markets rely upon are organized and sustained by nation-states. Thus Gamble urges caution in an age in which many are rushing to embrace ideas associated with globalization. More particularly, he defines governance as denoting 'the steering capacities of a political system, the ways in which governing is carried out, without making any assumption as to which institutions or agents do the steering'.

Kooiman (1993, 2000)

This Dutch political scientist is well known within the field of public administration, and his work concentrates on the relationship between government and society. He suggests that the governance of modern societies is a blend of all kinds of governing levels, modes, and orders. Kooiman argues that social-political governance implies 'arrangements in which public as well as private actors aim at solving problems or create societal opportunities, and aim at the care for the societal institutions within which these governing activities take place' (2000: 139).

World Bank (1992) (see also Davis and Keating 2000: 3)

The World Bank adopts a simply expressed definition of governance, suggesting that it refers to 'the exercise of political power to manage a nation's affairs'. It then suggests that good governance is based on an efficient public service; an independent judicial system; the accountable administration of public funds; an independent public auditor, responsible to a representative legislature; respect for law and human rights; a pluralistic institutional structure; and a free press.

New Right US commentators, Osborne and Gaebler (1992), who argue that the role of government should be to 'steer not row'. The central theme of their thesis is that for too long government has focused on extensive state control of all aspects of social life, leading to an ever-expanding state sector, bureaucratic growth, inertia, and inefficiency. Osborne and Gaebler claim that the Weberian model of bureaucracy has become a 'bankrupt' tool for rowing. Instead, they argue (1992: 19-20) that the old model should be replaced by 'entrepreneurial government' based on ten principles:

entrepreneurial governments promote competition (1) between service providers. They empower citizens (2) by pushing control out of the bureaucracy, into the community. They measure the performance of their agencies, focusing not on inputs but on outcomes (3). They are driven by their goals—by their missions (4)—not by their rules and regulations. They redefine their clients as customers (5) and offer them choices . . . They prevent problems (6) before they emerge, rather than simply offering services afterwards. They put their energies into earning money (7), not simply spending it. They decentralize authority (8), embracing participatory management. They prefer market mechanisms (9) to bureaucratic mechanisms. And they focus not simply on providing public services, but on catalysing all sectors (10)—public, private and voluntary—into action to solve their community's problems.

The essence of entrepreneurial government is that the state should radically withdraw from government (less rowing) and instead should concentrate much more on governance (more steering). By this, it is meant that government should take responsibility for controlling policy management, leaving service delivery, i.e. how the policies are implemented or delivered, to other actors, especially (where possible) the private sector. This, they argue, would allow governments a more efficient and effective role in 'steering not rowing' the whole economy, social policy, law and order, etc.

Elsewhere, Rhodes (1996: 667) suggests that the concept of governance assists us, as students of political science, to understand the change in British government in the last quarter of the twentieth century. In particular, it helps to comprehend the blurring or even the dislocation that has affected the boundaries between the state and civil society.

The state becomes a collection of inter-organizational networks made up of governmental and societal actors with no sovereign actor being able to steer or regulate . . . A key challenge for government is to enable these networks and to see out new forms of co-operation.

In effect, what Rhodes is here evoking is an analogy of government 'steering not rowing', and the above quote is a plea that the Government should act as a capable navigator in a state that has become fragmented. This has led to the advancement of a new role for the state, one which rejects the traditional model of state control and replaces it by the creation of an 'enabling state'. Again, the politics of many of those who advocate this position needs to be recognized, for the logic of this position is that it prescribes a minimum state, a position more closely associated with neo-liberals on the right of the political spectrum than with the more interventionist position of social democracy and socialism on the (centre) left of the political spectrum, which prescribes a more active role for the state.

So far, we have established that the concept of governance has a multiplicity of meanings attached to it. At its primary level, it sensitizes us to the numerous actors, the variety of terrains, and the different relationships involved in the process of governing. Moreover, it implies that the traditional role of central government has in recent times been curtailed to the extent that government is now only one actor among many in the policy-making process. Thus, at the heart of the debate on governance is a tacit acceptance that the process of governing today involves a much more pluralistic conceptualization of power. Put another way, power has been dispersed away from the traditional central-state actors to many different and new arenas and now includes many, often new, actors within the political system. Within the British context, the concept of governance tends towards a position in which the Westminster model is no longer sustainable (see Chapter 3).

In order to take account of the changing nature of the British state in the last thirty years and to recognize that the terrain in which politics is conducted has become much more diverse and complex, Rhodes has provided his own organizing perspective on the British political system—the 'differentiated polity model'.

The differentiated polity model

A problem facing political scientists has been to try and capture both the diverse nature and complex characteristics of the present-day British political system. Rhodes's (1997) differentiated polity model is one of the most sophisticated attempts at providing a contemporary organizing perspective on the British system of government. He argues (1997: 7) that:

A 'differentiated polity' is characterised by functional and institutional specialisation and the fragmentation of policies and politics . . . This perspective is only one possible interpretation of British government, but it has three advantages. First, it identifies important weaknesses in the Westminster model. Second, it poses distinctive questions about British government. Third, it explains key problems confronting policy-making and implementation in the 1980s and 1990s.

The key characteristics of the differentiated polity are: governance; intergovernmental relations; a segmented executive; policy networks; power dependence; and a hollowed-out state. In the next section, we examine each of these characteristics.

Governance

For Rhodes, the key to conceptualizing governance is to think in terms of 'governing without government' (Rhodes 1997, Heywood 2000). Since the 1970s, the role of the state is seen to have altered to one where it now steers not rows. An expression that is often applied to this transformation is 'the enabling state'. This implies that the role of government should be to create the conditions in which other organizations, most notably those located in the private sector, can prosper. An enabling state can be seen as a direct reaction to the notion of 'big government', in which the state adopts an omnipotent role in all spheres of society. This was a strategy pursued by the Conservative Administration in 1979-97, with its attack on public-sector waste, inefficiency, and size, and the advocacy of markets to create greater choice. Alongside this, the role of the state has shifted from the corporatist model of mediating between labour and capital associated with the 1970s towards one which now mediates between the interests of consumers and producers at the sub-national, national, and international levels (see Saunders 1985, Cawson 1986). A clear example of a government pursuing such a strategy was the 1991 Citizens' Charter implemented by the Major Government, subsequently re-titled 'Service First' under the 1997 Labour Government. When, in subsequent chapters, we look in greater detail at the changing nature of the British state, what we will emphasize is that the approach of recent governments has been to adopt a strategy of 'more control over less'.

Inter-governmental relations

Rhodes suggests that the notion of inter-governmental relations (IGRs) is a helpful concept, as it sensitizes us to the interaction between all the various state actors. He contends that IGRs cover all public-sector organizations, including Westminster, Whitehall, the European Union, local government, quangos, agencies, regulatory authorities (Ofwat, Ofgas, etc.): 'the term not only draws attention to the range of governmental organizations involved in service delivery but also to the increasing influence of the European Union [EU] on UK policy-making' (Rhodes 1997: 7).

An important feature associated with inter-governmental relations is that of 'imbrication'. This is a term coined by Cerny (1990) to reflect the process by which the public, voluntary, and private sectors, their organizations, interests, and environments have become interlocked, interpenetrated, and intertwined to the extent that the capacity of the state to isolate and demarcate itself is clearly bounded. As Cerny (1990: 188) observes: 'the development of modern society and the structuration of the state . . . have involved a complex expansion and intertwining of both the public and the private sphere, with the growth of each enabling the other to grow too.'

A segmented executive

It has long been a criticism of British central government that the departmental structure creates policy 'chimneys' in which policy is developed within a department without consideration being given to the possibility that a policy initiative in one area may have unforeseen or unintended consequences elsewhere. In effect, the departmental structure conditions policy-makers to think vertically, within the confines of their own specific policy area, rather than horizontally on the impact of an issue across other policy areas in Whitehall. From another perspective, the issue of policy 'chimneys' is exacerbated by the pathology of departmentalism (see Box 2.2).

The concept of policy chimneys, combined with the pathology of departmentalism, portrays departments as forwarding their own interests, regards relations with other departments in terms of a struggle for resources, and argues there is a reluctance to cooperate between departments on issues which cross-cut departmental responsibilities. It is argued that this has become one of the besetting sins of the British system of government, which has intensified in an era of governance. This has led to the present Labour Government actively pursuing a strategy of joined-up government in an attempt to wire the British state together again. Furthermore, Rhodes asserts that the reality of the British political system is that departments engage in bargaining games with other actors in the policy arena in order to achieve their goals. Hence, the most appropriate way to represent the functioning of government in Britain is in terms of a segmented executive.

Policy networks approach

Policy networks are a way of analysing how, in an era when the policy arena is portrayed as being increasingly complex and diverse, government interacts with civil society, especially interest groups which are constantly voicing their own sectional demands (see Chapter 8). The policy network approach is based on examining a particular policy area—for example a policy of banning fox-hunting—and identifying the range of actors involved in policy-making. A policy network can include ministers, civil servants, special advisers (from the academic or professional community), pressure group representatives, etc. Around each policy—be it health, defence, welfare policy for lone parents, asylum seekers etc.—a different network will exist with a different range of actors involved. As such, what

Box 2.2 Departmentalism: the pathology of bureaucracy

The broadest meaning of departmentalism is the way in which a minister will pursue the narrow interests of his/her own department at the expense of wider government policy. In his book on ministers, Gerald Kaufman (1997: 15), a Labour Cabinet minister in the 1970s, refers to this occurrence as 'departmentalitis' : 'It stems from a preoccupation with the department to which the minister is assigned, to the exclusion of all the other considerations including the fortunes of the government as a whole.'

The manner in which the policy-making process has been organized around Whitehall departments has provided the structured context that has shaped the way agents, ministers, and civil servants act. One consequence of the establishment of departmental government has been the problem of departmentalism. The term covers a mix of political, policy, and governmental pathologies. Essentially, critics argue that the departmental perspective can adversely affect the wider system and the broader objectives of the government. In a major speech in 1999 Tony Blair complained of having 'scars on my back' from his attempts to get Whitehall departments to improve public services; they were slow to provide initiatives or respond to ministerial prompting. Civil servants, he implied, concentrated on protecting their turf and their own interests rather than advancing government programmes.

Departmentalism flourishes for many reasons. Politics in Whitehall—as elsewhere—is about spoils, about who gets what. This can cover resources, media attention, and political capital—for the minister and his/her department. Barbara Castle, as Employment Minister, reflected on a meeting with other ministers: 'I wasn't in a political caucus at all. I was faced by departmental enemies' (*Sunday Times*, 10 June 1973). She was complaining that ministers were protecting their departmental interests as ends in themselves rather than focusing on an overall programme. When Richard Crossman, as Minister of Housing and Local Government, in 1964 surrendered responsibility for physical planning to another department, he was immediately assailed by his formidable Permanent Secretary, Evelyn Sharpe, on the grounds that he had significantly weakened the capacity and standing of the department.

In policy terms, departments have accumulated 'wisdom', derived from experience about which approaches work best, which lobbies should be consulted and how to negotiate effectively with the Treasury and other departments. Civil servants educate the new minister to 'ongoing reality'. Ministers frequently bear the impress of their departments, singing a different tune when moving from one department to another in the same government. A minister's concern with protecting turf, within as well as between departments, means that coordination tends to be done at the lowest common level which can weaken cross-departmental initiatives. Departmentalism should therefore be understood as a pathology that prompts ministers to think of the micro-political interests of their department, at the expense of the macro-political goals of their own government.

the policy network approach provides is an alternative framework for analysing government. Rhodes (1997: 9) argues that policy networks are important:

All governments confront a vast array of interests. Aggregation of those interests is a functional necessity. Intermediation is a fact of everyday life in government. To describe and explain variations in patterns of intermediation is to explore one of the key governmental and political processes.

What the policy network approach suggests (see Marsh and Rhodes 1992, Smith 1993, Marsh and Smith 2000) is that:

- A range of institutions are important in the operation of central government.
- The distribution of power may be horizontal rather than vertical.
- Power is not concentrated in a limited number of institutions.
- Therefore, there is not a simple model of government and there are no firm boundaries in central government.
- Instead, to understand British government, it is important to focus on the interactions between different elements of the core executive.

A policy networks approach is important because much policy-making in central government is not through formal institutions but through contacts of informal networks. Therefore, it is important to understand how these networks operate and affect policy outcomes (see Chapter 10).

A key point is the extent to which, in an era of governance, policy networks have proliferated and power has increasingly been dispersed throughout the political system. Rhodes (2000: 60-1) argues:

Networks are the analytical heart of the notion of governance in the study of Public Administration . . . Governance suggests that networks are self-organising. At its simplest, self-organising means a network is autonomous and self-governing. Networks resist government steering, develop their own polices and mould their environment.

Rhodes's comments are important, for, if correct, they lead to a whole series of fundamental questions relating to the issue of power and the ability of central government to control the policy process. Yet his notion of 'self-organizing networks' is not without its problems. At both a theoretical and empirical level, it is almost impossible to substantiate an argument that networks can be self-organizing. At whatever level of abstraction, the state will always have a role. The role might not necessarily be that of an agent, actively participating in a network. Yet the state will always play a part in determining the structured environment in which networks are able to be established and function. So Rhodes's 'self-organizing networks' is a concept open to contention. Indeed, we would argue that what the state might decide to relinquish at any one moment, it may also, at some other point, chose to bring back into its own sphere of control. Again, the central issue here is concerned with questioning the nature of power.

In order to analyse such questions, we adopt the state-centric approach (see above and also Peters 2000) which is concerned with identifying the capacity of central government to exert control over the rest of the polity, the economy, and society. Clearly, if self-organizing, inter-organizational networks are a true reflection of the current British political system, then central government's power has been seriously checked, sovereignty no longer resides in Westminster/Whitehall, and power should be conceived of as pluralistic, dispersed between a whole range of actors, with no one actor dominating. It is this theme that we will critically analyse throughout this book.

Power dependence

Power dependence is a characteristic that we will look at in greater detail in Chapter 9. Here, a brief description explains interactions in the power system. At the primary level, power-dependence 'postulates that organizations depend on each other for resources and, therefore, enter exchange relationships' (Rhodes 1997: 9).

First, we should point out that the core executive is not a simple, unified whole: there will be divisions within Cabinet, between departments, and among civil servants and ministers. More broadly, Rhodes suggests that it is wrong to see politics as a zero-sum game with, for example, the Prime Minister dominating ministers, ministers dominating civil servants, and central government dominating local government or the European Union. Rather, there are a series of exchange relationships: each actor possesses resources which the other needs. Politics is about resource exchange in order to achieve goals or objectives. Hence, it is also implicitly about compromise. For Rhodes, power is better understood as an exchange relationship; for example, ministers need civil servants to provide advice and help in the implementation of policy. Civil servants need ministers to win resources for their department from the Prime Minister/Treasury/Cabinet and to promote and defend the department's interests in Cabinet, Parliament, and, increasingly, Europe. Thus on most occasions, and in most ways, power should be conceived of as a positive-sum game. Rhodes (1997: 9) concludes by arguing that power dependence is a vital component of the differentiated polity model:

> It explains why different levels of government interact. It explains variations in the distribution of power within and between policy networks. It also replaces the zero-sum concept of power of the Westminster model with a relational concept which emphasises resources, not personalities, and the context of the relationships, not individual volition.

The hollowing-out of the state

The hollowing-out of the state (see Fig. 2.1) is perhaps the most radical aspect of the differentiated polity model. Rhodes (1997: 17) observes: 'The phrase "the hollowing out of the state" summarises many of the changes which have taken, and are taking, place in British government.' He contends that central government's authority, autonomy, and power have been reduced by being dispersed:

- upwards to the supranational level, i.e. Europe, IMF, G7(8) etc.;
- outwards through privatization and market testing;
- downwards, through the creation of quangos, agencies, etc.

Rhodes (1997: 18) observes: 'hollowing out identifies key trends, focusing

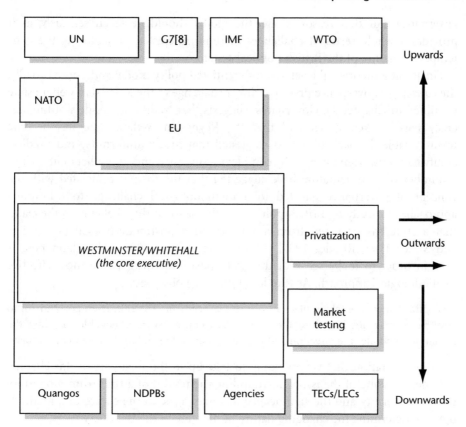

Figure 2.1 The hollowing-out of the state (*source*: Richards 1999)

attention on segmentation and its effects on executive behaviour and change, and its consequences for the UK bureaucracy.'

In order to determine the extent to which there has been a hollowing-out of the state, we first need to consider what are the perceived forces responsible for augmenting this process. It is suggested they could include globalization, internationalization, Europeanization, marketization and privatization. Each of these themes requires some detailed analysis. For example, the extent to which globalization has affected the autonomy of governments to control the policy arena remains a much-contested question in political science. We shall therefore explore each of these themes in more detail in Chapters 6–8, before returning to the core question of the extent to which the state has been hollowed out. Nevertheless, in relation to Rhodes's 'differentiated polity' model, here the key question is the extent to which hollowing-out has undermined the capacity of the core executive to control the policy process.

The importance of the differentiated polity model lies in the fact that it is one of the most sophisticated attempts to reflect the changing nature of the British state over the last few decades. It takes account of the issues presented by the concept of governance. For that reason alone, the model should be taken seriously, as it provides a whole series of challenges to those interested in exploring the contemporary nature of the British political system.

Finally, at a theoretical level, the differentiated polity model and, more broadly, the concept of governance present a direct challenge to the Keynesian welfare state (outlined in Chapter 3). Governance suggests that traditional models of bureaucracy have broken down and that the Keynesian welfare state has become unsustainable. In particular, it is suggested that order, uniformity, and predictability have now been replaced by complexity, diversity, and unpredictability. Thus, a number of commentators have suggested that the themes associated with the concept of governance has led to a methodological challenge to traditional approaches to studying British politics. At the heart of this challenge is the claim that a shift has occurred from a modern to a postmodern society (see Fox and Miller 1995, Rhodes 1997, Gibbins and Reimer 1999). The claim here is that, in order to make sense of this shift, postmodernism is the most effective methodological approach. As Rhodes (1997: 198) observes:

Dramatic changes are taking place in British Government. The shift from government to governance may not introduce the postmodern era, but it is impossible to refuse the invitation to ponder the direction and pace of change at the end of the twentieth century

It is this invitation that we are going to take up in the final part of this chapter, considering some of the issues surrounding the notion of a shift from modernity to postmodernity and the significance this may have on the choice of a methodology to determine the changing nature of the state in the last thirty years.

From modernity to postmodernity?

In Chapter 3 we examine the development of the modern state. We observe that one of the clearest manifestations of the modernist epoch is the Weberian bureaucratic state. During the second half of the twentieth century, however, many of the tenets most closely associated with the modernist world, but in particular with the nation-state and mass political parties, are no longer regarded as unquestionable success stories. For example, two world wars led to the questioning of the utility of the concept of the nation-state and prompted the search by some countries for alternative frameworks of political, social, and economic organization. The European Union, the World Bank, and the United Nations (in part) each reflect a lack of faith in the institution of the nation-state. Elsewhere, as society in the post-1945 era evolved, it has become much less homogeneous. Greater diversification in race, class, culture, leisure, work, etc. reflects the development of a much more heterogeneous society. The traditional dividing lines between capital and labour are still relevant, but as Keating (2000) observes, on many issues it is no longer the only or even the main determinant of political attitudes and expectations of government.

Keating (2000: 29) suggests that the influence of the traditional divide in attitudes to governance based on labour and capital has been 'overlapped by a number of other fault lines' between:

- the educated and knowledge rich and the knowledge poor;
- those who feel secure and embrace change and those who feel threatened by change;
- material and postmaterialist values;
- those who want maximum freedom for the individual to pursue their own interests and those who desire a society where communities are encouraged to co-operate together to enhance social capital.

These trends have made the task of mainstream, mass political parties that much more difficult. For many, mass political parties are no longer regarded as the best means by which individuals in society can express their opinions or channel a multiplicity of demands. In the second half of the twentieth century, the rise of single-issue pressure groups became a new feature in society (see Chapter 10). Increasingly, individuals have come to regard pressure group activity as a more effective means of achieving a direct impact on a political issue or debate. Mass political parties are increasingly portrayed as being no longer able to voice the concerns and sentiments of an increasingly diverse society. Thus, as the second half of the twentieth century progressed, the failure of political parties to deliver was reflected in a dramatic decline in their membership. Conversely, the membership of a wide range of interest groups such as Greenpeace, Life, ASH, Amnesty, and the National Viewers' and Listeners' Association grew.

Finally, another key institution associated with the modernist era, the Weberian bureaucratic state, has also become a target for much criticism. Hierarchy, uniformity, predictability, and unilinearity, all of which were originally regarded as positive characteristics associated with the Weberian model of bureaucracy, have been increasingly attacked as residual elements of an unresponsive, inefficient, inflexible, and non-innovative state machine that can no longer satisfy the aspirations of society. Fox and Miller (1995: p. xiv) are key exponents of this position. They argue that the ideals underpinning the Weberian State are moribund: 'the raw materials it [the Weberian State] once possessed are depleted, no spare parts are available, and the company that produced it went bankrupt in the mid-50s. Nostalgia for it only delays the need to ask each other: What should we do next?'

By the mid-1970s, politicians, practitioners, and academics were considering this very question, prompted by the development of a perceived crisis of the state. Alternative forms of state delivery were sought to address the perceived failings of the Weberian bureaucratic state, and it is here that the origins of governance, as a new state form, can be located. Postmodernism and the postmodernist state provide an alternative means of conceptualizing the political world and, more particularly, challenging many of the tenets associated with the modern state examined in Chapter 3.

What is postmodernism?

Postmodernism not only reflects a certain historical period but also represents what is referred to as a particular discourse. By this, it is meant that postmodernism provides a certain way of looking at the world and analysing politics. Whereas modernity provided a framework in which humankind attempted to understand the world based on the notion of 'foundationalism', 'rationality', and 'essentialist characteristics' associated with models of the nation-state, postmodernism views the world as being 'anti-foundationalist', lacking a single dominant discourse, and constantly engaged in a process of 'reflexivity', responding to old and new pressures, interests, processes, and structures. Postmodernists contend that society is no longer moving in a single immutable direction, but instead has become increasingly complex, disorganized and unpredictable, shaped by a whole series of new, competing, sometimes contradictory forces. In the light of this thesis and in order to understand the challenges presented by postmodernism, we first turn to the time framework in which the postmodernist epoch is seen to be embedded.

Postmodernism as an epoch

Political science is not the exclusive nor the original proprietor of the term 'postmodernism'. It is a label that is associated with many different strands of human activity, most notably art, music, literature, philosophy, drama, and architecture. Rose (1991) and Rosenau (1992) have each traced the term's origins back to an anti-modernist current in various Spanish and Latin American poetry writings between 1905 and 1914. Elsewhere, Arnold Toynbee used the term in 1939 to describe the triumph of mass society after 1914, and later C. Wright Mills (1959) used the term when referring to the 'fourth epoch'. Nevertheless, beyond the social sciences, architecture is probably the field with the most dominant usage of the term. Here, the term was thought to have first been used just after the Second World War, in relation to the 'postmodern house'. More recently, in architectural circles, the term 'postmodernism' has been used to describe a new architectural style associated with the 1970s and 1980s which broke the tenets of the previously dominant modernist architecture (see Table 2.1).

Returning to the social sciences: postmodernism really only began to challenge the embedded modernist discourse from the 1970s onwards. Those most closely associated with the first wave of postmodernist philosophical writings were Foucault, Lacan, Derrida, Wittgenstein and Deleuze. In particular, postmodernism was popular among Parisian street café philosophers in the 1970s and, elsewhere, in the anti-foundationalist writings of Richard Rorty in the United States. It was only in the late 1970s, however, that postmodernism began to provide an effective challenge to some of the accepted wisdoms of modernity. Thus it is only in the last three decades that the challenge of postmodernism has been taken seriously in social science circles. Now, our attention shifts to understanding postmodernism not as a period of time, but as a discourse.

The discourse of postmodernism

Postmodernism is the return of and revenge of the different, the assertion of the random non-pattern and the unassimilable anomaly. At risk, as the monolith fractures and then is deconstructed, is the loss of what western society took to be reality. (Fox and Miller 1995: 45)

Foucalt and Wittgenstein, two of the most famous philosophers of the last 150 years, remind us that language is a constant process of compromise and negotiation. The terms and discourses we use in everyday life are never neutral, but are value-laden, contingent, tied to particular periods, locations, situations, and conflicts. They are also closely associated with particular epistemes or modes of knowledge. In trying to compare and contrast the discourse of modernity with that of postmodernity, the use of language provides a useful tool. For example, one of the key themes in this book is to contrast the features of the Weberian bureaucratic state with that of the new forms of state delivery associated with governance. The language associated with the modern state could include hierarchy, responsibility, objectivity, homogeneity, unlinearity, predictability, and continuity. For those interested in understanding the nature of the state in today's society, many of these terms now appear inappropriate: they no longer aptly describe the way in which states are organized, nor the way in which they function. This has led to a growing number of critics who no longer accept that the characteristics of the Weberian state and, more broadly, modernity reflect the dominant features in today's society. As seen from the quote at the start of this section, postmodernism has provided a strong challenge to the established ideals of the society within which we live.

Traditional forms of ideology most commonly associated with modernity such as liberalism or Marxism have increasingly come under attack. The fixed nature of identity assumed by these ideologies has been criticized by postmodernists, who emphasize difference, fluidity, subjectivity, and relativism. The philosophical thrust of postmodernism has been important for political science—as it has challenged the assumptions of the existing, dominant ideologies about what identities are. Postmodernism emphasizes that identity (in our case, the identity of the state) is contingent, multiple, and constantly being renegotiated. For example, the metanarratives of liberalism or socialism are criticized by postmodernists for claiming an objective and immutable basis in their accounts of the social world. As Gamble (2000b: 20) observes:

Postmodernism in its various forms depends upon a radical rejection of the past and of all attempts to use the past to understand the present. Postmodernists want to sweep away all the grand narratives, all historical constructions of the past which attempt to provide meaning and direction to the present.

Postmodernists would criticise Marxist class analysis of society, arguing that class alone is incapable of defining an individual or of determining or framing the issues within which politics occurs. For postmodernists, the social world is seen as being much more complicated or, to apply a key postmodernist term, *fuzzy*. They argue that there is no single, immutable discourse, but instead numerous different narratives which give meaning to the way individuals live out their lives. So, postmodernists such as Laclau (1990: 76) argue:

Politics has to be pluralistic to take account of the many and overlapping identities and commitments which individuals have: the list includes race, gender, class, ethnicity, neighbourhood, locality, nation, work, household, age and sexual orientation.

There is no single established definition of postmodernism. Postmodernists would argue that the very nature of postmodernism, with its numerous competing discourses, does not lend itself to precise or rigorous definitions that can be found elsewhere, for example within the predominantly positivist world of the natural sciences. Hence, Gamble (2000b: 22) detects the irony of postmoderism: 'many variants of postmodernism reject not only all former narratives but all new narratives, since all narratives once they cease to be simple subjective constructions are vulnerable to the charge that they depend on foundations.' Nevertheless, postmodernists would broadly accept that, in the same way that the process of modernization in the form of mass political parties, the growth of the nation-state, the establishment of welfare states, comprehensive education, etc. was responsible for shaping modernity, the process of postmodernization has similarly shaped postmodernity. This then leads to the question of what characteristics postmodernists would identify as shaping advanced industrial society today. Gibbins and Reimer (1999: 22) argue:

In comparison with modernity, postmodernity has been identified with a move towards disorganised capitalism, with consumerism, with increasing speed and perpetual change, with an emphasis on surfaces and images, with the mass media, with globalization, with unpredictability, with a questioning of reality and even with the end of the social.

Within political science, one of the most accessible analogies used by those wishing to represent the shift from modernism to postmodernism is that of the change in the motor car industry during the twentieth century (see Jessop 1994, Ling 1998, Keating 2000; Box 2.3, Table 2.1)

If, in recent years, postmodernism has laid down a broad challenge to political science by providing an alternative discourse in which to try and make sense of political life, let us now narrow our focus to look at a postmodernist critique of the Weberian bureaucratic state.

Box 2.3 **From Fordism to post-Fordism**

Fordism is a word that is derived from the technique introduced by Henry Ford (1863–1947) to mass-produce a car that could be afforded by the majority of American households in the 1920–30s (see Jessop 1994). In order to produce a motor car at low cost, Ford envisaged a single, standardized production technique that was capable of producing mass numbers of identical cars at a low cost. The result was the Ford Austin motor car. Here, Fordism can be understood as being based on mass production of standardized goods, employing semi-skilled workers in Taylorist forms of work organization (see Keating 2000). However, as the disposable income of American households increased, so the demand for the cheap, mass produced, standardized Ford Austin fell. Consumers demanded much greater specialization and choice in the products they wished to buy to reflect their more confident economic status. In order to adapt to these new market demands, the Ford motor company introduced a number of new models to come off its assembly lines, at a greater cost to the consumer, but with more specialization in the final product in terms of different engine sizes, designs, colours and specialized features.

Political science has used the change in the production techniques of the Ford motor car to symbolize the broader changes in the process of capitalism in the twentieth century—a change from Fordism to post-Fordism (see Jessop 1994). At the heart of this argument is a recognition of the importance of speed and change in today's world. Initially, the production process underlying organized capitalism has been referred to as Fordism. Here, the emphasis is on the production of commodities and products on a mass scale at the cheapest possible cost to consumers. Fordism demands both a standardized production technique and centralized planning. Yet, with the increase in disposable income and a change in consumer tastes, Fordism became an increasingly outmoded form of production. Specialization, niche markets, short-termism, and flexibility replaced the standardized production techniques of Fordism. Post-Fordism reflected the development of a new phase in capitalist production. The analogy of post-Fordism is useful in demonstrating the much greater diversity of societies today. As Gibbins and Reimer (1999: 27–8) observe: 'Post-Fordism indicates that people have different needs; they cannot be treated like one homogenous group. This means that through the use of different products, and through fashion, people express themselves differently' (see Table 2.2).

Characteristics of the postmodern state

In this section, we identify some of the main characteristics which, postmodernists would argue, highlight the changing contours of the state. For postmodernists, what these characteristics cumulatively reflect is a new state form. Whereas the features of a modern state would include sovereignty, territoriality, single rule of law, nationality, centralization, unilateral defence, unified bureaucracy, policy autonomy, autonomous taxation, and welfare, the features of the postmodern state would include non-exclusive sovereignty and territoriality, cooperative or multiple rule and law, multilateral defence, shared citizenship, multiculturalism, devolution,

Table 2.1 The differences between Fordism and post-Fordism

	Fordism	Post-Fordism
Production	Mass production of identical goods using standardized, inflexible production processes	Batch production of varied or niche goods using a flexible production system
Consumption	Mass marketing; widespread consumption of increasing quantities of the same products	Niche marketing; widespread consumption of increasingly finely differentiated products
Social relations	Large homogeneous 'citizenries'	Fragmented identities and cultures
Culture	Mass culture spread through a mass media providing reproduced identical messages	Fragmented culture reproduced through diverse and multiple media, providing a diverse choice of highly differentiated messages
Economic policies	National strategies of maintaining high and stable levels of demand	Strategies aimed at enhancing particular aspects of competitiveness in the global economy
Social policies	Universal welfare provided through nationally coordinated, uniform, and unified bureaucracies	Means-tested welfare provided through a segmented and differentiated bureaucracy aimed at enhancing economic competitiveness
Political strategies	'One nation' appeals for mass support	Alliance of multiple identities behind symbolic and largely simulated strategic differences

Source: Ling (1998: 232)

non-bureaucracy, non-unitary, pluralistic policy, shared taxation, and trans-national welfare. A key point we will return to throughout this book is that the characteristics described in this section leads those who subscribe to them to argue that the Westminster model is now an inadequate, indeed flawed, organizing per-spective of the British political system that needs to be replaced by an alternative model which reflects the changing nature of the state in the latter half of the twentieth century. We consider here nine characteristics of the postmodern state. The central claim here is that there has been a shift from hierarchy to heterarchy.

A shift from hierarchy to heterarchy

The shift from hierarchy to heterarchy (see Parsons 1998) represents a shift from an organizational form which was clearly layered in a top-down manner to one in which there are many different but interconnected actors, each without a single dominant centre or core.

In practice, this implies a shift from the traditional Weberian model of hierarchy, in which Whitehall departments are the dominant actors in the policy process, to one in which the core executive is only one actor among many others, which can include markets, networks, and agencies now engaged in policy-making.

Clear lines of responsibility replaced by blurred or fuzzy lines of accountability

One of the perceived benefits of the Weberian, top-down model was that it provided clear lines of responsibility. Postmodernists would contend that there are now many different actors or bodies operating within the policy arena. One of the unforeseen or unintended consequences of this change is that lines of responsibility have become much more blurred. Previously, it was the case that, in theory at least, it was the Cabinet minister who carried ultimate responsibility for the actions of a department. Although this constitutional convention was open to manipulation depending on the political exigencies of the day, there was still less political space within which a Cabinet minister could hide. Now, by contrast, in a policy arena that has become much more cluttered, the opportunities afforded a Cabinet minister to avoid responsibility have greatly increased. This is most clearly demonstrated in the case of identifying the difference between responsibility for policy formulation and accountability for implementation. One of the most notable examples of this is the difference in interpretation of the notion of accountability involving Derek Lewis, chief executive of the Prison Service, and Michael Howard, Home Secretary, in the mid-1990s (see Box 2.4).

Hierarchical discipline replaced by regulation

This reflects a perceived shift from a directive relationship within the state associated in particular with the corporatist era of the 1970s (see Chapter 8) to one based on greater regulation. Rather than determining what you should do, the state regulates what you can do. It is a relationship based on trust: the state says that it will trust an organization to make a decision, but retains the right to hold the organization to account for those decisions. Clearly, the privatization programme instigated by the Conservative governments during the 1980s was one of the key dynamics leading to the shift from hierarchy to regulation. It is reflected in the numerous regulatory agencies, such as Ofwat, Oftel and Ofgas, that have been established by the state in order to monitor the activities of the now privatized utility companies.

Responsibility no longer gravitates upwards and is no longer clearly observable

Whereas, within a hierarchy, the further up an organization one goes the greater responsibility one will carry, in a postmodernist state, responsibility is increasingly dispersed to many different structures or agencies. To utilize the language of the postmodernist, a shift has occurred since the 1970s from an environment in which government was overloaded by responsibilities and demands to the present environment, in which the preferred strategy of government is to *download* responsibility to other organizations and agencies. Clearly, the process of establishing executive agencies from the late 1980s onwards is a prime example of government downloading responsibilities from the centre.

Box 2.4 An issue of accountability: the Michael Howard–Derek Lewis affair

By establishing Next Steps (now Executive) Agencies, the third Thatcher Government (1987–90) introduced a fundamental change in the way the Civil Service was both organized and operated. A much-contested issue concerning the establishment of agencies was that of accountability. In 1994, the events in the Home Office involving Michael Howard, then Conservative Home Secretary, and Derek Lewis, then Director-General of the Prison Service Agency, demonstrated the problems that arose when the lines of accountability in government became blurred by the creation of agencies.

The central issue in the whole affair revolved around who should take responsibility for the attempted breakout by IRA prisoners from a gaol in Cambridgeshire in September 1994. Three years earlier, a successful escape by IRA prisoners from Brixton Prison had seen the responsibility clearly laid at the door of the then Home Secretary, Kenneth Baker. Yet, following the 1994 incident, media attention centred on Derek Lewis, officially a civil servant, to account for the escape. The underlying point at issue was the argument of Michael Howard concerning the balance between policy (the responsibility of the Home Secretary) and operations (the responsibility of the Director-General). Responsibility for the escape was not clear-cut. It was not until the Prison Inspector, Sir John Woodcock, completed an inquiry that responsibility was apportioned. The report's conclusions were ambivalent: 'There exists some confusion as to the respective roles of the ministers, the agency headquarters and individual prison governors . . . The inquiry identified the difficulty of determining what is an operational matter and what is policy, leading to confusion as to where responsibility lies' [*Guardian*, 20 Dec. 1994). The Home Secretary, Michael Howard, argued that the escape was not the result of policy failure and hence that he should not take responsibility, while the Prison Officers' Association felt that 'Mr. Lewis was put there to deflect things from the Home Secretary' (BBC 1994). The crux of the matter was that ministers and civil servants did not agree on the lines of accountability. Eventually Lewis, not Howard, carried the can and was sacked, but the whole affair exposed the degree to which the creation of agencies had blurred responsibility in the policy process. The traditional, clear, hierarchical lines of accountability of the Westminster Model have been eroded, while the problem of accountability has become much more acute in an era of governance.

A shift from state central control to state steering

This is the notion that government has moved away from the modernist notion of control towards the more flexible (some argue) postmodern mode of steering (see below).

A shift from rigid to flexible and ad hoc organizational structures

As we shall see in Chapter 3, the traditional Weberian bureaucratic model is regarded as permanent and easily observable. The postmodern state is regarded as one in which rigidity has been replaced by flexibility, and in which institutions possess the ability to adapt.

Uniformity and predictability replaced by diversity and uncertainty

Similarly, whereas the Weberian state was regarded as being uniform and predictable, the postmodernist state portrays an environment in which diversity and uncertainty are the key characteristics. Thus, actors within the state, for example politicians and civil servants, require the capacity to be reflexive, in order to respond to the increasingly complex and changing environment in which they are now embedded.

Structures are no longer fixed but contingent

Structures in the postmodern state are regarded as fluid and constantly changing, in response to the environment in which they are located. Unlike the Weberian state which is established, stable, and possesses a functional bureaucracy (see Chapter 3), the postmodernist state is no longer fixed, but is contingent on its environment. So, for example, postmodernists would suggest that the task forces created by the present Labour Government are proof of a flexible state, adapting to problems in society as they arise, in areas such as teenage pregnancy or drugs.

A single public-service ethos replaced by a heterogeneous service culture

One of the characteristics of the Weberian state was that it possessed a single public-service ethos: state officials were conditioned by a culture based on public service and working for the public good. Most notably, the Whitehall culture was seen to be based on the conventions of neutrality, permanence, and anonymity. Civil servants were deemed to be free from corruption or bias. Postmodernists argue that there no longer exists a single organization (Whitehall) or unifying culture (a public-service ethos). Instead, there are numerous different state organizations, each possessing its own particular culture, which in turn prioritizes different features. These cultures may be conditioned by the needs of the market or of managerialism or self-interest, and they can come in many different shapes or forms (see Richards and Smith 2000). Thus, postmodernists would contend that there no longer exists a public-service ethos which socializes and conditions state servants in a particular manner.

The characteristics listed above reflect a number of arguments used by postmodernists to highlight the changing nature of the state and the erosion of the key tenets that had previously underpinned the Weberian bureaucratic model (see Table 2.2). It has led those who adopt a postmodernist position to argue that the sovereign nation is in the process of giving way to a much more pluralized form of civil society, in which the role of government is to 'hold the ring between a myriad of social and political groupings' (see Hall 1995, Giddens 1998). Thus, as Gibbins and Reimer (1999: 159) conclude:

The fuzzy logic of new technology will impact upon public management as 'what works here and now' replaces the practice of 'what worked there and then'. Pluralism, difference, eclecticism, complexity and flexibility will mark the new public administration.

At the heart of the postmodernist discourse is the assertion that one of the key

Table 2.2 The Weberian state vs. the postmodern state

Weberian bureaucratic state	A postmodern state
Government	Governance
Hierarchy (Weberian)	Heterarchy (networks etc.)
Power (1): zero-sum game	Power (1): positive-sum game
Power (2): concentrated	Power (2): diffuse
Elitist	Pluralist
Unitary, centralized, monolithic state	Decentralized, fragmented, hollowed-out state
Strong, central executive	Segmented executive
Clear lines of accountabilty	Blurred/fuzzy lines of accountabilty
State central control	State central steering
Single homogeneous public service ethos	Heterogeneous service cultures

characteristics of modernity—'determinism'—is being replaced by 'reflexivity' as political actors try to make sense of an increasingly complex and unpredictable world.

Conclusion: governance in a changing world

What we will address throughout this book is whether governance, and in particular Rhodes's differentiated polity model provides a new way to analyse the nature of the state. To adopt the words of Rhodes, does the differentiated polity model provide greater utility as an 'organizing perspective' of the British system of government, or does 'governance' provide us with a new, postmodern form of the state? Furthermore, to what extent do the themes captured in the differentiated polity model, and in particular the notion that power in the state is dispersed between many different institutions, reflect the actual reality of where political power in the British state lies? Finally, does the discourse of postmodernity and the postmodern state, reflected in many of the characteristics associated with governance, provide a more convincing narrative than that of modernity and the modern state?

KEY POINTS

- Governance is a way of understanding the various ways of delivering public services and organizing government that now exist.

- There are a number of competing views concerning what governance means, but essentially it refers to a shift from a one-way hierarchical system of governance to an environment in which the actors in the public arena have multiplied, the boundaries between public and private have blurred, and government's central control has receded.

- We argue that the key element of governance is the need to be sensitive to the range of actors now involved in delivering public services.

- Rhodes suggests that with the development of new forms of governance, the Westminster model has been replaced by a differentiated polity.

- Power dependence is an important concept for understanding the policy process. The term implies that no single actor has all the necessary resources for making policy, and therefore that different actors and institutions are dependent on each other.

- An alternative framework for understanding the changes in government is the shift from modernity to postmodernity

- The modern state is based on hierarchy, standardization, and planning from the centre.

- The postmodern state is fragmented, diverse, and concerned with reconciling conflicting visions of ways of life.

KEY QUESTIONS

1. What are the different interpretations of governance?

2. What are the key features of a postmodernist state?

3. What are the similarities between governance and postmodernism?

4. How relevant is the idea of a postmodern state?

KEY READING

The debate on governance is discussed in Rhodes (1997), Pierre (2000), and Pierre and Peters (2000). For governance and Britain see Foster and Plowden (1996) and Marsh et al. (2001). Policy networks are outlined in Marsh and Rhodes (1992) and updated in Marsh and Smith (2000). For an introduction to postmodernism see Lyon (1994) and for its implications for public policy see Fox and Miller (1995).

KEY WEBSITES

On British government and changes in organization see www.ukonline.gov.uk/ For some of the specific details look at www.10downingstreet.gov.uk/ On global governance see www.worldbank.org/wbi/governance/, www.governance.qub.ac.uk/ and www.nottingham.ac.uk/politics/european-governance/

On regional and urban governance see www.unesco.org/most/most2.htm, www.saltireguide.co.uk/register.html and www.cf.ac.uk/euros/welsh- For new forms of digital governance see www.digitalgovernance.org/governance/index.html. A useful introduction to postmodernism can be found at www.esher.ac.uk/scextranet/sociology/post-mod.htm

3

INTERPRETING THE MODERN STATE

INTRODUCTION

In Chapter 2 we examined a relatively new theme in political science—governance. The thrust of the debate on governance asserts that in the last thirty years, a new phase in governing has developed which has replaced a more traditional epoch in which government was seen to be the dominant actor in the policy process. This earlier phase we can refer to as an era of government. Here, the government was seen to centrally control the delivery of most public goods. Education and welfare were provided by the state, the major utilities were nationalized, and the government had considerable control over the economy. In this chapter, we argue that by the end of the twentieth century the British state became a large 'modern state'. However, the notion of a unified, hierarchical, territorially bound central state was always a caricature, and in many ways the British state was both centralized and fragmented. Undoubtedly, it provided many public goods (and still does), but the provision of these goods was often complex. So, the aim of this chapter is to identify the development of the modern state in Britain.

Modern states are now in existence through much of the developed world. For most of us, government regulates everything we do, from switching on the kettle in the morning until we turn off the light at night. However, the era of the modern state has been short. Its key features were established in the mid-nineteenth century, but their viability was already coming into question by the 1970s. But what is the modern state, and how does it affect the policy process? As a concept, the modern state contains two meanings: one is the state as it is today in modern times; the other is the notion of the state in modernity—a state that is seen to be rational and searching for progressive goals. This chapter will examine the idea of the state in modernity and look at the nature of the modern state in Britain. It will draw out the way the state has shaped the policy-making process. Its central argument is that whilst the state in Britain is undoubtedly modern, it is in fact a deformed modernity.

The modern state

What is the state?

Heywood (2000: 39) observes: 'The state can most simply be defined as a political association that establishes sovereign jurisdiction within defined territorial borders and exercises authority through a set of permanent institutions.' Although this is a useful starting point from which to explore the concept of the state, it is worth emphasizing that there is no single, short, and workable definition of the state—because the state is an inherently complex and ambiguous concept. The modern state consists of a range of different institutions, and these institutions will vary from country to country and across time. State institutions tend to be fluid, changing, and unsettled. For example, as we will later see, when the Labour Government won the May 1997 general election, the British state was a different entity from that inherited by the Conservative Government when it came to power under Margaret Thatcher in June 1979. However, at the most general level, there are a number of key characteristics which any modern state possesses. Below, we have adapted Heywood's definition (2000: 39) to identify six features of a state:

- The state exercises sovereignty: it exercises absolute and unrestricted power in that it stands above all other associations and groups in society. Thomas Hobbes (1588–1679) portrayed the state as a 'leviathan', a gigantic monster.

- State institutions are recognizably 'public', in contrast to the 'private' institutions of civil society: state bodies are responsible for making and enforcing collective decisions in society, and are funded at the public's expense.

- Institutional structures: all states depend for their existence on institutions. These can include a parliament or a congress, a judiciary, a civil service, local government, and a law enforcement agency. Moreover, all institutions have their own formal and informal rules and structures.

- The state is a territorial association: it exercises jurisdiction within geographically defined borders, and in international politics is treated (at least in theory) as an autonomous entity.

- The state is an exercise in legitimation: its decisions are usually (although not necessarily) accepted as binding on its citizens because, it is claimed, it reflects the interests of society.

- The state is an instrument of domination: it possesses the coercive power to ensure its laws are obeyed and that transgressors are punished. As Max Weber (1860–1920) put it, the state has a monopoly on the means of 'legitimate violence'. All states have access to coercive capacities (in various shapes and forms) by which to enforce order and underpin its claim to obedience. Even relatively democratic states such as Britain retain important coercive elements—witness the state's role in controlling the miners' strike in 1984, the poll tax riots in London in 1989, and the ongoing conflict in Northern Ireland (see Box 3.1).

Although, in general, all states often possess most if not all of the features identified above, we do not wish to suggest by this that all states are the same. States come in a variety of shapes and sizes (see Box 3.2). In order to understand the state in contemporary society, it is important to see it as a fluid entity which contains a range of elements: some are visible, such as Parliament; some are less tangible, such as regulations; and others are informal, such as important elements of the British constitution. From this perspective, Hay (1996: 8-9) defines the state as:

A series of dynamic and complexly interwoven processes and practices (occurring within specific institutional settings), and hence . . . the state [is] a dynamic and evolving system. Accordingly, we must reject the prevalent notion that the definition of the state may be used as a means to 'fix' and thereby render static what is, in fact, a constantly changing network of relationships and institutional practices and procedures. In defining the state, then, we should not place too much emphasis upon tightly delineating its structural form, function, content or boundaries. Indeed what might be taken as a characteristic, even defining, trait is the essential variability of the state.

In a public policy world that is constantly changing, Hay provides a useful definition of the state. Yet we have still to address the question of what is meant by the term 'modern'. In order to do this, we need to examine what is meant by modernity.

Box 3.1 The Government and Northern Ireland

Faced with growing violence between Catholics and Protestants in Northern Ireland, the Wilson Labour Government (1964–70) sent troops to the province in 1969 initially to protect the Catholic community from Protestant attacks. However, with the establishment of the Provisional IRA in 1970 and a growing perception that the troops were there to maintain the status quo, nationalist attacks on the army grew. As a consequence, the British army became increasingly repressive in its attempts to constrain violence. In 1972, thirteen Catholics were shot dead by the army during a march in Londonderry. In an attempt to contain violence and defeat the IRA, the security forces used increasingly repressive measures, including large-scale surveillance, internment, and (despite official denials) an alleged shoot-to-kill policy (see Stalker 1998). As the Marxist theorist Gramsci observed, state power is 'hegemony armoured by coercion'.

(*Source*: Coogan 1996)

Box 3.2 Different models of the state

The minimal (liberal) state

The concept of the minimal state is associated with the philosophy of classical liberalism. Those that advocate the need for a minimalist state hold an essentially negative view of the state, regarding it as a shackle on human behaviour. Minimalists argue that the role of the state should only be to prevent individuals from infringing on the rights and liberties of others. So, the state acts only as a protective body—its role being to ensure peace and social order. The broad functions of the minimalist state are: (i) to maintain domestic order, (ii) to ensure the enforcement of voluntary contracts or agreements made between private citizens, (iii) to provide protection from external attack. The state should not have a role in anything beyond these three functions. The New Right, in particular neo-liberals, are sympathetic to the idea of a minimal state.

The social democratic state

Unlike minimalists, who regard the state as a negative form, advocates of social democracy view the state in a positive light or as a force for good. At the heart of social democracy is the notion of social justice and the role that the state can take in achieving social justice. Social democratic states advocate an active role for the state in restructuring society, normally along lines of greater fairness and equality. The ideas of a social democratic state are based on the state actively intervening, of social engineering, as a means of increasing liberty and promoting justice.

The collectivist state

Both minimal and social democratic states, to differing extents, accept the operation of a market economy. Collectivized states reject the idea of a market economy and instead bring all forms of economic activity under their control. Communist regimes are often used as examples of collectivized states, in which all private enterprise is abolished to be replaced by the establishment of planned or command economies. The normative belief underpinning collectivized states is that all private property is abolished, replaced by common public ownership.

The totalitarian state

The totalitarian state can be found at the opposing pole to the minimalist state. It is based on the notion of the state being all-encompassing, controlling every aspect of human existence. So the totalitarian state dictates every aspect of life—education, religion, family life, culture, etc. Totalitarianism seeks total power over its subjects through the politicization of every aspect of social and personal existence. Civil society does not exist in totalitarian states, as there is only room for one view of how life should be lived—the state's view. It is argued that totalitarian regimes can be identified through six characteristics: (i) an official ideology, (ii) a one-party state, (iii) a system of terroristic policing, (iv) a monopoly on the means of mass communication, (v) monopoly on the means of armed combat, (vi) state control of all aspects of economic life.

The developmental state

A developmental state is one that intervenes in economic life with the overt intention of promoting industrial growth and economic development. It is an attempt to construct a partnership between the state and major economic interests. Examples of developmental states are Japan both before and after 1945, de Gaulle's France, with a government undertaking an interventionist role in the economy, Spain under Franco, or Germany after 1945. In all these countries today, the state has a much greater role to play in economic life than in countries such as the USA or the UK, which went through industrialization in the nineteenth century.

(*Source*: Heywood 2000)

What is modernity?

The modern state is often regarded as emerging from the period in which Britain entered into the industrial revolution—predominantly the nineteenth century. And yet to put an exact date on when the modern state in Britain first emerged is nonsensical. However, following the Glorious Revolution of 1689, a new intellectual, social, cultural, and political movement swept not just Britain but most of western Europe, labelled the Enlightenment. It is in the Enlightenment that we can trace the seeds of the modern state (see Harling 2001).

Modernity is seen to have developed during the nineteenth century from a philosophical belief in progress, a belief in evolution towards a better society. This was reflected in the development of new ideological schools such as Liberalism and Marxism. Modernity may be understood as stemming from the seventeenth- and eighteenth-century philosophical movement referred to as the Enlightenment. The Enlightenment period stressed the importance of reason and witnessed the critical reappraisal of existing ideas and social institutions. From a political-science perspective, an easy way of understanding the Enlightenment is to regard it as a reaction against the concept of absolutism or absolutist monarchical government. This developed after 1689 and was reflected in the rejection of the existing principle of absolutist monarchical rule which had been legitimized by the principle of the 'divine right of kings'. Hence, we see an absolutist system of government being discarded during the Enlightenment to be replaced by a new constitutional settlement which was to be based on legitimacy that could be rationalized (see Harling 2001).

The philosophical ideas emerging during the Enlightenment were developed during the nineteenth century and into the twentieth century, when the era of modernity is seen to have evolved. One way of trying to conceptualize what is meant by modernity is to consider two key words:

- *Foundationalism*—the belief that it is possible to establish objective truth and universal values which are usually associated with a strong faith in progress.

- *Rationality*—a doctrine associated with a group of seventeenth and eighteenth century philosophers, most notably Descartes, Spinoza, and Leibniz, based on the belief that it is possible to obtain by reason alone a knowledge or understanding of the nature of what exists. It is a belief that knowledge is deductive in character, and that everything is explicable and can be explained within one system. In its most popular sense, it is the rejection of religious belief as being without rational foundation, and with it the refutation of the notion of the divine right of kings.

Both these two terms are at the heart of 'modernity'.

More specifically, within political science modernity is a belief that there is a determinate universal, natural, a historical framework in which we can understand the world in which we live. This is based on:

- a belief in the power of reason and observation, i.e. that through reason we can develop and test theories of the world;
- a search for fundamentals or essentials. There are, in this sense, meta-narratives out there somewhere, which we as students of political science can search for in order to explain the secrets of the world which we inhabit.
- a faith or belief in progress and universal design. Underpinning this characteristic is the notion that we are committed to the ideal that we are assured of a steadily improving future.

More generally, one can observe that the construction of the state during the eighteenth and especially the nineteenth century is one of the remarkable achievements of the modern age. In the broader context of Europe we can see, from an assortment of relatively simple organizations, the emergence of a complex set of social institutions linked together by a variety of legal, financial, and ideological practices.

But this leads to a broader question: what is the importance of the modern state? There are a number of responses:

- The development of the state has shaped and transformed the nature of political power. The modern state has tremendous resources in terms of legitimacy, force, the ability to raise revenue, and a professional bureaucracy which have been unavailable at other times or in other types of organization. Therefore, nearly all social relations within civil society are either mediated through or regulated by the state (see Chapter 8).
- The modern state has become the primary means through which collective/public goods have been delivered. Before the modern state, public goods such as civil order, education, or a clean environment were either provided by private organizations, markets and the voluntary sector, or not at all. (For instance, armies were provided by barons, not the central state.) The modern state controlled, either directly or indirectly, the provision of most public goods.

How were the philosophical underpinnings of the modern state translated into something more tangible? The notion of government being rational and in touch with society led to the development of bureaucracy. Bureaucracy was crucial to the creation of the modern state because it enabled the state to intervene in more areas of society; it led to the administrative mechanisms for government becoming

> ## Box 3.3 **The modern state in postwar Britain**
>
> The state in postwar Britain was responsible for a range of public goods. Following the Second World War, health, education, social security, and law and order were provided by the state. The government also maintained responsibility for the level of unemployment and, through demand management, attempted to control the growth of the British economy. Through industrial policies, a growing number of instruments were created to enable the state to intervene in particular sectors of the economy. The 1972 Industry Act provided for a range of assistance to be given to industry. The 1974 Labour Government created sector working parties that covered 40 per cent of manufacturing output and undertook detailed discussions of the problems of particular industries. In addition, a vast array of industries and companies were directly owned by the state. By the 1970s, gas, electricity, water, coal, telecommunication, steel, and shipbuilding were all state-owned. There was public ownership of car manufacturers, computer companies, and even pubs (in Carlisle). Through the National Enterprise Board, the government could take stakes in private companies. At different points in time, major companies like Rolls-Royce, BP, and British Leyland were controlled by the state. The public sector accounted for 10 per cent of GDP in the 1970s and had a considerable impact on the operation of the private sector (Punnett 1994: 379). At its peak in 1977, public employment rose to 29.6 per cent of the workforce.
>
> (*Source*: Hogwood 1992)

more involved in a range of policy areas. The role of bureaucracy in the modern state was first analysed by the German sociologist Max Weber (1864–1920).

Bureaucracy and the modern state

For Weber, the state was a mechanism for 'rational domination'—which involved focusing on the development of permanent institutional structures and, in particular, the growth of bureaucracy as a response to changes in modern society. Bureaucracy was the epitome of a formally organised structure based on rational politics. Weber argued that the development of bureaucracy was a response both to the growth in democracy—in which mass citizenship placed increased demands on state administration—and to the growth of capitalism—which placed further demands on the state apparatus. Weber was influenced by the age in which he was writing—the latter half of the nineteenth century—when both democracy and capitalism were spreading across Europe. Bureaucracy arose through the state's need to organize itself in response to the growth of both these elements. Having examined explanations as to why states opted for bureaucratic growth and development, we now turn to the key characteristics associated with Weber's 'model of bureaucracy'.

Characteristics of a Weberian model of bureaucracy [adapted from Parsons 1998]

- A clearly identifiable hierarchy of relationships. There is a place for everything and everything is in its place. So, civil servants understand their relationship both between themselves and vis-à-vis their political masters, whilst politicians appreciate the limits to their political power. Within this context, there is seen to be a clear distinction between state bureaucracy and market modes of production. More particularly, public bureaucracies can be easily identified as being different from the marketplace.

  The most obvious physical manifestation of this element of Weberian bureaucracy is the organization of Whitehall departments. At the apex of a department is a Cabinet minister who has a number of junior ministers appointed to support him/her. Below this political tier are a whole series of hierarchical layers of civil servants, the most senior being the Permanent Secretary, while the most junior is a Clerical Officer.

- Clear lines of responsibility. Responsibility is closely tied to the notion of hierarchy. Where a hierarchy exists, as in the case of the departmental model, this increases the potential of knowing who is responsible for what. In particular, responsibility can be clearly identified vis-à-vis time, place, and person. This is captured in the notion of ministerial responsibility which argues that ultimately it is the Cabinet minister located at the apex of the department who is both responsible and accountable for the actions of the department. The strength of such a model, at least in theory, rests on its simplicity. Of course, the reality may differ somewhat from theory.

- Hierarchical discipline. Within the context of a Weberian bureaucracy there is a clearly established set of rules. Often, these are informal 'rules of the game' which participants have to learn to follow (see Rhodes 1988). The most obvious rules are established by the British constitution, which informs both ministers and civil servants of the boundaries within which they must operate. Elsewhere, the more recent findings of the Nolan Committee have conditioned the way in which Parliament acts, whilst the Civil Service Code sets the parameters within which a civil servant may operate. But the rules of the game are often manifested in more informal ways.

- Responsibility gravitates upwards. Within a hierarchical context, the higher up the hierarchy, the greater degree of responsibility an individual actor shoulders (see 'Clear lines of responsibility' above).

- There is an emphasis on control. Common processes ensure that bureaucrats operate through established procedures. Divergence from a given administrative norm is minimized. Thus, modernist administration is concerned with both control and process.

- Organizational structures are rigid and unilinear. Institutional patterns are relatively stable, and a line of command extends from the apex to the bottom.
- Uniformity and predictability. Following on from the last point, the machinery of government is organized in such a way that its various components are like one another. Thus, each part of the bureaucratic structure is similar to all other parts. As such, bureaucracy becomes predictable in the way it works. This is regarded as a positive asset.
- Structures are fixed over time and space. This is one of the most notable aspects of modern Weberian bureaucracy. The emphasis is on the fact that structures of the state remain continuous over time and space. i.e. they tend to stay the same for long periods of time. That is not to contend that they do not change at all, but change tends to be gradual, incremental, and occurring in phases.
- Clearly shared public service values. A key aspect is that those serving in state organizations have a common set of values. This is often referred to as a 'public-service ethos.' Officials are regarded as free from corruption or bias. In the case of Whitehall, officials are seen to be permanent, anonymous, and impartial. Clearly, this ties in with the 'rules of the game' above. Hence, the modern liberal state invokes the idea that the government should be so arranged that citizens and their representatives (MPs) should be able to know where to fix blame, or who to hold to account. There is strong linkage between layers and levels of authority. In effect, the model purports to show that politicians make policy assisted by their officials, and that it is they, as elected representatives of the people, who should be held responsible for their policies. Here, responsibility is both identifiable and transparent, and thus structures are fixed and observable

In principle, then, the modern state contains a number of key features:

- Institutional elements: the modern state is made up of representative institutions for obtaining legitimacy, and bureaucratic institutions in order to develop the capability for intervening in civil society. In addition, there are a range of institutions which regulate civil society and a myriad of informal institutions facilitating the activities of state actors and state group interactions
- Territorial integrity: these institutions operate within a defined area. There is a nation-state that has the authority to govern within particular boundaries.
- There are different levels of government, but it is the national state level that is primary.
- The state has mechanisms for intervening and to an extent controlling a relatively closed national economy.
- The state develops a range of social and welfare policies which are aimed at achieving social progress and maintaining legitimacy.
- Citizenship is the notion that people have the right to participate in political life, and this participation involves both rights and responsibilities.

(For a full discussion see Parsons 1998 and Jessop 1999.)

Thus, the modern state is a large, bureaucratic organization that governs a specific territory on the basis of a claim to legitimacy. It is characterized as hierarchical and centralized, and concerned with a modernist project: aimed at social improvement. More specifically, from a political science perspective, the concept of modernization refers to:

A bundle of processes that are cumulatively and mutually reinforcing; to the formation of capital and the mobilisation of resources; to the development of the forces of production and the increase in the productivity of labour; to the establishment of centralised political power and the formation of nationalised identities; to the proliferation of rights of political participation, of urban forms of life, and of formal schooling; to the secularisation of values and norms; and so on. (Habermas 1990: 2)

From this perspective, the modern state was predominantly capitalist, based on the concept of the nation-state, on secularization, industrialization and urbanization. These were all key trends that at various stages pervaded the nineteenth and twentieth centuries in many Western liberal democracies. They were accompanied by the growth of new classes, mass political parties, social mobility, welfare states, comprehensive education, and a staunch faith in scientific and technical knowledge. The world was understood to be a place which could be rationalized by observation; through modernist projects, most notably that of capitalism and the nation-state, societies could be assured of a steadily improving future.

Yet one of the consequence of the evolution of the modern state, and with it industrial society, was the creation of powerful economic groups which need to be ameliorated to safeguard social order (see Middlemas 1979). In Britain, the form of the modern state after 1945 is what Jessop (1994) refers to as the Keynesian welfare state (KWS)—a state that through Keynesianism and welfare policies directed both economic and social policy within the borders of its nation. Yet to what extent do these characteristics represent the modern British state during the course of the twentieth century? Our next section addresses this question. This state has often been portrayed in the British context as the Westminster model.

The Westminster model of government

The Westminster model has dominated studies of British government throughout the twentieth century, and is essentially an organizing perspective which defines an area to be studied. Here, the British state is seen to be unitary in character—by which it is meant that all domestic sovereignty [power] is formally concentrated in the Westminster Parliament. This is underpinned by the principle of parliamentary sovereignty. Constitutionally, this principle allows for the overturning of any law by a majority in Parliament. So, from this perspective, state power can be seen to be clearly located at the centre.

However, as we will see below, this model presents an oversimplified version of the British system of government. In many ways the British political system has been centralized, and is certainly closed and secretive. The closed and elitist system was justified by a parliamentary system based on legitimacy through representation, and on public servants who were conditioned by a public-service ethos and were therefore not self-interested actors. The ruling elite, in particular ministers and civil servants, could therefore be trusted to act in the public good, rather than for their own narrow or self-serving needs. However, despite the Westminster model's normative prescription of power being centred on Parliament, the British state contained many nineteenth-century features, its territory was contested, and there were tensions between the local and the national levels which weakened the utility of the model.

The Westminster model is built on the assumption that there is parliamentary sovereignty: all decisions are made within Parliament and there is no higher authority. Legitimacy and democracy are maintained because ministers are answerable to Parliament and the House of Commons is elected by the people. Decisions are taken by Cabinet and implemented by a neutral Civil Service. This view is derived from the Whig notion of the constitution being in self-correcting balance (Judge 1993). The main characteristics of the model are identified in Table 3.1. However, as with all models, it is only intended to represent an 'ideal type'. Thus, political scientists have long criticized this model for not describing the reality of the British system of government (see below). The model undoubtedly reflects important features of the British system of government, but it is also a legitimizing mythology. By this we mean that it justifies the maintenance of a closed and elitist system of government. The most important feature of this model is that it reflects how most politicians and officials perceive the system. Within this model, both groups are portrayed as representatives and servants of the people and answerable to them. But they have to act in the public interest rather than directly responding to their own interests or other special interests.

Table 3.1 Characteristics of the Westminster model

Westminster	Whitehall
Parliamentary sovereignty	Permanence
Governing party with a majority in the House of Commons	Anonymity
Cabinet ministers have collective responsibility	Neutrality
Party discipline maintained	Expertise/knowledge
Voters offered choice between disciplined parties	Informal 'village-like' networks
Accountability through free and fair elections	Accountability to political masters
Delivers strong Cabinet government (executive dominance)	Ensures defence of the public interest

Hence, it continues to inform and condition the way in which both sets of actors operate.

Identifying the modern British state

During the nineteenth century, British government and society was dominated by the notion of laissez-faire or liberalism (see Harling 2001). The role of the government was limited to maintaining the market economy and property rights, ensuring and protecting the freedom of individuals, and protecting citizens from external threat (Greenleaf 1983, McEachern 1990). As Harling (2001: 73) observes: 'there was little sympathy for central- or even local-government activism among the early- and mid-Victorians, most of whom were content with a frugal and disinterested state that left them tolerably alone.' Yet, it was in the course of the nineteenth century and throughout the twentieth century, that the modern British state developed; but, as Peele (1999: 74) observes, the process was gradual and piecemeal. The growth of the state was a response to a complex set of interweaving factors such as industrialization, concerns over public health, urbanization, and developing bureaucracy. The key developments in the nineteenth century were:

- The introduction of a range of social, health and education legislation that expanded the role of the state within these sectors. The key point here is that even at the high point of liberalism in the nineteenth century, the state was never solely a nightwatchman. The introduction of factory, education, and health legislation in the 1840s gave the state a special role (Mueller 1984).
- Growing public expenditure (see Fig. 3.1).
- The growth of the bureaucratic machinery (see Fig. 3.2).
- The development of collectivist ideas through the dissemination of the ideas of political thinkers such as Marx, Engels, Hobson, Hobhouse, and Weber as a response to the increasing complexity of a society undergoing an industrial revolution (see Box 3.4).

However, at the end of the nineteenth century the British state was still relatively limited in what it did, how much it spent, and how many people it employed. The predominant belief was still in a minimal role for the state, only intervening when faced with problems of internal or external disorder or when market mechanisms appeared to be failing (as in the case of providing public health). Before 1890, it was almost universally accepted that the level of government expenditure was kept at the minimum consistent with the provision of adequate protection against the Crown's enemies and the maintenance of order (Peacock and Wiseman 1967). Much of the social legislation was only implemented half-heartedly (MacDonagh 1958) and between 1841 and 1890 public expenditure declined from 11 per cent of GNP to 9 per cent (Peacock and Wiseman 1967).

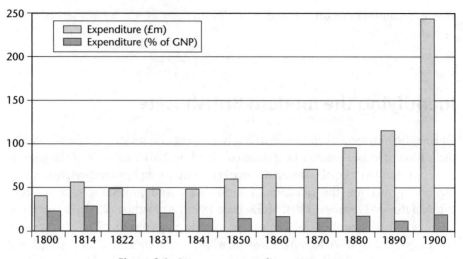

Figure 3.1 Government expenditure 1800–1900
Source: Peacock and Wiseman (1967: 37)

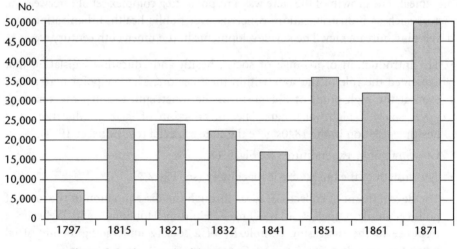

Figure 3.2 The growth of the Civil Service in the nineteenth century
Source: Mueller (1984: 174)

It was only in the twentieth century that the modern state really started to develop, when it acquired an increasing number of functions. As early as 1906, the state increased its role in the provision of welfare through health and unemployment insurance and old age pensions. Here, the Liberal governments between 1906 and 1915 advocated a more active role for the state in promoting social welfare. Harling (2001: 125) asserts that the Liberal governments 'provided an answer that sought to preserve free trade and commit the state to a mild form of wealth redistribution through progressive taxation'. As important, the events of the First World War had a real impact in transforming the nature of the state, and

Box 3.4 **Collectivism vs. liberalism**

Political philosophy has been a major factor in shaping the role of the state in the nineteenth and twentieth centuries. Put another way, ideas are very important in shaping the nature of the state in Britain. At the heart of the philosophical debate in Britain over the nature of the state, we can identify two intellectual paradigms. On the one hand, the laissez-faire or liberal paradigm stresses the importance of the rights of the individual, in particular property rights over collective benefits. Advocates of this paradigm are highly suspicious of the state, often seeing it as a force of evil needing to be controlled. They argue that any form of government intervention demands strong justification, and that the preferred solution to societal problems is to call upon charitable or private actors, not state agencies. The opposing paradigm is the collectivist model, which argues for the importance of state action in order to promote the collective good. It advocates an active role for the state in alleviating poverty, social injustice, and other pathologies it sees as symptoms of a market economy. Thus, the model places a higher priority on the use of state power, in order to promote collective good, than on the protection of individual liberty. 'This model ascribed no particular merit to the workings of the free market and saw governmental intervention as a rational force preferable to private philanthropy' (Peele 1999: 76; see also Greenleaf 1987).

During the late nineteenth century and throughout the twentieth, these two models have competed with one another for supremacy, as political parties, pressure groups, and social movements contested what the role of the state should be. However, a key point is that, throughout this period, at no time did either position completely eclipse the other (see Peele 1999). So, for example, as we saw above, at the height of liberalism in the 1840s the state was never relegated simply to a night-watchman role. If we look elsewhere, in peacetime Britain, the state both reached its greatest size and had the largest number of functions under its direct control in the late 1960s–70s. Yet, even here the state employed only 30 per cent of the workforce, and the private and voluntary sectors still played a substantial role in social, political, and economic life.

... with it the assumptions of the country's governing elite. An unprecedented degree of state intervention in the economy occurred between 1914 and 1918 and novel uses of discretionary powers were tolerated. (Peele 1999: 76)

During the interwar years, the Government became increasingly involved in the economy and the 'onward march of social policy' (Peden 1991: 105). During and after the Second World War, the role of the state in both the economy and social policy substantially increased. The Labour Government of 1945 continued the work started by the wartime coalition and established the welfare state, which provided free education and health care and a comprehensive welfare benefits system. On the economic front, the government committed itself to providing full employment, at least initially, planning the economy, and, through nationalization, acquiring control of large numbers of key industries. In addition, the government committed itself to Keynesian demand management, so accepting responsibility for the aggregate level of demand within the economy (see Pollard 1992). Individuals were no longer responsible for their own welfare, nor was the economy left to the market. These economic and social responsibilities were more or less maintained by all governments until 1979.

This greater economic role obviously increased the size of the state and raised levels of public expenditure. In absolute terms, the increase in state expenditure during the twentieth century has been enormous. Even as a percentage of GNP, it has increased from 11 per cent in 1910 to 52 per cent in 1979 (see Fig. 3.3). This increase in expenditure was accompanied by an increase in public employment. By 1976, 25 per cent of the population worked for the public sector in one form or another.

However, whilst the British state clearly became a large and influential organization in the twentieth century, it was in many ways a deformed modernity: it never strictly complied with the definition of the modern state. This was partly a consequence of the way in which the modernization process occurred in Britain.

An *ancien régime*

Anderson (1963) has argued that the British state never really modernized because the absence of a bourgeois revolution meant that many of the structures of pre-industrial society and the premodern state remained in place. Rather than Britain being a modern state, it is an *ancien régime* combining a premodern state, an anti-industrial commercial class, and a remnant of a landed aristocracy (hence the continuing role of the House of Lords and the monarchy in the political process).

The parliamentary state

The absence of revolution in Britain meant that much of the political development of the state in Britain was a process of negotiated change punctuated by moments of crisis, e.g. the Civil War and the Glorious Revolution in the seventeenth century

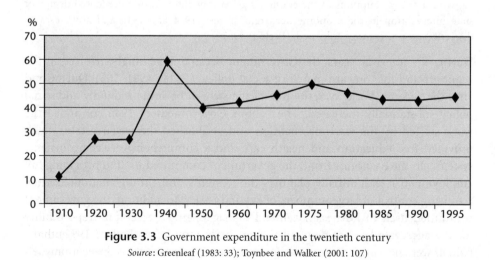

Figure 3.3 Government expenditure in the twentieth century

Source: Greenleaf (1983: 33); Toynbee and Walker (2001: 107)

and the Great Reform Act of 1832. As a consequence, Parliament gained a position as the key source of political authority as power shifted from the monarchy. There-fore, the evolution of the central state and administrative power has occurred within the framework of a parliamentary system (see Judge 1993). In the develop-ment of the British state, a crucial factor is how the growth of bureaucracy could be reconciled with parliamentary government and popular representation. Up to the mid-nineteenth century government departments remained very small, with officials appointed through patronage. In the 1840s and 1850s politicians such as Robert Peel and Lord Palmerston retained a rural, patrimonial view of trust. In the absence of enforceable contracts, the most trustworthy people are those you know—generally relatives or relatives of relatives. Consequently, they believed that patronage was a mechanism for preventing the evils of bureaucracy. However, patronage was not a particularly effective means of developing an effi-cient and bureaucratic state capable of delivering an increasing range of economic, welfare, and foreign policies.

At this time, owing to the limited size of government departments, most policies were not delivered by the central state but by boards such as the Poor Law Board, which were again based largely on patronage. They undermined notions of par-liamentary sovereignty because they made and delivered policy without direct reference to Parliament. However, this limited state was unable to cope with the demands of industrialization and imperial expansion. A resolution to the conflict between patrimonial forms of government and the need for greater state capabil-ities was necessary. One solution was the development of a Bismarckian or Bona-partist authoritarian state (see Moore 1967). Yet in Britain the representative gains of the middle class and the principle of parliamentary sovereignty made this path difficult. New forms of state that could deliver a growing number of public goods had to be reconciled with a role for Parliament.

Ministerial departments were nineteenth-century creations which developed as a mechanism for fusing the requirements of increased governmental activism, representative government, and parliamentary sovereignty. The two crucial elements inherent in this solution were ministerial responsibility and a merito-cratic and neutral Civil Service. Before 1860, most decisions were taken either directly by ministers, who had very little in the way of bureaucratic support—indeed, Peel use to answer all his own letters—or by boards. The use of boards was subject to widespread criticism from political thinkers such as Bentham and Mill.

The problem presented by boards, apart from issues of corruption or patronage, was that they broke the link between parliament and the decision-making process because decisions were not directly made by Parliament. Ministerial departments, on the other hand, allowed the expansion of government without threatening parliamentary sovereignty. They also ensured some popular representation because elected government ministers rather than appointees made decisions. Thus throughout the nineteenth century writers and thinkers such as Bentham, Mill, and Bagehot called for the development of ministerial departments as the key administrative unit because it meant that ministers, who were responsible to Parliament, and ultimately to the electorate, would make decisions:

> The Ministerial department came to have certain specific features. It was to be headed by a single political person, at once exclusively responsible, the most powerful and yet the most temporary element in the organization. Underneath the Ministers would be certain senior officers reporting directly to the Permanent Head and appointed like him in consultation with the Prime Minister and the general manager of the department. As the general manager he would also be the accounting officer. Thence downward there would be a continuing hierarchy. (Schaffer 1957: 60)

Thus, the administrative fusion of ministers and parliamentary sovereignty had important implications for the development of British government and the distribution of power within the core executive. Departments became the site of the majority of policy-making, with ministers having a monopoly of control over policy (Beattie 1995). As a consequence, a hierarchical form of government developed. In law, it is the minister who is responsible for the actions of the department. This, combined with political accountability, ensures that departments are centralized and hierarchical institutions with the minister at the top (Judge 1993).

These developments led to a further problem. If ministers are responsible for decisions, officials exist to implement their wishes; therefore departments founded on the principle of ministerial accountability require a professional, anonymous, and neutral Civil Service. However, officials have to reconcile neutrality with loyalty to the minister. Whilst officials are perceived as neutral, there can be no disunity between the minister and official because only ministers are held publicly to account. Officials in this sense cannot act in their own right.

Ministerial responsibility was also a means of reconciling the notion of democratic government with limited popular participation. Parliamentary sovereignty implied that MPs had to be representatives rather than delegates—if they were delegated, the people would be sovereign. Therefore, it was to the representatives rather than the people that the policy-makers were responsible. Thus, the establishment of departments placed policy-making firmly with the executive and away from electoral constraints. Ministerial responsibility created a direct chain of accountability from ministers to MPs, consequently allowing only a limited role for the citizen in the process of government. A common theme of 'liberal' thinking on representative government is that only 'educated' people can realistically be involved in government and therefore representatives have to use their own judgement rather than, to coin Joseph Chamberlain's (1836–1914) phrase, 'truckle with the multitude' (quoted in Jennings 1966: 1).

Consequently, the development of a professional Civil Service occurred coterminously with the development of departments. The Northcote Trevelyan report of 1854 proposed a professional, meritocratic, and permanent Civil Service with a degree of independence from its political masters (Northcote and Trevelyan 1954). This was crucial. With the increasing size and responsibilities of the state, politicians were unable to make all the decisions and control all the operations of a department. They needed advisers they could trust. First, officials had to sift, organize, and provide ministers with information on key problems, and on the available policy options. Second, ministers needed high-quality staff who could take decisions independently in an increasing number of areas. Third, there was a need for the administrative machinery to implement decisions in an increasing number of areas of civil society (Cronin 1991: 19).

Nevertheless, there was much opposition to the Northcote Trevelyan reforms, and it was not until 1870 that open competition for Civil Service posts was introduced. Even then, the Home Office and Foreign Office resisted reform for a number of years (Greenleaf 1987). Moreover, the reforms were evolutionary rather than revolutionary (Hennessy 1989) and did not undermine the nightwatchman state. They did, however, establish the basis of the modern Civil Service, which enabled the creation of a bureaucratic, administrative state. The aim of the reformers was not to expand the state, but to make it more economical and efficient (Greenleaf 1987; Hart 1972). Increasingly, its capabilities were, in a sense, a side effect. By abolishing patronage and creating a class of what later became known as policy advisers, the reforms enabled the development of a more effective Civil Service. Again, the notion that officials were neutral and anonymous reinforced the principle of ministerial responsibility and parliamentary accountability. Officials did not have to be accountable, because they were implementing the minister's will. This principle was firmly established by the Haldane Report of 1918, which recognized that 'civil servants as advisers have an indivisible relationship' with ministers (Richards 1997: 236) and so further ensured the unity of the central state. If ministers are responsible, officials cannot be distinct actors.

Departmental government, however, presented a potential threat to the indivisibility of sovereignty by placing policy-making in distinct, autonomous departments. The development of departments required the establishment of collective mechanisms within the core executive. The growth of collective government between 1854 and 1918 was much more erratic and ad hoc than the establishment of a professional Civil Service. The piecemeal nature of its development accounts for many problematic and contradictory elements in the modern-day core executive. These changes in the Civil Service were paralleled by changes in other parts of the core executive. During the second half of the nineteenth century the Cabinet became increasingly institutionalized, and power relationships within it changed: 'Most government tasks came to be formalised under the effective responsibilities of ministers' (Daedler 1963a: 18). In order to coordinate the work of ministers, the Cabinet grew and became much more rule-bound in its structure (Daedler 1963b). According to Mackintosh (1977: 143), the Cabinet became:

[t]he centre of political power; it was the body which determined policy. It was possible for Prime Ministers, Foreign Secretaries and even lesser Ministers to take some decisions on their own, but if there was any dispute or challenge from Parliament or the Press, the matter had to be settled in the Cabinet.

The two important factors in the developing of Cabinet were the First World War (1914–18) and the Haldane Committee Report (1918) mentioned above.

The Cabinet system from the mid-nineteenth century developed alongside a system of Cabinet committees (the first ad hoc committee was established in 1855 to deal with the Crimean War), the Cabinet Office (founded in 1916), and, from the 1960s, the Prime Minister's Office, as a means of imposing collective agreement on ministerial departments. Collective responsibility resolved a problem for government. Parliamentary sovereignty and accountability mechanisms led to the establishment of ministerial departments. Strong departments threatened the unity of sovereignty and therefore required the imposition of collective government. Collective government thus reinforces the power of the central executive by imposing on departments the requirement to accept the collective decisions of government whether or not they were involved in or agreed with a decision. In principle, it gives the Cabinet predominance over departments. Therefore, the institutional advantages of departments are, supposedly, counterbalanced by the constitutional advantages of the Cabinet. This explains why so much analysis in political science has been centred on the Cabinet rather than on departments; political scientists have accepted the constitutional precepts, rather than the institutional structures, as a more accurate indicator of the sources of power. Of course, it suited government to present this view because then it is seen as unified, strategic, and democratically accountable. However, as successive Prime Ministers have found, from Churchill's experiments with overlords in the 1950s to Blair's development of ministers for coordination in the Lord Chancellor and the Minister without Portfolio, imposing collective government on the institutionally strong departments is extremely difficult.

Consequently, the British system does not fit closely the rational and linear system of the Weberian model. There are complex tensions between the powers of officials, ministers, and the Prime Minister. Whilst in one way officials are neutral, in another way they are highly political because their role is to protect the minister; as a consequence, the policy process becomes one of making political decisions rather than rational decisions.

The continuing influence of liberalism

The British state developed in the context of liberal ideas from such thinkers as Bentham, Mill, Green, and Dicey. Consequently, Greenleaf (1983) identifies a continual tension between collectivist and libertarian thought. Whilst the state has become increasingly interventionist in the last 150 years, there have been important ideological limits on how much the state should intervene (see Box 3.4). There is a strong tradition that the British state should be limited; consequently there is no formally identified body of public law in Britain, and governments have rarely relied on detailed state planning as in continental European states (see Kavanagh and Seldon 2000: 343, 355). For instance, the comprehensive economic planning system created during the Second World War was quickly abandoned, and subsequently, the Conservative Administration (1951–64) took a relatively hands-off approach to the economy.

Territorial integrity

The boundedness of the British nation state has always been contested. First, until the Second World War, the British state was defined to a large extent by empire. As Gamble (1999) observes, the British state developed as an expansionist state, and the growth and sustenance of the empire was important in shaping both national identity and the nature of public service in Britain (for instance, the Northcote–Trevelyan reforms were largely a consequence of changes in the Indian Civil Service).

Second, Britain is not a nation-state, but a multinational state made up of England, Scotland, Wales, and Northern Ireland. This has led Mitchell (see Catterall et al. 2000) to speak of Britain as a union state rather than a unitary state, with Scotland and Northern Ireland at least having their own particular political systems within the UK. Scotland always retained its own education and legal systems, and the Scottish Office, established in 1885, had a considerable degree of autonomy. Northern Ireland had from 1921 to 1972 a devolved system of government, with the Government in London rarely intervening in the province.

A clear example of the fluid nature of the state can be seen if one examines the changing nature of the territorial dimension in Britain over the last few centuries. Scotland, Wales, and Northern Ireland have all been component parts of the British state for a long period. Wales was absorbed by Britain in 1536, Scotland by the Act of Union 1707, while the union of Ireland with Britain was achieved in 1801 and remained until the partition of Ireland in 1920 and the creation of Ulster in 1921. Each of these dates signifies a major change in the contours of the British state. More recently, the election in May 1997 of a Labour Government committed to the principle of devolution has once again led to the contours of the British state being remodelled. The Labour Government has set about redesigning the institutional makeup of Britain. It is in the process of redistributing power away from the centre, i.e. from Westminster to the sub-central level. The rationale underpinning Labour's devolution of power from the centre is that this will ultimately strengthen the Union. However, there is a counter-argument: that Labour has set in train an irresistible force whose momentum will lead to outright separation and the breakup of the UK. This has created the potential for 'leapfrogging' in Wales: having seen the power that has accrued to Scotland, Wales may demand more powers of independence for itself (see Chapter 10). But it should also be noted that the British state has changed its territorial arrangements at many points in history without disintegrating.

Local/national tension

Whilst the British system that evolved in the twentieth century was highly central-ized, as a consequence of parliamentary sovereignty and party discipline, it has to be remembered that the British state in many ways developed from the bottom up. Effectively, what occurred in Britain was that many services, including health care, education, and the provision of utilities, developed at local level and were national-ized in the course of the twentieth century. So, for instance, the creation of the National Health Service was the consolidation of many local authority and charity hospitals under Ministry of Health control. However, a consequence of this bottom-up process of state-building was that the local level continued to have considerable impact on the policy process. The fact that the local level remained important in funding, delivering, and regulating a range of welfare and other services leads Rhodes (1988) to question the idea that Britain is a unitary state.

Bulpitt (1983) surveyed the evolution of sub-central government in the UK in modern times and presents a contrasting interpretation to Rhodes. At the core of his observations was the argument that, between 1926 and the early 1960s, the relationship between the centre (e.g. Westminster/Whitehall) and the periphery (local government) took the form of a 'dual polity'. Bulpitt (1983: 235–6) argued that there existed:

A state of affairs in which national and local polities were largely divorced from one another. Those contacts which existed . . . were bureaucratic and depoliticised. In this period, the Centre achieved what it had always desired—relative autonomy from peripheral forces to pursue its High Politics preoccupations.

The crux of Bulpitt's argument was that central and local government coexisted independently of one another. Central government dealt with what Bulpitt referred to as 'high politics' issues, such as managing the economy, maintaining law and order, providing social welfare, ensuring the defence of the realm, and pursuing foreign policy interests. Local government, by contrast, addressed 'low politics' issues concerning education, social services, etc. As Rhodes (1997: 114) observes:

In sharp contrast to the French system, Britain has neither a Napoleonic tradition of using central field agents to supervise local authorities, nor a system of *cumul des mandats* whereby politicians collect electoral offices, leading to the close interpenetration of national and local elites. The British territorial code stresses the autonomy of the centre in matters of high politics.

As Bulpitt contends, however, the corporatist era of the 1970s witnessed the break-down in the relationship between the centre and the periphery. The centre became increasingly embroiled in 'low politics' issues. This, Bulpitt argued, compromised central government's ability to be seen as 'governing competently'. As a response, during the 1980s, the Thatcher governments sought to reassert a degree of auton-omy for the centre. They aimed to break what was regarded as the increasing power and overspending of local government. This was typified by the so-called 'loony Left' councils such as Camden, Haringey, and Liverpool in the 1980s, who had embarked on a series of policies to promote social justice in areas such as education, transport, health and social relations, policies which the Conservative Government regarded as a direct challenge to the moral agenda being laid down by Thatcherism.

The problem of the British state—which in many respects persists today—is that the tasks and functions of a large and interventionist modern state were grafted onto a system that was essentially nineteenth-century. Notions of the role of the Civil Service, ministerial responsibility, and the role of Parliament were created in the nineteenth century, and only adapted in a piecemeal and evolution-ary way. Moreover, the process of adaptation was through negotiation between governing elites, and therefore was not about modernizing government but about sustaining elite rule. It has only been at moments of crises of legitimization that significant changes have even been hinted at. The consequence is that the modern British state takes a very particular form. It was, to use Judge's (1993) term, a 'Parliamentary State' which, through party discipline and representative govern-ment, allowed a considerable concentration of power within the hands of the executive. The executive's power was to some extent built on a system of depart-mental government which relied on the loyalty of officials who, as we will see, had considerable influence over policy. It also relied on local administration for the implementation of policy, thus entailing considerable negotiation between the centre and the localities. It was through this framework that modernist features of the Keynesian welfare state were pursued, but the deformed nature of this modernity created many difficulties for the government in achieving its goals.

The state was (and is) undoubtedly large, centralized, and bureaucratic. After 1945 it controlled a wide range of policies, spent a vast amount of money and had a significant impact on the lives of most people. This peaked in the 1960s (see Box 3.5). However, there were significant limits on what the state could achieve and control. As we will see in later chapters, the British state has always been con-strained by external factors which are often portrayed as an explanation for not achieving domestic policy goals. It may even be the case that the maintenance of full employment was not a consequence of domestic control of the economy, but a result of the postwar boom fuelled by US expansion. Nevertheless, the development of the modern state did affect what British government did and the policy-making process.

The modern state and the policy process

Although the British state does not fit neatly into the characteristics of the modern state or 'government', the policy process did traditionally take a particular form:

- Central government set the agenda in most key policy areas. Whilst most policy

Box 3.5 **The 1960s: the high point of deformed modernism**

The 1960s was in many ways the high point of modernity. Living standards were rising quickly, and many people in Britain were for the first time concerned with satisfying more than their immediate needs. It was also the era when science seemed able to solve all problems. The space race was under way and the application of nuclear power to energy promised a solution to fuel shortages. Medicine was continually making break-throughs in the fight against new diseases, and many illnesses which had been killers only a few years before, such as tuberculosis and polio, were disappearing. This scientific optimism had an important impact on politics. In the late 1950s and the early 1960s, Britain's economy appeared to be lagging behind her competitors. The Conservative Government which had been in power since 1951 appeared increasingly embroiled in scandal and out of touch. Harold Wilson, the new Labour leader, promised a government inspired by the 'white heat of technology' which would finally modernize Britain through a programme of social and economic reform. Two central elements to this modernization process were the national plan and the Fulton Report on the Civil Service.

The national plan was seen as a rational and government-led response to the problem of stop/go which had slowed Britain's economic development. The British economy had a structural problem: periods of economic growth led to a surge in imports and a balance-of-payments deficit, which meant that the government was forced to cut back demand or face a sterling crisis. The national plan was intended to resolve this problem. The plan was to achieve 'a 25 per cent increase in national output between 1964 and 1970' (Cmnd. 2764: 1966), and the report stated that the government would use its economic power and influence to secure economic growth. However, the plan was never fulfilled because the sterling crises of 1965/6 forced the government into deflation rather than expansion.

The Wilson Government was also concerned with modernizing the process of government and there was much criticism at the time about the elitist and conservative nature of the British Civil Service. Labour set up the Fulton Committee in 1966 to inquire into the nature of the Civil Service. The main finding of the 1968 report was that the Civil Service was too generalist and amateurish, and needed much more scientific and man-agerial expertise. However, despite acceptance of the report, most of Fulton's recom-mendations were never implemented, largely because of Civil Service obstruction. More importantly, Fulton was never really intended to tackle the key problems of the British system of government. Its remit was issues of management and personnel rather than the machinery of government. Consequently, the ramshackle Victorian bureaucracy remained in place (see Hennessy 1989).

was delivered at local level, because central government controlled finance and legislation it had a major impact on health, education, and social policy. For instance, Labour and Conservative governments were relatively successful at driving through the shift from selective to comprehensive education in the 1960s (although even here a number of local authorities did resist).

- Policy-making was 'in-house'. Most policy was made within departments, with officials collecting information, advising ministers, and developing policy proposals. Departments were at the core of the policy process, and therefore had a considerable impact on outcomes.

- Policy-making within departments was hierarchical. Policy was developed by the top grades of the Civil Service, but within these grades all policy would be processed through a clear hierarchy up to the Permanent Secretary and the ministers. A retired, senior official gives a flavour of the process:

I remember back in 1969 in the Ministry of Power, what would happen was the principal would write two or three pages closely argued and put it up to his assistant secretary, who that night would add another two pages and would then pass it up to his under secretary who would add his own page and, if it was terribly important, it would then go through the deputy secretary and the permanent secretary and it would land on the minister's desk as a great thick thing which had contributions all the way from the top down. That was nonsensical but very typical of the way the Civil Service operated thirty years ago. (Marsh et al. 2001).

- Civil servants had a considerable influence on the policy process. Officials were the policy experts and had the necessary knowledge to make policy. Consequently, ministers were highly dependent on them (see Foster and Plowden 1996). In certain departments, for example the Home Office, it appeared that officials effectively ran the department, and ministers were seen as obstacles to its smooth running. Even as late as 1989, the former Home Secretary, David Waddington felt:

You were very much given the impression, when you went to the Home Office, that governments came and went and ministers come and go but things went on as they had always done. That they had responsibilities which went far wider than the political concerns of ministers who were here one day and gone the next and they had to operate grand empires whether it was the Prisons or the Immigration Service and it was a fair assumption that whichever party was in office, they would expect those functions to be performed in very much the same way.

- Only very particular outside interests were involved in the policy process. Policy-making in a range of key policy areas: health, education, agriculture, and criminal justice was made in a series of discrete and closed policy networks (see Chapter 8). Departments consulted outside interests, but these were particular groups that played by the 'rules of the game' and were not concerned with challenging the overall direction of government policy. These networks ensured that the government had legitimacy by claiming to consult concerned interests, but it also meant they could exclude 'radical' groups which might have upset the dominant policy groups (see Marsh and Rhodes 1992, Smith 1993, Richardson and Jordan 1979).

- In key economic areas, the government developed quasi-corporatist relation- ships with business and unions. The government developed established and institutionalized relationships with the TUC, the CBI, and individual unions and business. These bodies were often involved in detailed discussions of key elements of economic policy, in particular industrial policy and incomes policy.

For Middlemas (1979), trade unions and business became governing institutions and were incorporated into many levels of government through advisory
committees, quangos, and royal commissions. By 1966 the CBI was represented
on fifty-seven advisory bodies such as ACAS, NEDC and the Price Commission
(Newman 1981). Nevertheless, the arrangements were often unstable because of
conflict between business, unions, and government over policy issues, and in
1978–9 the unions and some businesses refused to implement the government's
incomes policy (see Chapter 8).

Conclusion: the British state and deformed modernism

The modern state is characterized as hierarchical, centralized, territorially bound,
and omnipresent. Many of these features could be identified in the British state
between 1945 and 1979, but it was also in many ways a deformed modernism.
Whilst the state was hierarchical and centralized, there were challenges from local
and non-state forms of administration. Whilst the public sector was large, there
was also a large private sector. Moreover, the territorial integrity of the UK has
always been contested. Yet it is also clear that the modern British state did take on
many functions; perhaps more importantly, policy-making was often closed,
secretive, and elitist.

So how should we interpret the modern (deformed) state in Britain? It helps to
return to the philosophical debate (discussed above) concerning the role of the
state. As we have seen, throughout the nineteenth and twentieth centuries this
debate has oscillated between two contrasting models—collectivism and liberalism, each located at opposing ends of a philosophical spectrum. The point was also
made above that at different stages the characteristics associated with one model
dominated but never eclipsed the other. A convincing argument can be made that
the height of collectivism in Britain occurred in the late 1960s—what we have
referred to as 'the high point of deformed modernism' (see Box 3.5). Yet it is
important to recognize that while, at this stage, both the private and voluntary
sectors still played an important role in social, political, and economic life, the
Government was undoubtedly the most powerful and important actor in the
policy process. It is from this perspective that we can label the period from 1945 to
the 1970s as an 'era of Government' in which there was a high concentration of
state powers. This then leads to the key question of this book: to what extent has
both the system of government and state powers been eroded, from the 1970s to
the present during the era of governance? Before this question can be addressed,
however, we first must analyse why it is that the high point of deformed modernism in the 1960s was then followed by a perceived crisis of the state in the 1970s.

KEY POINTS

- The state can be defined as exercising sovereignty, being public, having distinct institutional structures, being territorially bounded, having legitimacy, and using domination.
- The state is nevertheless a fluid and complex entity, with changing boundaries and networks of relationships
- Modernity is a belief in rationality, absolute truths, and progress.
- The modern state is a large bureaucratic organization that governs a specific territory based on a claim to legitimacy.
- The Westminster model provides the ideal type of the modern state in the British context.
- In the twentieth century, the British state took on many features of the modern state, including a large workforce, high levels of expenditure, a range of progressive policies, and an attempt to improve social conditions. It also retained features of a premodern state such as the House of Lords and a continuing role for the monarchy.
- In many ways the British state also continued to be fragmented, with a range of services delivered at the local level.
- In terms of policy-making, central government set the agenda, advice and decisions were made within central government, and officials had a central role in policy-making; policy-making was hierarchical, and whilst interest groups were involved, entry was controlled by the core executive.
- The British state can be described as 'deformed modernism'. Whilst it had many of the characteristics of a modern state, it also had elements of premodernism and local control over particular services.

KEY QUESTIONS

1. What are the key features of the British modern state?
2. What is the relationship between the Westminster model and the modern state?
3. Is Britain a deformed modern state?
4. How have premodern elements affected the nature of the British state?

KEY READING

On the premodern elements of the British state see Anderson (1963). On the development of the state see Smith (1999) and Harling (2001). For a discussion of the ideological imprint see Greenleaf (1983). For an examination of the Westminster model see Holliday et al. (1999). For the Parliamentary state see Judge (1993).

KEY WEBSITES

For a discussion of the modern state and its problems there is information at the sites of a number of think tanks including: **www.iea.org.uk/**, **www.demos.co.uk/pms2nded.htm,** www.adamsmith.org.uk/, www.cer.org.uk/, www.npi.org.uk/, www.ucl.ac.uk/constitution-unit/, www.fabian-society.org.uk/int.asp, and for a libertarian view www.digiweb.com/igeldard/LA/. There is also useful general information on British politics at www.ukpolitics.org.uk/

4

FROM MODERNITY TO CRISIS

INTRODUCTION

So far, we have examined the ideas underpinning the modern state and explored the challenge to it in recent years, in the form of governance and, at the philosophical level, postmodernism. Within this context we have described two contrasting models of the state, both of which attempt to provide an organizing perspective on the British polity. We observed that the original model used to describe the British political system was the 'Westminster model'. In the last thirty years, however, this model has endured sustained criticism by political scientists, who argue that it fails to properly describe both the nature and complexity of the British political system. Recently, the 'differentiated polity model' has been proposed by Rhodes as a more appropriate characterization of the British state, reflecting the changes that have occurred during the era of governance. Although we have outlined the details of these two different models and argued that they reflect two different periods in the evolution of the British state, we have not yet examined how and why governance presented such a serious challenge to the modern state. As historians continually remind us, in order to make sense of the present it is vital to understand the past.

In this chapter we look at the origins and development of the Keynesian welfare state. We explore its evolution in the postwar period as a key element of a modernist political project, and examine the subsequent development of a perceived crisis in the welfare state. We will argue that by the mid-1970s, there had developed the notion that the state had become overloaded, giving rise to the popular theme that the British state was becoming ungovernable. It is within this context that we explore the so-called 'ungovernability thesis'. The chapter will conclude by arguing that the perceived crisis in the Keynesian welfare state created a political vacuum which breathed life into an alternative political project for the state, based on a liberal democratic agenda which was subsequently augmented under the auspices of Thatcherism.

The Keynesian welfare state: a modernist project

War or revolution are always crucial periods in the development of a state. Each can provide a clear break from the past and a chance for a nation to start afresh with a new political project framed by a different constitutional settlement. In the last 150 years, Germany provides an obvious example of a nation-state which, either through war or revolution, has undergone a number of vastly contrasting political projects, each of which have signposted a clear break from the past. The Weimar Republic (1919–33), the Third Reich (1933–45), the Federal Republic of Germany and the German Democratic Republic (1945–89), and, following the collapse of the Berlin Wall, the subsequent reunification of East and West Germany all mark obvious disjunctures in the evolution of the German state. In contrast, the history of the British state is very different, marked more by continuity than discontinuity, with the relatively peaceful evolution of the parliamentary state over more than 300 years since the Glorious Revolution of 1689. Thus, in order to understand the nature of the British state, it is necessary to recognize the extent to which the past has shaped the present.

Clearly, the Westminster model discussed in Chapter 3 evolved out of past political practices that had been slowly modified over many years. Therefore, although in this chapter we are going to use the Second World War as a key period in which to contend that the Keynesian welfare state, as a modernist project, subsequently evolved, we want to point out that this political project arose within the confines of the parliamentary state which was little affected by the war. Moreover, the Parliamentary state reflects the ideas and values associated with a particular view of democracy that has slowly evolved in the last 300 years. These values and ideas can be referred to as the British political tradition (see Box 4.1), and it is the longevity of this tradition, responsible for shaping British politics, which distinguishes it from the traumatic experiences of many of Britain's continental neighbours. The key point here is that, although the Keynesian welfare state was a new political project borne out of the experience of war, it was a project both shaped and conditioned by the past, in the form of the broader structures of the parliamentary state, which itself was conditioned by the British political tradition.

The Keynesian welfare state and the war

In this narrative, the starting point is the period 1939-45, out of which the Keynesian welfare project developed. In effect, the Second World War was the catalyst which altered the trajectory of the British state and prompted widespread political acceptance of the need for a comprehensive system of welfare provision. However, we should not overlook the fact that the political elite were nurturing ideas of a greater role for the state, prior to the outbreak of war:

Box 4.1 **The British political tradition**

The institutions and processes of British politics are underpinned by a particular conception of democracy. This can be referred to as the 'British political tradition', and involves a limited, liberal conception of representation and a conservative notion of responsibility.

In this view, the British system is representative because there are periodic free and fair elections. There is little emphasis in the British system on demographic representation or on the notion that Parliament or an MP should forward the political views of constituents. As such, referenda are used in the British system not to discover the views of the electorate but rather to resolve irreconcilable policy differences among the leadership of the governing party. The past and planned referenda on Europe are ample evidence here.

As far as responsibility is concerned, the position is even clearer. Accountability does play a role in the British political tradition, in that the doctrine of parliamentary sovereignty rests in part on the notion that the executive is accountable to the voters at periodic free and fair elections and to Parliament between elections. However, despite David Judge's elegant defence (1993) of the role of Parliament, it remains true that the British system is characterized by executive dominance of the legislature. Perhaps more importantly, there is virtually no emphasis in the British political tradition on responsiveness—on the view that the government should be responsive to the electorate. Rather, the British political tradition emphasizes the idea that a responsible government is one which is willing and able to take strong, decisive, necessary action even if that action is opposed by a majority of the population. This view rests on the idea that 'government knows best': it advocates a leadership, rather than a participatory, view of democracy.

The key point here is that it is this view of democracy that has shaped the institutions and processes of the British state. So, the electoral system is one which produces—indeed, one could say is designed to produce—strong majority government. In contrast, proportional representation is opposed in large part because it produces coalition and hence, it is argued, weak government. Similarly, the obsession with secrecy in Britain exists to ensure that governments are able to take strong, decisive, necessary action with limited scrutiny of how and why they took that decision. In contrast, open government is opposed because it would mean that governments, and indeed ministers and civil servants, would always be looking over their shoulders at public opinion and, thus failing to take appropriate, if unpopular, decisions.

We can see that over the last few centuries the historical evolution of the institutions of government have been underpinned by a particular view of democracy—or, to put it in more abstract terms, that ideas about democracy, or, more particularly, ideas about democracy which were current in the late eighteenth and early nineteenth century, still influence both the structure and the nature of the British state.

(*Source*: Marsh et al. 2001)

One social historian (Gilbert 1970: p. vii) insists that even before the outbreak of the war, there had emerged amongst Britain's party leaders 'a private political consensus' that the state needed to ensure a national system of welfare provision for the most vulnerable sections of society. (Dorey 1995: 12)

Between 1918 and 1939, social deprivation and mass unemployment had been two prominent features of British society. The political elites in Britain were sensitized to the fact that, as part of a tacit contract to mobilize the population for participation in fighting the Second World War, it was important to promise a 'New Jerusalem' for a war-weary nation following the successful prosecution of the war (see Hennessy 1992). In practical terms, this meant that government should shoulder the responsibility for providing something worth returning to for those soldiers and their families after the horrors of war. Here, the principle of 'deferred gratification' was being applied, in order to help persuade British subjects to fight. Thus, the population would make sacrifices to the state as part of the war effort, based on the tacit agreement that the state would have obligations to provide for the population on their return from war. This theme is captured by Goodin and Dryzek (1995: 49) in their notion of 'justice deferred': 'The poor are asked to make a wartime sacrifice for which they simply cannot be compensated during the war itself. Their pay-off can come only later—by which of course their contribution has already been made.'

   Here, we also witness a lesson learnt from the earlier failure of the British governing class to provide something more substantial after the 1914–18 War, when the promise of 'homes fit for heroes' failed to materialize because of the imposition of economic constraints. In 1939 the governing elite recognized that another failure to deliver on promises made prior to war could ultimately lead to social and political instability, which should be avoided at all costs. Finally, the Second World War also played a crucial role in changing the political attitudes of the nation as a whole (see Box 4.2).

The emergence of the Keynesian welfare state

It was out of the context of the Second World War that the Keynesian welfare state emerged. In recent years a key debate has developed within political science centred on the extent to which, in the period after 1945, there existed a degree of political consensus among the main political parties in the development and consolidation of the Keynesian welfare state. In some ways this debate is crucial for our understanding of this state, as it provides the analytical framework in which to understand the development of the modern state. So in the next section we examine the original thesis of the postwar consensus associated with the work most notably of Addison (1975), Kavanagh (1987), and Kavanagh and Morris 1989) and then look at those who criticize this approach; Pimlott (1988), Rollings (1994), Kerr (1999).

Box 4.2 **The impact of war**

Among the electorate as a whole, the sacrifices of the war years gave rise to heightened expectations about the securing of a better world when arms were finally laid
down. In this respect, the war was like its predecessor of 1914. But there were important
differences. With government encouragement, the Second World War was seen as being
fought for the benefit of the common man. It was a 'people's war', and it would be the
people as a whole that would gain ultimate victory. The ethos of the First World War had
been altogether more conservative. Insofar as the earlier war had promised improvements for the common man—'a land fit for heroes to live in'—these hopes had been
largely disappointed. Yet, as the Second World War progressed, there developed an
overwhelming determination that such disappointments should not be repeated. This
war also disrupted civilian society, with all its deep-rooted class-based structures, to a far
greater degree than had its predecessor, adding further to the egalitarian thrust which it
produced. Some observers were not slow to recognize that, whatever it did to Britain's
position in the international arena, the war might become a catalyst for major social and
political change. Speaking in December 1939, the Conservative Anthony Eden declared
that the war would 'bring about changes which may be fundamental and revolutionary
in the economic and social life of this country.'

(*Source*: Dutton 1997: 12)

The postwar consensus debate: advocates

The narratives attached to the idea of a postwar consensus are important, as they
provide the terrain on which much of the literature on the development of the
British state in the latter half of the twentieth century has been debated. The
postwar consensus (PWC) thesis is represented most forcefully in the work of
Addison (1975), Kavanagh (1987), Kavanagh and Morris (1989), and Seldon
(1994). Although these authors differ somewhat, they broadly agree that this consensus reflected both a style of government and a broad range of policies which all
governments attached themselves to up until 1979. Thus, for Kavanagh and Morris
(1989: 3–4) consensus is used in two different senses. The first refers to a particular
style of government based on consultation between government and the major
economic actors, in particular trade unions. For these authors, the skill of governing was to focus on the harmonization of the demands of groups in civil society, as
much as imposing a set of policies on them. The second sense in which consensus
is used refers to the range of policies pursued by both parties, when in government
between the 1940s and 1970s, based on (i) 'Beveridgism'—a commitment to the
collective provision of a comprehensive welfare service, in order to promote social
citizenship—and (ii) Keynesianism—the government's use of particular fiscal and
monetary policies in order to stimulate the level of aggregate demand in the
economy with the aim of securing full employment. Kavanagh and Morris identify
what they believe are the key policy areas on which, after 1945, there was biparti-
sian political consensus (see Box 4.3). They argue that these policy areas were

Box 4.3 Policy grounds for consensus?

Full employment

A commitment by the political elites that unemployment which was such a predominant feature of the inter war years, would not be allowed to persist in the post-1945 era. The principle of a job for men [sic] for life became enshrined at the heart of the emerging consensus and was captured in the 1944 Employment White Paper. The role of government was to manage demand as a means to achieving full employment.

A mixed economy

This comprised two elements: an active role for government in managing the economy in order to pursue particular social and economic objectives and, secondly, a willingness of British governments for the first time to nationalize and to take over ownership and responsibility for a number of strategically important industries. Between 1946 and 1949, the Bank of England, coal, rail, civil aviation, iron and steel, road passenger and freight transport, electricity and gas were all nationalized. This created the structural basis for the postwar 'mixed' economy. More importantly, this large-scale programme of nationalization represented a fundamental transformation in both the boundaries and responsibilities of the state. The Conservatives, although ideologically never committed to nationalisation and state ownership, accepted both on grounds of political pragmatism.

Social welfare provision

Perhaps the most obvious and politically significant component of the postwar consensus was the welfare settlement. This born out of the 1942 Beveridge Report on *Social Insurance and Allied Services* which Labour and the Conservatives, for different reasons, both accepted (see below). Thus, both the main political parties attached themselves to the necessity and legitimacy of state-funded welfare provision, committing themselves to: a universal national insurance scheme; a comprehensive national health service free at the point of access to all; free and compulsory education; an extended state housing sector.

Conciliation of the trade unions

This was also a key constituent of the consensus thesis based on the conciliation and incorporation of the labour force within a wider political settlement—later this was labelled as a corporatist settlement. This, at least in theory, referred to the notion of the consultation and incorporation of labour as well as capital within the political decision-making process. Here, it is worth pointing out that one of the key authors of the consensus thesis, Kavanagh (1987), accepts that this is the weakest link in the consensus debate, in that, in particular under Conservative administrations, the trade unions were only consulted with a begrudging acceptance.

Foreign and defence policy

A consensus to maintain Britain's world role, through the development of a new 'special relationship' with the United States, a new independent nuclear capability, and the creation of a new Commonwealth from the crumbling remnants of the old empire, from which British politicians could project their global horizons.

established during the Labour Attlee Government (1945-51) and thus refer to them as the 'Attlee Settlement' (see Kavanagh and Morris 1989: 4–6).

It was on these pillars that a perceived postwar consensus between 1945 and the 1960s developed. More particularly, it is argued that during the period from the 1940s until the mid-1970s, these various commitments led both the major political parties to develop the Keynesian welfare state. As Kavanagh and Morris (1989: 6) contend:

These policy goals formed something of a social democratic package. It was a middle way, neither free market capitalist (as in the United States) nor state socialist (as in Eastern Europe). Success in the war had vindicated the active state and it was widely felt that the postwar reconstruction of society and economy should similarly be guided by the government.

The postwar consensus debate: critics

Kerr (1999: 67), a key critic of the whole notion of consensus, acknowledges that it is 'one of the most central and recurring themes within narratives of postwar political development'. Recently, the theme of consensus has been much criticized within political science for being both analytically flawed and empirically unsubstantiated. Empirically, a number of authors have questioned the extent to which policy in the period from 1942 to the mid-1970s can be regarded as the culmination of bipartisan agreement by the political class in Britain. Here, the argument of Pimlott (1988: 503) carries weight, for having researched the official records of governments during this period, he concludes: 'the consensus is a mirage, an illusion that rapidly fades the closer one gets to it.' Pimlott argues that both the Conservative and Labour Parties during this period remained ideologically divided, that the politics of the period reflected deep inter-party conflict across many policy areas, and therefore that the narrative of consensus misrepresents the reality of the time. Seldon (1994: 502–3) captures the essence of the Pimlott critique: 'consensus might appear to have existed . . . when looked at from a very broad perspective. But when viewed from close to the ground, or from the documents, the reality was very different.'

At an analytical level, Kerr (1999) has attacked the consensus narrative as a tool (discursive construction) that has been used by political scientists in order to explain the subsequent exceptionalism of the Thatcherite project. For Kerr (1999: 71), the consensus thesis has endured because it

serves a purpose which goes beyond merely explaining the period to which it has been applied. Primarily, it has been used to highlight the supposed radicalism of both the Attlee and Thatcher governments. In effect, then, it is as inextricably bound to our understanding of these administrations as it is to the era of supposed bipartisan convergence after the war.

Kerr substantiates his argument by observing that the consensus thesis emerged during the 1970s. This was a period marked by deep inter-party conflicts, hastening the advent of the Thatcher Government. As such, for Kerr, the consensus thesis was used more as a tool in order to explain what was subsequently perceived as the unique nature of Thatcherism, rather than as a rigorous, analytical account of the postwar era in British politics. He concludes that the PWC thesis provides a 'framework designed to highlight specific contrasts between Thatcherism and its historical antecedents' (p. 73).

This then leads to the question: was the postwar consensus a reality, or a rhetorical device used by those on the New Right during the 1970s to argue that an alternative political project to the Keynesian welfare state was required? In the next section we explore the nature of the consensus by using the welfare state as a case study, in order to gauge the extent to which a consensus existed. However, here it would be appropriate to state what our own position is on the Keynesian welfare state, in order to contextualize this analysis:

> The Keynesian welfare state can be regarded as very much a part of a modernist ideology—a belief in a better future (a key tenet of modernism). In order to deliver this improved society, the state would provide the engine that would drive the whole project forward. Thus, we would argue that after 1945, the key themes associated with this period of government were: (i) an active role for the state, (ii) the development of a modernist, state driven political project within the existing framework of the parliamentary state.

The postwar consensus—myth or reality? A case study of the welfare state

Until the early 1990s, the stature of William Beveridge, author of the 1942 Report *Social Insurance and Allied Services* and radical reformer of social welfare provision in Britain, remained predominantly untainted. Indeed, it can be argued that Beveridge cast a shadow over social policy throughout the second half of the twentieth century. There are two broad views on the importance of Beveridge.

Beveridge the radical reformer

Until recently, this has been the more popular perception of Beveridge. This view argues that William Beveridge was charged by the wartime national government with tidying up social legislation which had grown up in an ad hoc fashion in prewar Britain. From here, Beveridge has been seen to have fashioned an agenda which allowed him to present a 'revolutionary blueprint' for an all-encompassing system of social insurance in postwar Britain. However, more recently this perception has been criticized.

The revisionist critique of Beveridge

This view argues that the Beveridge Report was certainly something more than tidying up prewar arrangements, but it was also something less than a 'social revolution'. The revisionist critique argues that the post-1945 welfare state owes less to Beveridge and much more to:

• the state interventions by the Salisbury Conservative governments of the late nineteenth century;

- the innovating Liberal Administration of Campbell-Bannerman and, more latterly, Asquith, between 1906 and 1915;
- Finally, this critique points to the fact that the idea of a national health service first arose in the Dawson Report (1920) and was later raised in the (1926) Royal Commission on National Health Insurance. (For a general overview see Harling 2001.)

Thus, revisionists argue that by 1939 Britain already had a relatively advanced system of welfare provision, even if it had evolved in a rather incremental and ad hoc manner. One's views on the PWC debate determines whether or not one embraces the 'radical reformer' idea or 'revisionist critique' of the impact of Beveridge and his report on the development of the welfare state. (See Box 4.4) In order to assist in determining the impact of Beveridge on social policy in Britain, we need to examine the nature and impact of his 1942 Report.

The Beveridge Report and the modern welfare state

The 1942 Beveridge Report proposed a scheme to combat what its author regarded as the five diseases of society: 'Want, Disease, Ignorance, Squalor and Idleness'. It argued that the state should be the guarantor to every citizen in Britain of social security from 'the cradle to the grave'. The Report proposed that the main features of a new welfare state should be fairness, community, and collectivism. Beveridge's

---

Box 4.4 Two stories of welfare in Britain

The 'exceptionalist narrative' This begins by observing that the ideas in the Beveridge Report (1942) provided the founding charter of a radically new postwar system based on social security and social citizenship. Britain then proceeded through a period of ideological agreement in the 1950s and 1960s, followed by a crisis of faith in this established order in the 1970s. This resulted in a radical shift rightwards under the post-1979 Conservative Administration and thence to a new post-Thatcherite social/welfare policy consensus replacing the previous Keynesian welfare consensus and grounded on a new neo-liberal terrain.

  The 'incrementalist or continuity narrative' This begins with the idea that the present roots of the welfare state in Britain can be located in the interventions by Conservative governments at the tail end of the nineteenthth century and the early twentieth century, consolidated by the Liberal Administration of 1905–15. It contends that the Attlee Government of 1945–51 adopted the *conservative* (with a small 'c') Beveridge Report, which simply tidied up prewar arrangements. Subsequently, postwar governments, up to *and including* the Thatcher Administration, have engaged in a piecemeal programme of welfare modification, in an attempt to meet the burgeoning demands of an ever-expanding welfare state. The emphasis here is much more on continuity based on longevity throughout the twentieth century, rather than a narrative which argues there were two clear epochs in the development of the state: that of 1939–79 and from 1979 onwards.

vision was that the state should consolidate the existing but separate schemes of pensions and unemployment and sickness benefits. The aim was to pull all three together to create a universal national insurance scheme.

In practice, this entailed replacing the previous and much-despised means test. Social security would become part of a comprehensive plan for welfare, supported by a national health service and full employment. As Dorey (1995: 13) observes:

Beveridge believed that as far as possible, welfare provision should be linked to national insurance contributions, partly in order to finance the social security system . . . but also to maintain a semblance of individual responsibility, to prevent the idea that people were getting something for nothing. Entitlement would therefore be determined at least in part by what people had themselves paid in whilst working. At the same time, Beveridge envisaged that by linking eligibility to contributions, people receiving social security payments would no longer feel that they were the recipients of charity, with all the humiliation and stigma that this often entailed. Instead they would recognise that their welfare benefits were not hand-outs, but entitlements.

On this basis, the Beveridge Report established six defining principles:

- Full employment. The 1944 coalition Government formally accepted that post-war governments should seek to achieve the goal of 'a high and stable level of (*male*) employment' (emphasis added). It can be fairly argued that this was the most central pillar in postwar policy.

- A national minimum. Central government should provide a common safety net of a national minimum, to protect the poorest and weakest in society. Thus, the state must take on the responsibility of setting a national minimum wage and a certain standard of living for those unable to work.

- Equal and free access to health and education. This entailed the removal of the price barrier to access to health and education, which were deemed to be the basic rights of every citizen.

- A crucial role for the centre. In order to attain the above goals, the central state needed to take on clear responsibilities for key areas of social policy, including social security, health, education, and housing.

- State provision. Not only should central government be given a large role in financing social services, but the services themselves should be placed in the hands of state agencies.

- Continuity. It was argued that continuity should be introduced across all the various welfare areas. This was symbolically undertaken on 5 July 1948, 'Vesting Day', in which the legislation on the NHS came into force.

Analysing the Beveridge Report

At the time of the Report's publication, it was greeted with widespread popular support. For example, *The Economist*, a journal which has never been an advocate of radical reform solutions for society's ills, particular those proposed by those on the centre-left of the political spectrum, commented on 5 December 1942:

(The Report) . . . is one of the most remarkable state documents ever drafted . . . The true test of the Beveridge Plan is whether or not it will inspire, regardless of vested interests, a nation-wide determination to set right what is so plainly wrong and a series of prompt decisions by the Government to ensure that whatever else the war may bring, social security and economic progress shall march together.

In some ways the widespread acceptance of the Report was not surprising, as it was a mixture of fiscal caution, and radicalism in its commitment to full employment and a National Health Service. Let us demonstrate this point:

The fiscal caution of Beveridge

- The level of benefits he envisaged in order to secure basic subsistence were set extremely low.
- Full employment was conceived only in terms of full, *male* employment. Beveridge did not consider the role of women in the workforce (see Box 4.5).
- Non-means-tested pensions were to be phased in only over a twenty year period, in order to allow for the build up of contributions.
- Family allowances for the first child were abandoned in the final Report in order to save the Treasury an estimated £100 million per annum. (For more details see Pierson 1991, Hay 1996, Harling 2001.)

The radicalism of the Beveridge Report

Paul Addison, in his classic work on postwar British politics, *The Road to 1945*, observes that what was really radical about Beveridge was 'The assumptions he made about other areas of government policy in the postwar period: most notably, the commitment to support full employment and to introduce a National Health Service' (Addison 1975: 43)

It can be argued Beveridge's proposals were modest; and, in the austere climate of postwar Britain, they were never fully implemented (see below). However, Beveridge was certainly responsible for providing the framework in which British social policy evolved after the war, even if the Report itself was relatively conservative in what it proposed, while elsewhere the evolution of the welfare state after 1945 generated a whole debate on the implications for the nature of citizenship in Britain (see Box 4.6). Yet the important question here is: to what extent did the Beveridge Report receive bipartisan political support? For this is a key element in determining the extent to which the postwar consensus was a reality, and not just a narrative device utilized by the New Right in the mid-1970s.

The entrenchment of the welfare state: how much consensus?

In this section, we will assess the degree of consensus that actually existed between the two main political parties in relation to Beveridge. First, it must be pointed out that the reason Beveridge proved so enduring was because his Report could be interpreted in different ways. Those on the Left argued that the Report's basic thrust was towards the notion of collectivism and the establishment of universal

---

Box 4.5 **The patriarchal state: Beveridge and the feminist critique**

One of the most powerful revisionist critiques of Beveridge can be found in feminist literature. Here, the issue of full employment provides demonstrable evidence of the patriarchal nature of the British state. For when Beveridge conceived of the notion of full employment as a goal that governments should aspire to, his conception excluded or ignored over half the population—women. A contemporary commentator on Beveridge, T. H. Marshall, averred that by the 1950s, 'the basic right is the right to work' (1950: 10–11). Clearly, both Beveridge and Marshall overlooked the fact that this basic right was to be conferred only on the male population within the British state. As Hay (1996: 51) observes: 'the basic right to work . . . is clearly highly significant. That it should have escaped them [Beveridge and Marshall] that this right was to be denied to over half the population, those who did not conform to the image of the male bread-winner it implied, is scarcely less significant.'

Feminist commentators such as Pateman (1989), Dietz (1992), Pascall (1993), and Fraser and Gordon (1994) suggest that a deeply patriarchal welfare state has evolved. Here, a key argument is that the state benefits system ensures the maintenance of structured inequalities within society based on gender. These commentators not only draw on evidence from the limited notion of full employment but also argue that the creation of the welfare state did nothing to readdress issues such as the sexual division of labour and the unpaid domestic labour of women. Pateman (1989), in particular, effectively demonstrates the disproportionate 'importance of women in the welfare state and the importance of the welfare state for women'. She argues that evolution of the welfare state has created an environment in which state welfare agencies act as a major source of paid employment for women, yet, ironically, these agencies act in a manner which systematically exploits female labour by a rigid gender segregation of both tasks and remuneration. Furthermore, the welfare state is wholly dependent on the performance of unpaid domestic labour, which is predominantly undertaken by women. Finally, the one area in which women have been predominantly excluded is in the policy-making process, in particular high-level administration of the welfare state. Pateman (1989: 183) concludes that 'welfare policies have reached across from public to private and helped uphold a patriarchal structure of family life'.

---

welfare provision, which, they contended, would make private provision increasingly irrelevant. Those on the Right rejected this collectivist narrative, and instead argued that the Report could be interpreted on more individualistic lines. In particular, they focused on the passage from Beveridge (1942: 6–7) which argued:

The Welfare State should not stifle incentive, opportunity, or responsibility, in establishing a national minimum. It should leave room and encouragement for voluntary action by each individual to provide more than the minimum for himself and his family.

Indeed, it was the very ambivalence of Beveridge which allowed a broad swathe of opinion across the political spectrum, from both Left and Right, to embrace the Report. Here, of course, the irony is that, by claiming the Report for their own,

---

Box 4.6 'Citizenship and social class'

Citizenship concerns the relationship between the individual in society and the state. Ideas about citizenship centre on a debate concerning the nature of the reciprocal rights and duties of the state and the individual citizen. Clearly, the development of a welfare state will have a direct impact on the nature of citizenship, and in particular will alter the balance between rights and responsibilities of state and citizen. Thus, the creation of a welfare state affects the nature of citizenship.

   T. H. Marshall's (1950) famous essay 'Citizenship and Social Class' is an account of the evolution and extension of the rights of citizenship under capitalism, and in particular examines the relationship between citizenship and the welfare state. Marshall distinguishes between 'bundles of rights': civil, political, and social. It is the third bundle, social rights, that has proved the most controversial. These constitute a loose aggregation of rights covering a ' whole range from the right to a modicum of economic welfare and security to the right to share to the full in the social heritage and to live the life of a civilized being according to the standards prevailing in society' (Marshall 1950: 8). Marshall argues that citizenship implies social rights which guarantee the individual a 'minimal social status' and, in so doing, allows the individual to exercise both political and civil rights. It is in this respect, that Marshall's thesis has received much criticism. As Heywood (1997: 397) observes: 'The idea of social rights . . . has stimulated significant divisions, because it implies a level of welfare provision and redistribution that . . . the New Right have regarded as both unjustifiable and economically damaging. Marxists and feminists have also criticised the idea of citizenship, the former on the grounds that it ignores unequal class power, and the latter because it takes no account of patriarchal oppression.' (See Box 4.5.)

---

both the main political parties glossed over the fact that Beveridge was a lifetime member of the Liberal Party.

   Second, Beveridge published his Report in 1942. Hence, it is important to note that the future trajectory of the British state in the postwar period had been laid out before the election of the Attlee Government in 1945. When published in 1942, the Report received the blessing of the then National Government (made up of cross-party cabinet members) and so both sides of the political spectrum were attached to the Report's recommendations. Thus, the 1945–51 Attlee Administration, which alongside the Thatcher Administration is often labelled as a radical postwar government, is more appropriately conceived as the recipient and, subsequently, the implementer, of an already defined plan of social welfare reform. This, then, casts a certain degree of doubt over the extent to which the Attlee Government really was radical (see Johnstone 1999). Indeed, Hobsbawm (1993: 22) makes this point:

Even if Labour had not won [in 1945] we would have had a very marked advance towards a welfare state; if there had been a postwar Churchill government, I think this is a fairly safe counter-factual proposition.

Thirdly, it has been argued that the ideological consensus between both parties elevated the 'welfare state' above party politics for the next thirty years. However, in reality, the commitment to a 'comprehensive' welfare state was just one foundation, albeit a very important one, of the newly established terrain of postwar British politics. As noted above, there was also the commitment to full employment, a mixed economy, and a role for employers and employees in policy-making. Thus, there was effectively a shared bi-party commitment to the new terrain of collectivist politics.

Hence, on the contested question of consensus, we would suggest that, in the initial postwar period there was, at one level, real consensus, and that most of the immediate postwar social policy initiatives had been developed under the wartime coalition. This can be demonstrated by the broadly bipartisan nature of the legislation passed on welfare policy in this period.

- The Family Allowance Act was passed before the advent of the Labour Government of 1945.
- The Conservative minister R. A. Butler introduced the Education Act (1944).
- In 1944, the White Paper on Employment committed both parties to full employment.
- The 1946 National Health Service Act made it impossible, for electoral reasons, for the Conservative Party to repeal it.

As Dorey (1995: 13) notes:

The publication of the Beveridge Report and the recommendations contained therein received widespread political support, with many Conservatives echoing Labour's endorsement of the proposals, although some, including Churchill himself, were concerned at the costs that implementation of the Beveridge report would entail. However, Churchill's consternation at the financial implication of implementing Beveridge's proposals was ultimately subordinated to recognition of the political and electoral costs of not accepting them.

Thus we would contend that, at least initially, a degree of convergence emerged around the Beveridge Report, enabling the establishment of a coordinated welfare programme in the 1945–51 period. However, the acid test of the extent of convergence would always come about with a change in government. This happened in 1951.

Life after Attlee: testing the welfare consensus

For Labour, the 1951 election campaign was fought on the grounds that a Conservative victory would create a divisive domestic political arena in which the firm foundations laid by Labour for the welfare state would be dismantled. Their campaign nevertheless proved unsuccessful: despite winning the largest number of votes of any party, Labour lost the election. Harling (2001: 165) argues that 'the chief reason why Churchill and the Conservatives returned to office in 1951 was that they crafted a libertarian electoral campaign that capitalised on the mounting frustrations of consumers who had had enough after a full decade of state-imposed austerity'. Nevertheless, the narrow margin of victory ensured that the new Conservative Government lacked a proper mandate to undo Labour's postwar legacy (see Porter 1994: 281). Indeed, as one historian of Churchill's postwar government concludes: 'one of the most remarkable features of the Government was the extent that the Conservative policy followed on logically from Labour policy in the preceding six years' (Seldon 1981: 421). Certainly, in the area of social policy there was considerable continuity in the early 1950s. For example, between 1945 and 1955, when housing was a particularly pressing issue, it appeared at times that both Labour and the Conservatives were in competition to see who could build the most homes. There of course remained many areas of contention between the two main political parties. The Conservatives were critical of Labour's widespread plans for nationalization. They were also not ideologically committed to the NHS, but electoral exigencies ensured that they continued to support the newly emerging health service programme. Elsewhere, the Conservative minister Peter Thorneycroft's resignation from the Treasury in 1958 over the Cabinet's unwillingness to back cuts in social expenditure provides evidence that even during the 1950s some Conservatives believed the cost of the welfare state was rising too high. It is evidence such as this that Pimlott draws on to argue for the 'myth of consensus'. Elsewhere, Deakin (1987: 68) insists that, while 'real convergences in policy between the major political parties and individuals within them certainly took place ... there was far less homogeneity than is usually believed'. Perhaps Lowe (1990: 182) offers the most penetrating analysis of the extent to which consensus was a reality:

The period from 1945 to the 1970s has been portrayed as one of political consensus. This is justified in relation to the basic framework of welfare policy, where there was a continuing all-party commitment to the mixed economy, the maintenance of full employment and a minimum standard of social security. However, there was bitter animosity between the two major parties ... as well as fundamental differences in their underlying philosophies. Labour's priority was to engineer a more equal society through greater state intervention and, if necessary, higher taxation, the Conservatives were willing only to accept that degree of intervention and taxation which was compatible with market efficiency and personal initiative.

What we wish to suggest is that after the war both main parties were pursuing rather different agendas through their separate interpretations of the Beveridge settlement. Furthermore, both parties were constrained by electoral imperatives: the Conservatives by the popularity of the welfare settlement, hence a commitment to collectivism, Labour by popular resistance to even higher levels of taxation.

Increasingly, throughout the period 1950–1970s, the welfare state became the object of official complacency and the breeding ground for well-organized, vested producer interests (see Chapter 5). This encouraged an attack from a number of critics on both the Left and Right. Each used a whole range of statistics to illustrate the ever-growing burden the welfare state was placing on the economy. For example, between 1945 and 1975:

- The proportion of GDP spent on welfare services rose from 5 per cent to 20 per cent.
- The proportion of the population above pensionable age moved towards 17 per cent.
- Expenditure on the NHS rose from £500 million in 1951 to £5,596 million by 1975.

Critics from the New Right commented that these changes greatly increased levels of state expenditure, while also generating enormous new lobbies of political interest (see below). For us, the key point here is not to advocate arguments either for or against the notion of consensus, but to observe that mainstream opinion in both the Conservative and Labour Parties remained committed to maintaining the Keynesian welfare state. This was reflected in the exponential growth in spending on social and welfare services throughout the postwar period (see Table 4.1).

Political and economic decline: a breakdown in the Keynesian welfare state?

By the 1960s, the Keynesian welfare state was beginning to attract criticism from both sides of the political spectrum prompted by Britain's so-called relative political and economic decline (see Coates and Hillard 1986, which summarizes the debates on both the Left and Right concerning decline). Pierson (1991) argues that the viability of a successful welfare state is dependent on economic growth. He observes that within the British context the welfare state was predicated on an argument that Keynesian economic policies would induce capital investment, which in turn would stimulate economic activity and, in so doing, secure full employment. The net result would be that the Treasury would then be able to accumulate the requisite revenue in order to meet the increased demand for

Table 4.1 The growth of state welfare expenditure, 1931–1975

| | % of GNP | | | | | |
	1931	1937	1951	1961	1971	1975
All social services	12.7	10.9	16.1	17.6	23.8	28.8
Social security	6.7	5.2	5.3	6.7	8.9	9.5
Health	1.8	1.8	4.5	4.4	5.8	7.1
Education	2.8	2.6	3.2	4.2	6.5	7.6
Total state spending	28.8	25.7	44.9	42.1	50.3	57.9

Source: Gough (1979: 77)

spending on health, education, welfare, and social services. Pierson concludes (1991: 131):

It was economic growth that made a reconciliation of the opposing interests of capital and labour viable and sustainable. Fittingly, what has been described as the 'Golden Age' of the welfare state was also a period of unprecedented and unparalleled growth in the international capitalist economy.

Unsurprisingly, when Britain appeared to be entering into a period of decline, siren voices were heard concerning the financial burden the welfare state placed on the economy. Thus, while it is possible to trace Britain's political decline back to the late nineteenth century, public awareness of this decline only emerged at the end of the 1950s (see English and Kenny 2000, Tomlinson 2001). This was reflected in a spate of satirical books, magazines, and television programmes, most notably the irreverent *That Was The Week That Was*, all based around a similar theme—what's wrong with Britain?

Defining decline

The impact of decline on the Keynesian welfare state was critical; but before we explore this theme it is important to determine what is actually meant by the term 'decline'. The term is a value-laden, not neutral concept. Gamble (1994a, 2000a) observes that the nature of decline is a political construction. For the recipients of the word 'decline' have their thoughts then organized in a particular direction, forcing them to look at the world in a certain way. Gamble argues that the popularization of the word and the imagery associated with it, from the 1950s onwards, subsequently shaped the political agenda: 'Decline is . . . politically constructed and needs to be understood through the political debates which have taken place on its dimensions, its causes and its remedies' (2000: 5). The point here is that groups or actors opposed to the Keynesian welfare state actively promoted the word 'decline', in order to substantiate the notion that the politics of the postwar period was failing. This was a strategy which would then allow them to assert the need for an alternative programme to rectify the problem of decline.

We must also recognize that, in the British context, 'decline' has different definitions.

Absolute political decline
This refers to Britain's absolute decline in Great Power status, from the ruler of a third of the world by the end of the nineteenth century to the decline of the British empire after 1945 and, finally, to Parliament's acceptance of a European regional role by joining the EEC in the early 1970s. Perhaps the defining moment when the public became aware of the decline in Great Power status was in 1956, when Britain was forced to withdraw from its invasion of Suez because of pressure from the United States (see Sanders 1990).

The relative decline of the British economy

Here, 'decline' is understood vis-à-vis Britain's main industrial competitors. It is important to be clear on this point. In absolute terms, the British economy was more prosperous in the 1960s than it was at the turn of the century. However, relative to its closest competitors, for example France or Germany (both of whom were in the EC), the British economy was not performing as well. As English and Kenny (2000: 279) observe: 'the key question concerns *relative* performance and potential, and here there has been a striking diminution in power. This is true both militarily and economically, the two realms being interwoven and each significantly affecting national prestige and confidence.' The idea of decline was firmly driven home to the British public throughout the 1950s, not only through Britain's withdrawal from empire but also as the British economy became increasingly prone to sterling crises, that is, dramatic fluctuations in the value of the pound. Furthermore, not only was there both relative political and economic decline, but the key pillars of the postwar consensus—full employment, a mixed economy, social welfare, the conciliation of trade unions, and an active role for government—were being criticized. Britain's relative political and economic decline should be seen in the context of a long-term trend which developed over many years and which the public only really became aware of after the 1950s. However, in the short term it was events in the 1970s which collectively became the trigger that led to a perceived crisis in the Keynesian welfare state.

A crisis of the state: the 1970s

The 1970s was a crucial decade for the process of delegitimizing the Keynesian welfare state. As Pierson (1991: 141) observes:

It was in this period of the early and mid-1970s that social democratic confidence in the competence of the mixed economy allied to greater social equity came under increasing challenge. It was also ... the period of the flowering of New Right and neo-Marxist accounts of the welfare state, both of which concentrated on the ubiquity of crisis arising from the inherently unstable and contradictory elements within the postwar welfare capitalist consensus.

The sense of crisis in the 1970s was very real (see Hay 1996). Depending on one's political perspective (see Coates and Hillard 1986), there are a number of competing explanations as to the cause of the (perceived) crisis in the British state during the 1970s. Here, we are not going to reiterate the various debates, but instead we shall examine some of the key pressures on the state during the 1970s that led those on both the Left and Right to argue that a crisis was imminent. We have divided these pressures into three broad groups: economic pressures, the welfare state, and the need for state modernisation—although it should be pointed out that these groups are not mutually exclusive.

Economic pressures

These took the form of both exogenous and endogenous pressures. We have already discussed Britain's relative economic decline, exacerbated by the end of the postwar boom and the withdrawal from empire. More particularly, this was revealed through the collapse of Bretton Woods (1972: see Chapter 6), the OPEC oil crisis (1973/4), the power of the trade union movement (for example in 1974, when the trade union movement was held responsible for the downfall of both a Labour and Conservative Government), and the IMF crisis (1976), which finally signalled the demise of a Keynesian demand-side economic strategy. Some authors have argued that the British economy based on a Keynesian demand-side strategy would have been able to cope with any one of the economic pressures listed above, and possibly all of them, if the economy had been growing at the same rate as Britain's nearest European competitors (see Pierson 1991). However, this was not the case, and so pressure increased for reform. One of the most obvious targets for any reform was the source of the largest drain on public finances—welfare spending. This then leads to the second pressure area—the welfare state.

The pressure from the welfare state: a crisis of modernity

The political elite hailed the Beveridge settlement supported by Keynesianism as a radical break with traditional notions of the role of the state and the collective provision of welfare. It was clear that during the 1950s and 1960s expenditure increased greatly on welfare policy, and the perception was that, both in terms of the private economy and collective provision, Britain had never had it so good (see Table 4.1). However, even by the 1960s and especially the early 1970s, the limits and problems of modernity were becoming apparent, and a number of people identified an array of problems with the welfare state:

- The welfare state was much more expensive than had been anticipated by Beveridge and the other architects of the postwar system. For instance, the presumption was that as people became healthier and wealthier, the demands on the NHS and welfare benefits would become less. In fact, they became greater, as people wanted better health care and demanded a greater share of economic growth. These problems were further exacerbated because the whole system was premised on full employment (see Pierson 1991). Thus, rising unemployment created many more stresses on the welfare system than had been anticipated. This created what Offe (1984) and others saw as a fiscal crisis of the state, where state expenditure outran state income. Indeed, as early as 1968 the Labour Government had to make significant cuts in welfare expenditure in order to reassure the markets (Bale 1999).
- A number of people argued that the welfare state was not achieving its goals.

Two key arguments were put forward. First, the main beneficiaries of the welfare state were the middle class. They were the people who benefited most from the expansion of education and had the knowledge to use the benefits system and NHS to their best advantage. Secondly, partly as a consequence, the Beveridge system had done little to reduce inequality. Indeed, according to some writers, whilst absolute poverty had declined the relative difference between the rich and the poor had become greater. Townsend (1979) developed an important critique of those who saw the welfare state as reducing poverty. His argument was that poverty was not an absolute, in the sense of not having access to essentials, but was relative, in that it should be defined in terms of deprivation vis-à-vis the prevailing norms and standards of a particular social world. So there is poverty when people lack the resources to obtain the standard of life and activities that is the norm in a society (see Scott 1994 for a discussion). Townsend was concerned with the overall level of deprivation rather than with a crude measure of income inequality. He estimated that in 1968 a third of households were living on or below the poverty line. This compared to the 30 per cent Booth and Rowntree discovered in York and London at the end of the nineteenth century (Scott 1994). His conclusion was that the type of welfare policies that had been introduced had not reduced poverty.

- There was a growing dissatisfaction with the welfare state amongst the working class, as they were facing the burden of growing taxation to pay for it and felt they were receiving minimal benefit. In 1945 the average manual worker paid very low, if any, income tax. Throughout the 1960s and 1970s, the level of income tax for average earners grew significantly. As Whiteley (1983: 175) points out: 'The income tax threshold as a percentage of median earnings fell from 61 per cent in 1971–2 to 47 per cent in 1978–9.' This increasingly created a situation where those below the poverty line were paying income tax. Moreover, their perception was that the public services were getting worse and that benefits were going to welfare 'scroungers'.

- Claus Offe (1984: 153) points to an important paradox of the modern state: 'while capitalism cannot coexist with, neither can it exist without, the welfare state.' His point is that whilst, for the modern capitalist state, the cost of welfare is extremely high and affects profitability, capitalism benefits greatly from the provision of public education, subsidized housing, free health care, and social security. Indeed, as Offe observed and the Thatcher Government realized, capitalism finds it very difficult to operate without the welfare state.

This perceived crisis in the Keynesian welfare state resulted in a number of responses from the Left, Right, and Social Democrats. For many on the Left, the system was not an attempt to produce greater equality but was essentially a sop to the working classes in order to ensure order within capitalist economies. The welfare system was not really concerned with providing equal rights or abolishing poverty, but with ensuring that there was a healthy and educated workforce and, in effect, providing concessions in order to prevent the overthrow of capitalism.

The argument of the social democratic Left was that the problem was not with the system itself, but rather a consequence of broader economic problems and the system being more liberal than social democratic (see above). Anthony Crosland's solution to the crisis was to see it, not as the end of social democracy, but as an opportunity to implement real social democracy through a proper Keynesian system in order to encourage economic growth and greater redistributive taxation. This would then lead to real equality of opportunity. In a sense, the strategy that the Labour Right adopted was twofold: to try to cut the costs of welfare, and to attempt to incorporate unions into decision-making, as an alternative mechanism to welfarism for maintaining social order (see Chapter 8). It was the failure of both of these strategies that created the space for Thatcherism and the New Right.

The Right, as we will see in detail below, believed that the welfare state produced perverse outcomes. In terms of the welfare state, three key arguments were developed. First, that the amount spent on welfare was undermining the productive economy and increasing Britain's relative economic decline. Second, that welfare was increasing a dependency culture, where people were relying on the state rather than families or their own initiative for economic support. The level of social security was in fact providing disincentives for people to work and creating rigidities in the labour market. Third, that the shift to a more egalitarian society was preventing people being enterprising because nothing could be gained from risk-taking.

So far, then, we have seen that broad economic problems, coupled to a welfare state that was seen by some to be failing, provided the key pressure points. The third pressure point came from the perceived failings of the state itself.

Pressure for state modernization

From the early 1960s, there was concern that the state had not adapted to meet the needs of the late twentieth century and that Britain was still served by an amateurish and elitist state. Both politicians and, more particularly, civil servants were identified by some as the 'guilty parties' responsible for Britain's relative decline by failing to modernize the state, in order to adapt to the needs of the late twentieth century. For Westminster and Whitehall, the 1960s in particular was a decade in which both institutions endured a sustained attack based on the perception that Britain was still served by an amateurish, Edwardian bureaucracy and plutocratic politicians who adopted an elitist, narrow, and secretive approach towards policy-making. The critique was wide-ranging, from media commentators to official government-sponsored reports:

- In June 1961, the Plowden Report was published by a Treasury-based committee which had conducted an investigation into the Treasury's control of expenditure. The report was critical of the amateurish and short-term approach the Treasury had adopted, especially in relation to expenditure projections. The

Plowden Report can be seen as a turning point in the life of the Treasury, as it marked the beginning of a period in which the emphasis shifted to a more professional management approach (Chapman 1997: 43). (See Box 4.7.)

- Anthony Sampson's *Anatomy of Britain* (1962) was highly critical of the 'unloved Establishment', highlighting the narrow, interconnected, oligarchic nature of Britain's political elite—both ministers and civil servants.

- W. L. Guttsmann's (1963) *The British Political Elite* surveyed the demographic makeup of politicians between 1868 and 1955, questioning whether Britain had a ruling class or power elite. He claimed that in Britain, the movement between:

elite groups with the consequent accretion of responsibility in the hands of a narrowing circle of men, who often make decisions of the utmost gravity, is one of the essential features of the much used and much misused term *Power Elite*. Behind the individuals who make what may appear to themselves and others isolated decisions and behind the events of history linking the two, are the major institutions of modern society. The hierarchies of state, and corporation and army constitute the means of power. As such they are now of a consequence not before equalled in human history. These three institutions interlock as decisions tend to be total in their consequences, the leading men in each of these three domains of power tend to gather together to form the power elite. (p. 357)

- The 1964 Fabian Report *The Administrators* focused on the closed and secretive realm of Whitehall, which it regarded as being isolated from both the world of business and, more generally, society.

- More formally, the Fulton Committee was established to examine the structure, recruitment, and management of the Civil Service. Here, the debate centred on the competing needs for increased effectiveness, efficiency, and economy (see Richards 1997). This led to the Fulton Report (1968) and subsequently to Heath's White Paper *The Reorganization of Central Government* (1970).

- Finally, in 1968, four former civil servants, Thomas Balogh, Roger Opie, Dudley Seers, and Hugh Thomas, wrote a highly critical appraisal of Whitehall and its role in the policy-making process, which they pointedly entitled *Crisis in the Civil Service*.

Collectively, by the mid-1970s, these pressures led to a growing perception of a crisis in the Keynesian welfare state. Like 'decline', 'crisis' is not a neutral, value-free term. Here, it is useful to turn to t'Hart's (1993: 41) observation: 'the most important instrument of crisis management is language. Those who are able to define what the crisis is all about also hold the key to defining the appropriate strategies for its resolution.' As the perception of crisis permeated the national mind-set during the 1970s, it was the 'ungovernability discourse' that became the dominant narrative associated with crisis. The New Right co-opted the narrative of 'ungovernability' in order to define the crisis, and in so doing they successfully pursued a strategy of delegitimizing the Keynesian welfare state. Having diagnosed

Box 4.7 The Treasury, professionalization, and public expenditure

Following the publication of the Plowden Report in 1961, the Public Expenditure Survey Committee (PESC) was created. It was made up of the principal finance officers of all the major spending departments in Whitehall. The role of PESC was to consider reports from the Treasury on the forecasts of all departments' expenditure. The rationale underpinning the committee was to introduce both a planned approach towards public expenditure and, in so doing, regularize the system—in particular, to assess the overall projected spending of all departments against forecasts of the growth of national income. Previously, as the Plowden Committee had observed, the approach to expenditure had been piecemeal and ad hoc and the Treasury had failed to adopt a strategic overview on projected government expenditure. PESC was coupled to the introduction of Programme Analysis and Review (PAR), in which different departmental programmes were costed and their benefits assessed. PAR was intended to ensure that departments had clear objectives and stated their priorities. The perceived benefit of both PESC and PAR was that, after 1965 (when the process was conducted at Cabinet level), decisions on government programmes and expenditure could be prioritized based on an overall strategically assessed view (see Chapman 1997). It could be regarded as an attempt to professionalize the Treasury's approach to public expenditure. Lipsey (2000: 153) argues: 'PESC was for years the most important single determinant of what went on: the stuff of official wheeling and dealing, the focus of ministerial hopes and fears, and ultimately, the most significant influence on what individual citizens did or did not get by way of public services.'

Lipsey (pp. 157–8) observes that PESC went through a number of phases: the first, 1969–76, involved planning in real terms only—which 'led to spending spiralling out of control'; this was followed by the introduction of cash limits, a requirement of the 1976 IMF loan negotiated by the Callaghan Government. The next phase was an attempt to plan spending in cash terms alone, which also 'ended in disaster, with minor fluctuations in inflation mattering more to the true level of public spending than the decisions of Cabinet'. The final phase was the introduction of the Star Chamber by the 1979 Thatcher Government to resolve difficulties that arose between the Treasury and other departments. In 1992 the Star Chamber was replaced by the Cabinet's Economic and Domestic Policy (Expenditure) Committee (EDX), which had responsibility for considering pressures for greater spending by some departments within the constraints of available financial resources.

The life of PESC and its successor, EDX, ended under the 1997 Labour Government, which introduced the Comprehensive Spending Review (see Chapter 10). Here, capital and current spending were separated from each other, and departments were asked to complete comprehensive spending reviews (CSR) of everything they did. The Treasury would then issue each department with figures based on their CSR which would set out their spending for the next three years. The effect was to increase the power of the Treasury over departments and induce departments to think in the longer term, rather than overspend in their first year.

Clearly, a path can be traced from the publication of the Plowden Report in 1961, and the subsequent establishment of PESC, to the introduction of CSR in 1997, in which the Treasury has made numerous attempts at professionalizing its management of public expenditure and, in so doing, controlling it.

the crisis, the New Right were then placed in a strong position to offer their own prescription for how to rectify the failings of the postwar period.

The ungovernable state: the overload thesis

The concept of overload first appeared in 1975: in the US, in Michael Crozier's *The Crisis of Democracy*; in the UK, in Tony King's 'Overload: Problems of Governing in the 1970s'. The key theme of the overload thesis was that since the 1940s there had been in Western democracies a clearly identifiable rise in public expectations of what government could provide for its citizens. It was argued that, inevitably, governments had failed to deliver on many of these expectations or demands, which in turn had resulted in a serious decline of public confidence in government. Anthony King (1975: 166), the key articulator of 'overload' in the British context, summed up this argument in a striking aphorism which laid the failure to meet the expectations of the nation clearly at the door of the government:

Once upon a time, then, man looked to God to order the World. Then he looked to the market. Now he looks to government. The differences are important. God was irremovable, immutable. The market could be removed or mutated but only, it was thought at a very high price. Government by contrast, is removable, mutable—and corporeal. One blames not 'Him, or 'It', but 'Them'.

Within political science, the overload thesis soon generated its own cottage industry, with numerous authors from across the political spectrum supporting the overload argument, but for a variety of different reasons (see Box 4.8).

The core of the overload argument is relatively simple:

- During the postwar period there was an ever-increasing tendency by the state to intervene in all areas of political life—economy, civil society, etc.
- As the reach of the state spread ever wider, this resulted in the politicization of more and more areas of social and economic life in Britain.
- The central effect was to create an environment in which society had ever-increasing expectations of what government should and could deliver.
- This, in part, could be demonstrated by the rapid increase in pressure groups in the postwar period, each with their own sectional interests and all laying claims at the door of government.
- The effect of this was to create a political market place for votes.
- Political parties, who, through general elections, are in the business of competing for the individual votes of members of pressure groups, make more and more promises to satisfy their various demands.
- This creates an environment in which the state inexorably grows as governments try to satisfy promises to an ever-increasing range of pressure groups.

Box 4.8 **The literature on overload**

US neo-conservatives

Daniel Bell, *The Cultural Contradictions of Capitalism* (New York: Basic Books, 1976)

S. M. Lipset, *Dialogues on American Politics* (Oxford: Oxford University Press, 1978)

Samuel Huntingdon, 'The Democratic Distemper', *Public Interest* 41 (1975), 9–38

Irving Kristol, *Two Cheers for Capitalism* (New York: Basic Books, 1978)

The Liberal economists

(UK) Samuel Brittan, 'The Economic Contradictions of Democracy', *British Journal of Political Science* 5 (1975), 129–59

(UK) Peter Jay, 'Englanditis', in R. E. Tyrell (ed.), *The Future that Doesn't Work* (New York: Doubleday, 1977)

(Canada) Dan Usher, *The Economic Prerequisite to Democracy* (New York: Columbia University Press, 1981)

Neo-marxists

Claus Offe, 'The Theory of the Capitalist State and the Problem of Policy Formulation', in L. N. Lindberg et al. *(1975) Stress and Contradiction in Modern Capitalism* (Boston: D. C. Heath, 1975).

Jurgen Habermas, *Legitimation Crisis* (New York: Beacon Press, 1975)

Others

R. Rose and G. Peters, *Can Governments Go Bankrupt?* (New York: Basic Books, 1978)

J. Douglas, 'The Overloaded Crown', *British Journal of Political Science* 6(4) (1976), 483–505

W. Parsons, 'Politics without Promises: The Crisis of Overload and Ungovernability', *Parliamentary Affairs* 35(4) (1982), 421–35

(*Source*: Birch 1984: 135–60)

- The result is that the social democratic model leads to political overload, ungovernability and financial crisis. The state has over-stretched itself. (See also Hay 1996.)

As Birch (1984: 140) observed:

When unrestrained demands by voters and pressure groups go along with competitive bidding votes by politicians, the combination endangers sound economic policy-making. The problem is likely to be exacerbated by the readiness of sectional groups possessing economic power, notably trade unions, to employ it for political ends.

Ironically, the overload thesis provided an ideal opportunity for those on the Right to claim that there was a crisis of legitimacy of the state, a claim more often associated with those on the Left. As Dorey (1995: 278) argued, if the trend towards governments attempting to satisfy the ever-increasing demands of society was not arrested, then eventually both authority and legitimacy of government and the political system would be undermined:

Although 'legitimation crisis' is a concept usually associated with the Left, it does tie in very closely with much of the neo-conservative critique, for as the economist Samuel Brittan observes [1983: 17]: 'If a succession of governments ... stir up expectations only to disappoint them, there is a risk of the whole system snapping under the strain'.

Conclusion

The overload thesis provided a powerful critique of the consensus politics of the postwar era; moreover, it was particularly effective at delegitimizing the modernist Keynesian welfare state which governments since 1945 had pursued. An alternative was needed to fill the ideological vacuum created by the delegitimation of the existing orthodoxy. Under Margaret Thatcher, who became leader of the Conservative Party in 1975, elements within that party sought an alternative agenda. Thus, when elected in 1979, those on the New Right within the Conservative Party used the notion of political, social, and economic crisis, perceived or otherwise, to justify an ideological programme to transform what they regarded as an over-extended state. For the neo-liberal wing of the Conservative Party, the solution to overload was a clear set of responses: reduce the size of the state, combat inflation not unemployment, disengage from the economy, and cut direct taxation. Demands of the electorate would thus be shifted away from the state to elsewhere, most notably the marketplace, in order to satisfy expectations. Hence, the problem of overload would become a legacy of the past. It is the growth of the New Right and its alternative political project for the state, in order to fill the vacuum left by the failing Keynesian welfare state, that we examine in the next chapter.

KEY POINTS

- The evolution of Britain as a modern state was premised on two key components: a Keynesian economic strategy and a universal welfare system.

- There is controversy within political science as to whether or not the pursuit of Keynesianism and a welfare state led to the development after 1945, of a broad bipartisan political convergence. This can be referred to as the postwar consensus debate, and it remains a contested issue.

- Irrespective of one's views concerning this debate, from 1945 until the 1970s the state exponentially grew in terms both of its contours and of its expenditure.

- By the 1960s, signs of political and economic decline led to increasing criticism from both sides of the political spectrum, suggesting that the Keynesian welfare state was failing.

- In the 1970s, a powerful critique of the British state had developed and was referred to as the 'overload or ungovernability thesis'. The critique's impact was crucial in delegitimizing the Keynesian welfare state and creating a political vacuum.

KEY QUESTIONS

1. To what extent did both main political parties commit themselves to Keynesianism and universal welfare after 1945?

2. Is the postwar consensus simply a rhetorical tool used to highlight the exceptionalism of Thatcherism?

3. Provide an analysis of the decline of the British state in the postwar period.

4. Why was the overload thesis so successful at delegitimsing the Keynesian welfare state?

KEY READING

Key texts on the development of the Keynesian welfare state are Addison (1975) and Dorey (1995). For arguments that advocate a postwar consensus, see Kavanagh (1987) and Kavanagh and Morris (1989). For a critique of the postwar consensus, see Pimlott (1989), Seldon (1994), Hay (1996), and Kerr (1999). On the issue of decline, see Hay (1996) and Tomlinson (2001). For the key literature on overload, please refer to Box 4.8.

KEY WEBSITES

The websites related to the crisis of the state and problems associated with the welfare state and Keynesiansm are similar to those in Chapter 3. The most useful websites are: those of think tanks including; www.iea.org.uk/, www.demos.co.uk/pms2nded.htm, www.adamsmith.org.uk/, www.cer.org.uk/, www.npi.org.uk/, www.ucl.ac.uk/constitution-unit/, www.fabian-society.org.uk/int.asp, and for a libertarian view www.digiweb.com/igeldard/LA/. There is useful general information on British politics at www.ukpolitics.org.uk/. There are also a number of sites related to the welfare state: the Department of Health www.doh.gov.uk, and for the National Health Service www.nhsconfed.net, the Department for Education and skills www.dfes.gov.uk/index.htm, the Department for Work and Pensions www.dss.gov.uk. For general welfare issues, a useful site is the National Institute for Social Work, www.nisw.org.uk. Secondly, for discussions on the economy, the Treasury website is: www.hm-Treasury.gov.uk; the Bank of England www.bankofengland.co.uk, the *Financial Times* www.ft.com, and *The Economist* www.economist.com.

5

INTERNAL CHALLENGES TO THE MODERN STATE: THE NEW RIGHT

INTRODUCTION

In the previous chapter, we examined the growing criticisms of the Keynesian welfare state in the 1960s and 1970s. In particular, the notion of the British state being ungovernable emerged as a critique of the existing system of governance. At the time, the notion of ungovernability gained resonance with a wide public. It was believed that government had become overextended and was unable to deliver successfully on its myriad of commitments. There are those who argue that the 'overload' critique was both flawed and erroneous in its analysis (see Hay 1996, 1999b). Indeed, we have a number of sympathies with such observations. Nevertheless, the key point is that the popular resonance of the 'ungovernability' thesis meant that it delegitimized the orthodoxy surrounding the Keynesian welfare state. This in turn created a political vacuum. If, rightly or wrongly, the existing orthodoxy was deemed a failure, something had to fill the political void that had opened up. In this chapter, we set out to examine what we have labelled the internal challenge to the modern state. This internal challenge came from the New Right. As Dorey (1995: 275) observes:

> The collapse provided neo-conservatism with both the intellectual authority and the political space with which to launch a counter-attack against the social democratic values and policies which had guided post-war Governments—Labour and Conservative—hitherto.

Dorey (1995) argues that the emergence of a new critique identified both postwar

Conservative and Labour governments as equally responsible for pursuing policies which had led to the perceived state crisis of the 1970s. Both Conservative and Labour were culpable, as they each implicitly accepted the premises and principles of Keynesian economics and the universal welfare state. The effect of this was that neither sought to reverse the collectivist tide when in power.

In this chapter, we analyse the alternative agenda provided by the New Right, which it was hoped would fill the emerging political vacuum of the 1970s. In particular, we examine the growth of the New Right and its success at undermining the Keynesian welfare state. We look at the New Right's theoretical account of the nature of bureaucracy, most notably public-choice theory and the extent to which the newly elected Conservative Administration of 1979 sympathized with the New Right's analysis of bureaucracy in its subsequent application of private-sector managerial and business models to public services (New Public Management, or NPM). We assess the impact of NPM on the policy-making arena and conclude by considering whether or not the Conservative's reform led to an internal 'hollowing-out of the state'.

Filling the political vacuum: the growth of the New Right

Where did the New Right come from? Heywood (2000: 69) argues that its origins and ideas can be traced back to the 1970s. The New Right's growth occurred in conjunction with the apparent failure of the Keynesian welfare state, signified by the end of the postwar economic boom, and increasing concerns by the political elite over social breakdown and the decline of authority. The term 'New Right' was first attached to a group of monetarists from Chicago University, who were inspired by the writings of three eminent economic and political thinkers—Friederich von Hayek, Robert Nozick, and Milton Friedman (see Box 5.1). Their arguments centred on the rejection of the idea that governments should intervene in the economy because it distorted the market and so produced adverse outcomes. They rejected the political goal of full employment through stimulating demand within the economy (a key tenet of Keynesianism), and instead argued that government should focus on reducing inflation by controlling the money supply. In the immediate aftermath of the Second World War, the idea that governments would *not* take an active role in artificially stimulating employment was almost unthinkable. Soldiers needed jobs to return home to. But with the increasing criticisms surrounding Britain's relative economic decline from the late 1950s onwards, the notion took root that the Keynesian demand-side economic strategy pursued by both postwar Labour and Conservative administrations was failing. Alternatives were needed, and it was the monetarist ideas that first surfaced from the Chicago School of economists which began to gain currency in a number of elite political circles. Indeed, forced into devaluing the pound in 1967 and needing financial support from the IMF, Roy Jenkins, the Labour Chancellor in 1969, promised 'severe restrictions of the

Box 5.1 The intellectual origins of the New Right

The seeds of New Right thought can be traced back to the eighteenth- and nineteenth-century classical political economists such as David Ricardo, John Stuart Mill, and, most notably, Adam Smith, author of *The Wealth of Nations* (1796). Yet the three seminal thinkers most associated with the genesis of the New Right as it became known in the second half of the twentieth century were Friedrich von Hayek, Robert Nozick, and Milton Friedman.

Friedrich von Hayek (1899–1992)

Hayek was an anti-modernist who achieved fame with his critique of collectivism and planning in his most famous book, *The Road to Serfdom* (1944). His ideas were later developed in *The Constitution of Liberty* (1960) and the three volumes of *Law, Legislation and Liberty* (1973, 1976, 1979). Hayek's work is organized around four main themes: (a) Planning is mistaken: Hayek objected to planning, arguing it was both politically dangerous and economically inefficient. He believed that centralized economic planning by government reduced individual and group liberty, upset the balance between political institutions by making the executive too strong, and undermined the rule of law. This then led to pressure for yet more controls as the 'logic of intervention' fed on itself. (b) The complexity of society: Hayek believed there was a spontaneous natural order in society which was the outcome not of a plan or of a design but of human behaviour. He spoke of the need to submit to the undesigned rules and conventions of social life. This view was informed by his scepticism concerning social engineering, which those on the Left prescribed. He dismissed the belief that state intervention can improve social life. (c) The importance of markets and prices for the allocation of resources: Hayek believed that the spontaneous interaction of buyers and sellers was more efficient than the activity of planners. (d) The framework for social and economic activity and upholding the rule of law: Within this framework, government had an important but limited role. Hayek was critical of the belief that government should have a role in promoting social justice or compensating those adversely affected by the market, e.g. the unemployed. Government's role was to uphold the rule of law, to enable conditions in which the market could prosper.

Most of Hayek's writing was done after 1945. He attracted controversy in Britain because he challenged the belief in the so-called 'middle way' which combined both freedom and planning, prevalent in the moderate 'one Nation' wing of the Conservative Party and among the Labour Party elite such as Attlee, Gaitskell, and Wilson.

Robert Nozick (1938–2002)

Nozick was an American academic who had a notable impact on the intellectual development of New Right ideas. His two key works were *Anarchy, State and Utopia* (1974) and *Philosophical Explanations* (1981). He drew ideas from the work of the seventeenth-century British political philosopher John Locke in order to develop a contemporary form of libertarianism. Nozick averred that the state should enforce a strict defence of property rights, if and where the wealth of an individual had been properly and justly acquired. His position advocated such themes as a minimal state and a low tax threshold, and were seen as a direct attack on social democracy, welfarism, collectivism, social justice, and 'big government'. He became a champion of the New Right who vociferously advocated his 'rights-based theory of justice' as a rebuff to the dominance of collectivism that had developed in many Western liberal democracies in the post-1945 period.

Milton Friedman (b. 1912)

Friedman is an American economist who came to prominence from the 1960s onwards. He became one of the key proponents of monetarism and the market economy and directly attacked the existing orthodoxy of Keynesian economics. His most notable publication, co-authored with his wife, Rose, was *Free to Choose* (1980). This placed monetarist ideas firmly in a free-market context. It had a number of themes which became popular among the New Right: the inefficiency of government and the failure of state-driven programmes; the benefit of low taxes; the need to denationalize (privatize) and deregulate industry and services; and the abolition of rent controls, minimum wages, regional and industrial subsidies and employment legislation. All the above were seen as barriers to the efficient working of a market economy. Friedman argued that government's role should be limited to provide law and order, defence, and the provision of essential services. Capitalism, or the voluntary interaction between buyers and sellers of goods and services, created economic freedom, which in turn was essential for political freedom.

Hayek, Nozick, and Friedman are regarded as providing the core for the intellectual growth of New Right ideas. Indeed, it was Hayek who stressed the importance of ideas and the role of authors, academics, journalists, etc. in shaping the climate of opinion.

money supply' (Denham and Garnett 2001: 180). As Kavanagh and Morris (1989: 43) observe:

The ideas of Friedman received an airing in Britain in the late 1960s, in the columns of Peter Jay, the economics editor of *The Times*, and Samuel Brittan, the economics commentator of the *Financial Times*. Friedman's and Hayek's ideas were also promoted in the seminars and pamphlets of the free market publishing house, the Institute of Economic Affairs.

Coupled to this was the growth in Britain of New Right think tanks from the late 1950s onwards which sought to change the climate of opinion in Britain, away from the dominant discourse of collectivism. Such groups included the Institute of Economic Affairs, the Centre for Policy Studies, the Adam Smith Institute, the Social Affairs Unit, and the Social Market Foundation. It was these organizations that were responsible for disseminating the ideas of the New Right among leading Conservative Party members.

New Right ideas always had some hold within the Conservative Party because, despite the dominance of one-nation Conservatism, there was always an element of support for laissez-faire ideas. In the 1970s, however, with increasing economic problems, the New Right had a growing influence on party policy. In particular, Enoch Powell and Keith Joseph began to explicitly push for new right economic ideas, and this had a significant impact on the proposed economic policies in the 1970 Conservative Party manifesto.

The Heath Government was committed to disengagement from the economy and reducing public expenditure (Cairncross 1996). However, in the early 1970s even Conservatives like Keith Joseph were careful to retain a commitment to state intervention and collective provision, and Heath was still attached to the goal of

---

Box 5.2 The Heath Government, 1970–1974

After the apparent failures of the Labour government and the economic problems that continued to face Britain, the Heath Government was elected on a promise of reducing government intervention in the economy, reducing taxation, cutting public expenditure, and reducing subsidies to industry. However, faced with continuing economic problems and, by 1972, the collapse in economic growth and the prospect of unemployment reaching one million, Heath abandoned his proto-Thatcherite policy. Rolls-Royce was nationalized and the Government introduced the Industry Act, a highly interventionist strategy. The point is that whilst Heath was prepared to adopt some of the New Right's policy prescriptions, he was still attached to the principles of the Keynesian welfare state.

---

full employment (see Box 5.2, Denham and Garnett 2001, Campbell 1993). It was only with the failure of the Heath Government (1970–74) to solve the problems of the economy or to control the unions that unmodified New Right thinking started to have an influence amongst people like David Howell, Keith Joseph, Geoffrey Howe, and Margaret Thatcher. From this group, we can see the first real challenge to the dominant, orthodox thinking within the Conservative Party known as 'one nation' Toryism which had embraced consensus politics after the war. When in 1975 Thatcher became leader of the Opposition, monetarist and new right thinking had a much more consistent impact on party policy, as a response to the perceived failure of the Heath era.

If the Conservative Party was to thwart the steady drift in British politics in an increasingly collectivist direction, then it needed to provide an alternative political programme which would win over the hearts and minds of the nation. As Dorey (1995: 276) observes:

The essentially 'consolidationist' approach adopted by Conservative Governments during this time was to be replaced by a much more confident, combative style, whereby Conservatism and the Conservative Party were expected to go on the offensive, and consciously embark on a mission to reverse the principles and policies of postwar British politics . . . Central to the neo-conservative critique of British politics since 1945 was the role of the state.

Keynesianism had advocated state intervention in order to stimulate the rate of employment in the economy. The New Right argued that the 'market' should determine employment levels. By following the signs relayed by the market, this would prove to be the most efficient and effective form of economic management. The extensive and invidious degree to which the state impinged on the working of the free market and the liberty of the individual was the cause of Britain's long-term economic decline. Put another way, the key component responsible for impeding the effective and efficient working of the market was the size and scale of state intervention in the postwar period. Furthermore, the New Right argued that state intervention led to the distortion of the market, which then created further problems in the economy and in so doing induced the state to intervene further in an attempt to rectify the situation. If the predictions of the New Right were correct and this trend was followed through to its eventual logical end, there would be an exponential growth in state intervention to the point where the state would finally control all economic activity. For the New Right, this was the nightmare of social democracy, predicted by Hayek (1944), in which society would embark 'on the road to serfdom'.

Finally, there was a complementary set of arguments put forward by New Right economists concerning the extent to which the inefficient and uneconomic public sector had 'crowded out' the much more efficient, profitable, and wealth-creating private sector (Bacon and Eltis 1976). The 'crowding-out' argument posits that:

- It is only the private sector which engages in the creation of financial capital, i.e. the making of economic wealth.
- It is only the marketplace that engages in the production of goods and services from which a profit is made.
- The public sector is financed by the state through direct or indirect taxation, in order to provide goods and services free at the point of delivery.
- As such, the public sector is dependent on the wealth generated by the private sector in order to finance its activities.
- Hence, the public sector acts as a parasite on the back of the private sector.

This argument, when applied to an environment in which the public sector is rapidly growing, led Bacon and Eltis to conclude that the effect is to place greater demand on, or in some cases squeeze out, the private sector—the very sector on which the public sector is financially dependent. This problem is exacerbated by governments, who then have to raise further revenues from the private sector in order to fund the expanding public sector. The net effect is to reduce demand in the economy, as fewer goods are being sold, whilst also fuelling inflation as employees demand higher wages to ameliorate the impact of the higher taxes they have to pay.

For the New Right, the solution to the problems associated with the Keynesian welfare state were, at least theoretically, obvious. The state needed to take on a much more minimal role in society. It should concentrate on ensuring law and order, protecting or defending the realm of the nation, providing a minimum welfare net for those who could not provide for themselves, and, finally, create an environment in which the free market could thrive. It is on this last point that the New Right launched an attack on what it regarded as the overextended, bureaucratic state that Britain had slipped into in the 1970s, which, it argued, actively hindered the effective functioning of the free market. The state had to be cut, in order to create the conditions in which business could prosper. Moreover, the New Right argued that the Civil Service was too attached to notions of 'big government' through its own self-interest. Consequently, the New Right adopted a public-choice model of bureaucracy which provided a critique of existing patterns of government organizations.

Public choice and bureaucracy

First, it should be noted that there is not one single public-choice model, but a number of similar models derived from the same theme—that bureaucrats are utility maximizers. In other words, civil servants are concerned with their own self-interest rather than the public good. Furthermore, the public-choice critique portrays the relationship within the core executive as a zero-sum game in which bureaucrats control ministers. The origins of public-choice theory stem from the United States and are associated with authors such as Downs (1957) and Niskanen (1971).

Initial public-choice arguments suggested that powerful bureaucrats maximize their departmental budgets, in order to serve their own personal preferences, providing themselves with greater security, prestige, income, and influence. Such authors argue that the state is a monopoly supplier, and thus public services are supplied at higher than market cost, producing Pareto-inefficiency. This means that officials do not serve the interests and goals of politicians but instead maximize their own interests, and in so doing provide goods and services at a higher price than the private sector. Moreover, officials, relieved of the discipline of the market, continually over-staff and overspend, without any control directly from politicians or indirectly from taxpayers. A common example public-choice theorists often utilize to demonstrate their arguments is the dramatic rise in the size of bureaucracies since 1841 (see Table 5.1).

Table 5.1 The growth of the British Civil Service, 1841–1997

Year	No. of civil servants
1841	16,750
1871	53,874
1901	116,413
1922	317,721
1939	387,400
1943	710,600
1950	684,800
1976	751,000
1979	732,300
1997	472,412
2001	500,123

During the mid-1970s, the public-choice critique of Whitehall found a home in New Right think tanks such as the Institute of Economic Affairs and Centre for Policy Studies and with Conservative politicians such as Keith Joseph. They used the critique to argue that Whitehall was a natural ally of the Labour Party because of its belief in the merits of action by the state, and also demonstrated the failure of the Heath Government to implement public sector cutbacks in the 1970s. The prescription by the New Right was the need for a series of reforms designed to curb bureaucracy's budget-expanding tendencies—in effect, rolling back the state.

The most sophisticated contemporary public-choice model of bureaucracy is that presented by Patrick Dunleavy in what he refers to as his 'bureau-shaping model' (Dunleavy 1991). His work on bureau-shaping has justifiably received a great deal of attention both at a theoretical level and as an explanation of recent changes in the public sector in Britain and elsewhere. For Dunleavy, the key issue is not that bureaucrats attempt to maximize budgets, as these are usually beyond their direct control and rarely will they receive any benefit from an increase. Instead, senior bureaucrats are concerned to maximize their status and to shape the nature of their work in a way that gives them most satisfaction. For Dunleavy, senior bureaucrats seek out the exciting world of advising ministers at the heart of the policy process, rather than dealing with the mundane and often difficult role of managing a large organization. For these reasons, when high-ranking officials are faced with institutional-wide cuts, what they try to do is to hive off the difficult and the mundane tasks into agencies and keep for themselves the interesting work of developing policy and advising ministers.

The bureau-shaping model thus generates three propositions:

- Senior civil servants have less interest in the management of their departments and more interest in their role as policy advisers.

- The development of Next Steps agencies in Britain in the late 1980s was encouraged by senior civil servants as a way of hiving off mundane administrative tasks.

- The outcome of the Conservative reforms has been to take managerial responsibilities away from senior civil servants and allow them to concentrate on policy advice. (For details see Dunleavy 1999, Dowding 1995, and Marsh et al., 2001.)

Dunleavy's model is premised on the notion that senior civil servants, not politicians, controlled the bureaucratic reform process of the 1980s–90s. More broadly, all the public-choice models argue that it is officials who hold greater power over their ministers. Furthermore, the public-choice models were seized upon by the New Right in order to underpin their normative prescriptions for the reform of the state. So in the next section we examine the extent to which the Conservatives after 1979 used the theoretical analysis of the New Right in order to inform their programme of state reform.

The Conservative Party and the reform of the state

In order to understand the post-1979 state reform programme of the Conservatives, it is first important to examine their period in opposition between 1974 and 1979. After the Heath Government's electoral defeats in 1974, and Thatcher's succession as party leader in 1975, Conservative attitudes to the state and, more particularly, the Party's attitude to the Civil Service were re-examined. As we saw above, the new Thatcherites argued that state institutions, including the Civil Service, enshrined a deeply entrenched, corporatist settlement. This led some to contend that there was government overload. Concurrently, public-choice analyses of bureaucratic behaviour were embraced by a number of centre-right think tanks. Their analysis of the public sector was that it was 'flabby': a result of public servants not being exposed to the rigours of the market.

The idea of government overload coupled to public-choice accounts of bureaucratic behaviour provided a political discourse about the role of the state which the Thatcherites embraced. As Campbell and Wilson (1995: 304) observe. 'Thatcher herself brandished Niskanen's work on bureaucracy at her colleagues and pressed them to read it.' This was supplemented by empirical evidence from the 1978 publication of Leslie Chapman's *Your Disobedient Servant*—an insider's account of gross inefficiency within a Whitehall department.

The New Right discourse was accompanied by the evolving critique that the Civil Service was over-powerful and too wedded to a postwar settlement and the postwar consensus (see above). Those on the Right asserted that any government with a radical agenda which wished to break free would be hampered by the Civil Service's commitment to this consensus. They argued that the way in which senior mandarins had constrained the Fulton Committee's remit, and subsequently, systematically emasculated its report, provided ample evidence of the Civil Service's resistance to change (see Kellner and Crowther Hunt 1980; Richards 1997).

In this context, it is not surprising that a number of commentators suggest that, in order to understand the post-1979 reforms, it is important to analyse the role of the emerging New Right within the Conservative Party. These explanations fail to recognize the structural context within which the Party operated. In particular, the composition of the Conservative Party in the late 1970s and the political priorities of the newly elected Conservative Government acted as powerful structural constraints on the initial growth of the New Right political discourse in the Conservative Cabinet. New Right ideology did not dominate the Conservative Party in the late 1970s, nor was Thatcher's position as leader unchallenged. Here, it is important to note that the Parliamentary Conservative Party has always been a broad church (see Gamble 1994b, Ludlam and Smith 1996, Hay 1996, Kavanagh 1997, Gilmour 1997, Heath 1998). Certainly, under Thatcher, the Opposition front bench contained an array of individuals with differing political views, and between 1975 and 1979 the 'neo-liberal' wing of the Party was not dominant (see below).

It is thus unsurprising that the Shadow Cabinet had an ambivalent attitude towards the Civil Service.

Thus, in 1979, although the Conservative Party did have available an alternative coherent ideological discourse from the New Right, as an antidote to the failings of the Keynesian welfare state, the tensions both within the Party and within the Cabinet meant that the discourse was never wholly embraced. These tensions created a fault-line within the Party, and were reflected in the contrasting views on two wings of the Party:

- The neo-liberal wing: advocates a minimal state to maximize the condition of liberty and freedom. This wing of the Party wished to see radical reform of the state and, in particular, Whitehall.

- The neo-conservative wing: advocates an interventionist and authoritarian state, in order to centrally impose a rigid morality upon society. This wing of the Party believed the Civil Service, and more particularly the existing constitutional arrangements, needed defending (see Box 5.3).

It is important to emphasize that owing to the inherent ideological tensions within the Conservative Administration when it was elected in 1979, there was no coherent programme for reforming Whitehall. The battle for ideas between the two wings of the Party continued to be contested throughout much of the 1980s. However, as Hay (1996) observes, neo-liberalism had a much stronger hold over the formulation of Conservative policy, while neo-conservatism exercised a greater hold over Conservative backbencher opinion. As such, it was the ideas of the neo-liberals that dominated front-bench thinking in relation to the state. Yet they were constrained from following through the logic of this particular branch of Conservatism to its natural conclusion, for fear of alienating their own more neo-conservative minded backbenchers (see Richards and Smith 2000). When analysing the Conservative reforms of the state after 1979, it is important to recognize their piecemeal and evolutionary nature, rather than the implementation of any ideologically radical, clearly defined blueprint. Box 5.4 summarizes the key themes that shaped the thinking of the neo-liberal wing of the Party vis-à-vis the state. In the following section we will examine the degree to which this analysis of the state was acted upon after 1979.

Many of the various elements of the Conservative approach to the public sector were cobbled together to form what has subsequently been labelled the New Public Management [NPM] (see Box 5.5). NPM is essentially an attempt to impose coherence on a diffuse and often contradictory set of ideas, and it is not without its critics (see Marsh et al. 2001). It also refers to an attempt to reform the public sector through the application of private-sector techniques, and especially the introduction of markets and private-sector management into the delivery of public goods. In many ways it relates closely to governance, because it is a belief that the standardized systems of rules and hierarchy which hitherto had governed the public sector may no longer be appropriate to all areas of the public services.

Box 5.3 Neo-liberalism and neo-conservatism

Neo-liberalism

From the mid-1950s, a number of neo-liberal think tanks were established on the periphery of the Conservative Party advocating free-market liberalism. The key political figure behind the resurgence of this brand of classical liberalism was Keith Joseph, and the most established think tank associated with this position was the Institute of Economic Affairs (IEA). The IEA was probably the most important external influence on the Conservative Party during the 1980 and 1990s. Elsewhere, Keith Joseph also founded the Centre for Policy Studies, which had the closest relationship with Thatcherite policy. There was also the Adam Smith Institute, established in 1977, whose main concern was with public policy-making and it was closely associated with such proposals as privatization and compulsory competitive tendering. These particular think tanks constituted the 'big three', a triangulation in neo-liberal intellectual thought. Many of the ideas of Thatcherism stem from these think tanks. They also helped shape the ideas of neo-liberalism into practical policies.

The key precepts of neo-liberalism:

- the reassertion of the free market, the principles of laissez-faire economics and a belief in the sanctity and supremacy of market mechanisms as a means to deliver equitable outcomes, i.e. the morality of the market
- the maximization of individual liberty and freedom through the 'rolling back of the state from the economy'
- monetarism: a belief that inflation, not unemployment, was the major problem of the British economy, but that this could be controlled by regulation of the money supply
- the cutting back of the welfare state, which was regarded as stifling the potential of the free market and encouraging a culture of dependency

Neo-conservatism

The wing of the Conservative Party that advocates neo-conservatism can be closely associated with such campaigning pressure groups in Britain as Mary Whitehouse's National Viewers' and Listeners' Association and the anti-abortion lobby. Intellectually, the neo-conservative resurgence was most closely associated with the Salisbury Group and its journal, the *Salisbury Review*. One of its most prominent thinkers is the philosopher Roger Scruton.

The central principles of neo-conservatism are:

- a centrally imposed moral authoritarianism by the state enforcing a return to traditional values of the family
- the reassertion of the values of respect, discipline, and moral decency
- the active intervention of the state to police and coerce deviant miscreants
- the dismantling of the welfare state and the 'dependency culture' it has spawned
- the assertion and promotion of the institution of the patriarchal nuclear family
- the defence of the values of patriotism, nationalism, British identity, and 'the British way of life'
- The restoration of social hierarchy and tradition

Box 5.4 **A neo-liberal view of the state**

Neo-liberals are inherently suspicious of the state. They regard state activity as interfering in the natural order of life—be this in relation to the functioning of the market or the way in which social relations within society are formed and played out. Thus neo-liberals strongly advocate what is referred to as a 'minimalist role for the state'. This is based on the following key tenets:

- The importance of individual liberty: individuals should not have the right to coerce other individuals to do as they wish, so why should this principle not be extended to the state, which after all is itself only an amalgam of individuals?

- Greater freedom means greater innovation and progress. Innovation would not occur where the state owns or controls the means of production.

- Incentive is seen as the great innovator, while state intervention is perceived as leading to caution and inertia.

- Free markets are vital for social coordination: unlike a totalitarian state, a market economy evolves unconsciously, without depending on coercion, by relying on millions of individual actors constantly responding to price signals.

- Planned societies are less free. They involve social engineering—the Soviet Union being a classic example—but social engineering in whose interests?

- Social justice carried out by the state is inherently unfair: implicit in the term 'social justice' is the notion that certain individuals enjoy rewards they do not deserve, while others have rewards removed that they should be entitled to.

- State power can be unfairly monopolized, as interest groups form and are granted special treatment. The natural workings of the market are then upset.

- As a consequence, consumers pay more and get less, as agencies of the state become increasingly captured by the individual interests of particular interest groups.

(*Source*: Dearlove and Saunders 2001)

Therefore, a range of ways of delivering public goods should be investigated. Walsh (1995) points out that NPM is intended to improve control of work practices, but to try to make that control indirect rather than direct. In other words, it is a belief that market incentives can improve the efficiency and effectiveness of the public sector. Underpinning this process are changes in information technology which allow organizations to become much more flexible. The problem with the NPM was that much of it was contradictory:

- It is sometimes difficult to cut costs and improve service delivery.

- Shifting power from professionals to managers can create problems in services such as health and education.

- The introduction of targets and performance indicators in many ways is closer to central planning than the introduction of markets and can produce perverse

---

Box 5.5 New public management

The key features of new public management are:

- a belief in the superiority of the market and therefore an attempt to introduce markets and quasi-markets into the public sector
- the notion that organizations should be flexible and responsive rather than hierarchical
- decentralization and de-layering of decision-making, with the disaggregation of government into agencies
- the use of performance indicators and output targets as mechanisms for the creation of incentives for more effective work practices
- a focus on efficiency
- management by results and a much greater emphasis on the role of managers and their freedom to make decisions
- the use of new technology
- an increased role for audit

(*Source*: Ling 1998; Rhodes 1997; Walsh 1995)

---

results as organizations bend to meet targets rather than achieve the broad range of goals that they were created to deliver.

Nevertheless, as we will see below, the Conservative administrations were strongly influenced by private sector business and managerial models in their reforms of the central state and the public sector as a whole. The problem was, of course, that it was not a coherent package of reforms, and was often used for legitimizing or justifying cost-cutting and the introduction of crude managerialism.

Conservative reform of the state, 1979–1997

In reforming the state, the Conservative governments drew on many elements of New Right thinking and managerialism. There were concerted attempts to privatize and hive off organizations, to increase the role and effectiveness of managers, to increase the role and impact of markets, to de-layer management, and to increase the role of target-setting and auditing.

Structural and managerial reform of Whitehall

During the 1980s, the Conservatives undertook a series of managerial and structural reforms of the British bureaucracy. Underpinning these reforms was a belief that officials spent too long on policy-making to the detriment of efficient management (see Adonis and Hames 1994). The key reforms were: Raynerism, the Financial Management Initiative, and, most importantly, the introduction of the Next Steps reforms in 1988. We will examine each of these in turn:

Raynerism in the Thatcher years

A key theme the Thatcher Government wished to pursue was to increase efficiency throughout the public sector and, in particular, Whitehall. To aid them in this goal, Derek Rayner, the joint managing director of Marks and Spencer, was appointed as a part-time unpaid adviser. He was allocated a small 'Efficiency Unit' in the Cabinet Office, in order to conduct a series of in-depth 'scrutinies' into various aspects of departmental government work.

The Efficiency Unit's objectives were clear: to undertake a series of scrutinies and provide a

critical examination, to a tightly controlled timetable, . . . of a particular policy, activity or a specific aspect of organisation in central government, with a view to reducing the cost of administration and increasing efficiency and effectiveness, especially by cutting out unnecessary work. (Allen 1981: 10–16)

Rayner appointed civil servants, rather than outside consultants, to carry out the efficiency studies. One former civil servant, John Cassels, argues this was an important, but correct, decision:

I think Rayner was very shrewd in having them [scrutinies] done by civil servants, because he understood perfectly well that if you get civil servants to do them it was infinitely preferable to getting in consultants. He relied on departments and people acting on his behalf i.e. Clive Priestley and his minions, to be sure that they did choose ambitious people, and then these ambitious people did their studies. Although, in form, the whole thing was frightfully constitutional, everyone knew that if Rayner supported the outcome of the report, Margaret Thatcher would also and so someone had better do something about it. My own view of that was that it did get some changes done, but there was a huge element of fraud about it as well. (See also Richards 1997.)

The strategy Rayner felt most appropriate for successfully delivering results was one of divide and rule. Rayner actively fostered a culture within the Civil Service of different units competing against one another.

When the scrutineers were sent out to the various departments, they were detailed to ask three simple questions of each department examined;

- What is it for?
- What does it cost?
- What value does it add?

By December 1982, when Rayner had decided to return full-time to Marks and Spencer, 130 scrutinies had been conducted which had produced £170 million savings, with £39 million once-and-for-all savings and a further £104 million of possible economies identified. In terms of personnel, the targeted figure for cuts had been surpassed, the number of Whitehall posts being reduced by 108,000 (Hennessy 1989: 596).

Later, as Hennessy (1989) noted, Rayner conceded that the unit would have had only a marginal impact if it had not been for 'the unique political imperative created by Thatcher, as support for the initiative was not extensive among other ministers or at the highest echelons of the Civil Service' (Hennessy 1989: 595) He continued: 'The Rayner experience was similar to the Fulton reforms in that both demonstrated how vital the importance of Prime Ministerial patronage was: Wilson lost interest; Thatcher did not.'

Yet, despite this political clout and the seemingly impressive statistical results, the scrutinies were not a total success. Clive Ponting was less than thrilled by Raynerism, but, ironically, was later awarded an OBE for his scrutiny of the MoD. He argued that, similar to previous attempts at reform, Whitehall had absorbed Raynerism. He felt Rayner had underestimated the ability of Whitehall to 'fudge' implementing reports it believed were detrimental to the service. He argued:

The classic Whitehall response follows a fairly predictable sequence. The department will generally welcome a report, argue that a detailed study is required, and then set up a committee report on possible implementation of the proposed changes. Those responsible for the existing, criticized system will be well represented on this committee and psychologically opposed to major changes. After a few months a report is produced saying that some, but not all, of the proposed changes should be workable but need further study. A number of sub-committees are convened to look at all these detailed areas, there are difficulties about implementation and possibly more studies are needed. After a couple of years, everything has been so reduced to questions of detail that the general problem has been largely forgotten. A few minor changes can be implemented as the 'first steps' towards the full reform package. Gradually the whole process grinds into the sand of bureaucratic inertia and little, if anything, is achieved. (Ponting 1986: 214)

Ponting's view, though arguably jaundiced, touches on the limitations of the scrutinies. This was confirmed by a 1985 Efficiency Report which concluded that the scrutinies were not the unparalleled success as first thought:

. . . only half the planned savings had been made and even then they had taken twice as long as expected. Officials have been actively opposed to carrying out the studies, and the so-called action-plans have usually only been little more than a time scale for taking decisions in the future with no commitment to change anything. Whitehall has seen the whole process as one of 'damage limitation', implementing as little as possible but just enough to avoid the accusation of outright obstruction. (*Guardian*, 1 November 1985)

Undoubtedly, the scrutinies did make a number of major economic savings, whilst also introducing a more cost-conscious atmosphere to Whitehall. However, the fact remained that the scrutineers' broader goals were not achieved. Officials at the highest level in Whitehall were unwilling to embrace the findings. Raynerism facilitated a climate for further change, but in terms of logistics it fell short of its own goals. Its failure was in its scope: it had no mandate to examine the individuals who were to be in charge of implementing the scrutinies' findings. It was obvious to all those who had been involved in this first stage of reform that something greater than Raynerism was needed.

The Financial Management Initiative

In 1982, the Government launched the Financial Management Initiative (FMI), conceived by Michael Heseltine whilst he was Minister in the Department of Environment (DoE). Heseltine had introduced a Management Information System for Ministers (MINIS) at the DoE, which aimed to inform him of 'who did what, why and at what cost'. MINIS was accompanied by Joubert, an organizational structure that apportioned the DoE into 120 'cost centres', each with an annual budget to cover running and staff costs. This enabled the minister to compare actual expenditure with planned expenditure and to conduct systematic budget reviews. Heseltine argued that MINIS improved both the efficiency and the effectiveness of the DoE and he subsequently introduced it to the Ministry of Defence, when head of that department. Elsewhere in Whitehall, Heseltine's initiatives were greeted with a certain degree of scepticism, yet the one key department that did support his scheme was the Treasury. The Treasury and Civil Service Committee, in its 1982 *Report on Efficiency and Effectiveness in the Civil Service*, was

highly critical of the absence of any clear orientation towards the achievement of efficiency and effectiveness at the higher levels of the Civil Service, and of the limited attempts to set operational objectives, measure outputs and results, and thus to guide the proper use of resources. (Drewry and Butcher 1991: 204)

The Committee recommended that an equivalent of MINIS should be introduced to all departments. This formed the basis of the Government's 1982 White Paper announcing the FMI (Cm. 8616). The aim was to extend MINIS and Joubert to all government departments. Thus, the paper called for wholesale reorganization and a new style of management, based on devolved authority and accountable management. The aim was to:

... promote in each department an organization and system in which managers at all levels have:

a) a clear view of their objectives and means to assess and, wherever possible, measure outputs or performance in relation to those objectives;
b) well-defined responsibility for making the best use of their resources, including a critical scrutiny of output and value for money; and
c) the information (particularly about costs), the training and the access to expert advice that they need to exercise their responsibilities effectively. (HC 1982: 236–1)

Thirty-one government departments were required to assess their operating procedures and develop techniques to improve financial management. They were not required to adopt a standard approach. Each department came up with its own variation of MINIS, the DoE blueprint. For example, the Department of Energy introduced DEMIS, the Department of Trade and Industry produced ARM, the Ministry of Agriculture, Fisheries and Food had MINIM, and the Lord

Chancellor's Department adopted LOCIS. A small central body was established to oversee and guide the progress of these initiatives; originally known as the Financial Management Unit, it was later replaced by the Joint Management Unit (JMU). A process of decentralized budgetary control was also introduced. Departments were divided into 'cost centres', and managers were introduced who were accountable for budgets allocated.

Whether or not it can be argued that the FMI stands on its own as a step forward in Civil Service reform, it certainly broke new ground. It encouraged a greater cost consciousness by individual departments and, with it, the greater economies that the Government demanded. It also provided officials with a clearer view of policy objectives. The FMI signalled the first moves towards a programme of decentralization for Whitehall, which were later to reach fruition in the Next Steps reforms. As Barney Hayhoe, the then Minister for the Civil Service, concluded, the FMI meant

a push to greater decentralisation and delegation down the line . . . will represent a highly significant change in the culture of the Civil Service . . . Recruitment, training, promotion, prospects and practice will all be affected. (HC 1982: 918)

The efficiency scrutinies, MINIS, Joubert, and the FMI can be regarded as the heirs of Fulton based on the principle of economy. FMI was not a period of revolution for Whitehall, but of piecemeal change, a shift away from the previous emphasis on effectiveness. The culmination of these changes provided the foundations for the Government's largest scheme of reform—'Next Steps'.

Next Steps

A central element of NPM was the belief that organization should be hived off and that there should not be a single organization for all tasks. From a public-choice perspective, principal-agent theory was a mechanism for introducing market mechanisms into the public sector by creating contracts between the principal (the controller of services) and the agent (the deliverer of services). These ideas underpinned what were to become the Next Steps Agencies. In 1986, an internal Report by the Efficiency Unit to the Prime Minister criticized the time senior officials spent on policy as detrimental to efficient management, and questioned whether a unified Civil Service could act as the most effective framework in which to conduct government business. The suggestion was that the system needed to be broken up into units. The Report was referred to as 'Next Steps', and because of its potential to court controversy, it was suppressed until after the election of 1987 and published in 1988.

The Report recommended that, where appropriate, semi-autonomous agencies should be established to undertake executive functions of government. The broad aim was to have a core of policy-makers at the centre, remaining in Whitehall, while government services were delivered by agencies round the country. For example, the DVLA was set up in Swansea and, on a much grander scale, the Benefits Agency was established nationwide. A broad range of agencies was created, each with an accountable chief executive, providing a service along similar lines to a business operating in the private sector. Next Steps was not a radical departure from earlier attempts at reform; rather, it was a reaction to, and consolidation of, previous ad hoc attempts at change. Indeed, the incremental manner in which the Conservatives arrived at Next Steps is symbolic of the whole process of evolutionary transformation during the 1980s.

Although, superficially, Next Steps can be regarded as a reform programme based on an organizationally informed agenda, the rationale underpinning the initiative was political. The Conservatives believed that hiving off departmental administrative functions would leave ministers with a smaller policy-making elite based in Whitehall, whose role would be to assist the Government in its broader, strategic goals. As such, it would make it much easier for ministers to make policy. The extent to which this happened casts doubt upon Dunleavy's bureau-shaping model, which argues that the reform process was driven by the senior mandarins for their own self-interest. In this account the politicians drove the reform process, in order to restore executive authority, while at the same time establishing a more efficient model of the way in which to conduct government business.

Despite internal opposition, Next Steps eventually overcame the residual barriers erected in Whitehall. Initially, the Treasury was much opposed to the agencification process, while, more broadly, other departments were apathetic, in large part because they failed to appreciate the radical nature of Next Steps. Thus, by the time of Thatcher's resignation in November 1990, only thirty-four agencies had been established, accounting for 11 per cent (6,800 officials) of the Civil Service.

The goal of agencies was to improve the implementation of policy by separating it out from the making of policy. However, the reality is that the development of agencies has had a major impact on the policy process not least because a precise distinction between making and implementing policy is not easy to maintain. For instance, in the early years of the Child Support Agency, there was considerable debate about how the organization implemented policy. Indeed, many people believed that the way it attempted to pursue fathers for maintenance was a policy matter rather than an issue of implementation. It is also the case that the core department will rarely make policy without consultation with the relevant agency. To some extent a large number of policy ideas come from within the agency. According to a DSS official: 'I have three sections here, and one section is almost entirely devoted to liaising with the agency. That equates to the amount of time I also spend talking to the agency and the people who deliver . . .'

The Major Years, 1990–1997

The Major Government's attitude to the public sector in many ways reflected the arguments put forward in *Reinventing Government* by Osborne and Gaebler (1991). Here, the authors argued that liberal democrat governments should 'steer rather than row the economy'. The role of government should be to create the framework in which the private sector can flourish. In effect, governments were there to enable. Thus, the state should become an 'enabling state' for the private sector. For the Major Government, the Thatcher reforms of the 1980s had been about making the existing state apparatus more efficient. But by utilizing the 'steering not rowing thesis', the theme the Major Government adopted was that the market should be brought to the state. If the nationalized utilities could be privatized during the 1980s, ran the argument, why shouldn't the same principle be applied to the remaining public sector, and in particular the Civil Service? So the Major era of reform can be regarded as a period when the market came to the state.

Under the Major Government the Next Steps programme intensified, so that by 1997, 138 agencies had been established which accounted for 66 per cent of the Civil Service (see Fig. 5.1).

The Citizens' Charter (1991) (Major's big idea!) was also introduced, which aimed at transferring power away from providers to consumers. In effect, this became a process of auditing the public sector—by publishing performance lists for schools, hospitals, universities etc. Hence, a number of commentators refer to this period as

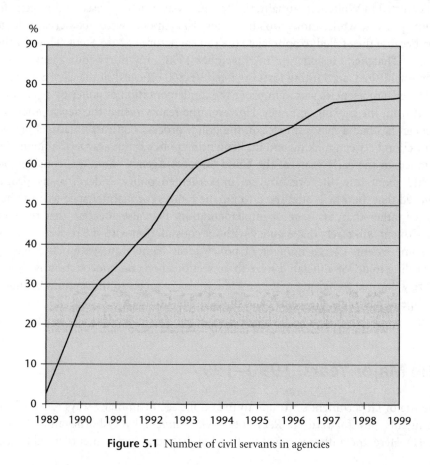

Figure 5.1 Number of civil servants in agencies

the onset of 'The Audit Society', in which market testing/privatization was introduced and performance tables became a key indicator in evaluating public services. Between 1993 and 1995, market testing produced £800 million savings, with over £2 billion of government work reviewed since 1992. Here, government services had to compete with the private sector—for example, HMSO became privatized. In terms of privatization, over £1 billion has been transferred to the private sector, 26,000 posts have been cut from Whitehall, and over 50 per cent of government work has been put out to the private sector.

More broadly, it is important to emphasize that the Conservative reforms directly affected the relationship between ministers and Whitehall. As a retired Civil Service Commissioner concluded:

If you are looking at the structure of the senior Civil Service, I don't think you can ignore the introduction of Agencies. They have very much affected the nature of the senior people advising ministers. I would say that it is one of the most significant changes to the Civil Service, since perhaps the Northcote–Trevelyan reforms. It seems unfortunate to me that it has been done without Parliamentary legislation. But if you are talking about the type of people now involved at the highest levels in the agencies, I think you will find a great deal of them come from the private sector. So you have got this infusion of people from outside. The reforms have produced tangible effects both for the Civil Service and the functioning of British Government as a whole.

Indeed, the broad, consensual view was provided by one recently retired Permanent Secretary:

So much has now gone out to Executive Agencies and they have largely an executive job to do. We have lost those days when you had the key policy makers also running the big executive functions, within a large department. That opens some new questions about the role of the Permanent Secretaries and higher civil servants in what is left of the policy making departments, as distinct from the Executive Agencies.

Clearly, the structural and managerial reforms between 1979 and 1997 produced a sea change in Whitehall. While Fulton was defused by the dynamic conservatism of the Civil Service, the reforms from Next Steps onwards have altered the balance of power between ministers and civil servants. As Metcalfe (1993: 352) concludes:

Management methods, concepts, models, and values have been accepted as an integral part of the way the business of government is conducted. Whether they are the right management concepts is open to debate, but then acceptance goes much deeper than almost anyone thought possible in 1979. It is difficult to imagine these reforms being reversed. . . . Without suggesting that a total transformation has occurred or that the changes have been completely successful, it is increasingly clear that a fundamental shift has been made which will have a permanent influence on the functioning of British government.

Personnel reform

The Conservatives' initial approach to the personnel reform of Whitehall was primarily political: it was a programme based on de-privileging the Civil Service. As one retired senior official argued: 'It soon became obvious that, from 1979 onwards, the Civil Service was no longer to be regarded as a "special case" and we were about to come under attack. Something unusual from a postwar Conservative Government.' Thus there followed a period in which the Civil Service Department was abolished (1981), there was a move towards a decentralized pay system following the Megaw Committee's recommendations (1982), and the Central Policy Review Staff, a think tank staffed by civil servants to provide policy advice to the Cabinet, was abolished (1983).

The Thatcher Government's strategy to realign the power balance between the ministers and Whitehall also embraced changing the culture and attitude of most senior civil servants. In order to do this, the Thatcher Government did not attempt to politicize the senior Civil Service by appointing a series of Conservative Party sympathizers to the most senior posts in Whitehall (see Richards 1997). However, given the longevity of Margaret Thatcher's time as Prime Minister, she had responsibility for approving a large number of appointments to the top two grades in Whitehall. In so doing, she personalized the appointment's system, ensuring that individuals who were 'managerially orientated can-doers' were appointed to a number of strategic posts (Richards 1997). This had an effect on the culture in the highest tiers of Whitehall which it was hoped would permeate downwards throughout the rest of the senior Civil Service. Senior officials began to concentrate more on finding ways to implement government policies, rather than adopting the more traditional 'snag-hunter' role of previous Whitehall generations. As one contemporary official commented:

I think what happened during the 1980s is that the Civil Service moved to recognising their job as delivering what ministers wanted. Can-do man was in and wait-a-minute man was out. Ministers not only knew what they wanted, but often how to get there. The Civil Service role as ballast was sidelined. There was no room for it. So officials buckled down and really got on with it.

Similarly, a retired Permanent Secretary emphasized:

I think Conservative ministers tended increasingly to want somebody to run the machine and do it effectively, but not to offer independent advice. That was the biggest change and I think this has had an effect to this day on the calibre of the people coming into the Civil Service.

In personnel terms, one of the key changes during the Thatcher period involved an increased emphasis upon the need to appoint efficient managers of the policy and implementation process, rather than policy advisers. Most notably, Permanent Secretaries became policy managers rather than policy advisers, and this change enhanced the ability of Conservative ministers to impose their will on the policy process. Here, the process of reform should be understood as political, involving the reassertion of ministerial power over the Civil Service. At a secondary level, however, it is also organizational and economic, emphasizing the need for senior civil servants to be efficient managers of the machine.

In the Major years, a whole series of personnel reforms were introduced: the Efficiency Unit's *Career Management and Succession Planning* (1993); a White Paper, *Continuity and Change* (1994); a second White Paper, *The Civil Service: Taking Forward Continuity and Change* (1995); and the Senior Management Review (SMR). Gradually, but in the view of many people too slowly, the system was changing from one in which individuals gained entry into a career to one in which an individual was appointed to a specific job. This was reflected in the two central aims of the White Papers: to break down the hierarchy in the upper echelons of the senior Civil Service and so increase delegation and diversity of advice within the policy-process; and, where possible, to eliminate layers of management among the 3000 top civil servants in Whitehall.

It was the 1995 SMR that had the most pronounced effect on the policy-making process. It led to the creation of the Senior Civil Service, the removal of a whole bureaucratic tier (Grade 3), and the devolution of responsibility down the Whitehall hierarchy. At the most formal level, the SMR was an organizational reform. Its rationale was to move closer to European models of bureaucratic organization; so, for example, Grade 2 Deputy Secretaries were to adopt the EU title of Director-General. The aim was to break down the traditional hierarchical (gradist) nature of policy-making in Whitehall, so that officials would now be known by their job titles instead of their grade. At the same time, the SMR was underpinned by a Treasury initiative aimed at reducing Whitehall departments to an elite core of policy-makers, with other activities being further contracted out either to agencies or to the private sector. In this sense, the reforms were justified in economic and political terms. They would result in cost savings, and give ministers greater control over the rump of the bureaucratic machine left at the heart of Whitehall.

Bringing the market to the public sector

Fundamental to the New Right project and New Public Management was the role of the market as a mechanism for delivering public goods in the most effective and efficient manner. The aim was either to return elements of government to the private sector (through privatization) or, where that was not possible, to introduce the market into aspects of the public sector (the creation of internal markets).

Privatization

For many Conservatives who were in office during the Thatcher/Major administrations, privatization was the most successful policy carried out during the eighteen years of Conservative government. The origins of this wave of privatization can actually be traced back to the previous Labour Government, when, as part of the IMF package in 1976, they were forced to sell shares in the then publicly owned BP as a mechanism for raising finance. The Conservative Administration of 1979 positively endorsed privatization; nevertheless the policy developed in a piecemeal and gradual way. It began by selling more BP shares so that it became a minority shareholder; it then followed a similar strategy for British Aerospace and then for Cable and Wireless. The first 100 per cent sale of a publicly owned company was Amersham International, and this was followed by the sale of the National Freight Corporation to its managers and workers. The first large-scale privatization, aimed at the general public, was British Telecom in 1984, the largest UK privatization. Following a large-scale advertising campaign, 2.4 million people applied for shares. The next large-scale privatization, British Gas, attracted 6 million applications for shares. By 1992 the Conservatives had sold off nearly all the major utilities and privatized companies. The only large companies left in public ownership were coal, British Railways, and the Post Office. The first two were privatized by the Major Government (Pirie 1993) (see Table 5.2).

For government, privatization can potentially have a number of benefits:

• it raises a substantial amount of money which the government can use for public expenditure and tax cuts;
• it encourages private investment in the utilities;
• it makes a considerable number of people shareholders, thereby attaching them to the private sector and market;
• it reduces the power of the trade unions, particularly in monopoly industries;
• it relieves government of responsibility for a whole range of problems, from the quality of water to trains running on time.

One of the biggest impacts of privatization was to change the mode of governance of a large part of the economy and the provision of public goods. For nearly forty years, responsibility for delivering different forms of energy, public transport, a range of public utilities, and even the production of a variety of manufactured goods such as steel lay with the government. With the privatization programme, the government was disengaging from the economy, effectively arguing that the market was the most effective way of delivering services such as water, gas, and electricity. However, the process of privatization was not a shift from state control to laissez-faire and in most cases, the government retained some mechanism of control over the newly privatized industries. In some industries the government retained, at least for a period, a 'golden share'. This meant that the government

Table 5.2 The key privatizations in Britain

Company	Date
British Petroleum	1979
British Aerospace	1981
Cable and Wireless	1981
National Freight Corporation	1982
Britoil	1982
Amersham International	1982
Association of British Ports	1983
British Telecom	1984
Cable and Wireless	1983
Enterprise Oil	1984
Jaguar	1984
British Gas	1986
Rolls-Royce	1987
British Airways	1987
British Airports Authority	1987
British Steel	1998
British Petroleum (second tranche)	1987
PowerGen	1995
National Power	1995
British Coal	1995
British Nuclear Power	1996
British Rail	1996

could have a substantial influence if it so desired. More importantly, the privatization process did not create competition in a range of areas, especially the utilities such as water, gas, electricity, and railways. Through privatization, therefore, the government introduced a system of regulation, setting up bodies such as Ofwat and Oftel which effectively restricted the price increases that the new private monopolies could impose if they were left to the market. Some of these bodies have been relatively effective. For instance, the railway regulators have imposed heavy fines for poor performance, and in 1995 the electricity regulator reconsidered the prices previously agreed. In 1997 both the water and electricity regulators imposed price reductions. As Feigenbaum et al. (1998: 80) point out: 'The regulators possess considerable power over the operation, service standards and pricing structure of the privatized utilities.' We have also seen with Railtrack that the government can impose direct government control if it believes that the standard of service falls below a certain level (see Box 5.6). Again, it appears that privatization marks a change in the nature of control rather than the end of control.

> ## Box 5.6 **Government and the failure of Railtrack**
>
> It is clear that in the case of railways there has been a significant shift from government to governance with the development of a complex network of service deliverers (see Boxes 11.1 and 11.2). Nevertheless, this does not mean that the Government has given up control. Indeed, in October 2001 the Government demonstrated that it was prepared to reconsider renationalization, in order to ensure the effective delivery of public goods. Here, the Government was faced with the problem of Railtrack going into receivership or alternatively, receiving even more government money. The company was placed in the control of Government-appointed administrators. Stephen Byers, the Secretary of State for Trade and Industry, said: 'I intend to renationalize the present system of regulation to provide a more united approach, with stronger strategic direction, while stopping the day-to-day interference in the industry' (BBC 2001c). The Government clearly wants to impose some central direction on the operation of the privatized rail system. Currently, the plan for Railtrack appears to be that it will be turned into a non-profit-making company, as this will end the conflict between the needs of shareholders and the interests of rail users

Marketizing the public sector

For the services that the government could not privatize, there was an attempt to introduce market criteria and managerialism as a way of making them more effective. As we have seen above, through the introduction of managerialism the government attempted to make the Civil Service more efficient and effective. But it also tried to introduce market criteria into education and health. The 1988 Education Act attempted to create competition in education by giving parents a choice of schools and allowing funds to follow the pupil. Therefore, if parents opted out of the worst schools and moved to the best schools, the worst schools would have to improve in order to attract more funds (Pirie 1993). Of course, the problem was that often there are limits to how far pupils can move: school performance is determined by catchment area rather than the ability of teachers. The best schools quickly became full, and so parents had little choice about where to send their children. The Act also gave greater autonomy to schools, allowing them to opt out of the control of local education authorities.

In the NHS, the Conservatives attempted to create a market by separating out the purchasers and the suppliers of services. The District Health Authorities were no longer the purchasers and providers of services. They were to become the purchasers and they could buy services from hospitals or NHS Trusts. Therefore, DHAs will seek the cheapest treatment and hospitals have an incentive to provide the cheapest service. In addition, GPs were allowed to become budget holders, which allowed them also to purchase services from hospitals or, if it was cheaper, provide them themselves.

Analysis: the Conservative years and state reform, 1979–1997: from public administration to New Public Management?

Whilst NPM was a mantra that echoed through the corridors of Whitehall and, as we have seen, appears to have influenced the reform process, it is important to recognize that there is no single definition of NPM. It is an amorphous term that contains elements of business/management theory fused with neo-liberal, public-choice accounts of bureaucracy. Indeed, Hood (1991)accepts that NPM is an 'ill-defined concept' which can be portrayed as a theme 'for all seasons'. This leaves open to question the utility of NPM as an analytical tool for understanding change in British government.

However, regardless of how we define NPM, it is clear that the process of state reform under the Conservatives was not based on a clearly constructed blueprint of reform, or even a loosely assembled range of goals. So, for example, Peter Kemp, one of the key figures involved in the Next Steps process, maintains that the Conservative Administration

had a vague feeling that there was something wrong with the Civil Service machinery of over half a million people . . . I think it is fair to say with all the reforms (and I accept there are some political overtures to some of them) there was a natural evolution . . . It was simply a case of tapping ahead with a white stick. Some of us felt—and Margaret Thatcher was included in our number from the point of view of the management and administration of the Civil Service and John Major from the point of view of customer service—that something was not quite right. It was a political feel at the top end, while it was official drive at the lower end.

Similarly, another retired senior official observed:

Some of the things that were being proposed were very vague and one or two things were accepted maybe two or three years later, while other proposals simply faded away. There was no real substance to the reforms up until the Next Steps.

These comments substantiate the observation of Hogwood (1997: 715):

The changes to the machinery of government were not the working through of some blueprint which the Conservatives had when they came into office in 1979. Changes to the structure of central government departments were undertaken on a largely ad hoc basis. While attempts can be made to suggest theoretical explanations for developments such as the establishment of Next Steps agencies, these explanations are poor at explaining the timing of the initiative and its evolution and the variety which exists among agencies and departments.

As such, the process of reform is much more properly understood as a response to a combination of political, economic, ideological, and organizational factors. The reforms were based upon a normative view that the private sector was dynamic and efficient, while the public sector was stagnant, reactionary, and wasteful. They reflected a process of strategic learning by a Conservative Administration in office for eighteen years. This learning was a response to lessons learnt from the previous decade and based upon an ill-defined, and often unpredictable, process of trial and error when in power. As Ling (1998: 118) observes:

> There is no evidence of a systematic and long-term plan for taking on and transforming the British state. In the years [after 1979], politicians and managers at the centre found themselves facing a variety of problems in managing the state system and responded with a large number of usually *ad hoc* responses.

Although it is important for students of public administration and public policy to be aware of the use of NPM as a framework for analysing change in British central government, it remains a problematic concept. In particular, it often leads analysts to portray the reform as part of a coherent neo-liberal agenda that swept through Britain and other similar liberal-democratic states, such as New Zealand, Australia, Sweden, Holland, France, Canada, and the United States. The NPM thesis suggests that the state changed from being stable, unilinear, consensual, centralized, rule-bound, and paternalistic to being responsive, flexible, dynamic, outcome-oriented, decentralized and enabling.

What in fact we can see is a conflict between competing approaches to Whitehall and the role of government. The traditional Whitehall culture was based on a notion of a public-service ethos, with officials as the key policy advisers within a hierarchically organized government. The Thatcherite vision of officials was that they were policy implementers who provide ministers with facts and not advice on policy (see Table 5.3). Moreover, the bureaucracy needed to be as close to a market economy as possible, and therefore should be flexible and fragmented rather than hierarchical and unified. The situation at the beginning of the twenty-first century is that the Civil Service contains elements of both cultures. It has retained much of its policy-making role, whilst losing the monopoly of policy advice it once had.

Of course, these changes in the structure of government are also causally linked to policy changes. The aim of the Thatcherite agenda was to move away from the policies of the Keynesian welfare state. It is certainly the case that Keynesian economic policy was abandoned and the Conservative governments of Thatcher and

Table 5.3 Competing cultural frameworks

	Values	Actions	Institutions
Managerialism	Efficiency Effectiveness Economy	Can-do Policy implementer	Flexible and fragmented
Traditional Whitehall culture	Integrity Neutrality Elitism	Policy adviser Fact imparter	Hierarchical and unified

Source: Marsh et al. (2001)

Major attempted to disengage from the economy. Rather than a commitment to demand management, the aim of the Conservatives was to improve the supply side of the economy through controlling inflation and reforming taxation. In addition, they rapidly reduced the amount of money spent by the DTI on regional and industrial policy. However, in areas of welfare policy, breaking away from the policies of the postwar era was much more difficult. Whilst, as we saw above, managerialism and markets were introduced, the fundamental elements of the welfare system—universal and free health care and education and a comprehensive system of social security benefits—remained in place. Indeed, despite the explicit Thatcherite goal of reducing welfare spending and cutting tax, both increased during the eighteen years of Conservative government.

So the Thatcherite period of government saw incremental rather than revolutionary changes in the nature of the state and policy-making. Many of the ideas that the Thatcher Government implemented were not developed by the New Right, but came directly from the Fulton Report in the 1960s. In addition, in terms of reforming policy the Conservatives were extremely pragmatic, and made changes in a way that would not alienate the core of voters who were attached to the key elements of the welfare state. However, the shifting culture of Whitehall and the changing role of ministers and officials (see Chapter 9) did produce a more complex process of policy-making, a shift from what some saw as government to governance. For instance, the policy of privatizing publicly owned utilities created a new, informal organizational network involving a government department, a private organization, and a regulator, rather than being completely within government.

Conclusion: an internally hollowed-out state?

When analysing the reforms of the state under the Conservatives, a number of key points need to be considered:

- The Conservatives pursued a course of reform which altered both public administration and concomitantly the structure of the state.
- Their reform programme was broadly ad hoc.
- It was based on a series of segmented measures which, retrospectively, can be portrayed as contributing to a process of evolutionary reform.
- Their programme lacked a blueprint, and thus contained a number of contradictory elements.

More specifically, because of the differing strands in the ideological makeup of the Conservative Party, both the Thatcher and Major Governments remained committed to retaining key features of the constitution. This acted as a fundamental constraint on the introduction of a more radical programme of reform.

Nevertheless, it can be argued that by 1997 the extent of state reform had ensured that the idea of social democracy based on collective provision, with the state playing a key role, had been seriously eroded.

Indeed, it is this final point that Rhodes (1997) dwells on when he claims that after the 1970s the state underwent a process of hollowing-out (see Chapter 2). The process is much more complex than that, however. Whilst the government introduced markets and privatized areas of government, it did this within the context of a legislative system and regulatory institutions that meant the state continued to be a key element in the process of policy-making. In educational reform, for instance, the government appeared to reduce central control by introducing parental choice and the local management of schools, but this was all done within a context of a national curriculum and testing which gave the centre much more direct control over the day-to-day operations of schools.

KEY POINTS

- Following the delegitimization of the Keynesian welfare state in the 1970s, it was the New Right that proved most adept at filling the political vacuum that had been created.

- The normative prescription of the New Right to combat decline was the state's withdrawal from both the economy and society and the pursuit of a monetarist, supply-side economic strategy.

- To accomplish this, after 1979 the Conservative Administration launched an attack on what it perceived as an over-extended, uneconomic, over-bureaucratized state.

- It pursued a wide-scale privatization programme, reduced its contacts with actors in civil society and reformed the public sector, most notably Whitehall, through financial cuts and the implementation of managerialism and market testing.

- The Conservatives' goal was to create an 'enabling state' in which business could prosper, but in which the rights of the consumer would be better protected against the demands of the producer.

KEY QUESTIONS

1. Why was the New Right successful in filling the political vacuum created by the delegitimization of the Keynesian welfare state?

2. How coherent was the last Conservative Administration's programme of reforming the state?

3. Did the reforms from 1979 to 1997 lead to an internally 'hollowed-out' state?

4. To what extent have the 'Beveridge principles' on which the welfare state was founded been eroded by the Thatcher and Major Governments?

KEY READING

For an account of the growth of the New Right and its ideas, see Kavanagh (1987), Cockett (1995), and Hay (1996). There are numerous accounts of the Conservative reforms of the state after 1979, of which we list a few selected texts: Gamble (1994b), Kavanagh (1997), Dunleavy (1991), Ling (1998), Richards (1997), and Thatcher (1993).

KEY WEBSITES

The website for the Conservative Party, where debates on reform of the state can be found, is: **www.conservative-party.org.uk**; for Conservative-oriented think tanks: **www.iea.org.uk/** and **www.adamsmith.org.uk/**. For changes to the Civil Service, a useful website is **www.cabinet-office.gov.uk**; on broader themes of reform and governance, see **www.Britishcouncil.org** and **www.fhit.org/democratic_audit/index.html**, and on quangos, see **www.cabinet-office.gov.uk/organisations.htm**. For websites on Europe and other supranational organizations see Chapters 6 and 7.

6

EXTERNAL
CHALLENGES TO THE
MODERN STATE I:
GLOBALIZATION

INTRODUCTION

As we saw in Chapter 3, one of the key defining features of the modern British state is the notion of territoriality: authority is bounded within a specific territory over which Westminster has ultimate control. This notion of territoriality grew out of the Westphalian concept of international society based on the idea that international relations occurred between sovereign and independent nation-states (see Jackson 1997). In Britain, this conception has been especially important because the notion of sovereignty has been an integral element in the process of legitimizing the parliamentary system. Sovereignty lies with Parliament, and there is no higher authority. This is a theme that continues to resonate throughout British politics, and particularly within the present ideological turmoil of the Conservative Party (see Box 6.1).

According to the governance literature, the cultural, political, and economic processes of globalization are permanently challenging these twin conceptions of territoriality and sovereignty. A whole range of factors—technology, transportation, computerization, the development of supranational organizations, the growth of transnational companies—have led to national borders being permeated, and now nation-states have to react to, and operate within, a global rather than national environment. It is argued that there is a hollowing-out of the state, as transnational institutions and forces increasingly become the sites of key decisions. The aim of this chapter is to examine this debate, and to assess the extent to which global pressures have led to new patterns of governance in Britain.

Unfortunately, when analysing globalization there is a need for a degree of caution. This is because globalization is not a neutral or meaningless label, but a value-laden and much-contested concept in both political and academic circles. When we are considering globalization within the context of governance, the key questions are:

Box 6.1 Britain and the enduring myth of sovereignty

Judge (1993) has illustrated how the notion of sovereignty is central to defining the nature of politics in Britain, and how the policy process is suffused with the legitimizing discourse of sovereignty. What is perhaps most surprising is how strong that notion of sovereignty remains today. For example, in a letter to the *Daily Telegraph* during the Conservative leadership contest of 2001, the former Prime Minister Margaret Thatcher criticized Kenneth Clarke, one of the contenders, for viewing 'with blithe unconcern the erosion of Britain's sovereignty . . . And in the strategic choice of whether Britain aligns herself with an emerging European super-state or whether our relationship with America should remain paramount, Ken would be on the side of Brussels' (*Daily Telegraph*, 21 Aug. 2001). What is striking is the degree to which Thatcher does not seem to see that the strategic choice was made long ago, and by the United States, not Britain. Britain really has had little choice but to integrate into Europe.

- What effect has globalization had on governance?
- Has globalization led to a more diverse and fragmented policy-making arena, which in turn has led to greater pluralism?
- Alternatively, has the impact of economic globalization (see below) led to a small number of very powerful transnational companies controlling the domestic policy process?
- Is globalization a recent phenomenon that has evolved in the last thirty years and which neatly dovetails with the governance era, or is it a process that has been occurring for more than 300 years?

The answers to these questions depend on what particular definition of globalization one adopts (see below) and the extent to which one either views globalization as a recent, immutable process which renders national governments impotent or, alternatively, consider it a much over-stated and over-rated concept, and conclude that nation-states remain the key sites of political power. We cannot provide a definitive answer to the questions posed above, because the nature of the subject is highly contested. Instead, we have set out to outline the different debates surrounding the concept of globalization. We have then assessed the British political elite's interpretation of globalization—which is perhaps the most important consideration, given that our task is to evaluate the present-day nature of the British policy process. For if Westminster and Whitehall consider globalization, in whatever form, to be a reality, they will act in a different way than if they regarded globalization as simply a debate discussed in university lecture theatres or late-night Radio 4 political chat shows, and which has no bearing on the 'real' political world.

Interpretations of globalization

There is now a considerable literature on the nature of globalization and its impact. But there is almost no agreement on what it is. Most people agree that something has changed, that the interconnectedness of the world—and the spread of that interconnectedness—has increased. People also agree that capitalism has become an increasingly dominant global force, and that this is having an impact on how people live and the sorts of choices that they can make (for reviews of the debate see Scholte 2000, Held and McGrew 2000). Many disagree over the meaning of the processes (see Table 6.1). For some, globalization implies a complete transformation of the pre-existing economic and political organizations and their replacement by a globally integrated state with transnational institutions of regulation (see Ohmae 1995). For others, globalization is seen as greatly exaggerated: what we are apparently witnessing is nothing new (see Hirst and Thompson 1996).

The causes of globalization

With little agreement over what globalization is, it is difficult to identify its causes. It is not a single and clearly identifiable entity but rather, as Gamble and Payne (1996) point out, an ongoing process. It has many elements and levels. It may be a process that continues infinitely, or unforeseen events may lead to the reassertion of national sovereignty. It is also difficult to distinguish between what is a cause of globalization and what is a consequence. Nevertheless, several economic, social, political, and scientific developments appear to have contributed to what people call globalization:

* The collapse of Communism. The end of the Cold War and the collapse of the Communist bloc allowed the extension of global markets and the ideological hegemony of liberal capitalism.

* The dominance of the US economically, militarily, and culturally. With the collapse of the Soviet Union and the continuing economic and cultural power of the US, the latter was increasingly able to set the economic and political agenda in international fora. It was thus able to extend a globalizing free-trade ideology.

* The collapse of Bretton Woods and the end of the postwar boom. Bretton Woods was essentially a system of fixed exchange rates underpinned by the US. In the 1960s, the costs of the Vietnam War and much higher levels of public expenditure forced the US to abandon the gold rate, and this undermined the system of fixed currencies. Devaluation allowed inflation to seep into Western economies and this, combined with the end of the postwar boom, forced economic restructuring in the 1970s and the 1980s. Generally, this restructuring took the form of a shift to liberal, free-market economic policies.

* The development of telecommunications and computing. A rapid development in these areas underpinned the existence of global markets (see below).

* The deregulation of the banking system and the liberalization of trade, exchange rates and investment. These measures were crucial to the freeing up of global

Table 6.1 Interpretations of globalization

Interpretation	Main argument	Main proponents
Globalization as totalizing process	The globalization of the economy and culture is resulting in the disappearance of national boundaries and the declining importance of the nation-state. Domestic states are being replaced by transnational states.	Ohmae (1995) Sklair (1995,1998)
Globalization as rhetoric	Globalization is not really occurring (or it is nothing new), but it is a useful rhetorical device for politicians either to hide policy errors or to promote the extension of neo-liberal economic policies.	Hay and Watson (1998) Hay (1999a) Hirst and Thompson (1996)
Globalization as imperialism	Globalization is nothing new, but is the continuation of imperialism by other means. Developing countries are no longer exploited through military conquest but through the exploitation of their resources and labour.	Hardt and Negri (2000)
Globalization as restructuring of state power	There are significant changes occurring in the economy, culture, and politics, but they do not mean the undermining of the nation state. It does mean, however, that the state is acting in different ways and making different choices. For some, it means policy being made increasingly in the interest of capital.	Mann (1997) Cerny (1990, 1995) Baker et al. (1998)
Globalization as Americanization	Globalization is not globalization at all, but Americanization: this is the successful export of US ideals, culture, and economic methods to the rest of the world.	Fukuyama (1992)
Globalization as transformation	Globalization is a continuation of patterns of global interaction that have occurred throughout history, but they are now having more extensive and intensive impacts on the way people live and the nature of politics and economics. This process is still occurring; therefore there is no fixed notion of what globalization means.	Higgott (1998) Held et al. (1999)

markets, and new technology allowed for the rapid movement of finance (see below).

- The growth of multinational and transnational corporations. The last twenty or thirty years has seen a rapid expansion in the number, size, productivity and levels of production of MNCs (see below).

- Migration. Greater levels of migration are changing the way that labour markets work and the perceptions of national borders and identities (see below).

Global changes and global challenges

For Castells (1996: 92) the key point is that for the first time we have a 'global economy' which has 'the capacity to work as a unit in real time on a planetary scale'. The development of this global economy has major implications for culture, politics, and society. Indeed, the development of globalization cannot be seen as having a single cause; it is in fact a complex interaction of many various factors (see Box 6.1). In terms of understanding the policy process in government, a central element in the process of globalization is the fact that 'the core Westphalian norm of sovereignty is no longer operative'. The state has lost 'exclusive authority' over a defined territory (Scholte 1997: 21). There are a number of changes in many facets of life which seem to be a cause and consequence of globalization.

Economics and globalization

The core element in the process and development of globalization is the economic change resulting from two crucial elements: the growth of, and liberalization of, capital and the rise, and increasing dominance, of multinational companies (MNCs).

The rise of multinationals

Held et al. (1999) illustrate how MNCs have become global players which 'account for the majority of the world's exports, while sales of foreign affiliates exceed total global exports'. This growth has been accompanied by the transnationalization of production and distribution being organized across borders (see Box 6.2). The extent of MNC activity is indicated by the growing levels of foreign direct investment (FDI)—in other words, the amount that MNCs invest in countries other than their own. In the period since the 1980s, FDI has been growing at four times the rate of world trade. Increasingly, this investment is occurring in developing countries and within manufacturing and services, rather than—as has traditionally been the case—in developing countries and in extractive industries. MNCs now account for about 75 per cent of world trade in manufacturing (Baker et al. 1998: 21).

> ### Box 6.2 **MNCs and transnational production**
>
> Some MNCs are now massive companies with sites of production in many countries. Often, the components for even simple goods such as a pair of jeans are produced in many different countries. For instance, Unilever has over 500 subsidiaries in over 90 countries. Normally, these companies establish affiliates, subsidiaries, or alliances in a range of companies. Even large multinational companies in industries like airlines have created strategic alliances with other MNCs. The WorldPartners Association is an alliance of 19 telecommunications countries in 35 countries. The levels of production of MNCs are massive: the sales of the 50 largest MNCs has risen from $540 billion in 1975 to $2,100 billion in 1990.
>
> (*Source*: Scholte 2000).

Multinational companies are much more difficult for governments to control. Their importance in terms of employment, investment, and overall economic growth is such that nation-states are dependent on them rather than the other way around. The relative mobility of these firms means that they can move production to cheaper labour markets, thus forcing developed nations into policies that reduce the cost of their own labour. The decisions of an MNC as to whether or not to invest in a particular region can have a tremendous impact on a city, or as in the case of the developing world, a whole country. As Lindblom (1977) pointed out, this means that large companies can have a major impact not only on people's lives but also on the taxation, employment, and industrial policies of nation-states, as they compete to attract inward investment. For instance, much of the debate around the issue of Britain and the 'social chapter' was focused on the issue of how EU regulation could make Britain a much less attractive option for overseas investors. One of the key issues for the EU is to prevent member states from giving particular subsidies and tax breaks which encourage MNCs to invest in one EU country rather than another.

The growth and liberalization of capital
According to Castells (1996: 93)

Capital is managed around the clock in globally integrated financial markets working in real time for the first time in history: billion dollars worth of transaction take place in seconds in the electronic circuits throughout the globe. It is now the case that due to the expansion of capital and technological change savings, investments and currencies are now interconnected worldwide.

The turnover of the currency markets is now greater than the world stock of foreign exchange (Higgott 1998). In Britain between 1985 and 1991, transnational financial flows increased from £366.1 million to £1,016.6 million (Castells 1996: 94). Susan Strange (1998) focuses on the rapid expansion that has occurred in financial markets between the 1960s and the 1990s. The number of people, organizations, and investments involved in international markets have dramatic-ally increased. As a consequence, all these actors are using their money to play the casino of international markets, and the result is large-scale instability in curren-cies, prices and stocks and shares (Strange 1998). This makes life extremely dif-ficult not only for governments, who are unable to control the amounts of money moving in the international economy, but also for individuals, who lose jobs and pensions as a consequence of erratic market movements. As we will see below, the paradox is that, whilst governments have been behind the liberalization of mar-kets, they are now trying to develop new forms of regulation to control the forces they unleashed. This again illustrates the complexity of governance, because the reality is not a shift to a smaller role for government but unintended consequences producing greater attempts at government control. As Jessop (2001) observes, one form of regulatory failure leads to new forms of regulation.

Nevertheless, it appears that economies are more open, foreign direct invest-ment has increased, international financial dealings have become more rapid and much greater, and the global market is increasingly beyond the control of nation-states. The globalization of market forces has made national economic management much more difficult.

Technology and globalization

Underpinning the so-called processes of economic globalization are important technological changes in three key areas: computers, telecommunications, and transport. Two fundamental changes were the combination of computing and telecommunications that allowed much greater, cheaper, and more efficient inter-national networking which, in the words of Giddens (1990), compress space and time. According to Castells (1996: 45)

This networking capability only became possible, naturally, because of major developments both in the telecommunications and computing networking technologies during the 1970s. But, at the same time such changes were only made possible by new microelectronic devices and stepped up computing capacity, in a striking illustration of the synergistic relationships in the Information Technology Revolution.

The combination of smaller, faster, more powerful computers combined with fibre optic cable technology which allowed the transmission of more information at higher speeds, provided the basis for 'ubiquitous commuting and for real-time, untethered, interactive electronic communication' (Castells 1996: 46). Even thirty years ago, computer hardware was large and slow and software was in its infancy, while international telephone calls were expensive and difficult. With the rapid development of the Internet in recent years, it is possible to have constant inter-national contact at low cost. Developments in IT have potentially a notable social impact on society. As Keating (2000: 16) observes:

. . . technology enables the processing of far more information and is more demanding of analytical skills. There is a risk, however, of a new divide emerging between those who are *knowledge-rich* and can adapt to the new technology and those who cannot.

Politics and globalization

For many writers on globalization, the process of change in the international system has had a dramatic effect on the role and nature of the state and has led to new forms of politics and new layers of governance. There is a wide range of often contradictory arguments concerning the impact of globalization on the state: some commentators see the nation-state disappearing altogether, whilst others argue that it has become stronger (see Ohmae 1995 and Payne 2000). For Held et al. (1999: 49):

'Global politics' is a term which usefully captures the stretching of political relations across space and time; the extension of political power and political activity across the boundaries of the modern nation-state. Political decisions and actions in one part of the world can rapidly acquire worldwide ramifications. In addition, sites of political action and/ or decision-making can become linked through rapid communications into complete networks of decision-making and political interaction.

Thus, the globalization of politics has a number of different dimensions:

The context of government

One of the simplest ways to understand globalization in terms of government is the way in which it changes the constraints faced by the state and the sorts of relationships that governments have with other states, international institutions, and transnational bodies. Cerny (1995: 595–6) makes the point that by 'reshaping the structural context of rational choice itself, globalization transforms the ways that the basic rules of the game work in politics and international relations'. In other words, globalization changes the options and degree of choice available to state actors. This is not to say, as some interpreters of globalization do, that national governments no longer have any importance, but rather that the things they are able to do are different, and are done through a new array of institutions and relationships. Gray (1998) argues that, because of tax rivalry in competitive global markets, states do not have the option of pursuing the counter-cyclical policies that were undertaken by the Keynesian welfare state, and as a consequence social democracy becomes unviable, since it relied on a closed economy, where states could raise the necessary taxation to fund welfare states and interventionist economic policies.

An illustration of the constraints of the global economy is provided by Britain's forced exit from the exchange rate mechanism (ERM) in 1992. For the then Conservative Government, the ERM became the linchpin of their economic policy: it was an external mechanism for controlling inflation and ensuring that the pound was a strong currency. Despite the belief that the ERM was a way of dealing with external threats to sterling, it actually created a new set of risks. During and following the April 1992 general election, the Prime Minister, John Major, and the Chancellor, Norman Lamont, maintained that membership of the ERM was a central pillar of the government's economic policy (Thompson 1996). However, on 'Black Wednesday', 16 September 1992, the government was forced to leave the ERM because of a series of events beyond their control:

- The pound was in a structurally weak position. The rate of the pound within the ERM was £1 to 2.85 Deutsche Marks (DM), which many considered too high. This was made worse by the deep recession affecting the British economy, which, in a situation of free-floating exchanges rates, would have ordinarily resulted in the pound being devalued.

- US interest rates were exceptionally low at 3 per cent and German rates exceptionally high at 10 per cent as a consequence of unification. The result was that investors moved from dollars to DM, and as a consequence the DM rose relative to the pound.

- The events that took place in the immediate run-up to the French referendum on the Maastricht Treaty, and a number of polls indicated the French would vote no. With a no vote, the ERM would have collapsed. Dealers believed this would result in the end of tough anti-inflation policies and split EC currencies between the weak and the strong. Sterling was perceived as weak, and therefore would fall in value. Dealers therefore sold weak currencies to buy strong currencies.

- The Italian lira was perceived as particularly weak, and there were strong indications that it would be devalued. Consequently, a large number of small investors bought DMs with liras, gambling on its devaluation. The sale of liras also had the effect of raising the value of the Mark.

- The President of the Bundesbank made a statement indicating that he thought certain currencies within the ERM would have to be devalued. The markets believed this comment was aimed at sterling.

Shortly before Black Wednesday, the Bank of England spent £10 billion to no avail trying to defend sterling. The German and French central banks were also buying sterling. On Black Wednesday itself, in order to stop sterling leaving the ERM, interest rates were raised by 2 per cent and the Bank of England was 'buying pounds at a rate of tens of millions every few minutes' (Stephens 1996: 149). But the Bank did not have the resources to compete with the international markets. Its foreign exchange holdings were only 10 per cent of the daily turnover of the foreign exchange markets; speculators knew that the pound would be devalued, and that within even a few hours they would be able to buy back at a large profit the sterling they had sold (Stephens 1996). The government had no choice but to leave the ERM. Black Wednesday provides a useful case study, depicting a national government being rendered impotent in the face of external forces over which it had little or no control. However, it also worth considering that, had Britain devalued sterling before entry, or even before Black Wednesday, the government could have avoided forced exit. In other words, the debacle was a consequence of human choice, not external forces.

The permeability of boundaries

In the process of globalization, the threats to sovereignty are two-sided. On the one side, as we have seen above, globalization appears to reduce or change state choices; on the other, it undermines the territorial integrity of states. A number of issues, relationships, and networks can be seen to cross boundaries.

- Issues such as immigration and environment are increasingly difficult for nation-states to control.
- A range of institutions (as we will see below) such as the IMF or EU can make authoritative decisions that bind nation-states.
- People are developing cross-boundary identities; for example, in certain parts of the EU a European identity is becoming increasingly strong (see Hooge and Marks 2001).
- Governmental and non-governmental institutions are increasingly involved in cross-boundary networks that are becoming the sites of decision-making and service delivery. For example, the University of Kent has announced that it is setting up a Trans-Manche University with a French university which will enable students to study for a transnational degree.
- Military responses to international crises increasingly involve a range of nations, for example Kosovo, East Timor, and Macedonia. In Afghanistan during 2001, although the US was the main military actor, it was concerned to have as broad a support as possible for its actions against the Taliban and Al Quaida.

Transnational governance

Transnational governance depends on two different forms of argument: the weaker form of this argument is that there are now layers of organization that compete with and on some occasions override the state—this is what Held et al. (1999) and Scholte (2000) refer to as 'multi-layered public governance', or what (as we will see in the next chapter) is often referred to as 'multi-level governance'. The strong form sees the subsuming of the national state into a transnational state.

Multi-layered governance

Multilayered governance can take two forms. The first form can be the cooperation of international governments to solve domestic or international problems. Examples of this type of governance are the G7 (now G8) organization of leading economic states. For instance, in 1997 the finance and employment ministers met to discuss unemployment. The importance of the meeting was that it was an international discussion to solve what had always been seen as a domestic problem. It 'represents an attempt to manage or "govern" those aspects of political life which escape the control of any single state' (Held et al. 1999: 52–3). A second important example is the way that governments have attempted to deal with the issue of global warming. In 1992, in Rio de Janeiro, leading industrial countries agreed to try to limit their emissions of greenhouse gases. The original agreement was not binding, but subsequently a binding agreement was developed at Kyoto (see Ward et al. 2001). After disagreement between the EU and the US in November 2000 and George W. Bush's decision not to ratify the treaty, however, it appears to have collapsed. This failure highlights the complexity of the debate over globalization. The discussions concerning climate change have been global, with a growing realization of the need for global solutions. Yet the support of nation-states was required for the global solution to be put into operation, and domestic politics within the US effectively resulted in the US vetoing the agreement.

The second form of multi-layered governance is the creation of permanent transnational organizations. There are now a growing number of transnational organizations with the power to make authoritative decisions concerning nation-states (see Archer 2001). Probably, the most important is the United Nations (UN). The UN essentially creates a system of international regulation by which all member states should abide. Held et al. (1999: 65) maintain that the UN has developed frameworks of regulation in areas as diverse as decolonization and international air traffic control and so 'helped to engender a system of global governance'. This system of global governance has extended into other areas. As Held et al. point out, there is now a developing international human rights regime which 'consists of overlapping global, regional and national institutions and conventions' (p. 67). In the case of Britain, human rights are guaranteed by the International Bill of Human Rights, the European Court of Human Rights, and now with the incorporation of the European Convention on Human Rights into British law by the British courts (see Box 6.3 below and Chapter 7).

International regimes also clearly exist in the case of trade policy. World trade is now governed by the World Trade Organization (WTO). All member states of the WTO have to alter their statutes to conform with WTO regulations. The WTO Trade Policy Review Body examines the trade measures of member states and the decisions of the WTO panel of experts are binding (Scholte 2000). The WTO has had a dramatic impact on policy in Britain or, more accurately, in the EU. The EU had tried to ban the import of beef implanted with growth hormones, but the WTO ruled that this was a restraint on trade and forced the EU into allowing the import of American beef.

The transnational state

It has been argued by a number of people that the developing global interconnectedness of the economy has led to the development of a transnational capitalist class. According to Robinson (2001: 158), 'Globalization, therefore, is unifying the world into a single mode of production and a single global system and bringing about the organic integration of different countries and regions into a global economy.' As a consequence, nation-states can no longer sustain: 'independent, or even, autonomous, economies, polities and social structures'. With the development of this global economy has come the still-continuing evolution of a trans-national capitalist class, made up of the executives of transnational corporations, globalizing state bureaucrats, globalizing politicians and professionals, and consumerist elites such as the media. For Sklair (1998), these actors represent a global ruling class which has a common set of interests. The transnationalization of class relations and the economy are, according to Robinson (2001), leading to new forms of political institutionalism—the development of a transnational state. For Robinson, the transnational state develops out of existing states and so consists of 'transformed national states and diverse supranational institutions' whose role is to ensure the domination of the interests of the transnational capitalist class. So nation-states are transformed through the way they have had to adapt to the new global system, which places them in new relationships with other nation-states and the developing transnational economic and political institutions (see Table 6.2).

From this perspective, the state is utterly transformed as a consequence of having to respond to the demands of globalization. The complexity and extra-territoriality of transnational capital that developed in the 1980s meant that pressure grew for transnational political institutions. At the same time, the global elite needed state and transnational regulation to help create a single global market. For example, the WTO operates both as a mechanism for extending free trade and global markets and as a transnational organization, to help regulate what is beyond the reach of traditional nation-states. For Robinson (2001: 188), the development of a transnational state does not mean the end of nation-states, because they act

... as transmission belts and filtering devices for the imposition of the transnational agenda. In addition they perform three essential functions: 1) adopt financial and monetary policies that assure macro-economic stability; 2) provide the basic infrastructure necessary for global economic activity and; 3) provide stability.

From this perspective, both the last Conservative Administration and the present Blair Government can be seen as preparing Britain for a place in a global market. Their concern has been to extend global competitiveness by developing domestic policies of market liberalization at home whilst committing Britain to trans-national institutions which entrench the free-market liberal policy in the global system and effectively prevent the British state from developing an alternative economic approach. Of course, from this perspective, the reluctance of British governments (or, in the case of the Conservatives, almost complete refusal) to join the European Single Currency is difficult to understand. This is the sort of institution that a transnational capitalist class would strongly support: it imposes currency stability and low inflation policies on governments and thus makes European capital increasingly competitive in a global market.

New forms of politics

Held et al. (1999) point to the ways in which the development of new structures of decision-making have affected the policy process, so that there are now a growing range of international pressure groups and non-governmental organizations: 'In

Table 6.2 The institutions of the transnational state

Name	Date founded	Type	Function
International Monetary Fund	1945	Economic	To provide monetary stability through loans to countries with balance of payments problems.
World Bank	1945	Economic	Originally to assist with European postwar recovery. Now to provide assistance to developing countries to develop their economies.
European Central Bank	1998	Economic	To establish and operate Single European Currency and to run monetary policy within member states.
Bank for International Settlements	1930	Economic	Provides a forum for cooperation for central banks.
World Trade Organization	1995	Economic	Deals with the rules of trade between nations. It attempts to ensure free trade throughout the world through nation-states.
United Nations	1945	Political	Initially the main function was to maintain international peace and security, but it also has a wider range of functions including education, development, and humanitarian aid.
G7 (8)	1975	Political/economic	Group of the leading seven (now eight, with Russia) economies in the world which meets regularly to discuss economic strategy and on occasions coordinates economic activity.
Organization for Economic Cooperation and Development	1945	Political/economic	Initially established to assist with rebuilding of European economies after the Second World War. Now aimed at promoting economic advice and free trade.
North Atlantic Treaty Organization	1949	Political/military	Defence alliance between most of western Europe and North America. Aim of providing common defence initially against the Soviet Union.
North American Free Trade Association	1993	Economic	Free trade between US, Canada, and Mexico.
European Union	1956 (as a common market)	Political/economic	Economic integration and political cooperation between member states.
Asia Pacific Economic Cooperation (APEC)	1989	Political/economic	Regional cooperation and free trade within twelve Asia/Pacific states.
Association of South East Asian Nations ASEAN	1991	Political/economic	To promote regional and economic cooperation and free trade area.

1909 there were 37 IGOs (international governmental organizations) and 176 INGOs (international non-governmental organizations), while in 1996 there were nearly 260 IGOs and 5,472 INGOs.' In a whole range of areas, pressure groups are organizing across borders and lobbying on international issues, especially groups concerned (ironically) with opposition to globalization and global capitalism (see the discussion in Chapter 8).

Migration and globalization

A key cause of globalization is the increasing fluidity of movement of people who are partly responding to new global labour demands and at the same time transmitting ideas and cultures across national boundaries, and possibly developing new senses of identity. The world has seen different periods of migration, with (for example) high levels during the nineteenth century to the 'New World' of the Americas and Australasia. What has occurred during recent times is economic migration from the poorer developing world to the richer developed world. Held et al. (1999) estimate that between 1965 and 1995 there were over 100 million migrations. This is perceived as a growing problem within the EU and the USA. The concern in the British case is that once immigrants enter the EU, which has a very large border, movement into Britain is then relatively easy.

Culture and globalization

Globalization is not only a political and economic phenomenon; it is also cultural. One of the key themes in the writings of the nineteenth-century English novelist Thomas Hardy was that with the arrival of railways into rural Dorset the traditionally closed communities were opened to information, values, and people which disrupted their traditional values and customs. For Hardy, these external forces ultimately led to personal tragedy and the disappearance of a particular way of life. Similarly, Anthony Giddens, in his 1999 Reith Lectures, tells the story of how a family in primitive living accommodation in the middle of Africa can watch a pirate video of a Hollywood blockbuster before it has been premiered in Los Angeles or London. In both cases, technology is portrayed as undermining traditional cultures and ways of life, thus leading to homogeneity across national and rural/urban boundaries. For many writers on globalization, one of its key elements is the development of a uniform worldwide culture. Sklair argues that it is the development of a culture of consumerism which underpins the voracious appetite of global capitalism for expanding markets and ever-changing demands. For example, let us consider the cyclical nature of the mobile phone market in the UK in recent years.

- In the late 1980s, during the first wave of the product, there is an aggressive marketing policy, in order to promote mobiles as a 'life necessity'.

- The success of this campaign leads to the market becoming saturated, once the majority of consumers are convinced of the need to possess a mobile phone.

- A second wave then takes place in the mid-1990s, in which companies continue to develop new mobile phone technology, such as WAP and internet functions, rendering it essential (in the eyes of the retailers) for consumers to replace their first-wave phone with one developed in the second wave.

- There then follows a new, third wave of phones from 2000 onwards, in which the retailers continue to upgrade both the technological capacities and the design features of mobile phones. They then, again, embark on a new phase of marketing, based on the theme that the new phones are far superior to the second-wave models.

- The redundant handsets from the first and second wave of marketing are reconditioned and exported to Third World economies, where there still remains a healthy market for the older models.

Held et al. (1999) suggest that the religious and empire elements of a global culture have a long lineage. However, the development of global infrastructures, greater cultural exchange, and the commodification, and strength, of Western popular culture has led to a more extensive and intensive global culture. The development of technology such as telephones, satellite/cable televisions, and computers allows for a much more rapid exchange of cultures; but a further important factor, as Held et al. (1999) point out, is the spread of shared language. In addition, they point to the growth of twenty to thirty large MNCs which 'dominate the global markets for entertainment, news, television etc.' (p. 347), leading to the globalization of culture. This does not necessarily imply a uniform world culture, but it does highlight a much greater and more rapid cultural interaction.

The problem with the global culture argument is that little attention is paid to the nature of culture and its meaning to individuals. It is hard to question the notion that certain cultural icons like Nike, Coca-Cola, McDonalds, or Madonna are recognizable around the world, but this in a way is an indication of global capitalism rather than global culture. What is cultural about them is what they mean to the individuals, not what they are as objects—the cultural difference is in the meaning of McDonalds in Manchester, Mumbai or Moscow. Moreover, these signs are dominant because of massive corporate advertising, which means that they overshadow, but do not necessarily overwhelm, local cultures. Local cultures are sustained by the everyday actions and interactions of individuals and not by the production of Hollywood films or the standardized production of beefburgers.

Robins (1997) indicates the globalization of culture through his example of a trip to the off-licence: 'You cannot but be aware of the increasing globalization of the markets for wine.' Whilst that is true in Britain, with its history of open markets and food importation and lack of wine production, it is not true in Spain or France. There, if you walk into a supermarket or off-licence, you will only see Spanish or French wine, and, more specifically, in France you will probably only see the wine of that appellation. This is despite the existence of a single market and currency in the EU which should mean that French and Spanish wine are the same price in the other countries and easily accessible. Global markets do not necessarily destroy local customs. The French tend to regard French wine as the best, and whatever the rules of the SEM, such wines are sold more cheaply than those from other EU countries. Consequently, in France integration into the EU has not produced globalised wine sales.

The other argument from the globalization literature is that technology and travel have created greater cultural diversity than ever before. New forms of media create relatively cheap spaces for subcultures to exist. The internet has acted as a catalyst for bringing together diverse people with similar values in a way that was impossible before. The authors of this book support, respectively, Exeter City Football Club and Bournemouth A. F. C. Both clubs may be a minority interest and receive little if any media attention, but the Internet has provided a medium in which interested but dislocated supporters, not just within the UK but also in other countries, can spend hours discussing the minutiae of each club and the likelihood of the team avoiding relegation each season!

Migration has allowed the possibility, if not always the success, of multi-cultural communities. Satellite and cable television create channels for the most obscure of interests. As Robins points out, 'globalization is also linked to the revalidation of particular cultures and identities'. Consider which is more culturally homogeneous, 1950s Britain or twenty-first century Britain? Greater education, travel, and access to media have complexified rather than simplified culture. It is within the context of globalization that both new and old cultural, regional, and national identities like Cornishness or Basqueness have taken hold (Hooge and Marks 2001). Moreover, external influences are not accepted, unmediated, into existing cultures. As Appaduri (2000: 230) points out, new cultural influences tend to become 'indigenized in one way or another'.

Globalization and British government

According to Higgott (1998: 20), 'The reconfiguration of UK politics, especially the management of the functions of the state, is thus increasingly determined by—or at least influenced by—the perceptions of the impact of globalization.' It is clear that government increasingly involves a wide array of international and transnational networks. Economic policy, for instance, will involve the WTO, the EU, the G8, the World Bank; in particular, what happens in the United States, especially in terms of interest rates and economic growth, has a large impact on the British economy. Environmental policy likewise is made in the context of domestic demands, international treaties, and EU regulation. As Tony Blair (1999a) recognizes, Britain has

a formidable network of international contacts. Our extraordinarily close relations with nations in every part of the globe through the Commonwealth. Our membership of the UN, Security Council, of NATO and of the G8. The close relationship forged through two world wars and the Cold War with the USA. And our crucial membership of the European Union. We are at the pivot of all these inter-connecting alliances and groupings.

The consequences of these networks and constraints are illustrated by Rose (2000). He points out that, whilst the British Prime Minister may appear more powerful at home—in other words in relation to the Cabinet and Parliament—decisions are increasingly being made within the context of international institutions. The Prime Minister is often unable to achieve what he or she wishes because decisions are made elsewhere, in a domain where he/she is not dominant. In the EU, the British Prime Minister is one actor among fifteen and so not in a position to determine decisions unilaterally.

It is clear that notions of globalization and concerns over the impact of trans-national institutions are having a considerable effect on British governments. What is striking is that both Gordon Brown and Tony Blair accept that globaliza-tion is here to stay; for them the notion, if not the impact, is unproblematic. For instance, Blair (1999a) believes that 'People still underestimate the impact of globalization'; Brown has said: 'Globalization has happened', and talks of the global marketplace as being one of the key determinants of economic policy:

The first objective national governments must have, in a global market place, is to maximise economic stability. We have learnt that monetary and fiscal stability is a necessary pre-condition for national economic success. For in a global economy funds will flow to those countries whose policies inspire confidence and investors punish mistakes more quickly and severely than in the past. Both the old Keynesian fine tuning, and the rigid application of fixed monetary targets were policies designed for sheltered national economies and based on apparently stable and predictable relations which have now broken down in modern, liberalised and global capital markets. (Brown 1998a)

Thus, the decision to make the Bank of England independent in May 1997 was, according to Brown, central to providing the necessary stability in globalized mar-kets. In addition, Brown is committed to extending the global market by encouraging greater competition and pushing for more free trade. It has also led him to call, in a way which Sklair (1998) predicts, for a new global architecture of financial regulation, and in particular for 'a new permanent Standing Committee for Global financial regulation' which would provide some form of transnational regulation where national regulation has failed (Brown 1998b).

Blair (1999b) has been concerned with the political and ideological implications of globalization. He points out that not only are economics global but so is politics:

It is difficult to imagine circumstances in which Britain or other developed countries would be called upon to defend themselves alone . . . Issues of international trade affect UK companies crucially and UK living standards. It is impossible to remain aloof from third world debt or global pollution . . . In every sphere, increasingly nations are having to accept they can only advance their own interests by working with others.

For Blair, sovereignty is not about standing alone because:

it grossly underestimates the impact of globalization on the power of an individual nation state. If sovereignty means control over one's destiny and strength, then strength and control, in today's world, means forging alliances or falling behind.

Blair has pointed to the growing interdependence in the world, and the way in which events in one part of the world now have a consequence for the rest: 'national interest is to a significant event governed by international collaboration' (1999b). Like Brown, he sees transnational institutions as mechanisms for dealing with these problems.

What is interesting and surprising is that within the context of a continuing symbolic attachment to parliamentary sovereignty, Blair and Brown are redefining sovereignty to mean working within an international arena and through transnational institutions where Britain does not always control the outcome. This commitment to global politics and global economics has had a direct impact on policy choices. As we have seen, it means that Britain is committed to free trade and increased competitiveness. It has brought about changes in policy in relation to the Third World, with a commitment to reducing debt and providing greater assistance for health and education programmes. It has affected the way the government has thought about defence policy and Britain's links with a common European defence policy and relations with NATO. It has led to Britain becoming involved in debates about universal human rights and the appropriateness of humanitarian and international intervention. Blair sees it as having an important ideological dimension: 'In the field of politics, too, ideas are becoming globalised. As problems become global—competitivity, changes in technology, crime, drugs, family breakdown—so the search for solutions becomes global too.'

The argument of Hay and Watson (1998) and Hay (1999a) is that this support for globalization is a rhetorical device used by Labour to legitimize their pursuance of a neo-liberal agenda. Whilst there may be some truth to this, the belief in globalization seems to be heartfelt. As we have seen, it affects not only the Labour Government's economic programme but its political programme as well, leading to a very non-Thatcherite conception of sovereignty and the role of the state in international affairs. It is enlightening to compare the Thatcherite and Blairite notions of sovereignty. In the Thatcherite view, sovereignty is based on a notion of an independent nation-state, whereas for Blair it is an interdependent nation state that pursues interests through international organizations. Whereas Thatcher sees Britain's primary international partnership with the United States, Blair talks about the importance of the relationship between Europe (not Britain) and the United States. However, it is clear that, following the events of 11 September 2001 in New York and Washington, Blair sees Britain's relationship with the US as having a continuing and central importance to British foreign policy. Nevertheless, these distinctions in conceptions of sovereignty illustrate how the academic debate concerning globalization does reflect important developments in politics.

The faith in globalization can even be discerned in issues such as human rights, democracy, and the role of the courts. The cases of Pinochet and Milosevic illustrates that national leaders may have to account for their actions after they leave office, thus undermining the notion of sovereign states and the belief that national leaders are not answerable to a higher authority. Britain has been centrally implicated in the development of international law. The Pinochet case also illustrated the way in which the law on human rights is permeating national boundaries and providing a body of law that is above the nation state (see Box 6.3). Pinochet was dictator of Chile from 1973 to 1989, during which time he and his regime were allegedly involved in the deaths of many who opposed his authoritarian regime. In 1998, however, he was arrested in Britain on charges of torture and human rights abuse, following an arrest warrant issued in Spain. Spain then pursued his extradition, forcing Jack Straw, the then Home Secretary, into the position of having to decide whether to send Pinochet, as a former head of state, to Spain for trial. Ultimately, the decision was avoided: it was decided that Pinochet was medically unfit to stand trial. As this case and Box 6.3 indicates, governments are increasingly in a position of having to obey international laws that are not made by their national parliaments. There can be little doubt that this has changed the nature and meaning of sovereignty.

The problems of globalization

Whilst a number of academics, along with the Prime Minister and the Chancellor, believe that globalization has happened and has changed the nature of politics and economics, it is in fact a deeply problematic term, and one that needs to be used with more caution than has hitherto been the case. There are a number of problems with globalization:

(1) What is often debatable is whether changes in capitalism and society are causing globalization or whether globalization is causing changes in the economy and society. What is being explained and what is doing the explaining is not always clear.

(2) It is also true that international constraint and dependence are not new. Britain did not defeat Germany alone in the Second World War, but was part of an allied force which involved, most notably, the Soviet Union and the United States. Throughout the entire postwar period, British governments have found their economic policy undermined by the instability of sterling. In the case of sterling, vulnerability is not new: since 1945, and particularly since the 1960s, governments have attempted to manage the risk of sterling crises, although ultimately their attempts have ended in failure. Exchange rate instability is not the result of global

---

Box 6.3 Sovereignty and the European Convention on Human Rights

In October 1998 the Labour Government received royal assent for its Human Rights Bill, which incorporates a version of the European Convention on Human Rights (ECHR) into UK law (although this did not come into effect until 2000). This enables UK citizens to appeal to any level of UK courts on the grounds of a breach of the Convention. The bill was specifically designed by the Labour Government, in order not to breach the principle of absolute parliamentary sovereignty, while at the same time removing the European Convention's guarantee of effective redress to citizens whose freedoms and rights have been infringed. It is clear that, despite this weakening of the European Convention, the bill will still have a substantial impact on the rights and freedoms of UK citizens.

Throughout the passage of the bill, the Home Office Minister, Lord Williams, strongly defended it, arguing that it would in no way impinge upon the concept of parliamentary sovereignty by devolving power and responsibility to the judiciary. Despite the guarantees of protecting the freedoms and rights for the individual citizen, Lord Williams's pledge concerning the sanctity of parliamentary sovereignty appears less than certain. For example, on 27 January 1999, Jack Straw signed the 6th Protocol of the European Convention of Human Rights, part of which abolishes the death penalty in the UK. The implications for Parliament will be that future governments will not be in a position to reopen the debate on the death penalty without first overturning the entire ECHR. Therefore, although there has been much rhetoric from the Labour Cabinet to the effect that parliamentary sovereignty has in no way been damaged by signing up to the convention, the reality is that clear and discernible constraints have been placed upon Parliament.

---

change for Britain; it has been a postwar constant. According to Gamble and Kelly (2000: 5), 'To a greater extent than most other countries British policy, ever since the repeal of the Corn Laws in 1846, has been shaped by Britain's involvement in the global economy.'

Harold Wilson, who was acutely aware of the dangers of the financial markets early in his first administration (1964–70) (see Wilson 1971), initially developed a risk-avoidance strategy based on a vehement opposition to any discussion of devaluation. This was despite the fact that most of the experts (his economic advisers) and the Left (and some significant figures on the Right) of the Labour Party believed that devaluation was inevitable and desirable (see Cairncross 1997, Stones 1988). This strategy ultimately failed, and Labour was forced to devalue in 1967. The reason for this position was essentially structural: the existence of the sterling area meant that former colonies kept their reserves in sterling, but Britain's assets were always greater than her liabilities. Consequently, Britain could not afford to pay all the holders of sterling. They, on the other hand, were worried about their savings being devalued, and hence would sell sterling if there was a danger of devaluation (see Strange 1971, Sanders 1990, Stones 1988). As Stones (1992: 203) illustrates:

A shaky exchange rate is a cause for concern to all governments, but it leaves the government of a nation whose currency is used internationally in a particularly vulnerable position. In 1964 Britain's liabilities to overseas investors in sterling amounted to approximately £3,895m. and they remained well over £3,000m. up to the end of the Wilson government's time in office. By contrast, Britain's autonomous foreign exchange reserves were approximately £121m in 1964–5, totally inadequate to withstand even the slightest loss of confidence in sterling parity.

The markets would punish what they saw as excessive spending and borrowing, continually forcing Labour to retrench in order to reassure the markets. As Bale (1999) has demonstrated, Labour governments were often forced to make symbolic cuts in order to reassure markets. The impact of these external forces was greatest in 1976, when the Labour Government had to borrow money from the IMF in order to reassure the markets. In return, it was forced to cut public expenditure, public borrowing, and the level of public employment. This proto-Thatcherite monetarist policy was essentially forced on a Labour government by a transnational institution (although for a counter-view see Ludlam 1992).

(3) The third problem with globalization is that it is a process that is particular to regions and people rather than general. As Castells (1996: 102) observes:

The global economy does not embrace all economic processes in the planet, it does not include all territories, and it does not include all people in its workings, although it does affect directly or indirectly the livelihood of the entire humankind. While its effects reach out to the whole planet, its actual operation and structures concern only segments of economic structures, countries and regions, in proportions that vary according to the particular position of a country or region in the international division of labour.

One point that is often raised is that globalization is actually a Western and rich (rather than global) phenomenon. It is the well-off who have access to multinational culture, foreign travel and the Internet, while many of the poor are not within the global circuit at all.

(4) Homogeneity of economic and welfare policies are, it is suggested, one of the key features. However, it is not clear that these policy areas are as homogeneous as many would claim. Patterns of spending on welfare, even within the EU, vary enormously. Reiger and Leibfried (1998) make the point that the process of globalization in many cases has not resulted in the decline of welfare spending. Welfare spending in Britain, for example in social security expenditure, has continued to grow (see Table 6.3).

(5) Likewise Pollin (1998) has argued that, despite the constraints on national governments, there are a range of economic measures that they can take which will allow domestic economic expansions. An increasing number of authors are arguing that national models of capitalism continue to be important and to affect economic policy choices—or at least the way that different states respond to global pressures (see Hay 2000, Weiss 1998).

(6) Held and Thompson provide the most sustained critique of globalization,

Table 6.3 UK growth in social security benefit expenditure, 1949–2001

Year	Spending in real terms (£ million)	Spending adjusted to 1998–9 level (£ million)	Spending as % of GDP
1949–50	598	12,201	4.7
1959–60	1,350	18,443	5.5
1969–70	3,392	32,113	7.2
1979–80	18,777	51,648	9.1
1989–90	50,174	69,179	9.6
1996–97	92,212	97,182	12
2001–2	105,549	98,253	11.2

arguing that global trade is no greater now that in the pre-1914 era, and that the majority of trade is regional rather than global.

(7) It is also clear that Western, developed states, at least, remain powerful. The existence of most transnational organizations depends on the support of nation-states, and if the latter no longer see these institutions as useful for their own domestic interests, they can withdraw support, potentially leading to the collapse of the institutions. The most obvious example is the US and the Kyoto agreement of December 1997 on climate change and the agreement to cut gas emissions. Elsewhere, Britain's ambiguous relationship with European Monetary Union demonstrates that states are not forced into transnational institutions. If and when Britain does join EMU, it will be for reasons of domestic political interest, not through global pressures. (Although, of course, the nature of domestic interests may be strongly affected by factors outside the nation-state.)

(8) There is an assumption in much of the literature and political rhetoric that globalization is an inexorable process. However, it is clear that things can change. Countries may become more protectionist in the face of world recession; political resistance may affect the way changes in global capitalism work through. We need to be careful not to assume that there are no alternatives.

Conclusion: globalization and the power of the British state

According to much of the governance literature, globalization has been a key theme that has been attached to the 'hollowing-out of the state' thesis. Political decisions are being made either beyond governmental control or within inter-national or transnational networks where the government is one actor amongst many. Whilst it is clear that there have been significant changes in the international economic order and that these have had profound political and cultural impacts, we still need to treat the notion of globalization cautiously. First, there have always been constraints on nation-states, and the increasing constraints on Britain may be an indication of its relative decline, rather than a consequence of globalization. The constraints on the US are much less than the constraints on Britain. Second, whilst Britain has become involved in more international organizations, the reason for participation is often in order to pursue domestic interests. For example, agreements at G8 meetings have a limited impact on domestic policy. Gordon Brown is not precisely following the same economic policies as his counterparts in the US, Germany or Japan. They still face different economic pressures and different domestic demands. Third, even large multinational companies rely on powerful, developed states for stability, the rule of law, and the development of infrastructure and international regulation.

It would also be foolish to reject the idea that there have been no changes. Today, ministers and civil servants are operating in more international fora, more regularly, than ever before. Agreements on climate change and on world trade, and the developing international human rights regime, affect domestic goals. The point to remember is that these developments occur within a world of nation-states, and whilst they may affect what those states do, they are not near to eliminating them. The British government has developed new patterns of dependency and sovereignty which means it does not have complete authority within clearly defined territorial boundaries. The government is still important, however, and its relationship with international institutions and forces has a considerable impact on the way commitments are translated into domestic policy.

KEY POINTS

- For many people, one of the main challenges to the operation of the modern state is globalization.

- There are many different interpretations of globalization ranging from those who believe that the nation-state is being subsumed into transnational politics to those who believe globalization is a rhetorical device for legitimizing neo-liberal policies.

- The international economy has become larger and more interlinked, and there are an increasing number of international and transnational political organizations.

- However, it is also true that nation-states, national politics, and indigenous cultures continue to have an important impact on the operation of government.

- Whilst the context of government has changed and governments are faced by new international constraints, this does not mean that national government is now unimportant. Rather, the things that they do are different, and often they are working through a new array of institutions and relationships.

- Changes in international relationships and organizations have affected the way that the New Labour Government thinks about policy and the nature of sovereignty.

KEY QUESTIONS

1. What factors have led to globalization?

2. What are the main interpretations of globalization?

3. How has globalization affected British government?

4. What are the criticisms of globalization?

KEY READING

The best account of globalization is given in Held et al. (1999). The sceptical view is in Hirst and Thompson (1999) and Hay (1999b) argues for globalization as rhetoric. Castells (1996) provides considerable data and a remarkable overview. For a discussion of the impact on Britain see Krieger (1999).

KEY WEBSITES

www.globalpolicy.org/ reviews global policy-making in the UN. For New Labour's thinking, see Blair's latest speeches at www.10downingstreet.gov.uk/news.asp?SectionId=32. www.ifg.org/ and www.mmu.ac.uk/gsa/ provide useful information on globalization. www.jubilee2000uk.org/ looks at world debt and www.McSpotlight.org/ provides information on multinational companies and www.zpub.com/notes/aadl.html looks at the opposition to globalization. Nearly all transnational organizations have websites: see: www.imf.org/external/index.htm, www.bis.org, www.worldbank.org, www.wto.org/.

Organization for Economic Cooperation and Development: www.oecd.org

European Union: www.europa.eu.int

NAFTA Secretariat: www.nafta-sec-alena.org

ASEAN: www.asean.or.id/

APEC: www.apecsec.org.sg/

7

EXTERNAL CHALLENGES TO THE MODERN STATE II: EUROPEANIZATION

INTRODUCTION

As we saw in the last chapter, a key debate in politics has been the impact of globalization on the policy process. Some commentators have argued that one of the consequences of globalization has been the hollowing-out of the state (see Chapter 2). There can be little doubt that national governments have increasingly lost functions to the European Union (EU). Indeed, one of the most significant changes that has occurred in terms of British policy-making since 1973 has been the integration of Britain into the European Union.

This development, which has been gradual and to a degree ad hoc, has had a major impact on what UK governments do and how they do it. This chapter will develop three central arguments concerning the impact of the EU on the British policy-making arena:

- Since Britain's membership in 1973, the sphere of influence of the EU over UK policy has greatly increased.
- The degree of EU influence varies greatly according to the particular policy area.
- Most importantly, central government still plays a key (if not always determining) role in shaping and implementing policy.

What is important is not the extent to which the British Government has lost autonomy but its relationship to the EU and how this has affected the power of the national state. To see Europeanization as simply a loss of sovereignty or a loss of autonomy is simplistic, because membership of the EU has multiple and varying impacts which restrain some actors but give others greater leeway. The chapter will also indicate how the institutional response to EU membership has also been ad hoc, and therefore has had less impact on the internal workings of the core executive than might have been expected.

Europeanization

Given this chapter's concern with the impact of Europeanization on British policy-making and on the broader debate on governance, a question is: what do we mean by Europeanization? Landrech provides a useful definition (1994: 70):

Europeanisation is an incremental process reorienting the direction and shape of politics to the degree that EU political and economic dynamics become part of the organisational logic of national politics and policy making.

What Landrech is suggesting is that Europeanization is concerned with understanding the way in which EU policy and politics have become integrated into the national level of politics (see Jordan 2001). This could involve several different elements:

- the extent to which civil servants consider the EU constrains or facilitates domestic policy-making;
- developing institutional machinery to integrate and deal with European issues;
- the way in which EU policies have an impact on domestic politics.

In Britain, the extent to which the government has lost sovereignty to the EU has become one of the defining cleavages within British politics both between and within the parties (particularly the Conservatives) (see Baker and Seawright 1996). This political debate in some ways reflects a wider theoretical debate about the processes of integration within the EU concerning whether the EU has become a supranational institution, which to some extent operates above nation-states or whether it is intergovernmental, in which nations states use the institutions of the EU to pursue their domestic political goals within a particular institutional context (Moravcsik 1993; see Table 7.1). Indeed, Bulmer and Wallace emphasize the importance of domestic political traditions, institutions, and interests in shaping the preferences of national states at the European level (see also Bache 1998).

Table 7.1 Theories of EU integration

Theories	Functionalism	Intergovernmentalism	Domestic politics
Focus	Supranationalism	Relations between states	The impact of domestic politics on national positions within EU

Policy-making in the EU

As Figure 7.1 (p. 156) indicates, the EU creates a complex and interlinked decision-making process which although, formally, it appears relatively clear, in practice is complicated and confusing. The key institutions are as follows.

The Council of Ministers and European Council

The Council of Ministers and the European Council are in principle the supreme decision-making bodies of the EU. The Council of Ministers consists of ministers of European governments for key policy areas; for example, there is an Environmental Council of Ministers and an Agricultural Council of Ministers. Here, decisions are made on EU policy in areas under the first pillar (see Box 7.1); this is through Qualified Majority Voting (see Box 7.2), whilst for areas in the second and

---

Box 7.1 The three pillars of the European Union

Pillar I: The European Community

This broadly refers to the areas where decision-making is located purely within the community, and covers issues such as trade, agriculture, and the single market. It also includes EMU. Decisions through this pillar are made by qualified majority voting (QMV).

Pillar II: Common foreign and security policy

This was created in 1992 by the Maastricht Treaty on European Union, and established the framework for a common foreign and security policy. Decisions in this pillar are intergovernmental.

Pillar III: Home affairs and justice

This was also established by the Maastricht Treaty, and involves developing policy on home and justice affairs including immigration and border controls. It is intergovernmental.

Box 7.2 Qualified majority voting

With the Single European Act 1986, qualified majority voting (QMV) was extended to a wider range of areas, essentially as a mechanism to ensure the more rapid acceptance of measures to establish a single market throughout the EU. Previously, a single member could veto a measure even if the majority of other countries supported it. With QMV, a measure will be accepted, if it is supported by specific weighting of votes.

third pillar it is through unanimity. The reality is that these councils meet relatively infrequently, and the majority of decisions are made by national officials in the Committee of Permanent Representatives (COREPER) (see Wallace 2000). Moreover, with the development of joint decision-making (see below), the Council increasingly establishes 'common positions', which have frequently to be reconciled with amendment to legislation proposed by MEPs in a 'conciliation procedure' (Wallace 2000a: 19). The European Council is a summit meeting of the leaders of the EU member states, and tends to make decisions affecting the overall direction and future of the EU.

The European Parliament

The European Parliament (EP) has extended its role from a consultative one to one where in a range of areas it is involved in joint decision-making with the Council of Ministers. With each of the treaty reforms the EP has acquired new powers; according to Wallace (2000a: 21), it 'is now a force to be reckoned with'. The EP has a range of powers over the EU budget and some aspects of expenditure. Most importantly, in a range of areas there is now joint decision-making, whereby the EP is able to reject commission proposals.

The European Commission

The European Commission is effectively the bureaucracy of the European Union, comprising officials organized into twenty-three directorates-general. The role of the Commission is essentially to advise on and execute policy matters. As it is the largest institution within the EU and has the most expertise, it effectively has a considerable impact on a whole range of decisions made within Europe. The Commission is essentially the source of most EU policy proposals, and for many commentators the Commission is seen as the key agent in the whole of the decision-making process.

The European Court of Justice

The European Court of Justice (ECJ) has become a significant player in terms of EU legislation. The court resides in Strasbourg, and its role is to interpret and rule on EU legislation. It has established the supremacy of EU law over national law, and thus has a significant influence on the process of Europeanization. The ECJ is separate from the European Court of Human Rights, created in 1950 following the signing of the European Convention on Human Rights (ECHR). Individual citizens within member states can appeal to the ECHR if they feel their human rights have been breached. The ECHR was ratified into British law in 1998.

National governments and parliaments

As we will see below, national governments have a major impact on all aspects of the EU. National ministers and officials provide the staff of the Council of Ministers and the ambassadors who form the Committee of Permanent Representatives (COREPER). National governments also lobby the EP and the Commission and, through the presidency, shape the agenda for the EU. In Britain, Parliament reviews the implementation of EU legislation, and committees in the Lords and Commons review aspects of EU policy in depth.

The EU, governance, and state autonomy

In Chapter 2 we observed that a theme associated with the concept of governance is the notion that the state is undergoing a process of being hollowed out. One of the most important aspects of hollowing out is the extent to which power has shifted upwards from the national government to the international or transnational arena. As a consequence of this change, the state has become one actor among many in the policy process. This argument suggests that a consequence of EU membership has been that the state has lost a significant degree of autonomy; in a whole range of policy areas, competence has shifted to the EU (see below). It appears that the EU is undermining the sovereignty of the British nation-state because, in a range of policy areas, Parliament is no longer the highest authority. Thus, despite the argument that parliamentary sovereignty is retained because the UK has the right to leave the EU if it so chooses, the reality is that the role of Parliament is often to ratify decisions made in the EU. Consequently, the EU appears to undermine the territorial integrity of its member states; decisions made outside the nation-state at the European level are being implemented within Britain. For example, in a range of areas, especially agricultural policy and trade policy, domestic policy has effectively disappeared, with decisions being made in the Commission and Council of Ministers (see Boxes 7.3 and 7.4). Indeed, the Treaty of Rome ensures that European law takes precedence over British law, and European judicial rulings effectively mean that EU regulations take precedence over British law. Moreover, the development and extension of Qualified Majority Voting (QMV: see above) means that, increasingly, the British government can have policy imposed on it against its will.

These factors seem to suggest that the autonomy of the British state is greatly restricted by EU membership, and that policy-making has increasingly become a partnership between the British government, other member states, and the institutions of the EU. Indeed, in many ways Europeanization should not be thought of only in political terms. For example, the most important goal for English and Scottish Premier football clubs is not winning their respective league championships but securing a place in the European Champions' League. Elsewhere, European citizens are increasingly working in Britain (especially in the public sector), while the Internet and satellite television opens up a world of continental culture. We will illustrate two aspects of this process, the Europeanization of policy and the Europeanization of government.

The Europeanization of policy

For many, the treaty developments of the EU and the growing powers of the EP, the Commission, and the European Court of Justice means that policy is becoming increasingly Europeanized in a whole range of areas. Indeed, for some Eurosceptics the EU is reducing the role of national government to that of a local authority responsible for an extremely narrow range of functions. As Marks et al. (1996: 343) observe:

The scope and depth of policy making at the EU-level have dramatically increased. The EU has almost completed the internal market and has absorbed the institutional reforms of the Single European Act (1986) which established qualified majority voting in the Council of Ministers and increased the power of the European Parliament. The Maastrict Treaty (1993) further expanded EU competencies and the scope of qualified majority voting in the Council, and provided the European Parliament with a veto on certain types of legislation.

They argue that the way the EU is designed, the difficulty of controlling the Commission, the problems with agreeing to restrain the process of integration, the unique informational base of the Commission, the regulatory powers of the Commission and the European Court of Justice, and the unintended consequences of institutional change all make it difficult for national governments to control the EU. Moreover, with the implementation of QMV, individual states have lost control over a range of decisions and may often have to implement policies to which they are opposed (which is reinforced by the ECJ's enforcement of decisions) (Marks et al. 1996).

Cram (1996) suggests that the ability to control day-to-day decisions affects the long-term process of integration. In encouraging interest groups to operate at the EU level, for example, the Commission has encouraged a process of integration that was not agreed by nation-states when they became members.

With the power to initiate and draft legislation, the Commission has a tremendous impact on the shape of the policy agenda at the European level. This ability has been extended by the Maastricht Treaty, and it is increasingly difficult for nation-states to control policy at the EU level. Moreover, it is difficult for the Council of Ministers to swiftly agree a collective position between member states, and this 'induces it to rely on the Commission for leadership' (Marks et al. 1996: 365).

Marks and Hooge (2001) argue that there has been a significant and dramatic

Table 7.2 Policy competence in the EU

Policy competence predominantly located in the EU	Policy competence a combination of EU and National Governments	Policy competence predominantly located in national governments or through intergovernmental agreement
Agriculture	Environmental	Foreign affairs
Trade	Transport	Macro-economic policy
Fishing	Social policy	Health
Competition	Regional policy	Education
Consumer protection	Research and technology	Defence
Monetary policy		Drugs
		Welfare benefits
		Law and order

increase in EU competence since its creation. Table 7.2 indicates how most policy areas now have some EU element to them and there are a number where all or most decisions are made within Europe.

In discussions on the impact of Europe on British politics, Europe is often portrayed as an institution in simple, monolithic terms. This is partly the fault of politicians and the media for conducting a highly politicized, but limited debate in which Europe is seen in simplistic terms as being either good or bad. The reality, in policy-making terms, is somewhat different. In order to understand the relationship between the UK policy-making process and the EU, it is important to distinguish between individual policy areas.

Some departments have found that the EU is a useful actor in order to help achieve policy goals, while other departments either find that the EU is not central to their own policy agenda or specifically wish for a semi-detached relationship. The point here is that Whitehall's relationship with the EU is complex, and we need to disaggregate across all departments, in order to understand better each policy area. Every Whitehall department has a certain degree of interaction with Brussels, but there is variation in the degree of interaction. For example, departments closely involved in formulating British EU policy include MAFF (before it was abolished in 2001), the FCO, the DTI and the DEFTR. Officials from MAFF tended to regard the EU in a positive light, whereas other departments, such as the DSS and the Home Office, have a more detached relationship with the EU when it comes to policy-making and thus their officials tend to see the EU in less positive terms. But even here, we must be cautious in our conclusions: for example, although the Home Office has been slow in embracing Europe (see Marsh et al. 2001), Home Office divisions such as immigration and police are closely integrated with their European counterparts in some aspects of their policy-making.

In order to understand the relationship between Whitehall and Brussels, it is

Box 7.3 **Agricultural policy**

When Britain joined the European Community in 1973, agricultural policy was transformed. Britain effectively joined the Common Agricultural Policy (CAP), with agricultural prices and policy set within the EU by the Council of Ministers and the Commission. It meant essentially a change from a system of deficiency payments, where government paid farmers for produce that was not sold at a particular price, to one of price support, where import restrictions were removed between member states. With the CAP taking between 60 and 70 per cent of the total EU budget, it was obviously a major part of EU policy, and indeed the central role of agriculture in the EU was a consequence of the political and economic importance of the farmers at the time of the creation of the Common Market in 1956 (see Rieger 2000).

The EU has had a dramatic impact on the shape of agricultural policy in Britain. It has been responsible for (up until the 1980s) a dramatic rise in the income of many farmers; it has encouraged the development of arable as opposed to livestock farming; and it has produced an intensification of agriculture. More recently, cuts in the level of price support in the EU have seen an important restructuring of the agricultural sector in Britain. One consequence has been the decline in many farming incomes. In addition, government policy on BSE and foot-and-mouth has been directly affected by EU regulation, with the EU paying much of the compensation for the loss of sheep and cattle during the foot-and-mouth epidemic. Likewise, food regulations at the EU level have resulted in major changes in issues of food hygiene and the operation of slaughterhouses in Britain. However, it is important to point out that even in this most integrated of policy areas, important national powers have been retained. Member states retain the power to fix individual commodity prices (through the Council of Ministers) but perhaps more importantly, through Monetary Compensatory Amounts (MCAs), national governments were able to use exchange rate mechanisms to effectively increase, or reduce, the prices their farmers received.

important to recognize that in some policy areas the EU acts as a facilitator, whilst in others it acts as a constraint. The relationship is both complex and fluctuating. Finally, and more broadly, it is also important to remember, as we will see below, that in many areas the impact of national government remains the dominant factor in determining policy.

The Europeanization of government

The EU has had a significant impact on the operation of the British core executive in both institutional and cultural terms. The increased European activity and the ever-increasing number of directives from Europe meant that all European governments needed to develop a means of integrating their national decision-making machinery with EU decision-making. In Britain, this has occurred with limited formal institutional change at the centre. What has emerged is an informal yet

---

Box 7.4 **Trade policy**

The key element of the European Union and its original *raison d'être* was free trade within the community, and this required a common tariff for third countries. Consequently, membership of a trade bloc such as the EU means that trade decisions will be made by the transnational organization. As we saw in the last chapter, much trade policy is negotiated through other international organizations, such as GATT and now the WTO. This has led to the Commission rather than member states acting as the negotiator for international trade agreements. This then is the integrated policy par excellence. However, three points are worth bearing in mind:

- National governments are watchful over the shape and outcome of trade negotiations.

- The highly technical nature of trade negotiations (and the long periods of time they take) gives much autonomy to officials (both at Commission and national levels) in the negotiating and implementation process.

- The collective EU negotiations gives the EU considerable leverage in international negotiations, thus allowing national governments greater influence than if they negotiated individually (especially vis-à-vis the United States, which is such a powerful economic actor).

(*Source*: Woolcock 2000)

---

powerful elite comprising Number 10, the FCO, the Cabinet Office, and UKREP. Burch and Holliday (1996) point to the existence of a European network with the task of managing EU policy formation, centring on: a Cabinet Committee, the Overseas and Defence Committee (OPD(E)), which is chaired by the Foreign Secretary; the relevant official committee; and the European Secretariat in the Cabinet Office. Burch and Holiday (1996: 88) argue: 'Together these are the elements which form the core of the European network.'

In principle, the role of the European Secretariat is to coordinate the responses of Whitehall to the EU. It convenes meetings to ensure that: the British government has a response to all new developments at the European level; objectives of departments do not conflict; policy is consistent with the government's wider objectives; and there is proper implementation of EU decisions (see Spence 1992). In an interview with the authors, one senior Cabinet Office official described its role as 'to be the neutral umpire, the dispassionate chairman of meetings and therefore to resolve conflicts between various departmental interests'.

The FCO also has a coordinating function. According to Spence (1992: 60), 'The FCO provides the institutional framework for the day to day co-ordination of EC policy through the Permanent Representative in Brussels.' The FCO monitors information from Brussels, prepares briefs for the Council of Ministers, and has responsibility for political co-operation (Spence 1992). Whilst the coordinating role of the FCO is important for all departments, other departments are also aware that, unlike the Cabinet Office, the FCO has its own departmental interests, and they are thus perhaps more wary of its advice.

Generally, departments are satisfied with the process of coordination at the centre. An official in the Treasury described it as 'excellent', and the view from the DTI was that 'although to the outsider, the structure looks very complicated and to some extent duplicatory . . . actually it works quite well because we all know one another . . . and so a lot of it is done very informally.' Despite the division of functions between the FCO and the European Secretariat, there seems to be limited overlap. The departments find FCO and Cabinet Office knowledge of the EU useful, and there is a constant process of consultation between the departments and the coordinating machinery. Key policy papers have to go through the Foreign Office and the Cabinet Office and then on to UKREP. The Cabinet Office coordinates within Whitehall, but the FCO coordinates instructions to the British Ambassador at UKREP (see Figure 7.1). Every Friday there is a meeting involving the FCO, the head of the European division in the Cabinet Office, the British Ambassador, and the relevant departments, and any problems are ironed out here; if they are not, they go up to the Cabinet Committee.

As Bulmer and Burch (1998: 606) point out, 'a pervasive Europeanisation of British central government has been consistent hitherto with the "Whitehall model" of government . . . Rather, European integration has been absorbed into the "logic" of the Whitehall machinery.' This adjustment again emphasises the way in which regional and international pressures are mediated by existing state institutions. The impact of the EU on the formal structure, organization, and rules of Whitehall has been surprisingly limited. There has been little reassessment of notions of ministerial responsibility, collective responsibility, or even parliamentary sovereignty in the light of EU membership. How, for instance, can collective responsibility be sustained when decisions are taken in areas that have little or no relationship with the Cabinet?

Nevertheless, it is clear that the role of the coordinators has changed, and in one sense this change has been about ensuring the continuation of collective mechanisms. To some extent, the FCO believes that it still controls contact with Brussels. As one official observed:

Any input that an UK Government department wants to make into the system in Brussels goes through the UK Permanent Representative in Brussels. They are the people who talk to the Commission, talk to other member states and so on.

The formal position is that all EU issues are discussed and cleared through the FCO and Cabinet Office machinery. The reality, however, is that, as EU business increases and the process of coordinating all departments becomes more complex (Bulmer and Burch 1998: 14), the FCO and Cabinet Office are losing control and departments are increasingly conducting business directly with the Commission and other member states. Clearly, departments with regular EU contact, like the DTI and MAFF, are competent at conducting their own negotiations. Similarly, a DoE official observed that, except for major issues of legislation:

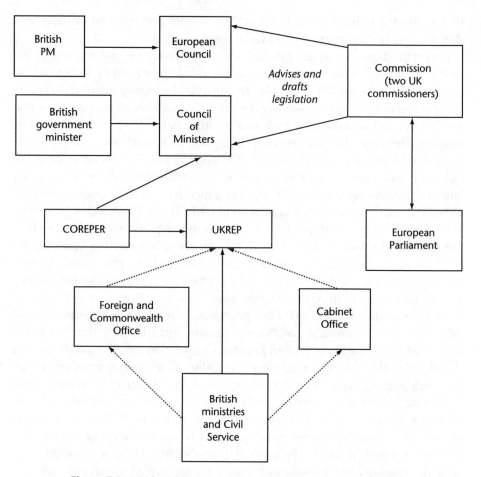

Figure 7.1 British and European institutions (*source*: Budge et al. 2001)

The majority of our links are bilateral . . . There is a continuous process of consultation and communication on a bilateral basis . . . We also have a lot of direct bilateral contact with officials in DG 11 in the Commission who are dealing with the areas that we are concerned with. We also have a lot of bilateral contact with our opposite numbers in the Environment Ministries in other member states.

The preferences of officials in relation to Europe have been influenced by the process of integration. The FCO and the Cabinet Office have effectively adapted to the need for coordination over European policy. According to Bulmer and Burch (1998: 10): 'The key departments—notably the Cabinet Office, FCO and the Treasury—seem to have reached an understanding quite easily and there were no significant department turf wars.' Increasingly, individual departments are developing close relationships with both the Commission and their opposite numbers in other member states. They are aware of the need to build coalitions. History does affect preferences, but institutional interests are of greater importance.

A continuing role for the nation-state

For many authors, much of policy and policy-making has become Europeanized, which has led to a hollowing-out of the state upwards towards the EU. Yet it is clear that the nation state continues to control considerable resources, and therefore the extent of Europeanization needs to be critically examined. Killick and Robinson (2001) make some telling criticisms of the notion of Europeanization:

- It is a vague concept applied to a wide range of phenomena such as government, policy, and culture.
- It is not an explanatory concept. It describes a process but does not explain why or how it occurs.
- It does not really distinguish between policy outcomes. There is no indicator of when something is an example of Europeanization or a concession to national interests (for example, as we will see below, membership of the Euro could be interpreted either as Europeanization or as the protection of domestic interests).
- Evidence of Europeanization, except in a few specific areas, is relatively weak.

To see Britain's autonomy, sovereignty, and culture being swallowed up by a creeping process of Europeanization would therefore be to oversimplify the process of change. In considering the limits on Europeanization, a number of factors have to be taken into account.

The power of the Commission

The Commission is a relatively small bureaucracy of approximately 15,000 officials. While it can make regulations, it lacks the capacity to implement them. In other words, it is dependent on member states for implementation. At worst, this means they can ignore legislation or subvert it; at best, they can act as gatekeepers. Nation-states have a number of strategies for avoiding EU regulation.

Non-compliance

There have been many cases where EU states have simply failed to implement EU legislation. One example is the free movement of labour. One of the key elements of the Single European Act (SEA) is that anyone within the EU can work in any country. However, in a whole range of occupations member states either refuse to recognize other countries' qualifications or simply will not employ people from other EU countries. For example, in Britain, the British Psychology Association argues that qualifications in psychology from non-British EU countries are not of the same standard; before EU nationals can be fully registered as psychologists, they have to gain a British qualification (judged by the BPA). In other areas, the situation is more acute. For example, it is more or less impossible for non-Spanish nationals to get a job in a Spanish university, even when highly qualified and of world renown. Contrary to EU law, Spanish universities refuse to recognize non-Spanish qualifications.

Subversion

Perhaps more effective and more difficult to challenge in the ECJ is the strategy of member states subverting the intent of EU legislation by following the letter rather than the spirit of the law. Effectively, this is what occurred with the Bathing Water Directive (see Box 7.5).

Gatekeeping

Subversion and non-compliance are difficult strategies for avoiding EU regulation because they can be undermined by legal action that can politicize issues in ways that governments do not desire. Perhaps the most effective way for governments to control the impact of EU legislation is through gatekeeping. The notion of a gatekeeper implies that, whilst decisions may be made in the EU that go against the interests of domestic states, nation-states retain a significant influence on EU

Box 7.5 **The Bathing Water Directive**

In 1975 the European Commission published proposals on the quality of bathing water. Britain was vehemently opposed to the proposals, both on grounds of the substantive measures and on the issue of whether it was within EC competence. Nevertheless, despite widespread opposition in Britain from 'the scientific establishment, Parliament, the water industry, the media and eminent lawyers', they were unanimously adopted in December 1975 (Jordan 2001: 87). Although the Department of Environment accepted the proposals their argument was that Britain needed to do little, as the concern was with water amenities, and the tidal nature of British shores kept these clean. 'After much delay, the DoE drew up a series of guidelines for regional water authorities, but emphasized the importance of interpreting them narrowly "to keep to a minimum any additional expenditure incurred"' (Jordan 2001: 92). As a consequence, the British Government designated only twenty-seven beaches in Britain, despite the fact that it has the longest coastline in the Community, compared to 3,308 bathing beaches in Italy and 1,498 in France. If beaches were not designated as bathing waters they did not have to comply with the European legislation, and Britain managed to subvert the legislation.

However, it is important to note that, over time, Britain has increasingly been forced into much greater compliance with the EU, first because the British Commissioner Stanley Clinton Davis forced the issue onto the agenda and secondly because political pressure at home and abroad increasingly attempted to embarrass the government. Finally, and perhaps most importantly, Jordan points out that the final and greatest pressure was the desire to privatize water: 'As the sale proceeded, it dawned on ministers that the City would not support the sale unless the liabilities (i.e. the cost of implementing EU rules) were made absolutely clear' (Jordan 2001: 10). Again, this demonstrates the unintended impact that the EU can have on domestic public policy.

policy, particularly regarding implementation, through their control of domestic resources (Bache 1998, 1999). Bache points out (1998):

The arguments of flexible gatekeeping assume national governments are crucial actors in the EU policy process, but not that an essentially intergovernmental interpretation of decision-making is necessarily accurate on all issues, at all stages of policy-making, over time. The concept of flexible gatekeeping does, however, suggest that a focus on initial decision-making, rather than the whole policy process can lead to an underestimation and thus misrepresentation of the underlying power of national governments able to mobilize considerable resources to shape outcomes at the implementation stage.

As Boxes 7.6 and 7.7 illustrate, whilst there were movements to Europeanize both regional policy and research and development policy, the British Government retained a high degree of control over the implementation of policy.

Scope of the EU

There are a number of crucial areas where the EU does not have competence. We have already identified a number of areas, such as regional policy, agriculture, trade and the environment, where the EU has significant but varying influence. There are also some highly important areas where it has minimal influence. Some key areas of policy, such as education, social policy, immigration, and macroeconomic

---

Box 7.6 Gatekeeping I: regional policy

The EU Commission has been increasingly concerned with developing a regional policy as an important element of both social and economic integration, and also as part of the bargain struck for creating the Single European Market. However, until 1988 European regional policy was to some extent undermined by the issue of additionality. The EU could not ensure that money granted to member states for regional policy was additional to existing expenditure. However, following the reforms to the programme in 1988, 'the additionality requirement was clarified and the partnership principle was formally introduced. This principle states that henceforth funds would be administered as partnerships between national governments, subnational authorities, the Commission and other relevant actors' (Bache 1999: 32). In addition to ensuring additionality, the Commission wanted to involve local and regional government and non-state actors in national policy on regional funds. However, what occurred in Britain was that, while some decisions were taken at local and regional level, the overall framework of the policy was still controlled by the centre. As a consequence, the British Government was able to ensure that its interpretation of additionality remained dominant. It was the government that distributed resources, and the fact that the Conservative Administration was hostile to local government and EU integration meant that it wished to control the detailed implementation of regional policy (for details see Bache 1998, 1999).

Box 7.7 Gatekeeping II: EU research and technological development policy

Although relatively small as a percentage of total research and development (R&D) expenditure, the EU had, through its various Framework Programmes, been increasing its degree of expenditure in this area. Under this development, an increasing part of Britain's R&D expenditure now has to go to the EU programme. For example, in 1996–7 total government R&D expenditure was £6132.6 m., and £373.3 m. went to the EU (Hill 2001: 113). In Britain, the Treasury has set up what is known as 'Europes'. Through Europes, the Treasury retrieves funds allocated to the EU by reducing related R&D expenditure in British departments. In other words, the money for the EU framework effectively comes from the existing expenditure of government departments and is not additional to it. This then creates an incentive for departments and research councils involved in research policy to lobby for a freeze on EU expenditure. This is because any extra money will come from their budgets. What has happened in this policy area is that the development of policy has not been dominated by the Office of Science and Technology. The dominant actor has been the Treasury, effectively a gatekeeper which has prevented the Europeanization of R&D policy (for details see Hill 2001).

---

policy, remain outside the remit of the EU (although there are varying degrees of cooperation in some of them).

Macro-economic policy

This is an intriguing case. The EU has attempted to develop elements of macro-economic policy, the Treaty of Rome calls for cooperation and coordination in economic policy and with the creation of EMU (see below) the EU is developing more powers. For instance, the EU is based on a common external tariff for trade. Whilst there has not, as yet, been a harmonization of taxation, all countries now have to impose VAT at a minimum rate of 15 per cent. In addition, in order for countries to join EMU, their public borrowing has to be below a certain level. However, it is still the case in Britain that the Treasury determines levels of taxation and public expenditure, while interest rates are set by the Bank of England Monetary Policy Committee, which has to meet inflation targets set by the Government. Artis (1998: 129) points out: 'No EU regulation or directive has so far had any significant impact on monetary policy in the United Kingdom, whilst the UK's participation in the Exchange Rate Mechanism (ERM) . . . was relatively short-lived.' So Menon and Forder (1998: 182) conclude that in terms of British macro-economic policy, 'EU institutions and policy had very little impact'.

Social policy

Social policy illustrates many of the contradictions of macro-economic policy. Whilst there is a desire for the EU to have an impact, and while a social dimension is seen as a key element of the Union, the actual amount of legislation is relatively small and its impact is perhaps even less. More particularly, social dimensions are often the consequence of other elements of EU policy like health and safety. Cram (1997: 28) illustrates this: 'The legislative profile of EU social policy . . . indicates the limited extent of binding legislation in the area of EU social policy: twenty-four Regulations, forty-two Directives; forty-nine Decisions.' The Maastricht Treaty did include a social protocol that contained measures on health and safety, education, and transferability of social security rights. There is not, however, any regulation on social security policy or attempts to standardize social provision. Nevertheless, whilst social security policy remains more or less autonomous and contact between the DSS and the Commission is not particularly extensive, the DSS does have a team of lawyers checking new rules against contravention of EU legislation.

The domestic impact on the EU

What occurs at EU level is often shaped by domestic politics rather than the other way around. Wallace (2000b) makes the point that much of EU policy is the extension of domestic politics to another arena:

Indeed much of EU policy is prepared and carried out by national policy makers who do not spend much, if any time, in Brussels. Rather what they do is consider how EU regimes might help or hinder their regular activities, and apply the results of EU agreements on the ground in their daily work. If we could calculate the proportions, we might well find that in practice something like 80 per cent of that normal daily life was framed by domestic preoccupations and constraints.

What is crucial to remember is that governments often do things for their own domestic reasons and interests, but blame the EU as a way of deflecting blame from themselves. What may seem to be a result of EU pressure is actually a consequence of domestic decisions. For example, regulations concerning the size of cucumbers, bananas, sausages, or other food products, which elements of the British press revel in reporting in order to deride the EU, are usually either a consolidation of existing national regulations or simply a myth perpetuated by the media.

A more significant illustration of the impact of domestic policy is in relation to economic policy during the Thatcher Administration. As Buller (2000) demonstrates, one of the reasons for Thatcher's apparent support for the integrationist Single European Act was that it enabled the Conservative Government to entrench its economic policy preferences (see Box 7.8).

> ### Box 7.8 **Britain and the Single European Act**
>
> Buller (2000) highlights the significant paradox of the Thatcher Government. Whilst it was profoundly Eurosceptic in terms of rhetoric, it pushed through the highly integrationist Single European Act (SEA). Buller's argument is that the Conservative Government of 1979 introduced monetarism as a mechanism for reasserting domestic autonomy and governing competence. However, with the apparent failure of monetarism, 'the Europeanisation of economic policy became an increasingly attractive solution to these governing problems'. The hope then of Thatcher and her allies was that the Single European Act would 'entrench the domestic commitment to the government's free market, supply-side policies' (Buller 2001). The SEA effectively exported the free market to the EU and prevented future governments from using import controls, restrictions on capital movements, and state aid for declining industries. The SEA entrenched Thatcherism, but in opening up a large number of areas to qualified majority voting it allowed the much deeper and rapid integration of the EU.

The EU and national autonomy

The EU may enhance the autonomy of some national officials and ministers. Much EU policy-making is highly technical, and consequently is carried out by officials with little reference to ministers and none to Parliament. Because of the complexity of the decision-making process, officials are in many ways left to make decisions. For former Labour Minister Tony Benn, Brussels was a 'mandarin's paradise' (See Marsh et al. 2001). Indeed, for a number of policy areas such as agriculture and trade, considerable responsibility for negotiating and making policy was placed in the hands of officials with little opportunity for ministers to amend what was already agreed. Likewise, ministers were often offered some protection in the EU: they could go to Brussels and argue a position knowing that it would not get through. They could thus support the Government's position, but in some cases achieve the policy that they prefer. For instance, one former Treasury minister argued that the Treasury could place limits on agricultural expenditure, but if the Agriculture minister went further in the Council of Ministers and rang up from the conference at 2 or 3 a.m., then the Treasury would 'have to agree what we had strongly opposed or risk an unplanned confrontation' (Barnett 1982: 158). Likewise, a former Conservative Minister of Agriculture said that he would be told to argue a certain line by the Cabinet and he would maintain that position in the Council of Ministers knowing that he would lose. While the autonomy of the government was reduced, the autonomy of the minister in this circumstance was increased.

Multi-level governance and the EU

When looking at the EU, one problem is that it is not easy to characterize it as just a different state form. The EU has the characteristics of a state, in terms of having authority, bureaucracy, and policies, yet it lacks many of a state's other features. In the words of Sbragia (2000: 220), 'The European Union makes binding decisions, but the symbol of its enforcement is the judge rather than the police officer or the soldier.' Thus, the EU has not replaced state structures, but it overlays and is embedded in state structures. The irony is that without state decisions and actions there would be no EU. This point is reinforced by Castells (1998: 330): 'the European Union does not transplant the existing nation states but, on the contrary, is a fundamental instrument for their survival.' As we saw above in Box 7.8, states can use the EU to pursue national or self-interest.

Thus, added to the complex mix of developing forms of governance is the EU, with its

complex and changing geometry of European Institutions that combines the control of decision making by national governments, the management of common European business by a competent, if unpopular, euro-technocracy, directed by the politically appointed European Commission, and the symbolic expression of legitimacy in the European Parliament, the Court of Justice and the Court of Auditors. (Castells 1998: 330)

The problem, of course, for the EU and indeed all member states, is that they exist with each other and because of each other. It is not a matter of the EU replacing the nation-state, but of the development of new forms of political conflict, dependence, and interdependence (see Box 7.9). States need the EU in order to provide markets, political security, and transnational response to international and global problems. The EU needs states for finance, legitimacy, and implementation. The impact of the EU on states is not unidimensional. First, it is a political process, which means states will concede or retain powers according to complex political negotiations dependent on interests and resources. Second, it is interdependent, and the EU is likely to need strong states to push through decisions, finance its operations, and implement its policies. Yet, at the same time, the EU has created new sets of interdependent relationships between:

• states and states;

• states and the EU;

• the EU and subnational and non-governmental organizations.

These relationships create new battles of legitimacy and authority between the nation-states and the EU over who can best deal with a particular problem (for example the issue of immigration) and who can best protect the interests of EU citizens (for example in the environmental area) (see Box 7.5 above). Thus, the EU creates a new political space (Sbragia 2000) in which the EU acts differently from a

> ## Box 7.9 Political conflicts between the EU and nation-states
>
> The issue of BSE clearly demonstrates how the EU and nation-states can come into conflict over particular issues. When in 1995–6 the extent of BSE was formally acknowledged in Britain, the British Government believed that it had undertaken measures that ensured that beef on sale was safe to the consumer. Nevertheless, following the Health Secretary's statement in March 1996 that there was a link between BSE and CJD, the EU banned the export of British beef. The then Prime Minister, John Major, felt that the ban created a 'crisis of confidence', and was political rather than being based on scientific evidence. Initially, he believed that the EU would lift the ban relatively quickly. However, when the EU Veterinary Committee maintained the ban, Major raised the political stakes and warned that Britain would use its veto and 'a policy of non-co-operation, if EU leaders did not relent on the beef ban' (Seldon 1997: 647). Government departments then drew up ideas for retaliation against the EU for the ban, while British action delayed a number of EU measures such as anti-fraud action which Britain had supported. Within the EU, there was an angry reaction by both the Commission and member-states to what was seen as unreasonable behaviour. The EU and the British Government began to work out a compromise, and on 17 June agreed an eradication plan. This was then put in place, with the final decision on lifting the ban resting with the Council on the advice of the Veterinary Committee. Consequently, the British Government was forced into a rapid and extensive culling programme in order to get the ban lifted (for details see Seldon 1997: 633–56).

nation-state but in which states are a crucial element in the relationships, processes, and conflicts within this space (see Box 7.9).

The factors of conflict and cooperation have led a number of authors to suggest that governance within the institutionalization of the EU is now multi-level. In other words, there is an increasingly complicated process of governance, with decision-making operating between different levels and these levels interacting to produce new forms of policy-making. The key premise of multi-level governance is that authority has dispersed away from centralized nation-states, and that different decisions are made at different levels of government. Some, for example, may be made by the EU, whilst others could be made by neighbourhood councils. From this perspective, the EU is not just a mechanism for the pursuance of national and domestic interests; through the complexity of the policy process and the development of new powers, the EU and other actors can act independently and beyond the control of the nation-state. In other words, 'governance must operate at multiple scales in order to capture variation in the territorial reach of policy externalities' (Hooge and Marks 2001: 7).

Hooge and Marks identify two types of multi-level governance. Type I is derived from federalism, and is based on authority being devolved to a limited number of non-overlapping jurisdictions. For example, central government may have responsibility for overall macro-economic policy, regional government for education, and local government for refuse collection. These patterns are relatively stable, and there is little, if any, overlapping of authority. At the same time, there are mutually exclusive jurisdictions with a range of functions. Regional government is responsible for education, health policy, roads, etc. within a defined space that does not overlap with any other authority.

In Type II, MLG jurisdictions are 'task-specific' and there are a vast number of jurisdictions which are not confined territorially. Authority is dispersed across a range of diverse authorities. Decision-making is thus polycentric and messy. For Hooge and Marks (2001: 19), the extent to which the EU is characterized by Type I or Type II governance is open to question:

The variability of territorial jurisdictions as a result of treaty derogation in the Maastricht Treaty, the establishment of three distinct pillars or governance systems for different policies and the creation of several independent European agencies all point to Type II governance, as does the growing possibility that some countries will engage in greater integration, while others settle for less in some areas. However, the bulk of EU policies, with the major exception of monetary union, apply to a single unified jurisdiction. The EU bundles together a variety of policy competencies that are handled outside the European Union by numerous, overlapping, and functionally specific jurisdictions.

With the establishment of the EU, authority is dispersed to various levels. Under Type I, MLG powers are clearly defined and assigned to particular authorities. Under Type II, the patterns of governance are complex and overlapping. In a sense, what has happened in the EU is that Type I has developed into Type II. What were clearly defined powers and jurisdictions have become blurred because of politics. Different institutions have seen the opportunity to utilize new levels of decision-making in order to influence the policy process. For example, local authorities and interest groups have chosen to interact with the EU Commission and develop policies in a way that had not been intended in EU treaties. Measures such as the Single European Act have produced unintended consequences that have expanded the competencies and range of the Commission. Within the EU, therefore, the process of multi-level governance may involve the development of a policy initiative within the Commission (perhaps as a consequence of lobbying by national and EU interest groups), the negotiation of the policy with national governments and agreement by the EP, and implementation by national government, perhaps through regional or local government (see Fig. 7.2).

The assumption underlying MLG is pluralism. Essentially, authority is dispersed, and decision-making occurs within a range of bodies through a process of negotiation. Policy-making is consequently about networks. However, what the MLG literature ignores is the power relationships between the various actors. Often (or usually), these multi-level relationships are based on asymmetries of resources, as was demonstrated in the gatekeeping examples above. The point here is that above governance there is meta-governance: 'governance in the shadow of hierarchy' (Jessop 2002: 125)—what appear to be self-organizing networks are in fact organized by various political authorities:

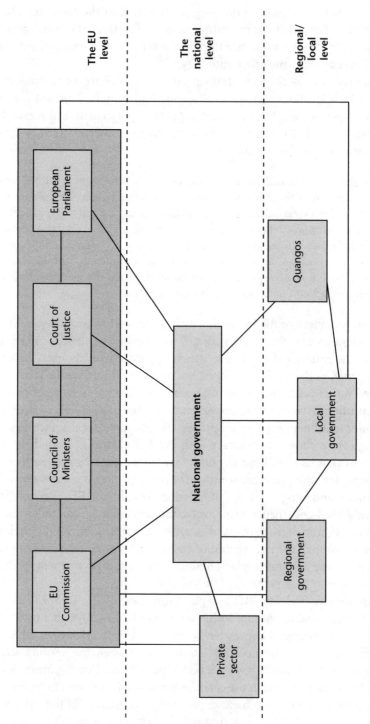

Figure 7.2 Multi-level governance[1]

The EU level

The national level

Regional/local level

European Parliament

Court of Justice

Council of Ministers

EU Commission

National government

Quangos

Local government

Regional government

Private sector

[1]Thanks to Ian Bache for assistance with this figure.

They provide the group rules for governance, ensure the compatibility of different govern-ance mechanisms and regimes, deploy a relative monopoly of organizational intelligence and information ... act as a court of appeal for disputes ... seek to re-balance power differentials by strengthening weaker forces or systems in the interest of system integration and/or social cohesion; try to modify the self-understanding of identities, strategic capaci-ties, and interests of individual and collective actors in different strategic contexts and hence alter their implications for preferred strategies and tactics; and also assume political responsibility in the context of governance failure.

Again, this illustrates the politics of the process. Nation-states and the EU have differing circles of influence, and over certain issues the EU and the nation-states (particularly more sceptical nations) compete for meta-governance, in order to be able to set the framework and devise the rules for particular policy areas. Different political actors and institutions, like voters and interest groups, are used in the competing battles for supreme political authority. In one sense the EU is depend-ent on nation-states, but the situation is complicated, because whilst there is only one EU there are many member states, and the Commission can play one state off against another. This is similar to what Wallace (2000b: 41) sees as the policy pendulum, with policy influence 'swinging between the national political arena of the participating members, on one hand, and the transnational arenas, with its European and global dimension, on the other'. When and where influence goes depends on context, functions, motivations, and institutions (Wallace 2000b: 44).

European monetary union

As we saw above, in Britain at least, the impact of the EU on macro-economic policy has been relatively limited. This, however, is likely to dramatically change if Britain joins EMU and adopts the Euro as its currency. Under this regime, monet-ary and exchange rate policy is determined by the independent European Central Bank (ECB). The bank sets interest rates for all the countries that are members of EMU. In order to join EMU, countries have to meet certain convergence criteria (see Box 7.10).

These criteria are institutionalized through the stability and growth pact. This means that the ECB can impose conditions on member states who are not operat-ing their economies within the requirements of the single currency regime.

At present, the impact of EMU is not simply the loss of autonomy. Dyson (2000) argues that different states have reacted to EMU in distinctive ways, according to their own cultural values and historical development. Consequently, within the context of EMU different states are making a range of macro-economic decisions. Dyson (2000: 650) observes:

It is inadequate simply to talk of the hollowing out of the state. The continuing relevance of the state as a unit of action in economic policy is confirmed by the absence of a structure of EU fiscal federalism, the lack of independent and discretionary areas of EU taxation, the

---

Box 7.10 **Convergence criteria for EMU membership**

- A rate of inflation which is no more than 1.5 times greater than that of the three best-performing countries.
- Deficits should not be greater than 3 per cent of GDP.
- Accumulated public debt should not be greater than 60 per cent of GDP.
- There has to be exchange rate stability, with currencies remaining within the normal fluctuation margins of the ERM for a minimum of two years.

---

continuity of state responsibility for welfare-state, labour market and employment policies, and the location of collective bargaining at the state and intra-state levels

In many ways, the state may gain through its reduced vulnerability to global markets.

The British Government and EMU

At the moment, the British Government's position on EMU is ambiguous. The Labour Government is committed to holding a referendum on British membership during its second term in office, but it will choose the timing. Before this referendum, five economic tests need to be met:

- British and EMU members' business cycles and economic structures have to be compatible.
- Is there sufficient flexibility to deal with problems?
- Would EMU create better conditions for making long-term decisions concerning investment in Britain?
- What impact would EMU have on the competitiveness of the financial service industry?
- Will EMU promote higher growth, stability, and stable employment?

The Government presents these tests as objective, whereas most are in fact highly subjective and political. The argument is that if Britain joined the EMU, economic autonomy would be lost. But, again, this is a similar case to the Single European Market. Whilst in some ways the autonomy of the Treasury would decline, what EMU would do would be to reinforce what is already government policy: controlling interest rates, in order to keep prices stable (the ECB's inflation target is between 0 and 2 per cent), and limiting the degree of government borrowing. One economic model suggests that Britain's inflation and output would be better if

Britain were in EMU (Barrel and Dury 2000)—for which, of course, the Government would take the credit. Alternatively, if problems arise, EMU and the ECB could be blamed and not the government. What is interesting is that the arbitrator of the tests on joining is the Treasury: what is in fact a highly political decision about Britain's future political and economic direction is being made by the Chancellor and not the Prime Minister (see Rawnsley 2001, Naughtie 2001).

Conclusion: power, governance, and the EU

Whilst Britain has undoubtedly become increasingly integrated into the EU, this does not mean that there has been an inexorable Europeanization or hollowing-out of the state. The development of the EU has complex and indeterminable implications for the power of the British state. It has to be remembered that in some ways there is an intricate battle between states and the EU over who determines the mechanisms of governance in a particular area. Often, states are in a strong position because of their financial and administrative resources. However, the EU also has important resources in terms of information, formal powers, and political alliances. Furthermore, the location of power depends on the policy area and the institutions involved. In areas like trade and agriculture, competence is clearly with the EU, but even here many decision are made by national government, and in a way the location of decision-making at the European level insulates policy-makers from domestic pressure and so increases their autonomy.

What this all means is that the EU alters the patterns of dependency in each policy area: who is powerful will depend on the circumstances at any particular moment in time. Whilst the EU has state-like features, it is not a state, and is highly dependent on nation-states for its existence. While the EU has changed the way that policy is made in Britain, it has not replaced the state as the main determinant of policy. Indeed, there is no indication from the actions of British politicians that a position in the Commission, or a seat in the EP, is preferable to membership of the Commons or the Cabinet.

KEY POINTS

- Since 1973, Britain has become increasingly integrated into the European Union.
- As a consequence, EU politics and legislation have increasingly become a part of national policy-making.
- There are now a number of policy areas where the EU is the main determinant of policy outcomes.
- For some people, integration into the EU has undermined parliamentary sovereignty.
- It is too simplistic to see government as beoming Europeanized. To some extent, the degree

of integration into the EU depends on the policy area and the interest of the policy actors involved.

• Likewise, there is a great deal of difference in the extent to which departments have made institutional adaptations to the EU.

• Governments are able to subvert EU directives through non-compliance, gatekeeping, and by ensuring that certain areas remain outside EU competence.

• What occurs at the EU is often shaped by domestic politics.

• The EU has not replaced state structures but overlays them, creating multi-level governance.

KEY QUESTIONS

1. In what policy areas has there been the greatest degree of Europeanization?

2. How has Europeanization affected the structure of government?

3. What is the impact of membership of the EU on discussions of sovereignty?

4. What is multi-level governance?

KEY READING

A good overview of the EU is given in George and Bache (2001). A detailed discussion of the key themes is provided in Wallace (2000a). A good example of the Europeanization of policy is provided by Jordan (2002). Hooge and Marks (2001) discuss the theory of multi-level governance. For an alternative perspective on Europeanization, see Buller (2000).

KEY WEBSITES

On the Maastricht Treaty see http://europa.eu.in/en/record/mt/top.html. On the Amsterdam Treaty see http://europa.eu.int/abc/obj/amst/en/index.htm, and on the Nice Treaty see www.europa.eu.int/comm/nice treaty/index en.htm. For British views on the EU, see www.fco.gov.uk/ and on Britain and the Euro see www.euro.gov.uk/home.asp?f=1. The official EU website is http://europa.eu.int/. The websites of the EU institutions are: www.europarl.eu.int/factsheets/default en.htm, http://europa.eu.int/comm/index en.htm, http://ue.eu.int/en/summ.htm, www.ur.eu.int/en/presid.htm, www.euro-ombudsman.eu.int/, www.curia.eu.int/en/index.htm. For information on pressure groups, see www.europa.eu.in/comm/secretariat general/sgc/lobbies/en/tabledom.htm. For information on the single market see www.europa.eu.int/pol/singl/index en.htm. For information on monetary union see www.europa.eu.int/pol/emu/index en.htm and www.ecb.int/

8

GOVERNANCE AND CIVIL SOCIETY

INTRODUCTION

A crucial aspect of the governance debate is the sense in which power has shifted from state organizations to groups and organizations which operate outside government and which collectively contribute to civil society. Here, civil society should be understood as being

distinguished from the state, and is used to describe a realm of autonomous groups and associations such as businesses, pressure groups, clubs, families and so on. In this sense, the division between civil society and the society reflects a 'public/private' divide; civil society encompasses institutions that are 'private' in that they are independent from government and organised by individuals in pursuit of their own ends. (Heywood 2000: 17)

In the last thirty years, groups and organizations in civil society have become increasingly involved in the making and delivery of policy (see Chapter 2). The recent trend has been for governments to turn to pressure groups and voluntary groups for the delivery of services. In addition, there is a greater awareness of the importance of voluntary groups and good citizenship as a mechanism for establishing trust and maintaining democracy (see Box 4.6). This chapter will look at how the role of these groups, referred to as non-governmental organizations (NGOs) within civil society has changed, and how new notions of participation have started to develop which challenge the traditionally restricted notion of democracy that is implicit within the Westminster model. However, as we have seen in other chapters, it is important not to exaggerate the degree of change, or underestimate the continuing role of the central state in regulating the relationships between NGOs and the government. We will begin by looking at the role of pressure groups, before looking at the role of voluntary groups and changing conceptions of participation.

Pressure groups

Traditionally, much of the analysis of the pressure group debate has been analysed from the perspective of pluralism (see Box 8.1). Intuitively, pluralism can be closely linked to the governance debate, in that a pluralist state in some senses is seen to reflect the demands in society and pressure groups are a mechanism for expressing those demands to the government. So, if governance sensitizes us to the increasing number of arenas in which politics is played out and to the greater number of actors involved in the policy-making process, then pluralism would appear to be a useful analytical model in order to understand governance and the nature of power. For, like some of the governance literature, pluralism sees power as being dispersed. Neither the state nor any group has a monopoly of power, and there are many constraints on the actions of the state. The central belief of pluralists is that it is relatively easy for pressure groups to form. Therefore, if the government does something that a significant number of people oppose, groups will form that will constrain what the government does.

Pluralism, with its relatively benign view of the state, was undermined both theoretically and empirically in the 1960s and 1970s (see Smith 1995). The persistence of structured inequality, rational-choice critiques of group membership, and a growing perception that government was not as open as it appeared to pluralists led to two important debates concerning the nature of group/government relations: corporatism and policy networks.

Box 8.1 **Pluralism**

The key elements of pluralism:

- Power in society is dispersed.
- If people are sufficiently concerned about an issue, they will form a group and pressurize government.
- Although groups may have unequal resources, groups lacking in one resource (money) will have another (good publicity).
- People have overlapping membership of groups—they are teachers, parents, consumers—and therefore no single group will become all dominant.
- Government gives access to groups lacking in resources because of the need to win votes.
- Most interest groups are concerned with a limited range of issues, and therefore different groups are involved in different policy areas.
- Government is constrained by 'potential groups'. If the interests of these groups are threatened, they will organize and force the government to take action.

(*Source*: Smith 1995)

Corporatism and policy networks

The concepts of corporatism and policy networks are based on the idea that relationships between the state and groups tend to be closed rather than open. Consequently, there is not a free flow of groups in and out of the policy process and power is concentrated rather than dispersed. These concepts are suited to understanding British policy-making in the postwar period for two reasons. First, as we have seen, the Westminster model and the British political tradition is based on a notion of power being concentrated within Westminster/Whitehall. Because of the limited notion of participation that exists within the British system, there is a limited role for pressure groups in the policy process. Second, the expansion of functions associated with the development of the modern state, meant that the state developed the need for groups for a number of reasons:

- Legitimacy: when the state was intervening in areas such as health or education, it needed the support of those affected by the intervention. Therefore, listening to these groups was important for maintaining legitimacy.
- Information: in fields such as education, medicine, or agriculture, groups often represent the experts in the field and therefore they can provide the information that is necessary for policy-making.
- Implementation: unless the state is going to create an enormous bureaucracy, it often relies on groups to implement decisions. For example, the Government could only create the NHS once it had the agreement of the doctors, and thus in 1946 the Labour Government had to make a large number of concessions to the doctors.
- Order: governments dislike uncertainty and disruption. If a group has a sufficiently coherent membership and economic resources, government will often attempt to placate the group rather than be seen to be out of control.

Relationships with groups thus provide a mechanism for the government to develop policy and deliver public goods in a legitimate manner which reduces the degree of uncertainty. At the same time, the government is unlikely to want to have contact with a wide range of groups with competing demands, because this will introduce greater complexity and conflict into the policy process.

The development of corporatism

Corporatism is a specific type of relationship between groups and government, where the leaders of the peak pressure groups become incorporated into the policy process and are then involved in the development of policy (see Box 8.2). Once policy is agreed, pressure-group leaders use their organization to implement the policy decision. For corporatists, groups are functional—they represent a particular sector of the economy, and each of these groups has a tendency towards monopoly: there will be one group representing doctors, one for teachers, one for

---

Box 8.2 Corporatism

The main features of corporatism:

- The dominant interest groups are functional groups with a tendency towards a monopoly of representation.
- Certain functional interests have privileged access to the state.
- Membership of the associations is often not voluntary.
- The groups often have a regulatory function.
- The policy process becomes hierarchical.
- Functional interest groups and state agencies enter into a closed process of bargaining over public policy.

(*Source*: Cawson 1986)

---

farmers, and so on. Often these groups have compulsory membership—for example doctors are expected to be members of the British Medical Association and often groups such as the BMA or the Royal College of Surgeons perform a regulatory role.

Middlemas (1979, 1986) regards the development of corporatism as a crucial element in the development of the postwar British state. Middlemas speaks of a corporatist bias of the state developing as a result of the need to resolve (or at least contain) the conflicts between business and labour. Therefore, the beginnings of incorporation of economic actors into the state was a direct result of the General Strike of 1926 (see Symons 1957). This process of integration was exacerbated by the Second World War, which increased the power of labour and created a need for the state to avoid strikes. Consequently, both labour and business were integrated into a wide range of policy-making arenas. Middlemas argues that in the postwar era trade unions and business became 'governing institutions'. They were in continuous consultation with government, and were represented on a range of advisory bodies, quangos, and royal commissions. Corporatism was seen as a way of maintaining social order and resolving Britain's economic problems. The government wanted to intervene in the economy and contain wage increases, and saw the cooperation of business and unions as essential to these goals. For example, the Conservative Government created the National Economic Development Council (NEDC) in 1962, as a forum for tripartite discussions aimed at improving the productivity of British industry. The Heath Government established an Industrial Development Unit to coordinate industrial policy, and the 1974 Industry Act created sector working parties to allow tripartite discussions of how to improve production in specific sectors of the economy.

Perhaps a more significant development, in terms of corporatist arrangements, was the development of institutions for controlling wage increases in the context of full employment policy and high inflation. Here, the government could control wage increases (and thereby reduce inflation) through encouraging wage restraint on the part of the unions. As a consequence, a whole range of income policies were discussed and developed with the trade unions and business. Negotiations were often conducted through formal institutions such as the National Board for Prices and Incomes, and the unions had a major role in the implementation of these agreements because they were charged with selling them to their members (see Box 8.3).

Despite the prevalence of the term 'corporatism' in both academic and journalistic writings in the 1970s, the concept was not particularly useful for analysing the role of pressure groups in British society. While a form of corporatism appeared to exist through incomes policy and bodies like the NEDC, the reality was somewhat different. Either these relationships were highly unstable—as in the case of incomes policy, where the relationships broke down after a short period—or they were not really policy-making institutions—as in the case of the NEDC, where policy was discussed rather than made. It was also rare, in the British case, that any group had a monopoly of representation; such groups therefore lacked the legitimacy to agree and implement a policy. Organizations like the TUC and CBI, with limited membership and often internally divided, found it difficult to act as corporatist institutions. Whilst institutionalized government group relations were a core feature of the modern state, perhaps a better way to conceptualize them is as policy networks.

Policy networks

The concept of policy networks accepts that relationships between groups and government are institutionalised—that is, there are relationships that are stable over time—but it also suggests that these patterns of interaction are segmented. In other words, the nature of the relationship between groups and government varies. In some they are relatively strong and closed, involving only a limited number of pressure groups, and there are high barriers to entry. In others they may be weaker

---

Box 8.3 Corporatism in action

During the high point of corporatism in the 1970s, government intervened in society by developing corporatist relationships with key economic and professional groups. For example, as a consequence of mortgage shortages at a time of rising house prices, the Department of the Environment entered into discussions with the Building Societies Association (BSA) to try to deal with the problem and these talks led to the establishment of a Joint Advisory Committee (JAC). In 1975, the JAC was used to establish borrowing guidelines for building societies which came directly from a bargaining process between the Government and the BSA. The BSA then ensured the implementation of the guidelines.

(*Source:* Boddy and Lambert 1990)

Table 8.1 Characteristics of the policy network spectrum

Dimension	Issue network	Policy community
Membership		
No. of participants	Many	Limited
Type of interest	Wide range	Economic/professional
Integration		
Frequency of interaction	Contact fluctuates	Frequent, high-quality
Continuity	Fluctuating access	Membership and values stable
Consensus	Variety of views	Shared basic values
Resources		
Distribution of resources within network	Often groups have few resources	All participants have resources to exchange
Distribution of resources within participating organization	Varied and variable distribution	Hierarchical
Power		
Nature of power	Unequal power, zero-sum	Power is positive-sum

Source: Marsh and Rhodes (1992)

and more pluralistic, containing many groups which have access to the policy area (see Table 8.1).

Marsh and Rhodes (1992) suggest that there is a continuum of policy networks, from relatively open issue networks to closed policy communities. In an issue network there are many actors, including government departments, pressure groups, and government agencies. Access to the network is relatively open, with groups moving rapidly in and out of a policy area. There is usually a high level of conflict over policy goals, and it is difficult to reach an agreement. One example of an issue network is postwar industrial policy. This involved the Departments of Trade, Industry, Employment, and the Treasury; it also involved some key actors such as the Prime Minister and the Chancellor. It included a range of pressure groups such as the CBI and TUC, and often individual unions and companies (the ranges of individual companies and unions involved were not stable). There was little agreement between these various actors and organizations over the nature of industrial policy. The Treasury and business generally wanted to limit government intervention in the economy (although particular industries such as cotton, steel, and car manufacture often called for government aid), whilst other sections, particularly the trade unions and the Department of Industry, supported an interventionist industrial policy. Consequently, there was little consensus in the policy area; it was highly political and the result was unstable industrial policy as governments shifted frequently from interventionist to laissez-faire policies (see Fig. 8.1).

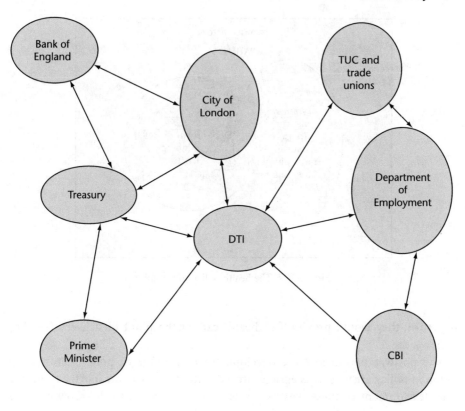

Figure 8.1 The industrial policy network

At the other end of the continuum a closed policy network is located: a limited and stable number of groups and government actors share a degree of consensus about the policy area and the policy solutions (this does not mean that they agree on everything, but that they agree on the basic premises of the policy). Access to a policy community is difficult, and only certain insider groups are likely to be included in the policy process. The relationship between group and government in a policy community is one of dependency. The group needs the government to provide certain benefits and the government needs the group to provide information, legitimacy, and (often) service delivery. In health, a closed policy community has existed for most of the postwar period. As noted above, once the 1945 Labour Government decided that it was going to create a national health service, it needed the cooperation of the doctors in order to implement the policy. Consequently, health policy revolved around the Ministry of Health (later the Department of Health), the BMA, and the royal colleges representing consultants. It was very difficult for other groups, such as nurses or patients, to have any say in the development of health policy or the running of the NHS. The community's consensus was built on the understanding that the doctors would have clinical autonomy;

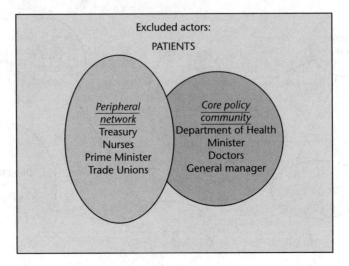

Figure 8.2 The health policy community

in return, they would provide free health care at the point of delivery (see Fig. 8.2).

The postwar period saw the development of a range of policy networks in different policy areas such as agriculture, education, energy, transport, and health. The development of these networks was a direct response to the growth of the modern state and for the need to intervene in society without developing an enormous and overbearing state bureaucracy. Thus, these networks had considerable advantages for government:

• They created mechanisms for government intervention.

• They simplified the policy process by excluding groups that did not accept the basic values of the policy sector.

• They made policy-making more predictable. Within a particular policy community, there is a range of possible solutions. For example, in the health policy community, a solution to the problems in health policy was not to make patients pay.

Nevertheless, the Thatcher Government was suspicious and critical of many existing networks, and attempted to break them up (see below).

Thatcherism and pressure groups

There can be little doubt that with the development of the interventionist, modernist state, interest groups became more integrated into the policy process. A central part of the policy process was civil servants consulting, often in great detail, with pressure groups before policy proposals were finalized (see Jordan and Richardson 1987). In some cases, such as incomes policy and farm prices, the process was one of bargaining rather than consultation. This did not mean that the policy process was pluralistic—many groups were excluded from any meaningful policy dialogue and, as we have seen, in a number of areas a few privileged groups were integrated into tight policy networks. However, as we saw in Chapter 5, the New Right and Thatcherite Conservatives were often suspicious of groups, blaming them for overload and un-governability. Interest groups were seen as protecting special interests, and thus opposed to attempts to extend the market and limit the role of the state. The Thatcherites accepted the notion that Britain was a corporate society, and saw this as one of the key factors in accounting for Britain's decline. What the Thatcher Government wanted to do was re-establish a direct link between individual voters and a sovereign Parliament, rather than work through group representation. The Conservative position was that government, not pressure groups, ran the country (Judge 1993). Richardson (2000: 1010) observes that Thatcher and her ministers

had their own ideas, policy frames and policy preferences . . . and relatively few of the new policy ideas emanated from the plethora of embedded policy communities around Whitehall that had grown up in the post-war years.

Consequently, there was an attempt to reduce the role of groups and undermine existing policy networks.

The Conservative Governments from 1979 to 1997 challenged pressure groups in a number of ways:

- They shifted the terms of political debate. As we saw in Chapter 3, a key element of the modern state was the assumption that the state resolved problems and delivered public goods. However, as the state was not a totalitarian state, it often had to deliver policies in consultation with, or with the assistance of, groups. The Conservatives attempted to change the debate so that the government was not always seen as the source of problems or solutions. For the Conservatives, solutions could be derived from the market, and groups were seen as often distorting the market. Therefore, if the responsibility for public goods were shifted away from the state, groups did not need to be involved in the policy process.

- They challenged intermediate and corporate institutions. New Right ideology led the Conservatives to believe in the direct contract between the voter and government, and to see that intermediate organizations such as pressure groups, churches, and local authorities should not have a role in making policy. Therefore, the Conservatives were committed either to abolishing pressure groups or to reducing their power. According to Gamble (1994b):

Legitimacy is withdrawn from voluntary institutions like trade unions and from public institutions like the BBC, the universities and state education systems, nationalised industries and local Government, until they have reformed themselves or been reformed from outside. A whole range of what we see as corporatist intermediate institutions, such as the National Economic Development Council, the Manpower Services Commission and Wages Council, were abolished by the Thatcher and Major governments.

- They privileged new interests. Whilst being suspicious of many interest groups, such as trade unions and even professional groups associated with the establishment of the welfare state, the Thatcher and Major governments gave access to a different range of groups. For instance, whilst in the 1970s it was the CBI that had good relations with government, after 1979 the Thatcher Administration was more open to the advice of the neo-liberal Institute of Directors.

- The Conservative Administration also depended more on ideological think tanks than on interest groups for policy advice. In policy developments such as the poll tax and welfare reform, think tanks were influential; in particular, they could be used to 'fly kites'. Often the Conservative Government would use right-wing think tanks to suggest a radical reform; they could thus gauge reaction, or get voters used to the idea, before proposing and developing the policy (see Cockett 1995, Hay 1996, Kandiah and Seldon 1996a, 1996b).

The Conservatives, then, were suspicious of the institutionalized relationships that developed between government and groups in the postwar period, and saw these policy networks as opponents of the types of free market policies and welfare reforms that they were keen to introduce. Marsh et al. (2001) demonstrate that there was a decline in the extent of consultation during the Conservative administrations. Most obviously, in a reaction to what the New Right perceived as a corporatist state, trade unions were almost completely frozen out of government. According to one official in the Department of Employment:

When I went in to the Department of Employment, the culture really was that they were the sponsoring department for the trade union movement. If the trade union movement didn't want it to happen it would not happen, even if there was a Conservative government and a Conservative Secretary of State. Now all that changed rapidly with the arrival of Norman Tebbit and it was quite amazing how the civil servants changed.

However, it was not only the trade unions that found contact with the government more difficult. Even in the DTI, contacts with business became less intense (Marsh et al. 2001: 192). In the area of social security policy, the government almost completely excluded pressure groups. According to one official, Peter Lilley, Secretary of State from 1992 to 1997, had no interest in consulting pressure groups and did not really care about the relationship with them. The government was also direct in the way it confronted some of the established policy networks. For the Prime Minister, changing policy often required changing the role of groups in the policy process, and therefore the Government explicitly attempted to break up policy networks in education, health, local government, and energy which were seen as major conservative forces stalling attempts to change policy. In a number of cases the Government tried to bypass the networks either by creating different networks or by overriding them. In education, for example, there was a conscious move to shift decision-making away from the network through creating more direct relationships between the Secretary of State and schools. In health, an

> ### Box 8.4 Undermining the health policy community
>
> The Thatcher Government was very concerned with the rising costs of the health service, and believed that to some extent the inefficiencies in the service were not due to under-funding but to the role of powerful interests within the health professions. Consequently, the Government was no longer prepared to allow the doctors to have a veto on health policy and hence wanted to eliminate them from the policy process. They did this in two ways. First, they introduced managers into the NHS and thus reduced the clinical auton-omy of doctors, because it meant that decisions had to made on grounds of cost and not just medical need. In addition, following the Griffiths Report, management of the NHS as a whole was devolved to the NHS management executive. Second, when this mana-gerialism failed to resolve the recurrent problems of the Health Service, the Govern-ment announced a thorough review of policy options for the NHS. Interestingly, the Prime Minister chaired the review with only peripheral input from the Department of Health, and there were no representatives of the BMA or the royal colleges. The health policy community was completely cut out of the reform process.
>
> (*Source*: Day and Klein 1992)

alternative network was created to look at reform of the NHS, and in energy, privatization destroyed the networks established for an energy policy based on publicly owned industries (see Box 8.4). Dudley and Richardson (1996) have highlighted how the growing opposition to roads (coupled to Treasury opposition to rising costs) led to the loss of power of the pro-roads lobby within the transport policy community.

Labour and pressure groups

According to Marsh et al. (2001), since Labour's 1997 electoral victory there has been a major increase in consultation and changes in who are consulted. Almost without exception, interviews by the authors with civil servants and pressure group representatives confirmed this view. The change was probably most notable in the DSS. One Grade 3 in the DSS stressed the greater consultation:

[The current Government] wants to bring [interest groups] in at a much earlier stage. Previously, we've generally had more of an idea and presented options, but now we are asking for everyone's views regardless.

Another Grade 5's response dealt with the changes in who was consulted:

One of the main differences between this Government and the last is that we now have more contact with [interest groups]. I think the last government did not welcome the voluntary organizations and, of course, they were not supportive of what the Government was trying to do. This lot [Labour] has relied on those voluntary organizations because they have been briefing them for the last eighteen years. I think their relationship with the people who used to brief them is difficult because they are now in government and they are going to have to take forward [changes] which do not necessarily tally with what they were doing before. But there is greater emphasis on presentation and selling policy under this government, and I think that will involve greater contact with the voluntary associations.

A DSS official concurred:

There is clearly a fundamental difference between this and the previous administration. The previous one really did not consult at all and so one might say they were more decisive. It was easier to get clear steers from them, but the current administration clearly has a large constituency out there that they are keen to keep on board.

The increase in consultation has not been confined to the DSS, although the contrast with the previous Administration is most stark there. Elsewhere, one of the civil servants in the DTI dealing with energy made a similar point:

[The difference] is fairly clear-cut. Pre-election we had very little contact with ... the unions associated with the nuclear industry, ... Friends of the Earth, and Greenpeace [or] local politicians from areas surrounding the nuclear plants. ... Post-election I've been in contact with them all on a one-to-one basis.

Not surprisingly, the view was confirmed by the interest groups. So, for example, an executive from the pressure group Gingerbread claimed:

I've had two meetings with the Head of Policy and they have phoned up and asked for another one. They want us on board and are prepared to put some effort in. Whereas previously, under the Tories, it was always us pushing at the door. So there is a difference; two years ago we simply wouldn't have been in this position.

These quotes suggest some of the reasons for the change. Clearly, the Labour Government has different policy objectives and is more committed to consultation. At the same time, however, it has debts to the groups that serviced it in opposition, so we may expect consultation with such groups to continue for some time. Part of the current exchange relationship involves access in return for services rendered in the past.

There are two important points to make concerning New Labour and interest groups. First, New Labour has probably had much better contacts with business than any previous Labour Government. Since the early 1990s, Labour has been cultivating links with business in order to change the perception that it is an anti-business party. Blair has explicitly stated that he does not wish to punish wealth creation, and has placed business people such as Geoffrey Robinson and David Simon into key places in his administration (see Cohen 1999, Walden 2001, Kavanagh and Richards 2002). In addition, in an attempt to reduce reliance on the trade unions, the government has encouraged businesses to make donations to the government. Whilst we could not suggest that this buys influence, it clearly gives access. In the case of the Bernie Ecclestone affair, the Labour Government received £1 million from the owner of Formula One racing. Once in government, there was a change in Labour's position on banning tobacco sponsorship of Formula One, although of course there is no indication of a connection between the two events (see Naughtie 2001, Rawnsley 2001, Toynbee and Walker 2001).

Second, whilst Labour was open to pressure groups early on in its first term, it quickly became more immune to their influence. Once the Government was established and developed new lines of policy advice from officials and task forces, the need for pressure groups diminished. Events such as protests against changes in disability benefits (1999) and the fuel protests (2000) have made the government less willing to listen to interest groups. In addition, it was wary about re-establishing the types of relationship that Labour had had with the trade unions in the 1960s and 1970s. During the 1997 election campaign, Blair stated:

We will not be held to ransom by the unions . . . We will stand up to strikes. We will not cave in to unrealistic pay demands from any one . . . Unions have no special role in our election campaign, just as they will get no special favours in a Labour Government. (Quoted in Ludlam 2001: 115.)

New forms of pressure-group behaviour

The sorts of relationship and the types of group involved in government have changed. New technology, new forms of information, new arenas of politics have undermined some of the traditional networks that existed in the 1960s and 1970s. This does not mean that pressure groups are unimportant, but now they are operating in different ways. There are three main elements to this change: the rise of new forms of political protest, pressure politics in the EU, and global political activity.

New forms of political protest

For much of the twentieth century, pressure politics revolved around economic and welfare issues, and consequently pressure politics was reflected in class cleavages. Consequently, corporatism was developed around the need to reconcile the interests of government, labour, and business. More recently, the role of pressure groups in economic issues such as wages appears to have lessened. Elsewhere, the key pressure politics issues seem to revolve around issues such as the environment, human rights, fuel taxes, transporting of livestock, and anti-road protests which either cut across class divides or are predominantly middle-class issues. This is reflected in the rise of new social movements and single-issue groups since the mid-1970s (see Grant 2000). The argument of those such as Mulgan (2001) is that people have become anti-party; rather than depending on parties for the representation of interests, they have therefore focused on single issues. This is a trend postmodernists use to substantiate their arguments (see Chapter 2). The 1990s in particular witnessed an escalation in single issues. Often, the tactics of the groups involved were not to work through established channels, but to use the media to arouse public sympathy.

The first element in this change in the nature of pressure politics was the rise of so-called 'new social movements' (NSMs). The main characteristics of NSMs are:

- They are primarily social: often the concerns of NSMs are cultural or lifestyle issues, rather than narrowly defined political issues.

- The groups are located within civil society: the focus of a number of NSMs is not usually changing the state, but changing ways in which social life can be organized.

- They attempt to develop alternative types of social organization: their concerns are participatory democracy, decentralization, small organizations, and community. Consequently, they tend not to form political organizations on a hierarchical basis (although in practice this often creates problems).

- Tactics are based on direct action: many new social movements see the state as essentially unreformable, and therefore contact with formal government organizations can dilute the goals of the movement. They rely on outsider tactics such as demonstrations or even illegal actions.

- Membership is not class based: NSMs tend not to be class groups, and they promote issues that cut across class. However, it is also true that their membership is predominantly middle class.

NSMs tend to have broad agendas that focus, as we have seen, on how society is organized and power distributed. They can have an important impact on established policy networks by politicizing the closed and settled agenda and introducing new ideas. For example, the agricultural policy community has had to face the challenges raised by the environmental movement, and this has led to more support for organic and environmentally sensitive farming. NSMs, in effect, work by changing the climate of ideas. In the 1990s, however, it appears that pressure-group activity moved away from broad movement to narrower, single-issue politics (see Box 8.5).

The last twenty years has seen a rise in single-issue politics. Some of these issues have been organized by combinations of existing groups, whilst others have developed around particular issues; in some senses these have been very successful. The 1990s reflects a trend of single-issue politics in which there are numerous examples of a range of interest groups having an effect on policy: the anti-poll tax campaign led the Conservative Government to abandon the Community Charge; the campaign against Genetically Modified Organisms (GMOs) resulted in the Government going through several changes of policy (see Box 8.6); the Snowdrop campaign against guns in society, which developed out of the Dunblane massacre led to the banning of handguns; and the Greenpeace campaign over Brent Spar

---

Box 8.5 **New social movements: the women's movement**

In the 1950s and 1960s there were increasing educational and employment opportunities for women, while full employment created increasing demands for women to return to the labour market. At the same time, a growing US literature questioned the traditional role of woman as housewives. In the late 1960s social movements developed around issues of civil rights and black rights. Increasingly, woman realized that whilst these groups were calling for equality, they were ignoring the role and position of women; as a consequence, women formed their own groups and started to campaign for their rights. The issue of the position of women became more salient when, in 1968, women workers in the Ford motor company went on strike over the issue of equal pay with men. Whilst the issue was not supported by the union, the women involved made connections with the wider women's movement. For the first time, more radical middle-class feminists joined with working-class women to promote a practical issue that affected many women. The strike attracted a great deal of publicity and resulted in the Minister for Employment producing an Equal Pay Bill (1975).

In the 1970s the British feminist movement began to grow rapidly, but it also split into different strands with different tactics. In Oxford in 1970 there was an attempt to unite these strands through a Women's National Coordinating Committee, which laid down some of the main aims of the women's movement: equal pay, equal opportunities in education, free contraception and abortion, and twenty-four-hour child care. The Wilson–Callaghan Labour Government (1974–9) introduced the Equal Pay Act and the Sexual Discrimination Act, and formally the women's movement achieved three of its four Oxford aims. Whilst in the 1980s economic recession and new right ideology was a setback for women, the movement has changed the debate about the role of women, and economic and social change has greatly affected the role of women in the labour market. Today, however, women have still not attained parity with men in pay, work status, or political representation.

---

effectively led to Shell Oil abandoning its plans to dump an oil platform in the North Sea.

Single-issue groups tend not to work through formal institutional channels, (although Snowdrop worked closely with the Labour Party), depending instead on public campaigns and demonstrations to raise issues. The campaign around GMOs was based to a large extent on the publicity generated by the destruction of GM crops. Generally, single-issue groups use a range of tactics of varying intensity from petitions and marches to the occupation of sites of road construction. These campaigns can be very disruptive to government. For instance, the fuel protest had a considerable impact on transport and the supply of goods, and consequently created a high degree of concern within government (see Box 8.7). Single-issues can disrupt existing networks by politicizing issues and producing public demands for policy change.

Box 8.6 Genetically modified organisms

Throughout the 1990s, the initial position of both Conservative and Labour Governments was to allow the food companies to continue with developing GMOs without government interference. Essentially, the Government was supportive of the testing of GMOs and did nothing to hinder their development. However, the Government quickly faced a pressure group and media campaign that highlighted GMOs as 'Frankenstein foods' with unpredictable consequences for human health and the environment. Through direct action and gaining media attention, groups like Friends of the Earth were successful at shaping the debate on GMOs away from the notion that this was a good development for human kind to one in which GMOs were seen as a tremendous risk. The consequence of this public concern was that food retailers began to regulate the use of GMOs themselves. A number of the large supermarkets banned GMOs and promised customers GMO-free foods. This illustrates the way in which changes in the processes of governance can affect pressure-group behaviour. The regulators of GMOs became private companies rather than the state. Nevertheless, public concern affected the Government's perception of the issue, and it established a Ministerial Committee on Biotechnology and Genetic Modification. It also reached an agreement with companies that GM crops would not be made commercially available before tests were completed in spring 2003. However, this did not stop food producers using GMOs.

Pressure groups and the EU

As we saw in Chapter 7, the EU is becoming an increasingly important element in the policy-making process in Britain. Particularly before the Single European Act and the Maastricht Treaty, most lobbying of the EU was through national governments but with the expansion of EU competence, new routes of influence for pressure groups have opened up. Indeed, in certain areas such as environmental policies (see Box 8.8) interest groups have had much more influence at the EU level than they have had domestically. The point about the EU is that it opens up new lines of access for pressure groups and leads to different types of network. Within the EU, power is much less concentrated than it is within the British state. Therefore, there are a number of different terrains and points of pressure, and groups can move from one to another if they are unsuccessful. In addition, the EU makes a virtue of its openness to interest groups and NGOs (see Prodi and Kinnock 2001). The downside is that lobbying the EU is much more complex: it needs a degree of coordination, access, and funds to travel that are not available to certain groups. As Mazey and Richardson (1993: 191) illustrate:

groups have to contend at the EC level with the phenomenon of an especially competitive agenda-setting process and attendant problems of uncertainty and unpredictability. Thus in order to be effective Euro-lobbyists, groups must be able to co-ordinate their national and EC level strategies, construct alliances with their European counterparts, and monitor changing national and EC agendas.

Box 8.7 **The fuel protest**

The issue of escalating fuel prices has been rumbling on since Labour was first elected in 1997. From the 1970s, governments have always had to deal with OPEC, the oil cartel that has traditionally had the market power to set the price for a barrel of crude oil. Between 1997 and 1998, OPEC had steadily raised the price of oil to almost £4 a gallon and the cost had been passed on directly to the consumer. Yet growing discontent over high fuel prices was not confined to Britain alone, but was spread throughout Europe and as far afield as Australia. Yet in Britain the tax on fuel was one of the highest in Europe; for every £1 spent on fuel, over 80 pence went to the coffers of the Treasury. Facing pressure from the road haulage lobby, as well as wider public discontent at the cost of fuel on the garage forecourt, the Chancellor, Gordon Brown, used his March 2000 budget to place a block on the environmental 'fuel duty escalator', the above-inflation increase in the tax on petrol. But, as OPEC continued to raise its prices throughout 2000 and the problems with Britain's rail network system persisted, popular discontent 'about fuel prices magnetised together an angry coalition of road hauliers . . ., fishermen and farmers . . ., and rural drivers who saw high petrol taxes as another assault on the way of life in the countryside by an unsympathetic and alien metropolitan government' (Rawnsley 2001: 397)

On 7 September 2000, the initial fuel protest demanding that the tariff on fuel be cut was a low-key affair in which a small group of mainly hauliers and farmers blockaded the Shell refinery in Stanlow, Cheshire. Very rapidly, however, their modest protest was mirrored elsewhere across the country. Fuel blockades were soon established in six out of the nine refineries. The impact was felt almost immediately, with growing queues at petrol stations as customers began to panic buy. The Government, and in particular the DTI under Stephen Byers, failed to appreciate the rapid change in events and were slow to react. Within days the issue caught the Prime Minister's attention for the first time following reports of petrol shortages in the north of England.

The Government's response to the growing crisis was to trigger 'Cobra', the Cabinet Office Briefing Room A used in times of crisis. The Civil Contingencies Committee that handled the crisis comprised Jack Straw (Home Secretary), Stephen Byers, Gus Macdonald (Transport), and Andrew Smith (Treasury Secretary), but Whitehall lacked a contingency plan. According to one Home Office minister: 'There was no plan at all . . . What you have to understand—it was then that I really saw it—is that the Civil Service is completely useless . . . You think you've got this Rolls-Royce service and it turns out to be a Robin Reliant.' (See Rawnsley 2001: 400.)

As the protests continued and their impact elsewhere became more apparent, for example in blood supplies to the NHS, so the public perception of a real civil crisis began to take root. With a general election looming, the last thing a 'remodelled' Labour Government required was the spectre of the 1979 'winter of discontent' coming back to haunt them in a new guise. The impact of the fuel crisis was quickly felt. Butler and Kavangh (2001: 19) observe: 'Public sympathy was largely with the protestors and the government's standing in the polls plummeted abruptly. In late September, polls briefly put the Conservatives ahead—for the first time since 1992.' Yet, the Government maintained a united front and, publicly at least, were unwilling to accede to the protestors' demands (see Naughtie 2001). In particular, Blair publicly declared: 'were we to yield to that pressure, it would run counter to every democratic principle that this country believes in.' With taunting tabloid newspaper headlines declaring 'Out of Gas' and 'Empty', the threat of both fuel and food shortages looming, and the MoD placing the army on emergency standby, the Government had little political room for manoeuvre.

A week after the initial protest, salvation for the Government came, first, in the form of the TGWU persuading its lorry drivers to resume their deliveries, the Road Haulage Association appealing to truckers to end their action, and the media, worried that their own papers would not be delivered, calling for the cessation of refinery blockades. The protest ended as swiftly as it had started, with a declaration by the organizers of a repeat action in sixty days if taxes on fuel were not reduced. This threat never materialized; in his November budget Brown cut the tax on fuel, although it was presented as a planned measure and not a concession to the fuel protestors. Rawnsley (2001: 414) concludes: 'The fuel blockade brought Tony Blair to the edge of the sort of reputation-ruining catastrophe from which Prime Ministers never recover. A ragbag of protesters—who even at their strongest never numbered more than 2,500 nationwide—paralysed the country and rendered the government flailingly ineffectual.'

Each element of the EU has its own mechanism for consultation with groups. As we saw above, the Commission is made up of a range of directorates-general (DGs) responsible for different areas of policy. Each of these directorates develop their own particular networks with interest groups. Some, such as the environmental DG, tend to be relatively open, whereas others, like the agricultural network, are fairly closed. Formal consultation with the Commission takes places through the EU's Economic and Social Committee (ESC) and the advisory committees of each of the DGs. The ESC comprises 189 representatives of employers, workers, and other groups. All commission proposals go to the ESC for comment, but it rarely has much influence on decisions. Advisory committees exist in each DG and are made up of groups directly concerned with the respective policy area. The concern of the advisory committee is to advise the Commission on the implementation of its directives. Therefore, the Commission has highly institutionalized contact with interest groups. The Commission, however, is also continually lobbied by both national and European groups. In the environmental sector, for example, the largest pan-European environmental groups meet with the Environment DG and discuss EU environmental policy and any problems that have arisen in the previous six months (Prodi and Kinnock 2001). For so-called third-sector groups, the Commission now provides considerable funding.

In terms of the governance debate, what is particularly interesting is the extent to which national pressure groups no longer depend on the nation-state as the key site of decision-making. They can use the EU as an alternative source of influencing policy. Fairbrass and Jordan (2001: 1) found

that British-based environmental groups (previously marginalised in the national arena) have mobilised at the EU level in order to press for environmental policy that may not have been secured had they relied on pursing their objectives with or via national policy-makers.

They demonstrate that, in areas such as biodiversity, habitat, and environmental

Box 8.8 **The Commission and interest groups**

What procedures is the Commission putting in place to take account of the opinion of interest groups?

To take account of the opinion of interest groups, the Commission may either establish consultation procedures on a formal basis, in the shape of advisory committees or groups of experts, or do so informally on an ad hoc basis. Very often the two procedures are used.

  When the Commission opts for dialogue by putting in place a committee, it lays down the rules of this formal consultation (mission, composition, appointment, and terms of reference) in the decision, creating the advisory committee. The selection criteria focus in particular on the degree of representativeness of the group to be consulted, with a view to a fair balance of the different interests involved. In other words, besides the economic sectors in question, more general interests such as the trade unions, consumers, and environmentalists are also represented.

  There is a Commission web page on special-interest groups:

http://europa.eu.int/comm/secretariat_general/sgc/lobbies/approche/ apercuen.htm

impact assessments, environmental groups were able to overcome the opposition of the British Government by lobbying at the EU level.

Whilst the Commission is the key site of pressure group activity, other institutions are also important.

The European Parliament

The European Parliament, as a consequence of joint decision-making (see Chapter 7), is now a major influence on policy at the EU level, and therefore an important target for lobbying by pressure groups. MEPs are relatively open to interest groups because they are a useful source of information and support. Groups also lobby the committees of the European Parliament and the informal groups of MEPs concerned with particular issues. Grant (2000) points out how the Parliament is generally used when lobbyists have failed to influence the Council of Ministers or the Commission. For example, in an attempt to stop the testing of cosmetics on animals, the lobby used the Parliament to influence the Commission, but this ultimately proved unsuccessful.

The Council of Ministers

The Council is the key decision-making body within the EU, but its meetings are closed and secret. This means that groups have little option but to lobby through national ministers and ministries, and are therefore dependent on their own governments defending their case. As a consequence, British officials in Brussels are both lobbyists and targets for lobbyists. Officials lobby both for national interest groups and for domestic government departments, and at the same time, try to make interest groups and departments aware of what the limits of negotiation are.

The European Court of Justice

The ECJ provides groups with an important source of influence at the EU level: they can often use European legislation to force national governments to implement EU regulations. This has had important implications for issues such as working hours, retirement, and the environment.

So the EU changes both the strategy of interest groups and the nature of the policy process. The EU is a complex process of decision-making, with many access points for groups. If they fail to influence policy in one arena, they can try in another. This means that the networks that develop at the EU level are different from those that develop at the national level. They tend to be more open and flexible because of the range of actors involved and the complex interaction of national and ideological interests.

Global political activity

With the development of global political institutions and transnational political problems, there has been a growth in global political activity. The globalization of pressure group activity takes five main forms:

The development of global pressure groups

This development is happening in two ways. New pressure groups are developing in order to deal with global issues. For example, the World Development Movement, founded in 1970, exists to tackle the underlying causes of poverty. It regards poverty as a global problem caused by the nature of markets and the problems of international debt, and consequently treats poverty as a global issue, dealing with transnational organizations such as the IMF and the WTO as well as with national governments.

Second, domestic pressure groups have developed or are developing international organizations. Groups like Oxfam and Friends of the Earth have now developed large international programmes in order to tackle transnational problems. There is now a range of international non-governmental organizations such as Amnesty, Greenpeace, the Ford Foundation, and Help the Aged which organize, operate, and lobby at the international level.

The development of transnational links between pressure groups

Increasingly, national pressure groups are working together and creating transnational networks, in order to deal with problems that have both domestic and global implications. In areas such as human rights, the environment, and prostitution, these networks have been important in forcing governments to rethink problems at the national and international level. Keck and Sikkink (1998) demonstrate how transnational advocacy networks were central to the recognition of AIDS as a global rather than domestic problem. Transnational networks, NGOs, social movements, government agencies, and officials worked together to place pressure on domestic governments and international institutions. The pressure of the network was able to highlight the fact that AIDS was not a problem of particular countries or groups within those countries, but a global problem that also had human rights implications. As a consequence of pressure, a joint UN programme on HIV/AIDS has been established (Lindquist 2001).

Groups opposing the development of globalization and global political institutions

In recent years there has been an important development of movements concerned with attempting to resist what they regard as the spread of globalization. In some ways this movement developed out of existing groups based in nation-states, who have subsequently formed a 'rainbow' alliance. The anti-globalization movement started off with the anarchistic, ecological, and anti-capitalist movements such as Donga, whose initial protests were anti-road. At the same time, movements started to develop throughout the world which were increasingly aware of the dislocation of powerful international institutions caused by the globalization of capital. In 1994 the People's Global Action movement started in Mexico, and in France the anti-McDonald's protests received much attention. In May 1998, the Reclaim the Streets movement organized a global street party in seventeen different cities. In June 1999, London witnessed the 'carnival against capitalism'. In some ways the most coordinated demonstration by these groups occurred in October 1999 in Seattle, when many thousands of protesters called for the reform of the WTO. The global coalition of protesters then reappeared in London, Melbourne, Gothenburg, and Genoa to coincide with international summits. This resistance to globalization takes two forms. On one side are those who are anti-capitalist and essentially influenced by the anarchist movement; on the other are those who see protest as a means of reforming global institutions, rather than subverting the whole process.

Pressure groups using the global arena to pursue domestic political objectives

For a long time a range of groups, but particularly human rights groups, have attempted to appeal to the international community as a way of putting pressure on domestic governments. In Burma, the supporters of Aung San Suu Kyi have continually raised her position with domestic governments, as a way of putting pressure on the Burmese Government.

The impact of external pressure on domestic policy

Grugel (1999) has demonstrated the ways in which external pressure from governments and NGOs has heightened the demand for democratization in a number of countries. Much of this pressure was from governments and transnational institutions, but NGOs also played an important role by supporting civil society domestically and helping groups to develop, in order to play a role in democratizing their societies. External pressure has also affected Britain. For instance, Britain was under considerable pressure from groups in Germany and Scandinavia to reduce the release of chemicals that were destroying their forests with the production of acid rain.

The period since the 1970s has seen a number of changes in the role of pressure groups and their impact on the policy process:

- The closed policy networks of the Keynesian welfare state period have either broken down, transformed, or become more open.
- Pressure groups appear to be using direct action tactics as well as institutional channels.
- Pressure groups are increasingly operating at EU and global level.

It appears that policy-making has become more complex, and that government has lost the secure and stable pressure groups that characterized the postwar period. However, it has to be remembered that the loss of institutional channels may be representative of a loss of influence by pressure groups. The increase in popularity of direct action is an indication that pressure groups are not having as much impact on government. Indeed, a feature of the period since 1979 is a decline in consultation with groups. As we saw above, although the Government made some concessions to dissipate the fuel protest, it really had little long-term impact on the role of government. However, one area that has changed has been the relationship between the government and NGOs in the delivery of services. In addition, changes in policy has made the Government think about issues of participation and about how people can be involved in the running of their communities.

NGOs and participation: the third sector and social capital

In an environment in which government is looking to new forms of service delivery, the voluntary sector is taking on public functions. The government created a competitive market in (for example) community care which has blurred the boundaries between the public and the private (Taylor 1996). The Conservative Government stressed the importance of the voluntary sector in providing public provision, especially in welfare. With the growth of community care, the voluntary sector has taken on an increased role in providing services which were previously supplied directly by the government. In particular, the role of the voluntary sector increased significantly with the NHS and Community Care Act (1990). According to Russell et al. (1997: 396):

The Act stresses the role of the local authority as an enabler of a mixed economy rather than a provider. A quasi-market is now being developed by statutory agencies making contacts with the private and voluntary sector for the delivery of services to users. This policy was given strong impetus by the requirements imposed on local authorities to spend the greater part of the Special Transitional grant funding for the initial implementation of community care in the 'independent sector'.

Consequently, Russell et al. (1997) discovered in their survey of voluntary agencies that between 1989–90 and 1993–4 the income of the sample organizations increased by 74 per cent and income from statutory sources increased in real terms by 145 per cent in real terms. Moreover, an increasing proportion of the income of agencies now comes from statutory sources (see Table 8.2). In certain areas such as learning disabilities, government grants count for 73 per cent of agencies' income (Knapp 1996).

An important illustration of these changes is the way in which private-sector organizations are increasingly taking on the provision of public goods. In the area of overseas aid policy, for example, the state, rather than providing aid, has increased funds to NGOs, and they implement a significant part of the aid programme on the basis that they have the knowledge concerning the situation on the ground. Another example is the changing status of the Rehabilitation Unit. At one stage the Unit was part of the DSS, it then became an agency and was finally privatized, with a voluntary organization being given state money to run the Unit.

It was not only in the area of welfare that the Government turned to voluntary associations. When Douglas Hurd was Home Secretary (1985–9), he coined the term 'active citizens' and launched a policy, Neighbourhood Watch, in order to encourage communities to watch out for and report criminal activity. In 1997 there were 161,000 Neighbourhood Watch schemes in Britain, but subsequently there has been little attempt to measure their effectiveness.

However, this shift to the voluntary sector cannot simply be seen as indicative of a declining role for central government. The irony is that, whilst the Government has introduced managerialism and the private sector to undermine bureaucracy and apparently empower the citizen, it has explicitly and deliberately expanded regulation, as a way of controlling these organizations in the delivery of services. The expansion of audit bodies increases bureaucracy, as organizations attempt to meet the rules, create the 'audit trails', and respond to their regulators. This regulation causes particular problems for voluntary groups. Many may be taking only a small part of their income from the state, but as a consequence all their work is shaped by meeting government demands. Moreover, the need to meet tough government regulation affects their ability to deliver services in what they see as the most effective way (Taylor 1996). Regulation in this area is often haphazard, and it puts severe strains on an organization, when *volunteers* find themselves subject to statutory regulation.

Table 8.2 Income of Voluntary Agencies from statutory sources as a percentage of total income

Year	1989–90	1990–1	1991–2	1992–3	1993–4
% of income	41.3	47.2	50.1	56.6	58.2

Source: Russell et al. (1997)

This raises a second problem: state financing of voluntary agencies within a state regulatory framework may not produce a thriving civil society, but may instead create the de facto nationalization of the voluntary sector. The danger for Rick Nye, the director of the Social Market Foundation (BBC 1999), is:

You lose some of the ethos you most value about the voluntary sector and they turn into contract chasers, people who are trying to fulfil the terms under which they have been engaged. And what you end up with is the worst of both possible worlds. You end up with a voluntary sector which in fact isn't voluntary at all, it is de facto an arm of state activity, and it becomes bureaucratized rather than actually drawing new people in with the ideas of giving their time and giving of their money.

It is relatively uncontentious to assert that at present many NGOs are doing little more than carrying out government policy, and that because of the amount of money that comes from the government they are highly dependent on the state.

Third, the devolving of issues to voluntary groups often does not reflect a concern with developing civil society but political pressure by governments to offload difficult problems. Many of the issues that have been contracted out have always been politically difficult, and now, whilst government is getting the services delivered, it avoids much of the political blame when things go wrong.

Pressure groups, participation, and governance

The changing role of pressure groups, NGOs, and voluntary groups has important implications for democracy, as it appears that citizens are using traditional political channels to a lesser degree. Although voter turnout figures remain constant at around 75 per cent for General Elections (see Table 8.3) and 35 per cent in local elections, it is in the area of political perceptions where worrying trends can be detected. A MORI poll commissioned by the Joseph Rowntree Trust examined the views of a cross-section of adults on politicians and the political process (see the internet page www.charter88/online/index.html). It revealed a low level of public confidence in the political system. Only 22 per cent thought that the political system worked well, and only 53 per cent stated that they had any interest in politics (*State of the Nation*, April/May 1995). The proportion of members of the public holding ministers in 'high' or 'very high' esteem was 9 per cent (down from 22 per cent in 1985) and for MPs, this figure was 7 per cent (down from 17 per cent

Table 8.3 Voter turnout in recent general elections

Year	1979	1983	1987	1992	1997	2001
% turnout	76.1	72.2	75.3	76.3	71.5	59.4

Source: Butler and Kavanagh (2001: 260–1)

Table 8.4 Political participation in various categories

Type of participation (% of people surveyed)	1979	1984	1989	1994
Helped with fundraising	26	26	34	27
Urged someone outside my family to vote	18	16	18	18
Presented views to an MP or councillor	15	15	15	14
Took active part in political campaigning	3	4	3	3
Stood for office	1	1	1	1
Been elected officer of an organization or club	13	14	12	11

Source: Parry and Moyser (1994)

in 1985). Table 8.4 displays the findings of a MORI survey on political participation. The table indicates that rates of activity have remained relatively stable, although involvement in politics remains a minority interest. Research also suggests that the active minority tend to be educated, middle-aged, and middle-class (Parry and Moyser 1994).

Although the membership of environmental groups has grown rapidly in recent years, the membership of political parties has been in decline since the war. The Conservatives had 2,800,000 members in 1952, but this figure had fallen to 400,000 and is still dropping (Davies 1995). The Young Conservatives had 160,000 members in 1949 but has recently been abolished due to insufficient membership levels (Davies 1995). The Labour Party has enjoyed a surge in new members, largely based on the appeal of Tony Blair and the public desire to oust the Conservatives after eighteen years. But size of membership alone does not reflect activity: the majority of members are inactive.

There also appear to be growing levels of apathy and political distrust, concentrated among the young. Research by Demos found a 'profound disconnection from the political process among young people' (Mulgan and Wilkinson 1995), which has been supported by studies elsewhere. A study for Barnardo's found that 59 per cent of young adults surveyed had 'no interest in politics' and that only 21 per cent supported a political party (*Independent*, 9 March 1996). Paradoxically, although young adults in Britain are not interested in politics or political parties (Allgier 1995), they are concerned with issues that they perceive as being apolitical such as racism, sexism, animal rights, and environmental issues.

The concerns about declining participation and a loss of trust in the political process have led to an important discussion about what is called 'social capital'. This refers to an argument developed by Putnam (1993) that participation occurs when the 'dense networks of civic engagement produce a capacity for trust, reciprocity and co-operation ("social capital"), which in turn produces a healthy democracy' (Lowndes and Wilson 2001: 629). In other words, the more people join together in face-to-face meetings either as neighbours or through clubs and societies (which may have nothing to do with politics), the more likely they are to work together in an attempt to solve problems that affect their community. Contact produces trust that enables people to work together without state compulsion to solve problems. From this perspective, vibrant voluntary associations are an indication of a healthy civic culture and wider political participation. In the United States, Putnam (1993) has argued that there has been a loss of social capital as people have turned their backs on voluntary associations, preferring to spend more time in the home. Hall (1999) has found in the British case, however, that on the whole there has not been a decline in the membership of associations—indeed, there is an indication of a rise in membership. Hall's conclusion is that this continued associational activity has coincided with high levels of political engagement in Britain. Yet he identifies a growing mistrust of politicians and an increase in direct action such as signing petitions and joining demonstrations.

The Blair Labour Government has explicitly attempted to encourage participation at the local level, underpinned by what it refers to as its 'democratic renewal programme'. Lowndes et al. (2001) observe that nearly half of all the local authorities in their survey were using innovative methods in order to encourage participation, such as citizens' panels, focus groups, and community planning fora. The Labour Government is concerned with issues of social capital and the low levels of turnout in local elections, and is therefore encouraging local government to adopt new forms of participation.

Conclusion

With changes in the nature of the state and public policy, the way that citizens relate to the state has changed. Traditionally, politics was seen as an elite activity, and interest-group participation tended to occur through closed policy networks where pressure-group leaders met with senior officials and ministers. In the 1980s these arrangements were challenged: the Conservative Government undermined many of the closed policy networks of the postwar era, and created new relationships with a different set of interests. At the same time, new forms of political participation occurred through the growth of direct action and attempts to encourage participation at the local level. How do these changes affect the policy process? In some ways, policy-making is more complex. With policy networks, government has considerable control over the political agenda—it is to an extent predictable. With the rise of direct action and interest groups operating at different levels, it is harder for the government to control the political debate, as we have seen in the case of GMOs and the fuel protest. However, this does not mean that the government has become powerless in the face of pluralist pressure groups. It is still government that makes the key decisions and has to react to pressure group demands. As a consequence, government is able to make concessions without changing the overall direction of policy. What we have seen in the voluntary sector is a shift to non-state groups delivering public policy. Yet these groups are often dependent on the state for funding, and are increasingly state-regulated. And this is not a new development—non-state groups have long developed and delivered public goods.

KEY POINTS

- The last thirty years has seen an increased role for groups in civil society in the policy process.
- There have been important changes in the closed policy communities that traditionally dominated key policy areas.
- The Thatcher Government in particular attempted to challenge the role of pressure groups in the policy process.
- The Labour Government, especially in the period following the 1997 general election, used pressure groups as an important input into the policy process.
- The rise of New Social Movements has seen some pressure groups operate outside the traditional political institutions.
- Globalization and European integration have changed the terrain upon which pressure groups operate. Increasingly, they are lobbying at the transnational level.
- Increasingly the voluntary sector is becoming involved in the delivery of public services.
- There is growing concern about the level of participation in politics today and the impact this is having on social capital. The government is looking at ways of enhancing participation in public life.

KEY QUESTIONS

1. How has the role of pressure groups changed in the policy process?
2. How have New Social Movements affected policy-making?
3. How has the role of voluntary groups changed in the delivery of public services?
4. What is the impact of declining political participation?

KEY READING

For an outline of the theoretical issues see Smith (1993). For very useful accounts of the role of pressure groups see Coxall (2001) and Grant (2000). Russell et al. (1997) investigates the changing role of voluntary groups. Putnam (1995) and Hall (1999) discuss participation and social capital.

KEY WEBSITES

Nearly every major pressure group now has a website. Some examples include: www.foe.co.uk/ www.charter88.org.uk

www.anl.org.uk/campaigns.htm
www.amnesty.org/
www.tuc.org.uk/
A useful website for looking at the work of new social movements at a global level is
www.protest.net/. Also useful is the Reclaim the Streets site: www.gn.apc.org/rts/. There are
also sites for volutary groups: www.oneworld.net/. For a comparative analysis of social capital,
see www.cspp.strath.ac.uk/index.html?catalog9 0.html. For an examination of civil society, see
www.civitas.org.uk/, www.oxfam.org.uk/. For a very useful site on encouraging participation at
the local level, see www.urbanwebsolutions.com/planning/ and for an example of a
participatory organization, see www.napp.org.uk/.

9

CHANGING RELATIONS BETWEEN MINISTERS AND CIVIL SERVANTS

INTRODUCTION

The image presented of the nature of governing Britain in the 1950s is one in which Westminster and Whitehall is portrayed as the central site of political authority (see Chapter 1). Here, ministers and civil servants are perceived as the key actors who determine policy outcomes. During the 1950s, in terms of policy the British core executive was regarded as the most powerful actor in the policy arena, and policy was made and implemented in a top-down manner (see Chapter 1). In this period, even the institution conferred with formal powers to restrain the executive, Parliament, was seen as ineffective at carrying out this constitutional role. For example, Hill and Whichelow (1964) addressed this theme in *What's Wrong with Parliament?* They observed the

ease with which a determined Government can achieve their ends, whether or not the House approves of them . . . The *raison d'être* of Parliament is called in doubt. In the public eye, the first thing that is wrong with Parliament is that it no longer controls the Government's handling of the people's money. (pp. 20–21)

The thrust of Hill and Whichelow's observations are not dissimilar to those of Lord Hailsham, Lord Chancellor in the first Thatcher Government, who viewed Britain as an 'elective dictatorship' in which there was a misuse of power by the executive.

The importance of these arguments, within the context of this chapter, is that commentators regarded the core executive (in particular ministers and civil servants) in the period after 1945 as omnipotent actors who dominated the policy process and operated with few constraints on their power. In this snapshot, then, policy-making is seen as taking place in a closed, secretive, and elitist world; it is top-down and the core executive is the central, most powerful actor (see Figs. 1.1 and 1.2).

If we now glance at the second snapshot—the 'picture of governance', taken some time in or after the 1980s—the scene has changed. The policy arena has become much more diverse and crowded. Policy-making is regarded as a process of interaction between many different actors, across a variety of terrains. Ministers and civil servants have been reduced to being only one group among many actors involved in the making and implementation of policy. Exponents of this view argue that the recent shift from government to governance has significantly affected both the role and the power of ministers and civil servants in the policy process. As Pierre and Stoker (2000: 29) observe:

Twenty years ago political institutions and political leaders were much more self-reliant, and it was assumed—for good reasons—that the state governed Britain. Today, the role of the *government* in the process of *governance* is much more contingent. Local, regional and national political elites alike seek to forge coalitions with private businesses, voluntary associations and other societal actors to mobilise resources across the public-private border in order to enhance their chances of guiding society towards politically defined goals.

As we saw in Chapters 7 and 8, the impact of the changing nature of the state in recent decades has led a number of authors to suggest that the process of governing Britain has now become a matter of multi-level governance, in which politics is played out over many different terrains involving a wide array of disparate actors (see Marks et al. 1995, Smith 1999, Jessop 2002, Pierre and Peters 2000). A key theme of multi-level governance is that both the power and role traditionally enjoyed by Westminster (ministers) and Whitehall (civil servants) in the policy-making arena has become much more circumscribed. In this chapter we will examine the changing role of ministers and civil servants in the context of changing modes of governance and, in particular, the changing nature of their relationships. We will also examine the way in which the increasing role of the Treasury and the Prime Minister has affected departments.

....

Ministers and civil servants: an interdependent relationship

The Westminster model is based on a number of assumptions that create a particular set of relationships between ministers and civil servants (see Chapter 3):

- Parliament is sovereign.
- Ministers are accountable to Parliament.
- Civil servants are neutral and loyal to ministers.
- Decision-making power is located in the executive.
- Government is legitimized by a public-service ethos.
- The system of decision-making is secret.

The constitutional position is that ministers decide, whilst officials advise and ministers then answer to Parliament. The underlying assumption is that officials are apolitical and do not have their own personal, political, or policy preferences to pursue. However, the secrecy of the British government hides some of the key elements of the roles and relationships of ministers and civil servants.

Unlike the image portrayed in either constitutional textbooks, where ministers are meant to be dominant, or the *Yes, Minister* model where officials collude to undermine and override their minister, the daily reality is that ministers and officials are dependent on each other. Ministers and officials have different resources, and in order to achieve their goals, they have to exchange resources (see Table 9.1). They are not competing with each other, but they are operating on different terrains. Ministers are concerned with particular policy decisions and officials are concerned with making decisions within a constitutionally informed framework. As long as they have ministerial (and therefore constitutional) cover, officials have considerable autonomy. They do not oppose ministers, but through their reproduction of the Whitehall game and by providing 'facts' for the minister, they determine the terrain on which ministers operate. They are then empowered to undertake decisions within an accepted (i.e. constitutionally proper) framework, reflecting the general goals of the ministers.

The basis of the postwar expansion of the modern state was the close interrelationships between officials and ministers, who were in effect working together to develop the welfare state. As we saw above, the British conception of democracy and representation assumes that decisions are made by those with knowledge and that the mass of people are excluded from this process, only exercising their democratic function every five years. The central presumption is that Whitehall knows best, and decisions can be made in secret through the complex interactions of officials and ministers. Commentators such as Marquand have referred to this as 'club government' (see Marquand 1991, Dunleavy 1999, Judge 1999). This system was convenient for both officials and ministers because the constitutional convention was that the minister decides but officials advise. This convention was useful to both sides, as it allowed ministers to appear decisive and officials neutral and apolitical. Moreover, the much more complex reality of policy-making was hidden by the ethos of secrecy.

Table 9.1 The resources of the Prime Minister, ministers and officials

Prime Minister	Ministers	Officials
Patronage	Political support	Permanence
Authority	Authority	Knowledge
Political support/party	Department	Time
Political support/ electorate	Knowledge	Whitehall network
Prime Minister's Office	Policy networks	Control over information
Bilateral policy-making	Policy success	Keepers of the constitution

Source: Smith (1999)

This interdependent relationship of ministers and civil servants was actually established by the rules set out in the Haldane Report of 1918. The aim of Haldane was to fuse together both sets of actors to form 'an ever-present, indissoluble symbiosis between ministers and civil servants so that they were almost one person' (Foster 2001: 726). In one sense then ministers and officials operate as a single actor, and it is the aim of a good civil servant to know the minister's mind (Richards 1997). As one official said in an interview:

Things actually work best when ministers and their staff have got a mutual understanding which was the kind of Civil Service I joined back in the '50s . . . it never struck me then that there would be any serious conflict between my minister and my bosses up in the office. They would all be in cahoots.

Another Home Office official gave a good indication of how the Haldane model worked:

Perhaps ten or twelve people would spend the morning discussing, for example, majority verdicts [for juries], which is what we brought in, which was a very important change. It is very difficult to say that the policy was decided by the Permanent Secretary or the Department or by the minister, it really developed from an interchange of views. *I thought this was perhaps the Whitehall machine at its best.* (Emphasis added.)

From this interdependent relationship, officials and ministers gave and received different things. Officials brought expertise, in terms of both policy-making and the bureaucratic process, loyalty, and the ability to protect ministers. Ministers brought the political authority for officials to act. Officials, who are regarded as neutral, therefore cannot act without ministerial cover. Ministers are the actors who have to authorize the decisions of a department. Without this ministerial support the officials can do little. This is why officials do not like indecisive or politically weak ministers. In order to illustrate the dynamics involved in the relationship between a minister and his/her department, let us consider what either a department or a minister is capable of achieving without the other. For example, a department can draft policy, but it cannot ensure it will become law; it needs a strong minister to gain approval for its initiatives. A minister who cannot win a battle in Cabinet or with the Treasury is a liability to his/her department. Moreover, it is usually only ministers rather than officials who can gain the support of the Prime Minister. Whilst the Prime Minister does not dictate policy, s/he can either veto a policy or, in alliance with a minister, get a policy through Cabinet and Cabinet committees (see Boxes 9.1 and 9.2). A minister without the support of his department, or a department that lacks an effective minister, is effectively rendered impotent. As a recent example, the DTI welcomed Peter Mandelson as their new Secretary of State, if only briefly (1999–2000), as the Department recognized the impact such a political heavyweight could bring with him. A number of civil servants referred to him as their first 'heavy hitter' in Cabinet since David Young (1987–9) and Michael Heseltine (1992–5) (see Marsh et al. 2001).

Despite the constitutional mythology maintained by the Westminster model, officials have highly political roles. Whilst officials are not political in a party sense,

---

Box 9.1 The role and power of the Prime Minister

The Prime Minister does have more resources than any other actor in government. However, the use of these resources depends to some extent on the political and economic
context and the support of the Cabinet and the Chancellor. Despite the focus of much of
the literature on the style of the Prime Minister (see King 1985, Foley 2000, Rawnsley
2001, Naughtie 2001), the reality is that the Prime Minister is in a highly constrained
position. Therefore, if s/he is to have an impact s/he has to ensure support and build
alliances. Nigel Lawson reveals that the Prime Minister's power is essentially negative:
'The Prime Minister's main power is the veto and that is the main way that the Prime
Minister exercises his or her power. The Prime Minister basically cannot force her proposal on a minister who is not prepared to go along with it, but they have a very
effective power of veto.'

Box 9.2 Cabinet committees

Much of the significant work of government is now conducted in Cabinet committees,
with only major strategic issues going to Cabinet. A matter will be referred to Cabinet if
there is a major change in policy, if there is significant conflict between departments,
or if there is a particular crisis such as foot-and-mouth. Cabinet committees are the
institutional mechanisms for combining departmental autonomy with collective
government. If ministers and departments are to succeed, they need to ensure that
their proposals are supported in these committees. Without agreement, they will get no
further. So, despite the decline in formal Cabinet, cabinet government through committee is still important. However, an increasing number of commentators believe that
committees are often being bypassed, as Prime Ministers increasingly work directly with
ministers or through ad hoc committees of ministers and close advisers. Nevertheless, it
is significant that Blair set up a War Cabinet to deal with the conflict in Afghanistan,
indicating the continuing legitimizing role of cabinet mechanisms.

---

they are political in two senses. First, they frequently make decisions of highly
political importance. Most decisions are not made by ministers, but by civil servants. These can be relatively small decisions but, for the person involved, highly
significant—such as whether someone receives a benefit or is given refugee
status—or relatively large-scale decisions—such as whether to grant an export
licence to an arms company. Moreover, when ministers make decisions, it is often
based on the advice of officials.

Second, officials fulfil an important political role for ministers in terms of the
political game in Whitehall and Westminster. They provide cover for ministers by
furnishing them with the answers they need for questions in Parliament and for
select committees. They can provide the form of words that can enable a minister
to respond to a question, but not necessarily to answer the question or even evade

the question. For example, in the BSE crisis, it would have been civil servants who composed the phrase: 'There is no evidence of a link between BSE and CJD.' They could say that because there was no evidence, but this did not mean that that there was no link between BSE and CJD.

The other important political role of civil servants is in Whitehall battles. Despite the myth of collective responsibility, central government is not a unified organization with ministers working together for the common good. Rather, it is the site of intense departmental conflicts. According to Ponting (1986: 102):

Much of the work of Whitehall is institutionalised conflict between competing interests of different departments. Each department will defend its own position and resist a line that, while it might be beneficial to the government as a whole or in the wider public interest, would work against the interest of the department.

Consequently, officials are often attempting to defend 'departmental turf' or working out alliances with other departments, in order to get departmental policy through. The Scott Report into the sale of arms to Iraq indicated the extent of conflicts between the DTI, the Ministry of Defence, and the Foreign Office (see Smith 1999). Likewise, one of the reasons for delays in making decisions in the BSE case was that MAFF was concerned to keep other departments off its turf.

This symbiotic relationship also meant that officials were highly influential in terms of policy-making. Below, an official provides a useful indication of how things have changed in recent years:

My clear impression is that civil servants had much more weight in 1947. The then Permanent Secretaries were powerful. Donald Ferguson obviously had a major influence on the promulgation of policy, and there was one minister and one Parliamentary Secretary. It was very clearly established that in the minister's absence the permanent secretary was in charge of the Department, and I think that they had very great weight in the promulgation of policy. That probably continued through to the '70s, but perhaps it was linked to the rather sharper, or much sharper, division between political parties from the '70s onwards. The influence of civil servants did become less, and there were more junior ministers around and they were given areas of responsibility and wanted to be consulted on those areas of responsibility and take decisions in them.

There was a sense that whoever the minister was, the department would generally continue on its own terms.

This relationship had important implications for the policy process. Despite attempts to standardize and to ensure rational processes of policy-making from Fulton (1968) to Blair (1997), the nature of the policy process changes frequently across time, policy area, department, officials, and ministers. The most common methods of developing policy were:

- The problem is identified, and an official, usually a Grade 7 (although there was variation from department to department) reviews the evidence, consults interests, and develops proposals which will then go to a Grade 3 or Grade 2 before being presented to a minister.[1] An example would be the development of the 1986 Public Order Act (see Hay and Richards 2000). The genesis of that review was a specific event: the murder of Blair Peach in 1981. For over five years the review slowly progressed, until an official was asked to draft proposals for a White Paper. The official was then charged with reviewing the existing legislation and consulting relevant bodies. He established a consultative group, which met very intensively over the first three months, reported back to the Home Office, and led to the drafting of the 1986 Act.

- The problem is identified and a committee is established to review and consult before reporting to a Grade 2 or 3 or maybe the minister. In health and social security policy, it has been relatively common when developing a major policy initiative to establish a formal committee involving ministers, officials, and outside experts to review policy and develop policy proposals. The 1986 Fowler Review set up 'review teams' which took evidence of various elements of social security policy. Some of these teams were chaired by the Secretary of State and involved outside experts.

- Response to a problem identified by an agency at operational level. This was the case over the payment of the Job Seekers' Allowance. Agencies play a crucial role in identifying problems with implementation, anomalies in policy outcomes, and contradictions in policy goals. Often, if they identify these problems in a non-political manner, they can be fairly successful at persuading the parent department to review the policy.

- Response to a crisis. Two classic examples are the Football Spectators Act (1989) and the issue of dangerous dogs (1991). There are enormous expectations on ministers to respond when things go wrong. This is particularly true in the Home Office, where the media pays a great deal of attention to issues of law and order, following events such as Dunblane (1996) or the inquiry into the murder of Stephen Lawrence (see Cm. 4262-I). The consequence is that ministers are often required to act quickly and legislation is to some extent made in an ad hoc manner—in the Whitehall phrase, 'policy-making on the hoof'. Thatcher responded directly to football hooliganism by pushing the Football Spectators Act with the aim of creating a membership scheme. The difficulties of the scheme were revealed in the more considered review of the Taylor Committee following the Hillsborough disaster, and the proposals were dropped.

- A policy is developed within the department and pressed on the minister. The classic example is the abolition of retail price maintenance which the Department of Trade kept pushing on ministers until it was finally accepted by the Heath Government (1970–4) (Lawson and Bruce-Gardyne 1976). Other examples are the decision to build pressurised water reactors that the Department of Energy first pushed on Tony Benn in 1974. He resisted, but they were later accepted by David Howell, Secretary of State for Energy 1975–9. In

---

[1] For aiding comprehension, we have used the pre-Senior Management Review grading structure.

the 1980s and 1990s, the DTI developed policy on information policy that it presented to ministers.

• Policies are developed by a minister either through ideology or as a response to a particular problem. This was Peter Lilley's approach when he was Secretary of State in the DSS (1992–7). Lilley was clear that he wished to reform social security because he thought that there should be less reliance on state provision. Consequently, he was the main force behind reforms in social security policy in the 1990s.

It is also important to note that there is a great deal of variation in the manner in which policy is made in each department; despite notions of a standardized Civil Service, departments have a great deal of autonomy in how they organize themselves. Nevertheless, it was the case that at the senior level decision-taking often occurred in a seminar-type forum where officials and ministers would discuss various ideas and come to an agreement about what was the best way forward. This, of course, assumed a seamless web between officials and ministers and no real tension in underlying beliefs and values.

Policy networks in Whitehall

The variable nature of policy-making points up the difficulty of applying policy networks to Whitehall.[2] Although there are clearly recognizable policy networks, rarely are they stable over a long period of time. Whilst there are a limited number of stable and well-institutionalized networks—for example the relationship between the Association of Chief Police Officers (ACPO) and the Home Office—the majority of networks are temporary, flexible, and fast-moving. As one Home Office official said: 'Yes there are a lot of policy networks but they are very individual in the Home Office.' The fluid nature of the networks within Whitehall is possible (whilst retaining an identity of networks) because the rules of the game are well established; when an official joins a network, s/he knows how to act and is aware of the sets of beliefs which underpin the system. According to one official, these networks are relatively fragmented because they cross-cut Whitehall:

Between the department and the Whitehall community, there were lots of horizontal linkages. They would start from a particular policy area of the department and (in the case of homelessness) end up in casualty departments, housing interests which take you into the Department of Housing side of the Environment, local authority interests which take you into the local authority side of the DoE, income support, social security interests because they are paying all the bills, the voluntary sector, the Salvation Army, Crisis, Centre Point. Organizations like that are dealing with the homeless, and they involve the Home Office because the Home Office then had responsibility for the voluntary sector and so it went on.

---

[2] For a full discussion on the nature of policy networks, see Ch. 8.

If you go to the simplest, most self-contained policy issue which just ran across all White-hall but actually began in the Department of Health—just think of AIDS, which if you had to find one person in Whitehall who was 'AIDS King' it was the Chief Medical Officer. But every Permanent Secretary was represented on a committee which at a ministerial level Willy Whitelaw chaired or the Cabinet Secretary.

Networks within the core executive, as opposed to those between Whitehall and outside groups, have a number of specific features:

- The absolute boundary of who is included is relatively limited, but within Whitehall the networks tend to be messy and ill-defined and thus closer to issue networks than policy communities.

- Members of networks will often be institutionally defined. People with specific roles will have tasks that include them in particular networks. At the same time, however, some networks may be interpersonal, and break down or change greatly with the removal of a particular individual.

- Many networks will be informal, and will exist in order to overcome the rigidities of formal hierarchies.

- At different times and within different networks, both ministers and civil servants act as gatekeepers, determining who is part of and who is excluded from participation (see Hay and Richards 2000).

- If networks are more often informal, then the institutionalization of power will occur more through cultures and values than through institutional forms. Thus, as Heclo and Wildavsky (1981) suggest, it is important to understand the actor's perceptions of the organizational forms which face them. It is also important to understand the way in which actors re-create those organizational forms (Giddens 1986).

Networks are important because much policy-making and intra-organizational contact in central government is not through formal institutions but through contacts of informal networks. It is important, therefore, to understand how these networks operate and affect policy outcomes. Moreover, networks involve the institutionalization of beliefs, values, cultures, and particular forms of behaviour. They are organizations. Organizations shape attitudes and behaviour (Perrow 1970). Networks result from repeated behaviour, and consequently relieve decision-makers from taking difficult decisions. They simplify the policy process by limiting actions, problems, and solutions (see Berger and Luckman 1967). They define roles and responses. In so doing, they are not neutral, but reflect past and present distributions of resources and conflicts. Thus, when a decision is made within a particular network, it is not based on a rational assessment of all the available information, but will reflect past practices, past conflicts, and the culture and values of the decision-makers. In other words, networks are important because they affect policy outcomes. They provide the structure for organizational power and reflect past conflicts. By examining networks, we are looking at how power relations are institutionalized (Marsh and Smith 2000, Richards and Hay

2000). However, changes in the mechanisms of governance have had an impact on the way certain networks operate.

The increased complexity and interconnectedness of the policy-making arena in an era of governance has led to departments interacting with one another more now than in the past. This process has come into focus recently with the Labour Government's strictures upon the need for joined-up government (see Chapter 10), but it is also a response to a significant long-term problem.

Obviously, Cabinet ministers and their departments interact with one another in a number of ways (and, as we have seen above, there is often conflict). We have already briefly dealt with the Cabinet as a forum within which issues which cross-cut departmental interests can be discussed and resolved. In most cases, however, both Cabinet ministers and their departments have a vested interest in resolving issues earlier in the policy-making process. Clearly, Cabinet ministers are constantly involved in an informal relationship with their Cabinet colleagues. Yet departments will also have a range of informal contacts with most other departments. Often these may just be based on a series of telephone conversations between the civil servants in departments who are most involved in some issue which cross-cuts departmental responsibilities. At other times the issue will be of sufficient (and most likely recurring) importance to warrant the creation of a committee which draws upon ministers and officials from all the departments involved. It is this context in which many, if not most, issues are resolved, because many of these issues involve the detail of policy.

Since 1997, the Labour Government has emphasized the problems that arise from the absence of adequate machinery to deal with issues which cross-cut departmental responsibilities (see Chapter 10). The argument which underpins this view is that departments operate as 'chimneys'—that informal processes of the type sketched out above are insufficient to overcome such departmentalism, and thus prevent more effective policy-making. This commitment to joined-up government has had a number of consequences that have affected both Cabinet ministers and their departments.

First, a number of policy units have been created which are specifically designed to address issues which previously have been the concern of a number of departments (see Chapter 10). It must be acknowledged that part of the Labour Government's argument is that, because such important issues cross-cut departmental responsibilities, they are the primary concern of no one and so receive insufficient attention. The policy unit of this type that has received most attention is the Social Exclusion Unit, located in the Cabinet Office; but there are others, including the Women's Unit, which was initially located in the DSS but in 1998 moved to the Cabinet Office.

These units are an important feature of some areas of social policy-making, and departments and their ministers have to deal with them. The Social Exclusion Unit, for example, is an important actor in many of the policy fields with which the DSS is concerned. In addition, some of its concerns impinge upon the interests of the Home Office. Certainly, these units represent a significant change in the

policy-making environment within which ministers and their departments operate, and provide an important part of the context within which some departments
interact.

Secondly, the emphasis on joined-up government has also encouraged ministers
and their departments to cooperate more on issues of common concern. This
trend has been accentuated by the change in the role of the Treasury identified
below. Recently, therefore, the Treasury has become a key element in the policy-
making process within a number of social and labour market policy areas, which
brings key departments together to develop an agreed and workable policy.

It is important to note that ministerial and departmental discussion and
cooperation, both within and between departments, are not new. However, there
are some key points to observe:

- The nature of the British system of government means that there has always
  been the need for inter-departmental consultation and negotiation.

- In an era of governance, governing has become increasingly complex, making
  inter-departmental consultation and negotiation even more important than in
  the past.

- Recent changes, not all to do with the change in government in 1997, have
  accentuated the process.

The case study in Box 9.3, a brief consideration of the relationship between the
DSS (previously DHSS) and the DFEE (formerly Department of Employment) in
the area of employment/benefits, illustrates these points.

The breakdown of dependency

Policy-making is based on interdependent networks that involve officials and ministers. There have been a number of occasions, however, when relations between
ministers and officials have broken down, and this has created problems both for
ministers and officials. The breakdown in relationships often occurs when trust
fails to develop between ministers and officials. The symbiotic relationship
between ministers and officials depends on each playing particular roles. Civil
Servants are happy to obey their ministers, if ministers have involved officials in
the discussion of policy. They are less happy when ministers attempt to impose a
policy which undermines the departmental approach or goes against the advice of
civil servants. Consequently, ministers who have not operated in the way that
officials want often encounter problems, frustrations, and delays (see Tony Benn
section in Box 9.5). Usually, a breakdown occurs when ministers have had distinct
policy proposals that run counter to the departmental agenda: the officials are
mistrustful of what the minister plans to do, and the minister believes that officials
will try to undermine his/her goals. When Michael Howard was Home Secretary

---

Box 9.3   **Relations between the DSS and DFEE**

There has always a close relationship between these two departments because the level of benefits will always affect the level of employment, and vice versa. However, the extent of contacts has fluctuated depending on the particular policies being pursued by government. For example, an official who worked in the DSS in the 1960s argued that a significant increase in contacts and consultation resulted from the introduction of the Earnings-Related Supplement in 1978.

Nevertheless, the contemporary civil servants in both the DSS and the DFEE agreed that, more recently, it was the introduction of the Joint Social Agreement in 1996 that encouraged the two departments to work more closely together. Initially, there was conflict between the two departments about who should lead on the policy; this was subsequently resolved in Cabinet. However, once the legislation was introduced it was clear that it could not be implemented without close contact and cooperation between the two departments. An interdepartmental committee was established. A number of representatives from interest groups involved in this committee have emphasized that it is now commonplace to see civil servants from the two departments sitting next to one another at a meeting (see Marsh et al. 2000: 129). Their collective view is that 'it is difficult now to spot which civil servant is from what department'.

Such interdepartmental consultation, in this area like many others, has been growing in large part because of the increased complexity created in an era of governance, coupled to more complicated legislation. This has meant that more issues cross-cut departmental responsibilities. However, this process has also been reinforced by the increased role of the Treasury in policy-making in some fields and by the Labour Government's commitment to joined-up government. So, in the 'welfare to work' area, a fairly tight triad based on cooperation between the Treasury, the DSS, and the DFEE was created after 1997. The civil servants involved (mainly Grade 5s and 7s) met regularly, discussed a broad variety of issues, and shared a broad commitment to a common policy. There appeared little evidence of interdepartmental tension, and all were signed up to the Government's labour market policy. Indeed, the major concern of the civil servants seemed to be with devising and perfecting ways of measuring effective policy delivery.

(1993–7), he had a clear idea that the best way to counter crime was through harsher prison sentences. This view ran counter to the departmental line that prison did not work as a deterrent. So in the Howard era, there was conflict in the Home Office.

The changing role of ministers

Traditionally, government at the centre has depended on a close and symbiotic relationship between officials and ministers, and it is within this relationship that the key decisions are made. However, the argument of the governance literature is that this relationship has changed or, to an extent, broken down: that the particular problems associated with Howard and Benn are becoming more general (Campbell and Wilson 1995; Foster and Plowden 1996). In order to evaluate this claim, we need to analyse the role of ministers and officials. In the 1970s, Headey (1974) examined the role of ministers, and suggested that they had a number of roles (see Table 9.2). When compiling this information, Headey did not suggest that all ministers perform, or give equal value to, all the tasks listed above. Instead, he argued that the minimum role a minister may perform is listed first in each category, with more activist or dominant roles listed later. Headey (1974: 54–5) then contended that, because of the multiplicity of roles listed in Table 9.2, a minister faces a basic dilemma:

On the one hand, their reputation in Whitehall and Westminster is bound to depend on appearing to perform a range of roles satisfactorily. A minister's future career . . . is damaged if he gets a reputation as a loser in the tight little world of London SW1 . . . where politicians are dismissed in cryptic single sentences: 'he is a light-weight'; 'he kicks the ball through his own goal every time he goes to Cabinet'. On the other hand, pressure of time, the totality of the demands made on ministers, make it well-nigh impossible for them to be consistently active in the performance of all their potential roles. Some kind of choice has to be made. A minister has to decide his priorities, decide in which roles he will be active and in which he will seek to achieve only a passing level in the eyes of the political world.

More recently, Marsh et al. (2001) have constructed their own typology of what they regard as the present-day role of ministers (see Table 9.3). This is an adaptation of Headey's original typology, in which they account for the changes that have

Table 9.2 The Headey typology: the potential role of Cabinet ministers in 1974

Classification of roles	The minister's roles

Roles as head of department	Policy leadership roles:
	  policy legitimation
	  policy selection
	  policy initiation

	Management roles:
	  departmental organization ('organizing')
	  departmental morale ('motivating': affective leadership)
	  'controlling': checking departmental performance

Role as a member of the Cabinet	Departmental battleaxe; fighting for parliamentary time, Treasury money, etc. Cabinet all-rounder
Role as parliamentary and party leader	Political troubleshooter Piloting measures through Parliament and the party so as to maximize support
Public relations and brokerage role	Consulting with department's interest-group clientele Selling values, policies, department, self to relevant publics

Source: Headey (1974: 54)

taken place in the last thirty years which have altered and added to the role of ministers.

Table 9.3 identifies four generic roles that ministers today perform: a policy role, a political role, a managerial or executive role, and a public relations role. These roles are not necessarily mutually exclusive. Indeed, they often complement one another. For example, if a minister is to be proactive in his or her policy-making role, s/he will need to perform managerial or executive functions; these could include deciding on the extent of intra-departmental and inter-departmental discussions and interest-group consultation. Subsequently, the minister needs to steer the policy through Cabinet and Parliament, perhaps, at the same time playing a public relations role, convincing the electorate of the benefits of a particular policy.

In the next section we will examine the four generic roles of ministers identified in the Marsh et al. typology, focusing in particular on the extent to which these roles have changed in the last few decades.

The policy role

In 1974, Headey identified three types of policy role: the policy initiator, the policy selector, and the policy legitimator (or minimalist). The Marsh et al. typology argues that it is useful to subdivide Headey's policy initiator role because, while many ministers attempt to initiate in narrow policy areas, there are some (albeit very few) who try to change a department's broader policy agenda; the latter is termed an 'agenda-setter' (see also Marsh et al. 2000, 2001). We look at each of these categories in turn.

Agenda-setters

These are ministers who act as 'agents of strategic change'. They attempt to instigate a permanent change in a department's institutionalized policy preferences and culture which privileges certain policy outcomes.

Table 9.3 Ministers' roles today

Policy role	Political role	Executive or managerial role	Public relations role
Agenda setting	Advocacy of department's position in Cabinet	Departmental management	Overseeing department's relations with:
Policy initiation	Parliament	Executive decision-maker	interest groups public media
Policy selection Policy legitimation	European Union Party		

Source: Marsh et al. (2001: 133)

In the last thirty years a number of Cabinet ministers, both Labour and Conservative, have set out to change the broad agenda or policy line in their department—they are 'agents of strategic change' whom we can refer to as 'agenda-setters'. For example, Roy Jenkins, the Labour Home Secretary (1965–7, 1974–6), successfully instigated change in the Home Office in the 1960s and 1970s, while Tony Benn tried but failed to change the policy agenda when he was Secretary of State at the DTI (1974–5) and, subsequently, the Department of Energy (1975–9). From the Conservative Party, Nigel Lawson had a crucial effect on the Department of Energy (1981–3); David Young changed the DTI (1987–9); Peter Lilley influenced the DSS (1992–7); whilst Keith Joseph (1979–81) tried but failed to make a significant impact on the Department of Industry. What is interesting is a comparison between those ministers who were successful and those who failed to change the agenda of their departments. Box 9.4 provides a case study of a Labour and a Conservative minister who were both successful at altering the agenda of the department over which they presided. There have also been instances in which a minister set out to act as an agent of strategic change and attempted to alter a departmental agenda, but failed. Again, examples can be drawn from both Labour and Conservative governments (see Box 9.5).

To explain why Joseph and Benn failed in their attempt to act as strategic agents of change, whereas Jenkins and Lawson succeeded, is no simple task. A combination of factors may be important: internal and external constraints, the personal relationships involved, the personal and psychological make-up of the minister, etc. The key point here is that there is no single, dominant factor we can drawn on to explain failure.

One other issue deserves comment here. Analysing those ministers who successful acted as agenda-setters highlights the fact that the Thatcherite project affected various areas of policy at different times. In industrial policy, for example, a change in the Industry Department's strategic selectivity occurred in the mid-1980s under Lord Young, while in the DSS and the Home Office, it was the Major Administration which fully implemented policy changes, initiated during the Thatcher era (Ludlam and Smith 1996). Any attempt to assess the legacy of a Thatcher or Major effect thus requires disaggregation across individual policy areas (Marsh and Rhodes 1992, Dolowitz et al. 1996).

Policy initiators

A policy initiatior is a minister who, though lacking the goals or vision of an agenda-setter, is nevertheless prepared to take on his or her department in order to initiate a specific policy that may run counter to the department's strategic preferences.

Some ministers do not aim to change the overall direction of their department, but are willing to attempt particular policy initiatives that may rub against the grain of the department's own culture. For example, Patrick Jenkin, the Conservative Secretary of State for the Department of Social Security (1979–81), admitted:

Box 9.4 Successful agenda-setters

Roy Jenkins, Home Secretary (1965–1967, 1974–1976)

In the 1960s, the Labour Home Secretary Roy Jenkins effectively shifted the Home Office away from an agenda of social conservatism to one of social liberalism. As he explained in an interview: 'I had a very clear programme and saw my role as opening up a number of windows in the stuffy atmosphere of the Home Office. This was not overly difficult to do. A lot of Home Office officials were very eager to respond to a new liberal wind blowing in. I felt it was time for a change . . . and I did not find it that difficult to shift Home Office opinion' (see also Jenkins 1991: 179–85). A now retired Permanent Secretary from the Home Office witnessed, first-hand, the effect Jenkins had on the Home Office: 'In 1966, Jenkins had a very large, very immediate, profound and lasting impact on the selection of people in the Home Office and the ability to convey and permanently register his view and aims in philosophical as well as purely policy terms. His influence went both deep and wide.' The agenda that Jenkins introduced into the Home Office left an imprint on the Department that lasted well into the 1990s. The Jenkins agenda survived a number of changes in government, including the advent of the ideologically driven Thatcher Governments of the 1980s. As one senior Home Office official revealed in discussing the change of government in 1979: 'One has to emphasize the surprising degree of continuity between the two different governments, which, despite the Thatcherite approach, remained unbroken up until Douglas Hurd left the Home Office in 1989. Indeed, the continuity remained intact from Jenkins in the sixties, all the way through to Hurd. During that time, the Home Office did have a sense of a great deal of continuity in what it was doing and what its approach should be.'

Nigel Lawson, Secretary of State for Energy (1981–1983)

Nigel Lawson was a Conservative minister who effected wholesale change in the Department of Energy's agenda. In his view, the free market should determine Britain's energy policy, and he used his earlier experience as Treasury Secretary to help force an agenda change in the Department. The success of Lawson's approach, with its emphasis on privatization and the gradual erosion of the Department's commitments in the energy field, eventually led to the Department's demise in 1992. In an interview Lawson argued: 'My belief was that what was needed in the energy field was to apply economic principles, which included privatisation, and the market approach. It wasn't difficult because the Energy officials lacked the Treasury's self-confidence and were not really capable of the same degree of sustained argument and really a meeting with them would be very much shorter. They would put forward a proposal and you would shoot it down. They would be sullen but well mannered and then they would rather ruefully accept what you were trying to do.' Lawson was almost universally admired by Energy civil servants. For example, a now retired Permanent Secretary of Energy argued: 'the most formidable Secretary of State was Lawson. He was formidable and influential; part of it was intellectual and part stemmed from his political skill.' Similarly, an ex-Permanent Secretary argued that Nigel Lawson was the crucial driving force behind the privatizations introduced by the DEn. His civil servants produced briefs and then met Lawson to discuss them. As the same civil servant said: 'these policy meetings were the highest point of my time in the Department. They were great fun and everyone enjoyed them.' The civil servants liked the period because Lawson had weight in Cabinet and the Department became much more important within Whitehall. Many of the energy

> privatizations of the 1980s occurred after Lawson's time, but the civil servants were all agreed that it was he who set the agenda. Indeed, the success of Lawson's agenda was confirmed by the abolition of the DEn in 1992. This was justified on the grounds that there was no longer a need for this Department, as energy policy should be determined by the market.

I was a mandarin's Minister. I remember that when I first went into the Department . . . I met a group of civil servants. They said: 'Patrick we can't tell you how encouraging it is that, for the first time, we have a Minister who takes the papers away, reads them, comes in the next morning discusses them and makes a decision.' I said, 'But that's what you are supposed to do, isn't it?' And they said 'Yes, but you're the first we've had for a long time.'

Jenkin was not concerned with challenging the agenda of the DHSS. The dominant view of most of his officials was, as one official put it: 'There was continuity there; although the parties changed, the policy didn't.' Nevertheless, although Jenkin was generally a mandarin's minister, he was also prepared to initiate policy against the advice of his civil servants, as he did when he abolished the earnings limit for pensioners in 1986.

Policy selectors

This is a much less ambitious type of minister, who, rather than being proactive in making policy, is instead prepared to choose a particular policy initiative from a range of options presented by the department.

Some ministers are content to play the role of policy selectors: choosing from the alternatives set out by officials. Douglas Hurd accepts that when he was Home Secretary (1985–9) during the third Thatcher Government, he effectively acted as a policy selector. In an interview, he acknowledged:

Despite having experience of the Home Office as a junior minister in the early 1980s, when I was appointed Home Secretary I saw my role much more as managing the department and keeping an eye open for any potential crisis looming on the horizon, rather than introducing my own social agenda on law and order. In my time, I ensured the Home Office was a fairly transparent department in which to work, as I was most concerned to consult widely and heed the views of my senior officials.

Policy legitimators/minimalists

These are ministers whose role and impact within a department is relatively marginal, and whose main function is to legitimize or rubber-stamp departmental policy.

It was Headey (1974) who conceived this particular role for a minister who, at most, merely legitimizes departmental policy; unfortunately, he provides no examples. However, the last Conservative Administration provides examples of a number of ministers who made almost no impact when in office and who we can label 'policy minimalists'. In most cases, this was because they were in office only briefly or became overwhelmed by events. For example, Peter Lilley's short tenure

Box 9.5 **Failed agenda-setters**

Tony Benn: Industry Secretary (1974–1975); Energy Secretary (1975–1979)

The Labour Minister Tony Benn was convinced that the Civil Service was conservative. He argued that officials did everything they could to frustrate any radical change (Benn 1980). As he said in an interview: 'civil servants think that continuity of government works within the department and people come in and stay for a year or two in the bridal suite of the Grand Hotel but they still run it . . . I think they do think that and it's your job not to get angry about that, but just to shift it.' Benn wanted the Department of Industry, and subsequently Energy, to become departments of economic planning more supportive of the interests of the trade unions than of business. However, according to Benn, the Permanent Secretary at the Department of Industry said: ' "I take it you are not going to implement the manifesto." He actually said it to me. I said, "You must be joking" and I circulated the manifesto to all civil servants and told them, "That's what we have been elected to do." ' Benn believed that his officials intentionally thwarted the implementation of his agenda. Yet one official who served under him felt: 'Benn was not thwarted exactly, but he was certainly subjected to a good deal of advice that he found unwelcome.' The problem was that Benn upset his officials by ignoring and questioning their advice and by developing an alternative advice network, using Frances Morrell and Francis Cripps as special advisers, whom one official called 'his rather pernicious political advisers'. He also used his contacts in the trade union movement as a regular alternative consultative outlet often playing off the advice he had received from within his Department with that which TU officials had provided. Although constitutionally permissible, these actions did not endear Benn to his officials.

Benn's second problem was his isolation in Cabinet. As a Cabinet colleague, Merlyn Rees, rather irreverently observed of Denis Healey's reaction to Benn in Cabinet: 'Denis would sit there and Tony would go on and Denis's view was a little bit like that of Enoch [Powell], that the logic was good but the conclusions were balls. Denis would say "And now here comes the bullshit." ' Ultimately, Benn failed in his task to alter the Department's agenda. Indeed, if anything, by alienating his officials, he created considerably more intransigence within the Department. Bereft of prime ministerial authority, there was little he could do to bring his officials into line.

Keith Joseph, Industry Secretary (1979–1981)

In 1979, the Conservative Keith Joseph was appointed Secretary of State for Industry. He was confronted by a highly interventionist Whitehall Department. His intention was to introduce a new laissez-faire agenda, and he even distributed the works of Hayek and Friedman to his officials in order to demonstrate his commitment to a new approach. However, despite the opportunity provided by the perceived failure of the interventionist policies of the Wilson–Callaghan Administration and the 1979 Conservative election victory, Joseph had little success in changing the Department's prevailing world-view. In the words of one official: 'Keith Joseph didn't throw [interventionist policies] out of the door straightaway, he was willing to examine with us, very carefully, what we were doing, why we were spending this money and what effect it was likely to have.' Despite his ideological preferences, he was unable or unwilling radically to change the policy direction of the Department. As a Conservative colleague of Joseph and subsequent DTI Minister, Kenneth Baker, argued: 'Keith Joseph had a much greater intellect than either David Young or myself. But that made him indecisive. He could see both sides of the problem and could be seduced intellectually, as was the case when he was in Education as well.'

at the DTI (1990–2) left no discernible legacy. Elsewhere, John Moore, Social Security Secretary (1987–9), despite a rhetoric promising 'big ideas' on the reform of welfare policy, became overwhelmed by the task and was quickly removed. Lord Carrington and Patrick Jenkin admitted that when they were put into the new Department of Energy, they were so overwhelmed by an energy crisis that there was little, if anything, they could do (see Carrington 1988: 262–3). Most notably, David Waddington, as Home Secretary (1989–90), argued that he was constrained both by the lack of time and by the impact of the riots at Strangeways Prison. Consequently, he accepted that he made little impact on the direction of the Home Office:

I wasn't really there long enough to bring about major change and, particularly with all the problems we had in prisons and the Strangeways affair, one did tend to be absolutely overwhelmed by events as they unfolded. There wasn't really a lot of chance to bring about radical change even if one had wanted to do so. But then again, we did just begin . . . it was when I was at the Home Office that we were shaping up to big decisions about introducing the private sector into the running of prisons, but the actual decisions were not being made.

Summary

It is important to recognize that the roles and relationships of ministers do vary across departments and differing ministerial styles. The Home Office, having a firmly embedded culture and being well insulated from wider economic vicissitudes, is perhaps the most inflexible department in Whitehall. Its officials have generally been the most successful at persuading ministers to accept the departmental line. The DTI, possessing a culture whose nature could at times be characterized as being Janus-faced, made it much more susceptible to frequent change. There is a clear causal link between the porous nature of a department's culture and its capacity to resist change. The study by Marsh et al. (2001) raises some important issues concerning the role of ministers.

- Ministers should not be divided between policy, managerial, and ambassadorial roles (see Headey 1974). All of these roles are component parts of a minister's remit and, indeed, all are mutually reinforcing.

- All ministers have a policy role, and this has cumulatively increased in the last three decades. Partly because of ideology, partly because of external advice, and partly because of increased public scrutiny of government activity, ministers are now more concerned with formulating effective policy and making a difference.

- The impact of ministers depends on four main factors: the nature of the minister; the nature of the department; the relationships between the minister and the Prime Minister; and the wider political and economic context. Thus, unlike Headey, we contend that the impact of a minister is not solely dependent on his/her perception of the ministerial role, but develops within a particular context and a certain set of structural relations.

A continuum of ministers' policy roles

Ministers cannot be assigned a particular role. It is more useful to conceive of what they do as being on a continuum which reflects the degree of activity involved in the four different policy roles of ministers (see Fig. 9.1). At one end of the continuum we can identify agenda-setters, those ministers who were proactive while in office. At the other end of the continuum we can identify policy legitimators, based on the minimal role they adopted as ministers. We can label this end of the spectrum the 'inactive' pole.

Despite the complexity and variability of ministerial roles, there are a number of points we can make about the position of ministers today:

- It would appear that ministers have assumed a more proactive role, that there is therefore more, rather than less, power concentrated in the core executive. One explanation of this greater emphasis on proactiveness by ministers might be that, in an increasingly complex and fragmented policy-making arena, ministers have to take greater action and become more directly involved in the policy process, in order simply to maintain some semblance of control.

- The balance of power between civil servants and ministers has shifted, with ministers becoming increasingly dominant. A number of authors (Campbell and Wilson 1995, Foster and Plowden 1996, and see below) claim that the Whitehall paradigm—or, to put it another way, the dominant position of the Civil Service within the policy-making arena—has been destroyed by the changes wrought during the era of governance.

- Ministers are increasingly looking to outside sources for policy advice. The number of special advisers (political appointments paid for by the taxpayer) has fluctuated over time, but there is no doubt that it has increased in the last two

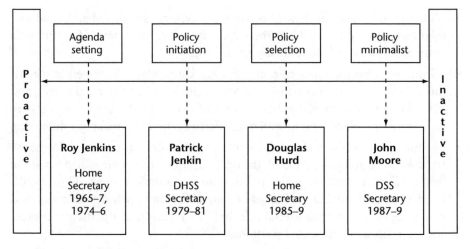

Figure 9.1 A continuum of policy roles

decades, most significantly since the election of the Labour Government in 1997. During the Major Government, for example, overall there were on average thirty-two special advisers, a number which rose to an average of seventy-four during the first term of the Blair Labour Government (see Table 9.4, Pyper and Robins 2000: 186, Toynbee and Walker 2001: 217). The cost of special advisers rose from £1.9 million a year under Major to over £4 million a year under Blair. Yet, as Toynbee and Walker (2001: 216–17) observe,

Many more special advisers were brought in to strengthen the influence of ministers over their departments, and to act as political brains bridging the divide between departments and politics. For all the venom poured on them by the Opposition, and resentment at usurpation from within Whitehall, the best of them were good brains collating bright ideas from outside the narrow Whitehall loop. They were able to explain policy better than civil servants, they made government more open.

Generally, advisers have tended to be of two types: policy advisers or public relations experts—in the current jargon, 'policy wonks' or 'spin doctors'. Both types of adviser can cause tension within departments, but the pattern is not uniform. One Treasury civil servant argued after the 1997 general election:

There is quite a lot of resistance [to special advisers]. Certainly for the first six to nine months [of the Labour Government] officials were heard to say: 'This will soon settle down and go back to normal.' But of course it never has. I think officials have increasingly understood that this is how it is going to be.

In contrast, a current DSS Grade 5 civil servant claimed:

I've never seen the current special adviser, which is some indication. I think the current adviser is more of a detail man, more than a spin doctor. The first lot of ministers had two advisers who were both into spinning rather than anything else. We had a fair degree of contact with them, which was fine. However, I think one of the advisers stirred up a lot of mistrust with the minister.

Of course, not all ministers have, or like, special advisers. One Labour DTI minister asserted:

I'm not all that keen on special advisers if I'm honest. I'm all for peer review but I don't think we make enough of our officials. They are very bright people and they certainly want to help and be part of transforming public administration . . . but in a sense they are being sidelined . . . they are now really there to [assess] radical suggestions coming from outside the department.

Table 9.4 Number of political advisers

Year	No. of advisers
1995–6	38
1996–7	38
1997–8	70
1998–9	72

Finally, a current special adviser in the DTI offers a more critical view from the 'other side':

I remember when I was a civil servant, I hated special advisers. . . . I think that the officials don't like advisers attending meetings with ministers and contributing, but what they hate most is advisers getting involved in the Department lower down. That is exactly what we have done to try to shape the way that policies are coming up by talking to more junior officials in order to see who is working on areas in which the minister is interested.

The pattern is complex and evolving, but clearly a minister with (a) special adviser(s) has to ensure that the relationship between the adviser(s) and the department is cooperative rather than competitive; this is an important new role for ministers.

In addition, the last Conservative Administration received an increasing amount of advice from consultancy firms. The use of consultants was a practice that continued throughout much of the 1980s, but in the Major years their use came under scrutiny, and was subsequently reduced on grounds of cost-efficiency. As one contemporary official observed:

Consultancy was the thing in the 1980s, but it was then rather criticized by Ken Clarke [Chancellor of the Exchequer 1993–97] in the 1990s due to the amount of money which was being spent on consultants. In particular, because he recognized he could get similar advice, at much cheaper cost to the taxpayers, from his own civil servants.

Thus at the start of the Thatcher Administration the use of consultants became an additional component of the policy-making process, and one that altered the balance of resources within the core executive. Their use was cut back during the 1990s, but they still remain a key alternative resource for ministers.

The changing role of officials

As we have seen above, from the 1950s to the 1960s officials were integral to the policy process and intimately involved in the making and taking of decisions. From the late 1970s onwards, however, ministers driven both by ideology and by the apparent failure of the Civil Service to solve Britain's recurrent social and economic problems developed a greater policy role. In addition, there was [as we saw in Chapter 4], a broader New Right critique of the efficiency of the Civil Service.

The changing role of ministers and the managerial reforms to Whitehall had a significant impact on the role of officials. They had to some extent a monopoly of policy advice, and an almost total monopoly of political advice (in the sense of how to play politics in the arenas of Whitehall and Westminster). A number of commentators (Campbell and Wilson 1995, and Foster and Plowden 1996) argue that the reforms of the Thatcher years destroyed the traditional role of officials. For example, according to Campbell and Wilson (1995: 60), the Whitehall model has been undermined with

civil servants increasingly defining their role as policy implementors rather than policy analysts, people who gave ministers what they said they wanted, rather than functioning as what they disparagingly call 'quasi-academics' who tried to show politicians the full consequences, adverse as well as positive, of their policy proposals.

In some ways, this is an accurate representation of changes that have occurred. After 1979 there was an attempt to assert a managerial culture over the public-service culture, and this has affected the nature of the relationship between ministers and officials (see Richards and Smith 2000). According to Foster (2001: 9), during the 1980s ministers continued to listen to officials 'but often seemed less responsive'. He also suggests that many ministers were indifferent to statistics, and this of course produced poor legislation, such as the poll tax and the child support agency. One of the traditional rules of the Whitehall system is that officials are the arbitrators of 'facts'. Ministers are expected to respect the official presentation of facts, when of course the facts can be interpreted in different ways. In a sense, the official version of the facts was used as the basis of policy but more ideological ministers in the 1980s had a different value set to draw on. This then created a conflict between the official framework of facts and the ministerial ideological framework.

It is increasingly the case that ministers rely much less on officials for policy advice. One of the main conflicts within the Treasury concerns the Chancellor, Gordon Brown, using his own advisers rather than Treasury officials in developing policy (see Naughtie 2001, Rawnsley 2001).

It is the case, however, that many officials rejected the notion that relationships had broken down in the 1980s and 1990s. According to one, commenting towards the end of the Major Administration: 'I think certainly the senior Treasury officials all get on very well with the Chancellor and the Chief Secretary.' It is also the case that, as in other areas, the personalism of the system and the degree of ministerial autonomy means that the nature of the relationship depends on the department and the minister. As one official pointed out:

Your experience around Whitehall depends very much on who your minister is and what his/her attitude is. Some ministers think they are there to run the Department and others think that the Permanent Secretary is there to do that and they are only there to give broad instructions. I think that will continue to vary depending on the personality and predilection of ministers.

Nevertheless, there have been some important changes in the day-to-day work of the senior Civil Service, and in some ways contradictory changes in the way their work is organized and what they do. There have been three important changes: an increased managerial role, a de-layering of the senior Civil Service and a greater role for Next Steps Agencies.

Managerialism

As we saw under the Haldane model (discussed in detail in Chapter 3), officials were integrated into the policy process. However, the managerial reforms introduced by the Thatcher Government (see Chapter 5) had a major impact on the role of officials. Senior officials are increasingly managing the department and policy advice, rather than being involved in day-to-day development of policy. One Home Office Permanent Secretary summed up this change:

I feel that all permanent secretaries, wherever you go, spend more time in the managerial role than they did fifteen years ago. A lot of the business of the Home Office, especially on the law side, is extremely difficult stuff. I'd say roughly I do a managerial part, a policy part, and an accounting officer part of the job. The balance depends on the time. I see my role as reading vast volumes of paper every night, and I read what goes through and if I feel things have not gone right I will intervene. If I feel the Home Secretary is doing something wrong, I will intervene and say 'This is wrong.' I'd brief myself and go and see him about it. If people came to see me and said they were worried about something that was going on, I would think about it and then go and see the Home Secretary

An official in the DTI said:

I don't mind spending my time on management. Indeed, I think I should, and the balance is about right. The balance is still approximately 60 per cent policy, 40 per cent management, but I think ten years ago it would have been 90 per cent policy and 10 per cent management.

De-layering

Whilst senior officials have taken on more of a managerial role, there has also been an attempt to break down the hierarchical nature of departments. In particular, the 1995 Senior Management Review saw the removal of one whole grade from the Whitehall hierarchy, and encouraged detailed policy work and policy advice to be handed down to lower grades of the Civil Service. A senior official in the DSS provides a good example of how things have changed:

The arrangement was that I have got a Grade 2 as head of policy and then he has four Grade 3s who are what we call Policy Directors who are responsible for the strategic direction of policy and who will have responsibility for seeing that some of the big policies are carried through . . . The benefit-based responsibility comes in at the Policy Manager level, Grade 5. There are twenty to twenty-five Grade 5s, each of them responsible for a particular benefit area, and their responsibility is to see to everything surrounding that benefit . . . Now a lot of the day-to-day work on the detail will be done right the way down. We have submissions going to ministers from HEOs, SEOs, Grade 7s. We push that kind of thing further down the Department than almost anywhere else.

In Foster's (2001: 733) view, the extent of de-layering and the increased contact between ministers and relatively junior civil servants has increased the likelihood of 'mistakes of fact and analysis'.

Agencies

The other great change that has affected civil servants has been the development of agencies (see Chapter 5). This has led to the majority of civil servants now working within agencies rather than departments (see Fig. 5.1). For senior officials, it means that a whole range of tasks has been removed from their responsibility. For example, senior officials are no longer concerned with the delivery of benefits; rather, they now manage relations between the department and their respective agencies. This in a sense creates new tensions and new roles for officials in terms of making and delivering policy. For instance, Foster (2001) points out that agencies challenge the Haldane principle that officials are the alter egos of ministers. There were several occasions under the Conservative Administration where acute conflicts developed between a Secretary of State and the chief executive of an agency because the chief executive believed that s/he had operational independence.

The changing role of the Treasury

For most of the postwar period the role of the Treasury was essentially negative: it attempted to stop departments spending. Often, it was not very successful in this goal because many of the welfare policies were demand-led: for example, the amount spent on health depended not on Treasury targets but on how many people needed to be treated. In the 1990s, both Conservative and Labour Governments attempted to make the Treasury more proactive. With the Fundamental Expenditure Review (1994) under the Conservatives and the Comprehensive Spending Review (1998) under Labour, departments had to justify their spending and keep within targets set by the Treasury. The Treasury, in particular under Gordon Brown, has become much more active in dictating policy developments within departments, especially in areas such as social security. According to Rawnsley (2001: 147), the Comprehensive Spending Review was 'an opportunity to delve deep into every department which he further exploited by binding ministers to his will with "public service agreements" with the Treasury'.

The Treasury now has spending teams, headed by a Grade 5 official, responsible for each expenditure area. In each department the key contact is still the Principal Finance Officer. Of course, the main responsibility of these teams is for expenditure. Inevitably, however, their brief involves policy, given the focus of the Treasury on improving economic performance. Once again, the DSS offers an excellent example of how this works. As Deakin and Parry (2000: 61) argue: 'After the 1997 election, the Treasury and the DSS formed something of an axis within government because of a shared ministerial agenda of targeting and means-testing.'

The Treasury's involvement in this policy area stemmed from at least two factors. First, Gordon Brown and a close colleague, Harriet Harman, the first Secretary of State for Social Security (1997–8), were both committed to a policy change which was at the core of the Labour Government's pledge to reform the welfare state. In the Treasury's view the New Deal, the flagship policy in this area, would contribute to a more skilled and flexible workforce and thus improve economic efficiency. And this policy was funded from the public utilities windfall tax, which also gave the Treasury a key concern in this policy area.

There is little doubt, then, that the Treasury is now crucially involved in labour market policy, most specifically in the Welfare to Work programme. It has established a Work Incentives and Policy Analysis Unit, and there are regular meetings between the teams responsible for this policy area in the Treasury, the DSS, and the Department for Education and Employment. Of course, this in part reflects the Labour Government's emphasis on joined-up government, but it also shows that the Treasury is now much more proactive in policy terms, when a policy area impinges upon its concerns. So, despite arguments concerning governance decentralizing control, recent years have seen much greater Treasury dominance.

The changing role of the Prime Minister

There has been much discussion recently concerning the increasingly presidential role of the Prime Minister (see Pryce 1997, Foley 2000, Hennessy 2001, Rose 2001). In addition, the importance of joined-up government and the increasing size of the policy unit has led to suggestions that the Prime Minister is becoming increasingly dominant in the policy process (Kavanagh and Seldon 2000, Riddell 2001, Rawnsley 2001, Naughtie 2001). One approach to the issue of governance is the strengthening of the centre. It can be argued that prime ministers have become increasingly proactive in policy-making and that they have had clearer policy visions. It is also true that Prime Ministers are less dependent on departments for advice and have, through the expanded policy unit, a source of independent policy advice that greatly increases policy-making capacity. In addition, both Thatcher and Blair have been much less willing to work through Cabinet or Cabinet committees. Instead, they have tended to work through bilateral relations with particular ministers, and once an agreement has developed between other ministers and the Prime Minister, it is difficult for a minister to block it. Since 1997 it has been the case that economic policy-making has been reduced to a tacit bipartisan coalition between the Prime Minister and the Chancellor.

However, despite the growing policy activism of Number 10, this does not mean that British government is now presidential:

- The majority of policy and decisions are still taken within departments. Even when the Prime Minister makes decisions on policy, they still depend on the expertise and information of departments for implementation.

- The Prime Minister is only human, and cannot control everything that goes on in government. Large chunks of Tony Blair's time has been taken up by Northern Ireland, Kosovo, crises like foot-and-mouth, and, more recently, the attacks on Afghanistan. He does not have the time to involve himself in the majority of areas of departmental policy.

- Many ministers have their own support and resources, and therefore the Prime Minister can only build alliances with them. He cannot, on most occasions, order them to follow a particular policy. It is clear that Gordon Brown has considerable autonomy, and that the Prime Minster is dependent on him for support.

- Despite increased staff, the Prime Minister's retinue is still small compared to the rest of Whitehall.

- Whilst prime ministers can act independently and without the support of their colleagues, to do so for any sustained period is likely to lead to problems. Thatcher was effectively forced to resign because she failed to recognize her dependence on her Cabinet colleagues (Smith 1999).

- Rose (2001) makes the point that whilst the power of the Prime Minister may have increased in his/her domain, the size of the domain has shrunk. The Prime Minister may have more control in Westminster and Whitehall, but globalization and Europeanization mean that s/he has less control over policy outcomes.

Summary

It is undoubtedly the case that a range of internal and external factors have changed both the roles of ministers and officials and the dynamics of the relationship between them. The main themes identified in this chapter are as follows.

- Ministers often have clearer policy ideas and will not always work to the departmental agenda.

- Ministers will use a range of sources for advice such as think tanks, task forces, and special advisers in developing policy. Indeed, officials may be excluded from policy discussions.

- Ministers are less trustful of officials.

- Officials are taking on a role that is increasingly managerial.

- Officials are less policy experts and more experts on policy implementation.

- Detailed policy work has shifted down the departmental hierarchy

- Prime Ministers have become more active in issues of policy but departments continue to be the sites of most policy-making.

- The Treasury is now a stronger constraint on the activities of departments.

Despite these changes, it is important to remember some key factors.

- The relationship between officials and ministers is highly variable. It depends on personalities, circumstances, and departments, and many officials and ministers have maintained relatively traditional relationships.

- The relationship between ministers and civil servants remains an exchange relationship. The nature of Britain's political system ensures that departments still want strong ministers, capable of defending their interests within Whitehall and beyond. On the other hand, ministers need good civil servants, capable of giving sophisticated advice, drafting good policy documents and legislation, and implementing policy effectively.

- The terms of the exchange are not equal or constant. Ministers are agents with significant resources. Only they have the authority to make policy. A department with a weak minister can achieve little or nothing. In addition, civil servants are trained, and most wish, to carry through government policy. As such, they expect ministers to make policy; indeed, they admire strong ministers with a policy agenda which they can get through Cabinet. Of course, not all ministers want to adopt, or are capable of adopting, such a proactive role.

The relationships involved in the core executive continue to be exchange relationships, but the exact nature of those exchanges is dependent on the skills, values, and interpretations of those occupying those roles. The personality of some ministers may push them towards a relatively inactive ministerial role. Others may feel too constrained by a departmental culture to innovate. However, ministers, and to a lesser extent civil servants, clearly do make a difference. The nature of the exchange is also affected by the broader context. So, for example, if a government—for example the Thatcher Government—holds the view that civil servants are too powerful, then this is likely to affect how ministers conceptualize the nature of the exchange between ministers and civil servants.

Most Conservative ministers also had a different view of what the relationship should be between ministers and officials than that enshrined in the traditional Westminster model. The Westminster model regarded officials and ministers as partners; civil servants could be trusted to exercise considerable discretion (Richards 1997, Richards and Smith 2000). In contrast, the Thatcher Governments were more critical of civil servants, whom they viewed as a cause of, rather than a solution to, what they saw as the core of the governance problem: weak, ineffective, government pursuing consensual policies because it was in thrall to particular interests. To break out of this stultifying embrace, government and ministers needed to exercise executive autonomy. To the Conservatives, the chief role of the Civil Service was not to advise on policy but to assist ministers in carrying out government policy. At the same time, the Conservatives were more willing to use special advisers (see above), although not to consult interest groups (see Chapter 8), as alternative sources of information. All this meant that Conservative ministers were encouraged to lead their department, to change departmental thinking, and, in Bulpitt's (1986) term, to project an image of governing competence. Foster (2001) avers that under New Labour the old Haldane style of relationships have not been re-established, with ministers relying much more on outside advice and special advisers.

Conclusion: pluralism, elitism, and the British system of governance

On the broader issue of power and the state, we wish to briefly return to Rhodes's differentiated polity model, outlined in Chapter 2. There we saw that the model is implicitly pluralistic in the image it presents. The model suggests that in an age of governance there are many actors participating in an increasingly fragmented policy-making arena. As such, the differentiated polity model is underpinned by the core tenet of pluralism: that power in the British political system is diffused.

It is the implicit pluralistic logic of this model that we suggest may need to be analysed in a critical light. The evidence we have presented here suggests that, despite the structural changes in the policy process over the last two decades—for example, the introduction of Next Steps agencies and the greater use of outside consultants and special advisers—the crucial actors in the policy process remain those located within departments, i.e. ministers and civil servants. These two sets of actors continue to act as the guardians of the policy process, which in turn continues to be predominantly top-down, closed, secretive, and elitist.

This then leads to the interesting question of why ministers and civil servants continue to subscribe to this particular narrow model of policy-making. They have continued to protect their dominant position in the policy process because it is in their mutual interest to do so. This is mainly a reflection of a particular view of democracy held by both sets of actors. This position can only be understood in its historical context, as part of what can be referred to as the British political tradition (see Marsh et al. 2001).

The British political tradition advocates a limited conception of popular representation and a conservative notion of responsibility. It is informed by a top-down view of democracy that downplays the importance of participation. Thus, there is virtually no emphasis within the British system on the notion that the government should be responsive to the population. Instead, ministers and civil servants believe in responsible, strong government, with its emphasis on the idea that the governing elite should be capable of taking strong, decisive action where necessary, even where that action is unpopular. It is a top-down view of democracy that asserts that government knows best. Both ministers and civil servants subscribe to this elitist, leadership view of democracy, and therefore have a shared interest in protecting it. So, despite the impact of governance, in which the structure, organization, and culture of the government machine has changed in the last two decades, in our view, power still remains predominately centrally concentrated, and is justified by the maintenance of a strong British political tradition (see also Chapter 11).

KEY POINTS

- Contrary to the normative assumptions of the Westminster model, a more appropriate reflection of the relationship between ministers and civil servants is one of co-dependency based on resource exchange.

- Power between ministers and civil servants is often better understood as a positive-sum rather than a zero-sum game.

- The context, resources, and structure of the different actors within the core executive changes over both time and policy area. This affects the nature of the dependency relationship.

- One of the more effective ways of understanding the relationship between actors within the core executive is the policy networks approach.

- Since the mid-1970s, ministers have become more proactive, and in particular the policy role of ministers has increased.

- Ministers have been increasingly willing to use sources of advice outside Whitehall.

- Senior civil servants have increasingly taken on a managerial role, with policy advice being pushed further down the Whitehall hierarchy.

- The emphasis in Whitehall has shifted away from policy expertise towards greater demand for more effective policy implementation.

- In the last two decades, the balance of power between ministers and civil servants has shifted, with ministers becoming more dominant; but they remained locked in to a co-dependent relationship.

KEY QUESTIONS

1. From your understanding of the contemporary role of ministers and civil servants, provide a critique of the Westminster model.

2. How and why has the relationship between ministers and civil servants changed in the last two decades?

3. Using the 'power-dependency' approach, critically assess the notion that the Prime Minister is *primus inter pares*.

4. What are the different sets of explanations that account for ministers and civil servants embracing an elitist model of the policy-making process?

KEY READING

The original and most enduring account of the relationship between ministers and civil servants, written over twenty-five years ago, is Headey (1974). The most contemporary and comprehensive analysis of their present role is Marsh et al. (2001); but see also Norton (2000). For a critical account of the effect of change on Whitehall, see Campbell and Wilson (1995) and Foster and Plowden (1996). An account of the power-dependent relationship between ministers and civil servants can be found in Smith (1999)and Rhodes (1997).

KEY WEBSITES

For websites of the House of Commons, see www.parliament.uk. The websites of the main political parties are: Labour, www.labour.org.uk; Conservatives, www.conservative-party.org.uk; Liberal Democrats, www.libdems.org.uk; SNP, www.snp.org.uk; Plaid Cymru, www.plaid-cymru.wales.com. For details on the work of both ministers and civil servants, a good starting point is www.open.gov.uk or, more specifically, www.cabinet-office.gov.uk. For debates on the role of ministers and civil servants, an interesting site is the Democratic Audit, www.fhit.org/democratic audit/index.html.

10 GOVERNANCE AND NEW LABOUR

INTRODUCTION

We have now established that two general key themes associated with the term govern-ance are fragmentation and the loss of power by the core executive to control the policy-making arena. The Labour Party under Blair has taken the perceived effects of governance seriously. For example, prior to winning the general election in May 1997, Tony Blair declared: 'People have to know that we will run from the centre and govern from the centre.' During Labour's subsequent first term in office (1997–2001), one of the key terms associated with their attempts at reform and renewal of the British state has been 'joined-up government'. These expressions of intent highlight the extent to which Labour has accepted the narratives surrounding governance and the pressing need to address the perceived problems of disaggregated policy-making and the loss of power from the centre of government.

In Chapter 1, we presented a snapshot of the British polity, taken in the late 1990s and labelled it 'An Era of Joined-Up Government' (see Fig. 1.3). Here, the picture is blurred. Labour's programme for achieving joined-up government is still ongoing: the snapshot has yet to develop fully. This means that here, any conclusions on the success of joined-up government can only be tentative. The actions that Labour has undertaken since 1997, however, have provided a number of signposts that indicate the likely course that their programme of state reform will follow. With this in mind, this chapter will assess the Labour Government's success at attempting to resolve one of the key challenges pre-sented by governance: the inability of elected governments to control and coordinate policy across the whole gamut of Whitehall. We will analyse the extent to which Labour has been able to 'wire the British polity back up', in response to the pathology of govern-ance: an increasingly crowded yet segmented policy-making arena which lacks control and coordination.

The chapter starts by providing an overview of the historical relationship between the Labour Party and the state. It then describes the state which the Labour Government inherited from the Conservatives after the 1997 election. The focus then shifts to the

Labour Government's programme of state reform. Initially, it examines the ideas under-pinning reform, 'the Third Way'. It then takes a thematic approach, focusing on the reform programme which has subsequently been pursued: the themes are reform of central government, devolution, regionalism, and local governance. The chapter concludes by addressing the extent to which fragmentation and conflict remains a key element of the policy-making process in Britain. Here, a series of questions are considered:

- What is the likelihood of success of the reform programme in enabling ministers to gain control of the policy process?
- What are the implications for the nature of power in the British polity?
- Is there a shift occurring from a pluralistic environment, as portrayed by the era of governance, to one in which the core executive once more controls the policy arena in a top-down, elitist manner?
- Alternatively, is the pathology of governance such that joined-up government is an unattainable goal and Labour's programme of 'wiring the system back up' is doomed to failure?

Labour, the state, and the Westminster model

Labour and the state

The Labour Party's attitude to the state is perhaps best understood as a product first of its own history and secondly of its experiences in power. McKibbin (1974: 241–2) emphasizes the importance of the trade union movement for informing both Labour's position on its own internal structure and its views on the nature of the state. The unions themselves had consistently supported the notion of statu-tory, national wage bargaining, and so had opposed any arguments that socialism could be achieved through a bottom-up, devolved model of government. Crucially, for much of the twentieth century this has informed the Party's own thinking on the unitary nature of the UK.

Secondly, the Party, or at least the Party leadership, has consistently maintained a peculiar reverence towards the British constitution (Harris 1982: 134). When in power, indeed, Labour has been primarily concerned with establishing its creden-tials as a legitimate and responsible party of government. As such, it has been willing to accept the constitutional status quo and the preservation of a system of government which, arguably, allows for the greatest centralization of state power of any contemporary, liberal democracy. As Marquand notes (1992: 44), the Labour Party's objective

has been to win power within the existing political system and to use it to change society in accordance with its ideology and the interests of its constituents. It has shown little sym-pathy for the proposition that a system permeated with essentially monarchical values might not be compatible with such a project.

Therefore, the dominant strand of thinking within the Labour Party throughout the twentieth century has broadly accepted the state as being neutral.

Labour leaders have also been optimistic about the ability of the state to achieve its political goals. In government, the Party has had a tendency to utilize the existing state institutions as part of a long-term strategy of reform based on the 'inevitability of gradualism' (see Jones and Keating 1985). This has been premised on the assumption of 'permanent revolution': a belief that once in power, Labour governments would retain power, thus allowing for a long-term process of incremental state reform (see Sharpe 1985: 14).

It was the two brief Labour governments of 1924 and 1929–30 which established both the ideological and political position which future Labour administrations would adopt towards the state. As Jones and Keating (1985: 43) observe:

[Ramsay] MacDonald's evolutionary brand of socialism was not concerned with destroying the state because he rejected the concept of class war and its corollary that the state was the instrument of one dominant class. Instead, he argued an expanded role for the state, creating socialist order out of capitalist chaos. MacDonald's constitutionalist strategy of gaining control of the state by parliamentary means, rejected any philosophy or policy which might call into question the very mechanism by which the socialist society was to be progressively introduced.

The willingness to pursue MacDonald's constitutionalist strategy has meant that the Labour Party leadership has not been willing to question the effectiveness of the long-established and firmly entrenched Westminster system of government. The history of Labour in government throughout the twentieth century has been conditioned by its willingness to accept the constitutional route, and in so doing embrace the Westminster model (see Box 10.1).

Labour and the Westminster model

Labour politicians have been conditioned, as much as Conservatives, by the Westminster model. As noted in Chapter 3, a key element of the Westminster model is the British political tradition which sees governing as a process conducted by a closed elite, constrained by an ethos of integrity and concern for the public good (Richards and Smith 2000) and contained within the framework of a balanced and self-adjusting constitution (Tant 1993). Within the model Parliament is theoretically sovereign, but as a result of the growth of both parties and bureaucracy in the last 150 years, the reality is executive or Cabinet sovereignty. A corollary of this model is the notion of ministerial responsibility, whereby it is ministers who make decisions and are at the head of hierarchical departments and accountable to Parliament. The primary source of legitimacy in Britain is thus Parliament (see Judge 1993). MPs are representatives and not delegates, and therefore act in what they see as the public good. Furthermore, the public in general do not have the necessary information available to make informed decisions. Therefore, secrecy is

---

Box 10.1 **Labour in power**

Attlee Government (1945–51)

Labour established itself as the party of the British state. This can be seen by; its programme to implement the Beveridge Report, state intervention, and nationalization, in an era which Miliband (1972: 272) refers to as the 'climax of Labourism'. Yet the political system and the constitution were left mostly untouched. The Attlee Government simply tiding up a few electoral anomalies and confirmed the limitations on the powers of the House of Lords

Wilson Government (1964–70)

A few minor attempts were made at reforming the machinery of government (through the Fulton Committee and a number of departmental changes). In this period, further attempts to reform the House of Lords were defeated by Labour dissidents voting with the Conservatives

Wilson–Callaghan Governments (1974–79)

In this period there was a half-hearted attempt to introduce devolution in Scotland and Wales. As Bogdanor (1997: 111–12) points out: 'During the . . . period of supposed post-war consensus, there were in fact quite striking differences between Labour and the Conservatives on social and economic questions, but they agreed wholeheartedly on the virtues of the Westminster model . . . For Labour has, historically, been a constitutionally conservative party, not a radical one. Indeed, for most of the post-war era, both Labour and the Conservatives have distinguished themselves from the Liberals by their support of existing constitutional arrangements.'

---

regarded by the political elite as the best means of ensuring that the right decisions are made in the interests of the people.

Underpinning this position is the fact that any significant shift towards greater openness increases the opportunities available to the media, the opposition parties, and interest groups to attack the government. This is clearly a reflection of the adversarial nature of the British political system. Yet publicly, secrecy has to be justified and assurances made that a closed system does not lead to corruption. The political elite argue that the ministers, and in particular civil servants, are imbued with a public-service ethos and thus serve the general, not their own, interest (see Smith 1999, Richards and Smith 2000). The relationship between ministers and civil servants is one of interdependence with ministers providing authority and officials expertise (see e.g. Fowler 1991: 112).

It is therefore significant that in the 1997 election campaign the Labour Party broke with its tradition and promised a wide array of constitutional and machinery of government reforms. Within days of electoral victory the Bank of England was made independent, and the first parliamentary session produced twelve constitutional Acts (see Hazell and Cornes 1999). Retrospectively, one of the defining features of the first term of the Labour Government has been its extensive programme of constitutional reform, marking a significant break from both its Conservative and Labour predecessors. To understand the extent of this reform programme, it is first necessary to describe the nature of the state Labour inherited from the Conservatives in 1997.

The state inherited by Labour in 1997

The state which Labour inherited from the Conservatives is one which has undergone a fundamental transformation yet remained, at least rhetorically, wedded to a set of constitutional arrangements which have changed only marginally in the last fifty years. But in the aftermath of electoral victory, the new Labour Government had no intention of unravelling the public-sector reforms introduced by its predecessors. As Massey (2001: 23) observes: 'Tony Blair was not about to reverse any of the Tories' substantive public sector reforms; he was and remains committed to consolidating and ensuring their implementation under his administration.'

Under the Conservatives, the make-up of the state dramatically changed (see Fig. 2.1), as a whole range of functions were siphoned off upwards to a supra-national level, mainly the EU, downwards in the form of agencies, regulatory bodies, quangos, and TECs and LECs, and outwards, most particularly in the form of privatization and market testing (see also Chapter 5). This process led some commentators to speak of a reinvention of government in which the state has been 'hollowed out' (see Rhodes 1997, Weller et al. 1997). Others portray the state as having undergone a process of reconstitution, in which its power and the size remains, but in a more diffuse, decentralized form (see Saward 1997, Richards and Smith 2000, Marsh et al. 2001). In a sense, the Conservatives created a hybrid state between the Keynesian welfare state and a neo-liberal notion of the laissez-faire state. They certainly disengaged from crucial elements of the economy through policies such as privatization and cuts in subsidies, but they were unable to break the welfare policies of the postwar settlement. Whilst they viewed state intervention as problematic, they were unable to overcome the weight of past institutional practices. So whilst there was a widespread introduction of managerial mechanisms, they were imposed largely on the existing structures of welfare provision such as the NHS and the benefits system (see Chapter 5). In other areas such as law and order, defence, and even education, the degree of state intervention increased (see Gamble 1994b). The state has undergone extensive reconfiguration, but the argument of the Government and senior civil servants is that these changes have no constitutional implications. The reality is, however, that they had dramatic implications both for sovereignty and for ministerial responsibility (Flinders 2002).

Paradoxically, eighteen years of Conservatism exposed the flexible nature of the British constitution as a myth—the constitution had remained static, while the state had been transformed. Nevertheless, the present Labour Government believes that the constitution only requires a degree of adaptation, not wholesale reformation:

The challenge facing us is that which confronted the Victorian reformers of the last century who, almost uniquely, gave Britain democracy without revolution. It is to take *a working constitution, respect its strengths,* and adapt it to modern demands for clean and effective government while at the same time providing a greater democratic role for the people at large. (Tony Blair, *The Economist,* 14 September 1996; emphasis added)

Next, we examine the philosophy underpinning the present Labour Government's view of the state. We then present a thematic presentation of the various areas in which Labour has reformed both the state and government. The analysis that then follows argues that by the end of its first term in office the present Labour Government had failed to understand the organic nature of the constitution. As Riddell (1998: 106) observes:

Many of these proposals tend to be viewed in isolation, with little attempt to relate them to their implications for the position of Parliament—and, in particular, of the Commons— but, in practice, many would have a much wider impact.

The Third Way and the state

Anthony Giddens (1994, 1997, 2000), author of *The Third Way,* has argued that the growth of economic and political internationalization, combined with much greater social diversification, has undermined the ability of the traditional state to promote or control social and economic outcomes (see Chapters 6 and 7). He contends that rigid hierarchical state structures, most often associated with Weberian models of bureaucracy and welfare states, are incapable of meeting the aspirations or fulfilling the needs of an increasingly heterogeneous society. As we saw earlier, in the 1980s and 1990s the response of the New Right to these problems was the pursuit of a neo-liberal project that advocated a much more minimal role for the state in society and a shift from collectivism towards individualism, but in fact this created a hybrid state. This had implications for both the existing bureaucracy and the welfare state. The changes pursued under Thatcherism nevertheless presented a number of unintended consequences. Giddens (1998: 27) suggests that

Tony Blair's election in 1997 confirms the failure of socialism as an economic system of management. Yet, rather than marking the 'triumph of Margaret Thatcher', it confirms also the failure of Thatcherism, and neo-liberalism more generally. Neo-liberalism was an attempt to respond to the new conditions in which we live—to the impact of globalisation and intensifying global economic competition. It was deeply flawed, not least because of its paradoxical mix of economic libertarianism and moral traditionalism. Thatcherism wanted to modernise the economy but 'de-modernise' other areas . . . It was the enemy of devolution, since Thatcher drained power away from local councils and other bodies to the central state.

A key suggestion was that, after eighteen years of Conservative governments, it was increasingly obvious that unfettered markets did not guarantee economic success, while at the same time they produced a number of unacceptable social outcomes (see Hay 1999a).

The Third Way attempts to resolve a crucial dilemma within the Labour Party— the need to accept some of the key reforms introduced by Thatcherism while not turning its back on Keynesian welfarism. Where the Keynesian welfare state marked the high-water mark of collectivism, the period since the 1980s has witnessed the promotion of individualism. Where once the state provided the basis on which social relations were formed, the market has increasingly usurped this role. Labour has had to come to terms with this trend and reappraise its traditional understanding of a society based on a hierarchical, bureaucratic state and universal welfare. What Labour has tried to do is re-engage with social problems—seeing them again as the responsibility of state action—but the Blair Government does not want to act on the basis of the postwar settlement. Essentially, the New Labour Government has attempted to resolve problems of social order, family breakdown, welfare dependence, education, and health through mechanisms that involve many of the instruments of the Conservative era. Consequently, they have tried to involve the private and voluntary sectors as well as the public sector. They have also been concerned with some of the issues raised through managerial perspectives and thus they have focused on changing incentive structures rather than on establishing new administrative structures. The importance they have attached to the Private Finance Initiative (PFI) or Public–Private Partnership illustrates the new types of relationship that have been developed between the public and private sector and the new ways in which Labour is thinking about state intervention (see Box 10.2).

Another example of the New Labour approach to intervention is its policy on teenage mothers. Through the Social Exclusion Unit the government has made great efforts to intervene in the area of teenage pregnancy, with the goal of reducing the number of pregnancies amongst the under-18s. The Government's method of dealing with the problem is through a whole range of mechanisms including a national campaign involving both the Government and voluntary organizations, a task force of ministers, independent national advisory groups, and local coordinators. New threats and incentives include more support for teenage mothers in housing and education and the targeting of fathers for maintenance by the CSA. The Government is attempting a strategy based on multiple service deliverers and policy-makers which are joined up at the centre (Cmnd. 4342, 1999).

The other solution offered by the Third Way is that of a society of stakeholders. Here, the state forms partnerships and networks based on trust between a whole range of groups in society, including businesses, employees, and voluntary and public sectors. As Freeden (1999: 1) observes of Labour's new realism:

The state is reduced to the status of one actor among many, both internationally and domestically, appearing as pathetically subservient to global economic forces, unwilling to generate policies through its bureaucracies because it no longer believes in the power of politics as a central force for change. Societies have simply become too complex for wielders of political power and authority to manage.

Stakeholding was a widely used concept in the early period of Blair's leadership of the Labour Party, but confronted with the radical implications of elements of stakeholding the emphasis on the idea subsided. However, Prabhaker (2001) has demonstrated how many of the ideas contained within stakeholding have influenced government policy. Central to the notion of stakeholding is the idea of the responsible and responsive individual—the notion of a developmental self, and the idea that through help and education people can improve. These themes do appear in Labour's health and education policies. Policies like the home–school contract build on conceptions of responsibility within stakeholder thinking. Moreover, a crucial element in education policy under New Labour has been the notion of building citizenship and awareness of rights and responsibilities. Again, these policies can be traced back to stakeholding (Prabhaker 2001). It is also the case that a wide range of departments are thinking consciously and explicitly about their 'stakeholders', those involved and affected by policy, and how to involve them in the policy process. To give one example, a recent analysis of policy-making in DEFRA pointed out: 'Policy affecting air quality potentially affects many stakeholders and the departments used several methods to consult them about the strategy' (HC 232, 2001–2: 4).

Box 10.2 Private finance initiative: the Third Way state?

The Private Finance Initiative was introduced by the Major Government as a mechanism for allowing private finance to fund public-sector projects. What is innovative about the projects is that private organizations not only fund and construct the capital projects but are responsible for their operation and maintenance, with the public sector leasing the building or paying a fee for the service. So, for example, a private consortium could build and maintain a hospital and the health trust would lease the building. In areas like prisons, a private consortium builds and runs the prison and charges the prison service for the provision of the facility. The Labour Government has been keen on PFIs, as a mechanism for improving investment in the public services. According to Ball et al. (2000: 96), '150 projects have been signed since May 1997, at a capital cost of £12 billion with projects worth an additional £20 billion over the next three years.' Some of these projects are solely private money, whilst others include money from the public and private sectors. For example, Newbury College has created a computer-aided design and engineering centre, funded by £474,290 from the private Thames Valley Enterprises and by an application of £488,000 from the Government Office for the South East. In addition, the private sector supplied £19 million of software. These partnerships clearly involve complex patterns of governance which further blur the public and private sector.

As we saw in Chapter 5, throughout the Conservative years the traditional public service model of a top-down, centralized, command-based bureaucracy was attacked. New forms of state delivery embracing private-sector business models were introduced, including contracting out and privatization, aimed at making the existing public services more efficient. The Keynesian welfare state underwent change, yet the extent to which collectivism and the traditional command bureaucracy was broken down between 1979 and 1997 can be overstated. Nevertheless, the politics of New Labour, influenced by Third Way thinking, has rejected a wholesale return to a centralized, top-down bureaucratic model based on command, or the maintenance of universal welfarism. As Giddens (2000: 42) observes:

The new political culture is sceptical of large bureaucracies and opposes political clientelism. Many citizens see local and regional government as able to meet their needs more effectively than the nation state. They support an increasing role for non-profit voluntary agencies in the delivery of public services. Hierarchy is viewed with suspicion, as are traditional symbols and trappings of power.

For Labour, Third Way thinking led to a number of radical solutions to the problems of the Keynesian welfare state. For example, Blair argued that only the Labour Party, the original architects of the welfare state during the Attlee Government (1945–51), would be capable of radically reforming the now malign institutions associated with welfare delivery. As Rawnsley (2001: 110) observes, Blair argued: 'It had taken de Gaulle, the great nationalist, to extract France from Algeria; so it would take a Labour Prime Minister to radically reshape the welfare state.'

New Labour has shifted its position on the state to argue that alternatives to traditional state formations should be sought. It advocates the idea of networks of institutions and individuals cooperating in mutually beneficial partnerships based on a relationship of trust. Labour is not seeking the outright abandonment of central bureaucracy or the welfare state. Nor does it advocate the wholesale use of markets; instead it embraces a mixture of both. The aim is to utilize a combination of hierarchies, networks, and markets, the mix of which is determined by the nature of the particular service to be provided. Labour's position is intended to overcome the problem associated with the latter Conservative years in which there was a failure to develop the notion of an evolving or mutually beneficial relationship between the public and private sectors. Instead, services were simply contracted out by the former to the latter.

The Third Way advocates a position in which the public and private sectors collaborate to provide the required services. No formal structure should be adopted to condition this collaboration; instead, different options should be available in order to ensure flexibility and responsiveness. The key to binding the various relationships together is one of trust. Such an approach, New Labour argues, will lead to the creation of a truly enabling state based on responsive relationships of trust within society. This theme has been amplified by Blair in the much used Labour soundbite 'Joined-up problems need joined-up solutions'. It is a theme which has been addressed in the White Paper *Modernising Government*

(Cmnd. 4310, 1999). The next section examines the reform of the state since 1997, and in particular considers how successful Labour have been in delivering a programme of reform based on effective coordination, so addressing the pathology of governance.

Labour's state reforms: a joined-up approach?

Contextualizing the reform process

Joined-up government was the media-friendly label attached to Labour's programme of reform during its first term in office. Since 1997, Labour's programme of reforming the state has been conditioned by a desire to ensure that the leadership of the Party would impose itself on the policy-making process while not at any stage losing control of its own Party. Why? There are three factors that have conditioned the way Labour has operated once in power:

- The first factor was party-related: the perennial tendency of the Parliamentary Labour Party when in office to descend into internal factions and divisive splits, and the concomitant desire of the new leadership team to attain a tightly disciplined, unified Party.

- The second was organizational: the potential for Cabinet divisions to appear when in government, as a result of the existing structures and functional patterns of the core executive.

- The third, more strictly institutional factor: the problem of fragmentation which the Labour leadership believed was a symptom of eighteen years of Conservative state reforms and the broader impact of globalization and internationalization (see Kooiman 1993, Rhodes 1997).

These three factors led the Blair leadership team to conclude that the Party, once in government, would have to strengthen the coordinating abilities of the core. In their view, the traditional departmental organization of government created a number of problems:

The 'tubes' or 'silos' down which money flows from government to people and localities have come to be seen as part of the reason why government is bad at solving problems. Many issues have fitted imperfectly if at all into departmental slots. Vertical organisation by its nature skews government efforts away from certain activities, such as prevention—since the benefits of preventive action often come to another department. It tends to make government less sensitive to particular client groups whose needs cut across departmental lines. It incentivises departments to dump problems on each other—like schools dumping unruly children onto the streets to become a headache for the police ... Over time it reinforces the tendency common to all bureaucracies of devoting more energy to the protection of turf rather than serving the public. (Mulgan 2001)

Accepting the Conservative inheritance

In examining the detail of Labour's approach to state reform, a key point is that in a number of areas Labour were willing to accept a number of the reforms that had taken place in the previous eighteen years of Conservative government. Conditioned by Third Way thinking, Labour rejected the option of bringing functions back into the public sector which had been privatized under the Conservatives. Geoff Mulgan, head of the Number 10 Policy Unit, has said: 'The new public management of the 1980s had successfully encouraged government to be more focused, more organized around targets and performance, and more governed by market forces'. As Blair (1998) contended:

Big government is dead. The days of tax and spend are gone. Much of the deregulation and privatization that took place in the 1980s was necessary. But everything cannot be left to the market. We believe there is a role for active government.

The Citizens' Charter was rebranded as 'Service First'. Labour introduced the innovation of a 'People's Panel', consisting of 5,000 members of the public, who are regularly consulted on a range of issues concerning the delivery of public services. But, more generally, any change here has been more superficial than real, and Labour were broadly willing to go along with the charter programme introduced by the Major Government in 1991. As Theakston (1998: 29) notes:

Acceptance of charterism and its themes of quality, responsiveness, individual empowerment and the shift from a 'producer' to a 'consumer' emphasis, was bound up with the wider transformation and modernisation of the [Labour] party in the 1990s.

The Labour Government believed that the Civil Service it had inherited had not been imbued with a Conservative 'mind-set' and so rejected the notion that the Civil Service had been politicized (see Richards 1997). Thus, there was no overturning of the existing senior staff after the 1997 election. Nor did Labour choose to take agencies back into the embrace of their parent departments. Instead, agencification continued, though in a more cautious manner. By April 1999 there were 107 executive agencies employing over 77 per cent of the Civil Service (see Fig. 5.1).

Joined-up government

The new Government was aware of a lack of any institutionalized coordinating body *solely* responsible for safeguarding and enforcing broad government strategy and preventing a slide into departmentalism. The Blair Government's programme for reforming the state was based on the notion of moving towards 'joined-up government'. In particular, there was much anxiety over whether the organizational structures and the existing operational style of the core executive were capable of delivering a coordinated policy programme. As Mandelson and Liddle (1996: 235–6) commented:

Blair needs to . . . get personal control of the central-government machine and drive it hard, in the knowledge that if the government does not run the machine the machine will run the government. At the same time, he needs to use all his ministers—and their civil servants and advisers—to the maximum effect in their departments, because the government's overall programme will depend on the successful implementation of each of its component parts.

The most effective antithesis to departmentalism is a strong coordinating agency located at the centre of the core executive. The problems of the British core executive has always been that it is institutionally strong in departments but institutionally weak at the centre. In particular, conflict arises between three coordinating centres: the Cabinet Office, the Prime Minister's Office, and the Treasury.

Under Labour, the initial focus was on policy implementation and coordination, in particular achieving effectiveness in service delivery. The key elements of the new (post-1997) thinking about policy are set out in the White Paper *Modernizing Government* (March 1999). For Labour, good policy-making is strategic, holistic, focused on outcomes and delivery, evidence-based, inclusive (in the sense of taking account of the impact of policy on different groups), and, finally, based on clearly defined objectives. Labour's approach to 'joined-up government' was a twin strategy of centralization and the establishment of ad hoc policy reviews (see Box 10.3). In addition, they have created incentives to encourage joined-up behaviour such as rewarding those who take a joined-up approach and designing targets that can cross departmental boundaries (Mulgan 2001).

Box 10.3 Changes to create joined-up government

- Greater focus on outcomes
- The creation of bodies like the Social Exclusion Unit and the Performance and Innovation Unit, which exist to analyse departments outside departmental boundaries
- The establishment of joined-up delivery units such as the Rough Sleepers Unit
- Introduction of joined-up budgets in areas like Surestart and drugs
- Ministers with cross-cutting portfolios
- Regular cross-cutting reviews of policy
- New budgets that cross-cut departmental boundaries
- The creation of new departments such as DEFRA which try to establish integrated approach to problems

(*Source*: Mulgan 2001)

Centralization and the core executive

There is a certain contradiction in commencing a section dealing with centralization by initially focusing on fragmentation. Paradoxically, however, within days of its electoral victory, one of the Labour Government's first actions was to augment the process of fragmentation by making the Bank of England independent and establishing the new Monetary Policy Committee, with the power to determine the base lending rate[1] (see Rawnsley 2001: 31–50). Elsewhere, however, throughout Labour's first term (1997–2001), the emphasis was on centralization and coordination across central government. Box 10.4 highlights the reforms at the centre that Labour has introduced. As Box 10.4 indicates, Labour established a number of units attached to either the Prime Minister's Office or the Cabinet Office, each with a role in bringing greater coordination to the heart of government. However, this did create a number of unforeseen and unintended consequences for the Labour Government. For example, the creation of the Minister without Portfolio role created conflict with a number of other high-profile Labour ministers who also saw their formal position as being responsible for cross-departmental coordination. In particular, the Lord Chancellor, Lord Irving, regarded part of his role as being, formally, to coordinate the machinery of government and, informally, to act as chief adviser to the Prime Minister. There were clearly tensions arising over the creation of these particular power bases at the centre of the Labour Government, and during the 1998 summer reshuffle the job of the Minister without Portfolio was merged with that of the Chancellor of the Duchy of Lancaster to create the new post of Minister for the Cabinet. This new portfolio included overall responsibility for the work of the Cabinet Office, including the Better Government agenda (see below), providing strategic direction to assist the Cabinet Office in cross-departmental coordination, and acting as Minister for the Civil Service.

Elsewhere, a new Centre for Management and Policy Studies has been created, incorporating the existing Civil Service College with the aim of introducing greater outside influence on policy thinking. A Management Board for the Civil Service has also been created, in order to emphasize and harmonize the corporate objectives of government as a whole. Whereas during the Conservative years reform was targeted at introducing and improving managerialism and economy in government, the present raft of reforms emphasize the need to improve on policy-making, in particular, policy-making which cuts across the old departmental boundaries (see Bichard 1999). As the present Cabinet Secretary, Richard Wilson, observed:

I do worry that the management reforms of the last decade [the 1990s] may have focused our energies very much on particular objectives, particular targets, performance indicators

---

[1] The reasons underpinning Labour's decision to grant independence to the Bank of England are predominantly historical. In the postwar period, previous Labour governments suffered from being perceived as unable to control the economy, an image reinforced through the devaluations which occurred during the 1960s and 1970s. By relinquishing powers over the economy to the Monetary Policy Committee, the Labour Government was relieving itself of certain key responsibilities, and hence dispersing accountability in relation to economic management (see Rawnsley 2001).

Box 10.4 **Reforming the centre**

Monetary Policy Committee (created May 1997)

This Committee has been conferred with the power to determine the base lending rate. The Committee is staffed by a range of independent economists, although the majority of its members are appointed by the Chancellor.

Minister without Portfolio/Minister for the Cabinet (created May 1997/June 1998)

The first Minister without Portfolio was Peter Mandelson; in the wake of various reshuffles in Labour's first term, Jack Cunningham and Mo Mowlam have also subsequently held this post, which has been given Cabinet status. The role of the Minister is to assure coordination in government policy. Effectively, the job is to act as a 'Number Ten Chief of Staff' (Kavanagh and Seldon 2001: 253) who will carry forward the implementation of cross-departmental policies.

Constitutional Secretariat (created May 1997)

Created to coordinate and provide the dynamism for the Government's programme of constitutional reform. The Secretariat reports directly to the Prime Minister and the Cabinet Secretary.

Women's Unit (created May 1997)

This Unit was created to provide support to the Minister for Women. Its role is to provide a voice in government for the specific needs of women through research, project work, and a longer-term goal of effecting institutional change.

Social Exclusion Unit (created December 1997)

The Unit is a cross-departmental team whose function is to tackle the wide range of issues, such as homelessness and teenage pregnancy, which arise from the inequalities of society. These have been labelled the 'wicked issues' which cut across the traditional boundaries created by Whitehall departments.

Policy Unit (expanded) (May 1998)

The Policy Unit effectively operates as a think tank within government, providing independent thinking across all policy areas. It is located in the Prime Minister's Office and headed by David Milliband with an expanded staff of about twenty which has developed much closer links with the Cabinet Office.

Strategic Communications Unit (created 1998)

A staff of six whose remit is to harmonize public relations initiatives of Cabinet ministers. Here, the emphasis is on the coherent and unified presentation of government policy across all departments.

Central Secretariat (created autumn 1998)

Its role is to advise on: ministerial responsibilities and accountability; issues surrounding the reform of the machinery of government; issues of propriety and ethics in government; and public appointments and public bodies. The Secretariat reports to the Cabinet Secretary who then conveys its views to the Prime Minister.

> **Performance and Innovation Unit (created October 1998)**
>
> Reports directly to the Prime Minister on medium- and long-term public policy chal-
> lenges that cross departmental boundaries. It also promotes innovation in policy and
> service delivery, in order to improve the implementation of the government's objectives.
> Its approach is to conduct short studies on relevant topics, and it reports directly to the
> Prime Minister through the Cabinet Secretary.

in return for resources and delegations. And that we have in some measure taken our eye off what we used to be good at—and still can do—which is working more corporately across the boundaries. And it may be . . . that personnel reforms that we have introduced have also given people a sense that they work more for departments rather than for the wider civil service. (Wilson 1998)

For Blair, political appointees and a strengthened policy unit are crucial elements in imposing coordination on government. The Labour Government has doubled the number of special advisers (political appointments) who assist minis- ters across Whitehall, from thirty-eight under John Major to seventy-eight under Blair in 2000. There has also been a growing debate (mainly within the media) over whether the British system of government is becoming more presidential (see Box 10.5).

In relation to centralization, one of the key tools available to the machinery of government to facilitate communication and coordination is information tech- nology. In particular, one of the aims of joined-up government is to introduce an intranet system compatible across all government departments, smart cards, and call centres. As Toynbee and Walker (2001: 215) observe, the *Modernizing Govern- ment* White Paper (March 1999) emphasized the importance the Blair Government placed on harnessing the new IT: 'By 2005 basic dealings with government, central and local, are to be conducted electronically.' Unfortunately, throughout Labour's first term there have been a number of IT embarrassments, most notably in the Immigration Division of the Home Office, the Passport Agency, the Lord Chancel- lor's Department, and the Department of Social Security, stemming from a combination of incompatible software packages and faulty computer hardware.

Ad hoc committees

The second element of Labour's strategy for joined-up government has been the innovative establishment of ad hoc policy reviews, popularly referred to as task forces. These bodies are located within central government, but have a mixture of members from the public, private, and voluntary sectors, MPs of all parties, trade unionists, academics, etc. who have been given a specific brief and asked to provide a response within a particular period of time. The most important element of this strategy has been the creation of task forces which cut across the traditional policy arenas of Whitehall to address 'wicked issues' such as homelessness, teenage preg- nancy, and drug abuse which have no single, departmental home. As Daniel (1997: 27) observes:

Unlike the Royal Commissions and reviews of previous governments, the task forces are not intended to sweep issues under the carpet. They are emblems of Labour's desire to be seen to be implementing manifesto pledges briskly and in a spirit of trust.

There is some confusion over the number of task forces that Labour have established during their first term. In part this is due to the lack of any clear definition as to what actually constitutes a task force. Barker (1998) observes that three different terms are often applied by different departments: 'review', 'task force', and 'advisory group'. Burch and Holliday (2000: 72) suggest that taking into account

---

Box 10.5 **Presidentialism in Britain: a bogus debate**

Under Tony Blair, the importance of the Prime Minister's Office continues to grow because Blair sees himself as having a continued role in the development of policy (see Kavanagh and Seldon 2001, Rawnsley 2001). This is indicated by Blair's attempt to replace the official appointment of principal private secretary with a political appointment as Chief of Staff. In the end, the official Civil Service post was retained whilst the Chief of Staff was given an explicitly separate political post. There has been a substantial increase in the number of political appointments at No. 10—individuals with predominantly media and public relations skills, as well as some with policy expertise. Previous prime ministers have kept such appointments in single figures. Twenty years ago Aberbach et al. (1981: 17) referred to the small number of such appointments as 'hybrids'. They mediated between bureaucrats and ministers or combined some of the skills of both. Their number is steadily increasing.

The changes at No. 10 since 1997 have led a number of commentators to argue that there now effectively exists a Prime Minister's Department. The same commentators also speak of a 'creeping Presidentialism' under Blair (see Kavanagh and Seldon 2001, Foley 2000). For example, Rawnsley (2001: 50) contends: 'In Britain's unwritten constitution a Prime Minister is *primus inter pares*, first among equals. Tony Blair recognised no equal in his Cabinet, and only his Chancellor was sufficiently strong to challenge that supremacy. This Prime Minister planned to be *primus*. From the beginning, it was designed to be a presidential premiership.' Furthermore, in a BBC2 current affairs programme (17 November 2001), one of Blair's former ministerial colleagues, Mo Mowlam, claimed that Cabinet Government was effectively 'dead' and that, since the attack on the World Trade Centre on 11 September 2001, Blair had in effect been acting in a presidential manner and excluding his cabinet colleagues from the decision-making process.

What these claims ignore are the structured lines of dependency which constrain all Prime Ministers (see Chapter 9). As the downfall of Thatcher in November 1990 demonstrates, a Prime Minister cannot function without the support of his/her Cabinet colleagues (see Smith 1994). Both sets of actors are locked into a relationship of dependency. Furthermore, the notion that a handful of political advisers in No. 10 can act as an effective bulwark against the size and power of the Whitehall machine is wishful thinking, and the presidential thesis should be viewed with scepticism. Britain retains a parliamentary system of government, including a Civil Service based on the principle of 'professional performance', *not* political affiliation to the governing party of the day.

all three definitions, Labour created 227 new teams within its first year (132 reviews, 61 advisory groups, and 34 task forces). Elsewhere, Platt (1998) suggests that during the Government's first twelve months, 192 policy reviews, task forces, and a Royal Commission were set up (see Platt 1998) The response to a parliamentary question from the Labour MP Oona King on 18 December 2000 was that there were over 200 'live' task forces, ad hoc advisory groups, and reviews in the period between 2 May 1997 and 31 October 2000. The figures remain contested, but as Burch and Holliday (2000: 72) argue, the key issue is not the number of task forces that have been created but:

That the New Labour Government is (i) not averse (indeed keen) to bring in outside experts and (ii) no respecter of departmental boundaries when it comes to problem . . . The task force approach is an excellent fit with Labour's general theme of a partnership approach to government and with its philosophy of assembling individuals with hands-on experience to focus on specific problems.

It is clear that these task forces include a wide array of individuals from the private sectors, public sector, voluntary groups, and traditional civil servants, and that often they are dealing with very specific policy problems. In addition, the range of topics is extremely diverse (see Table 10.1). It is also worth noting that some of these bodies are chaired by ministers, whereas others are chaired by official or non-government people. This raises interesting constitutional questions concerning the status of their reports. If a task force does not include a minister, it is unlikely that its report can have any real impact on decisions unless that is what a minister wishes. Some of the more high-profile task forces have been on youth justice, school standards, NHS efficiency, welfare-to-work, and football (for a sense of the range, see Table 10.1).

Joined-up government, centralization, and ad hoc committees: an analysis

By adopting an innovative approach to policy-making through the use of task forces and the establishment of various coordinating units at the centre, Labour has ironically exacerbated some of the tensions associated with governance: an increasing lack of control and coordination at the centre. Through its attempts at strengthening the centre, Labour has recast the old problem of competing power centres based on strong departments, but at a different level and in a different guise. As the Labour Government has attempted to improve coordination at the centre of the core executive, it has established a number of competing centres of power. Paradoxically, indeed, the unforeseen and unintended consequence has been to create confusion over where power at the centre resides (see Fig. 10.1) Various central bodies have become locked into a struggle for ascendancy, leaving those in the traditional government departments unsure over which power centre to engage with in order to secure their own departmental goals. It would, at least potentially, appear that Labour may have re-created and exacerbated the problem of ineffectual central coordination, rather than overcoming it.

Furthermore, the style Labour has adopted could in future lead to fundamental

Table 10.1: A sample of task forces, ad hoc advisory groups, and reviews established in Labour's first term (1997–2001)

Task force	Date	Ministers	Civil servants	Public servants	Voluntary sector	Private sector	Chair
Fuel Supply	Sept. 2000	6	1	1	0	0	Jack Straw, Home Secretary
Creative Industries	July 1997–June 2000	11	15	2	0	10	Chris Smith, Secretary of State for Culture
Advisory Group on Citizenship	Jan.–Sept. 2000	0	0	11	2	3	Prof. Bernard Crick
Promotion of Life-Long Learning	Mar. 1999–	0	8	5	1	1	Tim Dowe, DFEE
School Standards Task Force	May 1997–	3	3	16	0	2	Secretary of State for Education
Disruptive Passengers on Aircraft	Feb. 1999–July 2000	0	3	3	0	6	Michael Smethers, DETR
Youth Homelessness	June 1998–June 2000	0	8	6	8	0	Mike Baldwin, DETR
Integrated Sexual Health and HIV Strategy Steering Group	May 2000–	0	13	10	8	3	Dr Sheila Adams, Director of Health Services NHS Executive, and Prof. M. Adler
Modernization Action Team: Patient Care	Apr.–July 2000	1	2	10	5	4	Parliamentary Under-secretary for Health, Gisela Stuart
Cancer Task Force	Sept. 2000	1	7	12	3	1	Mike Richards, Department of Health
Working Group on Forced Marriage	Aug. 1999–June 2000	0	6	3	5	1	Lord Ahmed and Baroness Uddin
Human Rights Task Force	Jan. 1999–	3	5	3	6	0	Home Office Minister of State, Mike O'Shea
Rover Task Force	Mar.–July 2000	0	2	6	1	12	Alex Stephenson, Chairman, Advantage West Midlands
Task Force on Potentially Hazardous Near-Earth Objects	Jan.–Sept. 2000	0	0	0	0	3	Dr Harry Atkinson, Retired Chief Scientist

Source: Parliamentary Question of Oona King (House of Commons Official Record, 28 Dec. col 47, and Lord Tomlinson, House of Lords Official Recorder, 19 Dec. 2000).

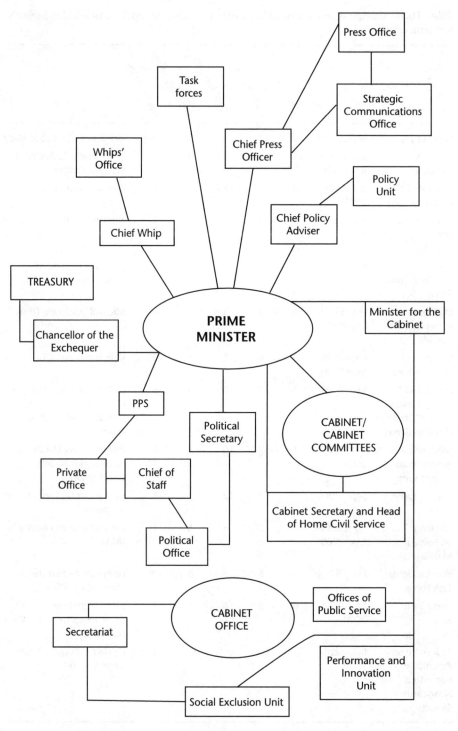

Figure 10.1 Complexity at the centre (*source*: Barberis 2000: 32)

splits within Cabinet and, more broadly, to policy drift in Whitehall, as the traditional networks for securing policy success have become blurred. In 1998 Sir Richard Wilson, the Cabinet Secretary, examined the processes of coordination in Whitehall and suggested that there needed to be greater cross-department coordination and increased strategic capacity. Two years later the Performance and Innovation Unit published a report, *Wiring It Up: Whitehall's Management of Crossing-Cutting Policies and Service*, which suggested there were six key areas in which to improve coordination in policy-making: stronger leadership, improved policy formulation and implementation, better-trained civil servants, flexible use of budgets, using external audits, and using the centre (Number 10, the Cabinet office, etc.) to lead the drive to joined-up government (see PIU 2000). It is in these areas that the future agenda for reform of the machinery of government will develop. But, as Hazell and Morris (1999: 152) highlight, 'there was no mention of the impact of constitutional change; and no awareness that there may need to be more radical reconfiguration at the centre as it adjusts to its new role at the centre of a quasi-federal, more rights-based, more transparent system of government'.

In office, Labour appears to have continued the Thatcherite tradition of bypassing the Cabinet system; Blair does not regard the Cabinet as an 'effective decision-making forum. Only on a few occasions has Blair allowed sufficient time for Cabinet to be discursive . . . he tries to focus on strategic issues' (see Kavanagh and Seldon 1999: 408, Rawnsley 2001). The preference is to work through bilateral meetings with Cabinet colleagues. Likewise, Cabinet committees are under-used. This leads Hennessy (1998: 3–4) to suggest that the Blair Government has abandoned Cabinet government, replacing it with a 'Napoleonic' style of government. Here, the implication is that strategies are centrally prepared and then imposed on departments, which are regarded as units whose function is one of implementation. Furthermore, instead of Cabinet, Labour seems to be relying on task forces[2] to deal with interdepartmental issues or problems, and this raises a number of constitutional issues. The key difference from Cabinet committees is that these bodies have been set up to deal with specific issues, and include a large number of outsiders (Daniel 1997). It is interesting that, of the formal task forces initially set up by the Labour Government in 1997, only four were chaired by ministers. These bodies indicate a more pluralistic approach to policy-making and less reliance on civil servants for advice. For traditional mandarins like the former Cabinet Secretary Sir Robin Butler, the use of so many outsiders is leading to poor advice, policy errors, and lack of accountability (*Guardian*, 5 January 1998). The absence of ministers does raise the question of the weight the final reports will carry within government. Unlike Cabinet committees, their decisions will not carry Cabinet authority and may lack the necessary departmental support to be implemented.

The Labour Government has attempted to address the fundamental problem of

[2] For example, in March 2001 it created a task force to counter the foot-and-mouth epidemic, the effect of which had been felt by a number of government departments, and demanded a coordinated response.

coordination which exists within British central government but, in a contra-dictory style, they have further fragmented the state with the creation of new institutions. However, these changes have been made without any reference to wider constitutional changes. The state and the constitution are perceived as mutually exclusive entities, thus limiting the radicalness of constitutional change. Change in the constitution is not regarded as directly affecting the way the nation is governed. The Blair Government is sustaining the principles of parliamentary sovereignty, secrecy, and elitism that underpin the core executive. Yet the problem for the Government is that the programme of constitutional reform is not con-sistent with these principles. For example, the key tenet underpinning their pro-cess of reform is increased pluralism, achieved by devolving power away from the centre. In practice, this is a principle that is in direct opposition to elitism and parliamentary sovereignty.

Having examined Labour's reform of the core executive and its attempts to achieve joined-up government, our attention now turns to the other reforms of the state introduced by Labour during its first term, in particular devolution and regionalism, electoral reform, parliamentary reform, and human rights. The rest of the chapter will highlight the tensions which may develop between Labour's notion of the state and the aims of its constitutional reform programme. The problem is that the programme of constitutional reform has produced direct chal-lenges to the various elements that collectively make up the Westminster model, which Labour claims will be strengthened, not further damaged.

Devolution and regionalism

Bogdanor (1997: 15) argues that '[t]he UK is a unitary, though not necessarily uniform, state'. In principle, parliamentary sovereignty means that there is a single authority that governs the whole of the nation of the UK. However, it is also clear that unique institutional arrangements have developed in particular regions, such as distinctive legal and educational systems in Scotland and varying forms of government in Northern Ireland. As Mitchell (2002) points out, the UK developed without disrupting the existing institutional arrangements. When Labour was elected to power in 1997, a number of serious stresses existed in the unitary nature of the UK (see Box 10.6). Labour's response to regional demands and concern over democracy was a commitment in its 1997 manifesto to devolve greater power to Scotland, Wales and Northern Ireland, and to England through the establishment of new English regional assemblies. Indeed, their commitment to such a policy is arguably one of the most radical elements in their agenda for reforming the state.

Labour's approach, in particular to Scotland and Wales, has been based on political pragmatism. Their programme of reform has been framed in the context of devolving greater power to the territories in order, paradoxically, to strengthen and

---

Box 10.6 **A disunited kingdom**

Until the 1960s there was very little discussion about the nature of the UK, and in a sense this was part of the postwar consensus that Britain was and would remain unified. The regions were given autonomy over particular areas of policy, but in return devolution was not discussed. However, from the 1960s onwards there was growing nationalist feeling within Scotland and Wales and an increased desire for some form of devolved government. In the case of Northern Ireland, there was a growing demand for a united Ireland in the Catholic/Nationalist community. Following a failed attempt to secure greater independence in the 1970s, after a 1979 referendum failed to secure the neces-sary majority for devolution, tension within the UK again grew in the 1980s, when people in Scotland and Wales increasingly felt that they were being governed by a government they did not elect. Whilst Conservative governments were being elected in the UK, support in Scotland and Wales practically disappeared. Moreover, the perception that England dominated Scotland was exacerbated by Thatcher's apparent belief that the UK was just an extension of England. As McConnell (2000: 220) observes: 'the Thatcher Government came to power in 1979 with moves for devolution apparently at a dead-end ... In retrospect, it is clear that devolutionary sentiments were not dead. Supporters of devolution were merely reeling from the shock of the referendum result and were about to be galvanised by the activities of the Thatcher and Major Governments between 1979–97.'

---

reinvigorate the unitary character of the British state, not as a transitory stage on the path to complete separation or federalism. The key dynamic underpinning this stance has been Labour's reluctance to risk the strong electoral position it secured in 1997 and reaffirmed in 2001, and which it had spent eighteen years striving to achieve.

In the following section, we will examine the variation in Labour's programme for devolution. Our approach will consider three principal problems arising from devolution:

- Devolution is a threat to parliamentary sovereignty.
- There is not one but at least four forms of devolution being developed.
- A consequence of devolution may be greater fragmentation and conflict within the British state, exacerbating the problems associated with governance.

Scotland and Northern Ireland: a real transfer of power

In this section we will examine the transfer of powers to Scotland and Northern Ireland. Although a different model of devolution has been pursued in each case, what links the two is that Westminster has relinquished real powers to both nations.

Scotland

In the case of Scotland, the Government's argument is that devolution neither threatens parliamentary sovereignty nor undermines the integrity of the UK. 'Sovereignty rests with Westminster because we are proposing devolution—local services to be run here by the people of Scotland. It's not separation' (see Riddell 2000: 105). However, the central tenets of the reform package have been to established a Scottish Parliament, based in Edinburgh, with powers to make law and to provide limited scope for raising taxes (see Box 10.7). Following elections held in May 1999, the Scottish Parliament held its first meeting in the following July. There has been a conscious attempt to reject the Westminster model. This can be seen in the way ideas embracing proportional representation, more sociable working hours, and the use of electronic voting methods have been instituted.

Despite Labour's reassertion of the sovereignty of the UK Parliament over the Scottish Parliament, however, a number of issues have arisen over the interpretation of the nature of sovereignty:

- The fact that MPs are pressurizing the Westminster Government to prevent Scottish MPs from voting on English matters (the 'West Lothian Question') indicates that the unified sovereignty of Parliament is not guaranteed.

- The de facto sovereignty of Parliament could be further threatened if proportional voting increases nationalist representation and breaks the links of dependence that would be maintained through a Labour Scottish Assembly.

- The rejection of the Westminster model may produce a less executive-centred, more open and responsive assembly, unbound by the Westminster traditions and consequently less elitist.

- The assembly may have greater legitimacy than Westminster, thus effectively restraining central government from ever reducing the powers of the Scottish Parliament.

Northern Ireland

The principles of parliamentary sovereignty are further stretched by the form of devolution in Northern Ireland. On 10 April 1998 the key parties in Northern Ireland, except the Democratic Unionist Party, signed up to the Good Friday Agreement. The key elements of this agreement and the key features of the Northern Ireland Assembly are outlined in Box 10.8.

The problem of devolution in Northern Ireland is the instability of the executive. Based on the notion of cross-community representation, it is unusual in that all parties with a certain mandate have a right to a position within the Executive. This means that the ruling body contains representatives of Sinn Fein and the Democratic Unionist Party. Consequently, agreement is difficult to achieve; *and*

> **Box 10.7 The Scottish Parliament**
>
> **Membership and organization**
>
> 129 Scottish Members of Parliament (SMPs). 73 SMPs are directly elected on a constituency basis, with the remaining 56 members elected by the Additional Member System drawn from a party list. The Cabinet is headed by a First Minister. The Secretary of State for Scotland retains a seat in the Cabinet in Westminster. Scottish ministers are entitled to participate in meetings of the EU Council of Ministers.
>
> **Duration**
>
> A maximum four-year term, but with the possibility of early dissolution.
>
> **Powers**
>
> The Scottish Parliament possesses legislative powers and is responsible for: health, education and training, local government, social work and housing, economic development and transport, the law and home affairs, the environment, agriculture, fisheries and forestry, sports and art, and research and statistics in relation to devolved matters. It is also vested with tax-varying powers in the range of + or − 3p, in relation to the basic rate of tax established by the Westminster Parliament.
>
> In conceding the above range of powers to a Scottish Parliament, the Labour Government made clear that the UK Parliament would remain sovereign. Westminster would retain powers over issues concerning: UK defence and national security; UK foreign policy, including relations with Europe; the UK constitution; the stability of the UK's fiscal, economic, and monetary system; common markets for UK goods and services; employment legislation; social security; and most aspects of transport safety and regulation.

already the assembly has been suspended on a number of occasions in 2000 and 2001, and was subject to a legal challenge over David Trimble's re-election as first minister and the timing of the next election.

Wales and England: a limited transfer of power from Westminster

A comparison of the various institutions established in Scotland and Northern Ireland indicates that they each have different models of devolution. However, both Scotland and Northern Ireland have been given considerable autonomy. In Wales and the English regions, policy competence is much less. While Scotland has experienced a real and discernible transfer of power from Westminster to Edinburgh, the same cannot be said for Wales after the new Assembly based in Cardiff first met in May 1999.

Box 10.8 **The Northern Ireland Assembly**

Membership and organization

The Northern Ireland Assembly is made up of 108 members, elected by a single transferable vote based on the existing Westminster constituencies in Northern Ireland.

Duration

First term is five years, subsequent terms are four years.

Organization and powers

- The Assembly operates where appropriate on a cross-community basis and is the prime source of authority in respect of all *devolved* responsibilities.

- The Assembly has authority to pass primary legislation for Northern Ireland subject to a number of checks, including the European Court of Human Rights and the Westminster Parliament, which continues to legislate on *non-devolved* issues.

- A North/South Ministerial Council has been established to bring those with executive responsibilities together in Northern Ireland and the Republic to develop consultation, cooperation, and action on matters of mutual interest.

- A British–Irish Council has been established under a new British–Irish Agreement to promote the 'harmonious and mutually beneficial development of relationships between the North, South and the mainland'.

Important elements of the agreement of Ireland bring non-Westminster elements into the policy process and further question the notion of territorial sovereignty within the United Kingdom.

Wales

Labour's proposals, set out in the July 1997 White Paper *A Voice for Wales,* aimed to revitalize Welsh participation in the political process and reinvigorate faith in the UK political system. However, it offered only executive, not legislative, devolution of power to the Principality. Unlike the Scottish Parliament, the Welsh Assembly has not been given either power to raise taxes or primary legislative powers. Instead, it only constitutes 'executive devolution' (see Box 10.9). The establishment of a Welsh Assembly has not created the same degree of tension surrounding issues of sovereignty as in Scotland, nor is it as likely to provide a staging post on the path towards full separation. However, the danger Hazell and O'Leary (1999) identify is 'leap-frogging', whereby a Welsh Assembly sees a successful Scottish system and starts to push for more powers. This may increase tensions with Westminster and lead to greater autonomy for Wales. Already there have been conflicts over BSE and foot-and-mouth; and the fact that Blair's preferred leader, Alun Michael, was forced out of office in 2000, to be replaced by Rhodri Morgan, indicates that the Welsh Assembly perhaps has already more independence that was at first intended.

Box 10.9 **The Welsh Assembly**

Membership and organization

The Assembly consists of 60 members elected by the Additional Member System. Forty members are elected on a constituency basis and the remaining twenty are taken from a party list. The Cabinet is headed by the First Secretary. The Secretary of State for Wales retains a seat in the Westminster Cabinet. Only the Secretary of State is entitled to participate in meetings of the EU Council of Ministers.

Duration

A fixed four-year term, in which early dissolution is not permissible.

Power

The Welsh Assembly does not have any legislative powers, nor does it possess any tax-raising powers. The Assembly possesses executive powers only and these cover the areas of health; education; industry and training; agriculture; environment; roads; planning; arts and heritage.

England and regional governance

In Labour's first term in office, of all the elements contributing to its programme of devolving powers away from Westminster, the case of the English regions has been by far the slowest and most haphazard. As Holliday observes: 'The UK is an instance of asymmetric devolution, similar to Spain's region-building of the late 1970s and early 1980s, in the sense that distinct regions are being given different sets of powers at variable times and speeds.' Labour has also sought some form of regional governance for England. The 1997 Labour manifesto embraced many of the proposals stemming from the 1995 Labour consultation paper *A Choice for England*. In particular, it advocated the creation of regional chambers based on ten Integrated Regional Offices, with coordinating functions over a range of policy areas. Furthermore, the manifesto proposed that, depending on the outcome of regionally held referenda, directly elected regional assemblies should be created. Again, as in the case of Wales, these assemblies would lack tax-raising or legislative powers, but apart from providing a strong coordinating role, they would perform a vital function in making sub-central government more accountable. However, the momentum behind regional devolution seems to be declining, and during Labour's first term in office only limited progress was made in this area. Indeed, in Labour's 2001 election manifesto, its commitment to regional devolution was further downgraded. Greenwood et al. (2001: 203–4) provide a useful analysis of the Department of the Environment, Transport and the Regions attempts to assist the development of regional government in Labour's first term by creating a number of Regional Development Agencies aimed at promoting regional economic growth (see Box 10.10).

Only in London, with the creation of an Authority and executive Mayor, has

Box 10.10 **English Regional Development Agencies and Regional Chambers, 1997–2001**

Regional Development Agencies
- One North East
- North West Development Agency
- Yorkshire Forward
- Advantage West Midlands
- East Midlands Development Agency
- East of England Development Agency
- South West of England Regional Development Agency
- South East England Development Agency

What are Regional Development Agencies?
- Non-departmental public bodies (quangos).
- Their remit is to further economic development and regeneration, business efficiency, employment, and inward investment.
- They are accountable to ministers and Parliament.
- They are bound to consult with regional chambers on strategy (see below).

Regional Chambers
- North East Regional Chamber
- North West Regional Chamber
- Yorkshire and the Humber Regional Chamber
- West Midlands Regional Chamber
- East Midlands Regional Chamber
- East of England Regional Chamber
- South West Regional Chamber
- South East England Regional Assembly

What are Regional Chambers?
- Voluntary organizations of local government councillors and other representatives of a region's economy, society, and environment.
- They are intended to scrutinize and advise the RDAs.
- They are intended to develop a role in the regional planning processes.

(*Source*: Greenwood et al. 2001: 204)

there been any real devolution within England. The March 1998 White Paper *A Mayor and Assembly for London* set out plans for the establishment of a powerful directly elected Mayor of London and a twenty-five member London Assembly which together constitute the Greater London Authority. The powers allocated to the elected Mayor, Ken Livingstone, cover transport, economic development, the environment, culture, planning, policy, and fire. The election of the Mayor of London and the subsequent tensions that have arisen between him and the Labour Government over the redevelopment of the London Underground system provide a clear example of the problems encountered when there are institutional clashes over spheres of power and authority.

An analysis of Labour's programme of devolution: fragmentation and conflict

Constitutionally and practically, it may not seem a problem that the constituent parts of the UK have different forms of devolution, but two issues arise:

- These developments undermine the notion that Britain is a unitary state because not all people are being governed in the same way.
- If devolution is popular in Scotland and Northern Ireland, pressures may develop for similar forms of government in Wales and the English regions. Such developments, and the pressures they may cause for greater independence, will further undermine the Westminster model as a value system for legitimizing government.

The notion of a unitary state is difficult to maintain when a range of forms of governance are operating within various parts of the UK. This problem will prove even greater if conflicts develop between Westminster and the regions. A crucial point is that devolution is not an end point, but a process of continual negotiation and development. Relationships will vary according to circumstance, political control, and the tactics of the various parties.

The Labour Government also maintains that devolution is not a threat to a unified civil service (Hazell and Morris 1999: 138). It is likely, however, that over time, varied traditions and cultures will develop in each of the regions which, in effect, may produce a range of types of officials. The desire for the new devolved bodies not to operate within the confines of the Westminster model means that civil servants are likely to work within different rules of the game, and therefore that political/official relationships will vary from the Whitehall model norm. Hazell and Morris suggest (1999: 138): 'There will be pressure from the Scottish Parliament and Welsh assembly to have their own civil service, like the Northern Ireland Civil Service.'

What devolution has produced is new structures of dependency within the British system of government (see Chapters 8 and 9). Whilst currently the most important relationships within the core executive are between the Prime Minister and departments, the Treasury and departments, and ministers and officials, devolution has established important new relationships between the centre and the regions. For certain policies, the Prime Minister and departments are dependent on devolved bodies for delivering policies, and important processes of exchange occur over issues such as finance and legitimacy. This may create an important constraint on the activities of the centre, especially if regional governments are controlled by nationalists or coalitions. These new structures of dependency are likely to make greater coordination and joined-up government difficult to achieve because the Government will not have direct control over the devolved bodies. The impact of these new dependency networks have been made apparent already in the area of agriculture, where the Welsh and Scottish bodies have levered extra assistance to all farmers and, in return, the Secretary of State for Agriculture has had to put pressure on his Welsh and Scottish counterparts to lift the ban on beef on the bone before he can do so.

It is important not to take too apocalyptic a view of the impact of devolution. Mitchell (1999: 608) points out that it is possible to classify Britain as a union, rather than a unitary state, where 'integration is less than perfect and that pre-union rights and institutional infrastructure preserving some degree of autonomy and serving as agencies of indigenous elite recruitment are preserved'. In other words, a strong degree of autonomy has always existed, especially in Scotland, and devolution is about changing the form of legitimation rather than governance. In addition, the choices made by the Scottish Parliament remain constrained, particularly by financial imperatives. Finally, the fact that all EU negotiations have to be conducted through UK representatives reinforces the position of national sovereignty. As far as the EU is concerned, the UK remains the nation-state that is recognised within Europe, and the Scottish Parliament and Welsh Assembly can only lobby informally.

Parliamentary reform

Electoral reform

During its first term, the Labour Government also embarked on a process of electoral reform which it hoped would modernize and revitalize Britain's democratic tradition. For example, as we have seen in the case of both Scotland and Wales, the alternative member system has been introduced, whereby at least half of the members are elected locally by first-past-the-post procedures, while the remainder are allocated proportionally at a regional level, with electors having two votes. In the European elections in June 1999, the regional list system was used, whereby electors voted for a particular party and seats were then allocated proportionally from a closed list of party candidates. In the case of the direct election for a mayor of London, a variant on the alternative vote system has been used. Voters ranked their preference between first and second choice, and votes were then redistributed until one candidate had 50 per cent or more of the votes cast. In the case of the London Assembly, electors voted for a first-past-the post candidate based on the fourteen area members, while the remaining eleven London-wide seats were allocated proportionally on a party basis.

The other main initiative instigated by Labour in relation to electoral reform has been based on Westminster itself. In December 1997 a cross-party electoral reform committee was established, chaired by the Liberal Democratic peer Lord Jenkins, to recommend an alternative, broadly proportional system to the existing first-past-the-post system, based on four criteria: stable government, an extension of voter choice, the maintenance of the constituency link, and broad proportionality. In October 1998 the *Report of the Independent Commission on the Voting System* was published which recommended the 'alternative vote plus' system. This is a mixed system containing two features: a constituency element and a list top-up. Electors would have two votes—the first for an MP (based on 500 constituencies) and the second for the party of their choice (open list), creating between 98 and 132 MPs drawn from 80 top-up areas across the country. Following the report's publication, the Government did not formally commit itself either way to its findings. There were immediately some dissenting voices, however, most notably Jack Straw and John Prescott. Subsequently, Labour has been slow to respond to the issue of electoral reform; there is a tentative proposal to hold a UK referendum, but a date has yet to be set.

There are a number of problems for Labour in relation to electoral reform. In one sense, it has conceded the principle that first-past-the-post is not a legitimate electoral system by abandoning it for all but central and local elections. At the same time, the national party is still schizophrenic on the issue. It is torn between the desire to have a majority, in order to implement the New Labour project, and seeing PR as a way of realigning the party system to ensure that Labour remains in office for a long period. Furthermore, it faces the problem that PR in devolved assemblies and possibly the House of Lords will give these institutions greater legitimacy than the Commons elected on FPP. This may reduce the power of the executive or force a shift to PR.

Such a sequence of events has a potentially serious impact on the Westminster model. If there is electoral reform for the Commons and coalition government becomes the norm, key elements of the Westminster system will change:

- Collective responsibility may be harder to maintain with multi-party government.
- Conflicts within the government could become party-based, as well as departmental. This would alter the nature of dependency within the core executive.
- A by-product may be greater openness, as parties leak in order to achieve their own goals. As such, the power of the executive may be more difficult to maintain.
- Policy could depend on compromise between coalition partners rather

than direction, and this may produce a role for backbenchers and parties in negotiating agreements in order to pass legislation.

• Opportunities for Parliament to win concessions from government will be increased. When parties are offered ministerial portfolios as part of a coalition deal, the autonomy of the minister will be increased. For example, if the leader of the Liberal Democratic Party is made Foreign Secretary in return for supporting Labour, the Prime Minister cannot sack him without the possibility of bringing down the government. Consequently, PR will change the relationship between ministers and the Prime Minister.

• Finally, different party and department agendas within government will again fragment the policy process and create new problems of coordination.

The House of Lords

Another arena in which Labour has acted from its 1997 manifesto has been the House of Lords. This has involved a two-stage process.

• Stage 1: remove the hereditary element of membership of the Lords.
• Stage 2: undertake a review process in order to remodel the existing body.

There was considerable controversy surrounding the first stage, which was completed during Labour's first term in office. During this period (1997–2001), both the Conservative and Labour leaders in the Lords resigned and the House itself adopted a discernibly entrenched position in relation to the lower chamber. Despite this, and following the 1999 publication of the White Paper *Modernising Parliament: Reforming the House of Lords,* Labour pushed on with the first stage of its strategy and removed all but ninety-three hereditary peers.

Subsequently, a Royal Commission was appointed under the guidance of the Conservative peer Lord Wakeham to look at suitable alternatives to the present arrangements. In its report, the twelve-member Commission supported a mostly appointed second chamber with a small indirectly elected element. This is not problematic for Labour, who, though committed to removing what it perceives as the antiquated, unjust hereditary element to the Lords, do not wish to see a newly constituted upper chamber with real power and democratic legitimacy capable of challenging the lower house (see Riddell 2000: 114). In the November 2001 White Paper *The House of Lords: Completing the Reform* (Cmnd. 5291), the final proposals were even less radical than many expected. One hundred and twenty members will be elected, 20 per cent will be appointed by an independent appointments commission, and two-thirds will be appointed by the parties reflecting their share of the vote. The Lords will thus remain largely based on patronage, and will continue to be subservient to the Commons and the Government (*Guardian,* 7 November 2001). However, the key issue is not so much how the Lords are appointed but what their powers are, and unless these are reviewed, it is unlikely that the Lords will become a more effective check on government.

Human rights

Another key area which is having an impact on the constitutional settlement inherited by Labour is that of human rights. In October 1998 the Labour Government received royal assent for its Human Rights Bill, which incorporates a version of the European Convention on Human Rights into UK Law (although this did not come into effect until 2000). This enables UK citizens to appeal to any level of UK courts on the grounds of a breach of the convention. The bill has been specifically designed by the Labour Government, in order not to breach the principle of absolute parliamentary sovereignty, while at the same time removing the European Convention's guarantee of effective redress to citizens whose freedoms and rights have been infringed upon. However, it is clear that, despite the bowdlerised version of the European bill which Labour has introduced, it will still have a substantial impact on the rights and freedoms of UK citizens.

Throughout the passage of the bill, the Home Office Minister, Lord Williams, strongly defended it, arguing that it would in no way impinge upon the concept of parliamentary sovereignty by devolving power and responsibility to the judiciary. Despite the guarantees of protecting the freedoms and rights for the individual citizen, however, Lord Williams's pledge as to the sanctity of parliamentary sovereignty appears less than certain. For example, on 27 January 1999 Jack Straw signed the 6th Protocol of the European Convention of Human Rights, part of which abolishes the death penalty in the UK. The implications for Parliament will be that future governments will not be in a position to reopen the debate on the death penalty without first overturning the entire European Convention on Human Rights. Although there has been much rhetoric from the Labour Cabinet to the effect that parliamentary sovereignty has in no way been affected by signing up to the convention, the reality is that clear and discernible structural constraints have now been placed upon Parliament.

Freedom of information

As with human rights, the Labour Government's proposals to introduce freedom of information legislation also have serious constitutional implications. The first stage towards introducing a Freedom of Information Act occurred in December 1997, when the Government published the White Paper *Your Right to Know*. Constitutionally, the key area of any legislation concerning freedom of information centres on reconciling ministerial accountability with a statutory right to information. Following the publication of *Your Right to Know*, it was clear that the Government's priorities lay in protecting the convention of ministerial responsibility. The key elements of the White Paper are: individuals would have a legal right to see almost *all* information; an independent commissioner is to be appointed to police the Act and handle appeals; the law is to be applied right across the public sector; and sensitive information is to be protected. The seven categories to be protected are: national security, defence etc., the internal discussion of government policy, law enforcement, personal privacy, business activities which could unfairly damage a company's commercial standing, the safety of individuals, the public and the environment, and references, testimonials, etc. Following the White Paper, however, the minister responsible, David Clarke, was sacked, and the development of the bill was passed to the more constitutionally conservative Home Office.

The bill drawn up by Jack Straw and the Home Office was the subject of widespread criticism, and was seen as a retreat from the radical proposals of the White Paper. The principal and crucial change is that under the White Paper the 'guiding principle was that disclosure should be the norm' unless the authority in question could prove 'substantial harm' to the public interest. As Hugo Young (1999) points out, it is 'virtually impossible to challenge' a decision if the government claims its interests could be substantially harmed. In addition, the commissioner who can decide on 'substantial harm' is no longer independent because the government can use a parliamentary order to exempt any information being released. According to Young (1999):

This bill is a triumph for the forces of reaction in Whitehall, a reward for the patience of mandarins. They opposed it from the start. They knew it would take time for ministers to lose their idealism, and arranged, with Straw's connivance, for time to pass.

Crucially, the bill excludes any documents relating to policy advice. This raises two problems. First, policy advice can be used to cover much of the information that is passed through Whitehall. Second, it is only through revealing the advice of ministers that the processes of policy-making can be opened up. Without this change, the policy process will continue to be closed and elitist and officials will not be held to account for poor or misguided advice. Indeed, it is only by opening up this procedure that citizens could really become involved in policy-making and the nature of advice given to ministers be improved.

Effective open government would ultimately destroy the Westminster model. It would end the closed, elitist value system that has underpinned the British system of government. Openness would create external supervision but, more importantly, expose the myth of ministerial and collective responsibility. It would reveal, as the Scott Report did, that officials make a whole range of decisions often without ministerial support. In addition, it would open up official advice to scrutiny and accountability, and allow outside groups to challenge the assumptions of official advice, thus allowing for more pluralistic and inclusive policy-making. For these reasons, the government does not intend to have open government. Freedom of information does not include advice to ministers, even though such a change is necessary to make the core executive democratic and open. Much of what will be revealed under the FOI Act is already available under the Conservative Government's changes. As Hazell and Morris (1999: 147) confirm:

At the policy level little will change. Departments will be required to publish all their internal manuals and staff instructions; but this requirement has already existed for five years under the Open Government Code of Practice. . . . Few if any policy papers will be released until after decisions have been made. Overseas experience suggests that will not be related to increased public participation in policy-making . . . To sum up, most FOI requests will be relatively low level; and FOI will not be the great reforming panacea which its proponents sometimes propose.

Indeed, the government's ambiguous attitude to FOI has been illustrated by the implementation process. Initially, the government intended to enact the legislation for central government by 2002. Now FOI will not be introduced until 2005, after Lord Irvine was overruled by the Prime Minister on the implementation process. Rather than allowing a phasing in of FOI, Tony Blair has insisted that it is implemented in all levels of government at the same time, delaying the process until after the probable date of the next general election (Campaign for Freedom of Information 2001). There appears to be no substantive reason for the delay, with many departments having already prepared for an earlier introduction.

Conclusion: Labour's first term—governance vs. joined-up government

During eighteen years of Conservative Government, the British state underwent a programme of almost continuous transformation. Where some commentators would have expected a period of consolidation under Labour, the Government has instead pursued a programme of reform which has again fundamentally redrawn the contours of the state (see Fig. 10.2). Labour's policies on the constitution and the state reveal a number of dilemmas. On the one hand, it has been radical; on the other, it is bound by tradition and pragmatism. Labour has grappled with many features of the constitution—devolution, electoral reform, and the House of Lords—but without recognizing the ways in which the core executive and the Westminster model are fundamentally linked to the reform process. Thus, many features of the constitution are being changed without any real consideration being given to its foundations.

This is a fundamental problem, because the changes that Labour are introducing have profound implications for the Westminster model which the government has failed to properly consider. It is difficult to have devolution, a bill of rights, and an independent Bank of England and maintain notions of sovereignty. The fragmentation of the policy process and proportional voting will threaten executive sovereignty and further reveal the tenuous nature of ministerial responsibility. The greater use of referenda will lead to questions concerning the centrality of Parliament. This reveals the contradictions of the reform programme. Finally, while notions of ministerial and collective responsibility are continually used to obscure

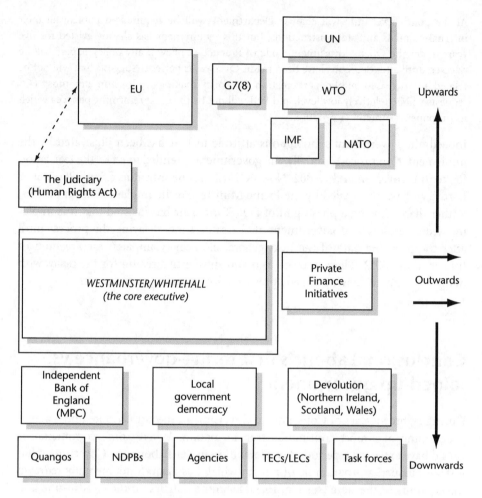

Figure 10.2 The reconstituted state under Labour

how decisions are really made, the system will remain difficult to democratize. Under Labour, the framework of the Westminster model remains, whilst key elements of the model are undermined. For example, the disaggregation of the decision-making process could make greater coordination and joined-up government much harder to attain. This leads us to suggest that, despite the flexible nature of the British constitution, under Labour its point of elasticity may be surpassed and the façade of the Westminster model left exposed.

Finally, if one adopts a holistic view of Labour's programme of reform, the degree to which, since 1997, political power has conditioned Labour's actions soon becomes apparent. As we have seen, Labour does have a state-led project to modernize British society and the polity. It is a project conditioned by pluralistic sentiments aimed at devolving power away from the centre, in part as a safeguard against any future Conservative Government using the state in the same way as occurred in the 1980s. However, the reality of implementing this project has not necessarily proved compatible with the dispersal of power. As this chapter has shown, during its first term Labour did not display wholehearted willingness to relinquish power in the way it promised prior to April 1997. Changes such as devolution, freedom of information, and electoral reform are considered within the context of maintaining the executive power which was so useful to the Thatcherite project. This creates an almost impossible task: New Labour is trying to reform the constitution and the state without surrendering the powers of the state. Consequently, reform will be deformed or limited, or it will produce outcomes which are unintended and (possibly) more far-reaching than the Government foresaw. Moreover, in office Labour has appeared willing to trust the nation(s) through the devolution of power to the periphery while still not trusting its own Party [witness the attempts to impose candidates in various elections]. Two decades ago, Beer (1982: 103) spoke of the Labour Party applying a political model based on 'pluralism without consensus'; today, we would wish to suggest that New Labour is applying a political model of 'plurality without pluralism'.

KEY POINTS

- Until the 1990s, the Labour Party was committed to a unitary model of the UK and maintained a largely uncritical respect for the British constitution, and with it a belief in the Westminster model of government.

- In the 1990s Labour rejected the corporatist model of state and civil society relations and accepted a number of Conservative reforms of the state.

- Since 1997 Labour has instead opted for a 'third way' approach involving the state, private, and voluntary sectors, in an integrated approach to providing solutions to problems in society. The most obvious examples are public–private partnerships and public–private finance initiatives.

- In order to address the perceived pathology of governance—that of fragmentation and a loss of control—Labour's solution has been to embark on a programme of joined-up government. This has involved the reform of the machinery of government, most notably in the strengthening of the centre of government, the creation of a number of new coordinating units, and the use of task forces.

- Labour has also redrawn the boundaries of the state by pursuing a programme of devolution and regionalism.

KEY QUESTIONS

1. Account for Labour's traditional willingness to accept the Westminster model of government.

2. To what extent have Labour's reforms of the state since 1997 undermined the Westminster Model?

3. Analyse Labour's programme of joined-up government as an effective solution to the problems associated with governance.

4. To what extent have Labour's reforms, in particular devolution, affected the nature of power in the policy-making arena?

KEY READING

For traditional accounts of Labour's relationship with the state, see: McKibbin (1974) and Kavanagh (1985). For literature on the Third Way, the key texts are: Giddens (1994), (1997), and (2000). There are many academic texts on Labour and reform after 1997, including Ludlam and Smith (2001), Coates and Lawler (2000) (eds.), and Savage and Atkinson (2001). For a more irreverent, but well-informed, journalistic account see Rawnsley (2001).

KEY WEBSITES

For websites on the Labour Party, see www.labour.org.uk; for information on reform of the House of the Lords, see www.parliament.uk. For Labour's programme of state reform, the Constitution Unit's site is very useful; www.ucl.ac.uk/constitution-unit. For details on the impact of reform on various departments, the best starting point is: www.open.gov.uk or, more specifically: www.cabinet-office.gov.uk. For issues concerning Labour's reform of the state, go to: www.fhit.org/democratic_audit/index.html or the site of Charter 88: www.charter88.org.uk. There are many sites on devolution, including the Scottish Parliament, www.scottish.parliament.uk, the Welsh Assembly, www.wales.gov.uk/assembly.dbs, the Northern Ireland Assembly, www.ni-assembly.gov.uk/ and the London Assembly, www.london.gov.uk.

11

CONCLUSION: GOVERNANCE, POWER, AND PUBLIC POLICY

Governance and understanding change in the British state

In Chapter 1, we presented a narrative of governance illustrated by three snap-shots of governing in postwar Britain: the first picture was an 'era of government', some time in the 1950s. It was argued that governing was a relatively straight-forward exercise. The policy arena had yet to fragment, policy-making was pre-dominantly a top-down process and central government was regarded as the most dominant and powerful actor in a relatively uncluttered environment. The key theme concerned the power and command-control that central government enjoyed in the making of policy. Our second picture was taken sometime in the early 1990s, and the scene depicted, labelled an 'era of governance', had notably changed. The policy arena had been extended to include a variety of new terrains, the number of actors located on these terrains had increased, and central govern-ment had become only one amongst many when it came to the making of policy. The key theme was the extent to which central government had lost the power to control a fragmented and disaggregated policy-making process. At best, the role of government in this picture was one of striving to achieve some semblance of coordination when it came to the making of policy. Our final picture, labelled 'an era of joined-up-government', is taken some time in 2001, as the Blair Labour Government reached the end of its first term in office. This picture is still in the process of developing, but a blurred image can be discerned of a government striving to reimpose its own power and command-control over the fragmented policy-making arena it believes it inherited from the Conservatives.

The images depicted above are useful, as they provide a characterization of the changing nature of the policy-making process in Britain over the last fifty years. As with all characterizations, however, they can be superficial, sometimes mis-representative, and so fail to capture the subtle nature of change over time. For example, is the image depicted in our first shot a true reflection of the nature of governing in the 1950s? Is it true that in the past policy-making was a simple top-down process, or is this a simplification? Secondly, our picture of governance in the 1990s presents a view of government struggling to maintain control, having being relegated to being simply one actor amongst many in a crowded and frag-mented policy-making arena. If this is the case, how can this be reconciled with the legacy of the Thatcher Administration and Thatcherism? The narrative of govern-ance, a hollowed-out state, and globalization all suggest that the power of the core executive has waned. Countering this is the view that the Thatcher Administration possessed the political tools to achieve a 'reordering of British politics' by creating a 'free economy and a strong state' (see Gamble 1994b, Kavanagh 1997).

What we hoped to have achieved in this book is to highlight the subtle nature of change, when it comes to making sense of what is meant by governance and assessing its impact on public policy. Change has been gradual and incre-mental, and in some cases the forces of change, most notably globalization, have been much exaggerated. For example, Hogwood (1997) provides a powerful cri-tique of the 'hollowing-out of the state' thesis by arguing that its conclusions are confusing: it suggests that 'hollowing-out' has led to a lack of control, but on whose behalf—the state or Cabinet ministers? As we saw in Chapter 9, other commentators (Campbell and Wilson 1995, Foster and Plowden 1996) have argued that more powers have accrued to ministers since 1979 than at any other time throughout the duration of the modern British state. There appear to be at least two countervailing critiques. How, then, is it possible to make sense of what appear to be contradictory analyses of the changing nature of the policy process? We suggest that one approach is to consider the impact of governance, in terms of the changing roles and arenas in which policy is made.

Governance and public policy: changing roles and arenas

In Chapter 2, we suggested that one of the broader themes associated with govern-ance has been a decline in the capacity of central government to control the policy-making arena. Indeed, we claim that this is one of the key issues in political science, as it raises a series of important questions concerning the nature of state power in contemporary British society. A criticism of much of the existing literature on public policy is that it focuses on micro-themes, such as processes and organizations. This leads to a tendency to gloss over broader macro-themes, including the changing nature of power in an 'era of governance'. In order to rectify this, throughout this book we have adopted the 'state-centric' view of governance identified by Pierre and Peters (2000). This approach considers the extent to which the capacity of central government to exert control over other areas of the state, the economy, and society has changed in the last thirty years. Thus, in Chapter 2 we set ourselves the task of considering the extent to which central government, or more specifically the core executive, still retains the power to steer or control policy through political brokerage, by defining goals and making priorities.

One way of accomplishing this task is to consider the way in which the arenas and roles of actors associated with the policy-making process have altered in the last three decades. Indeed, our own definition of governance encapsulates this exact theme:

> 'Governance' is a descriptive label that is used to highlight the changing nature of the policy process in recent decades. In particular, it sensitizes us to the ever-increasing variety of terrains and actors involved in the making of public policy. Thus, governance demands that we consider all the actors and locations beyond 'the core executive' involved in the policy-making process.

What we have been concerned with throughout this book is the nature of state power and how it has changed over time, as a consequence of exogenous and endogenous changes.

Governance and change over time

Much of the literature on governance (see Chapter 2) suggests that there have been major changes in the policy-making process. We would not wish to disagree with this argument. At the same time, other elements of the policy-making arena have endured, despite the pressure for change. In the last thirty years, we would suggest that some of the key areas of continuity and change in policy-making have been:

- The arena in which policy is made has altered. An obvious example here would be the impact that British membership of the EU has had on policy-making (see Chapter 7). Indeed, more broadly, British central government in 2001 is much more embedded in supranational organizations such as the EU, WTO, and G8 than in the 1950s. Elsewhere, the introduction of executive agencies, the growth in quangos, and, more recently, the devolution of power to the regions since 1997 have all created a greater diversity in the arenas in which policy-making occurs (see Chapter 5 and 10). In turn, these have altered the patterns of dependency between actors within the core executive.

- There have been shifting patterns, in terms of size and sphere of influence, between the public and private arena (see Chapter 8). This can be seen in terms of the extent of privatization that occurred throughout the 1980s and 1990s. But accompanying privatization has been the introduction of state regulatory bodies. Thus, the changing nature of the public/private arena is both subtle and complex. Elsewhere, after 1979, the role of interest groups in policy-making generally declined under Conservative governments, except where a relationship of high dependence already existed, for example in policing, health, and agricultural policy. By 1997 there were clear differences from the corporatist era of the late 1960s and 1970s (see Chapter 8). After 1997, however, New Labour brought with it to government an array of client-interest groups, and this had a reinvigorating effect upon civil society (see Chapters 8 and 10). Again, the pattern of dependency between central government and civil society has been a process of almost constant renegotiation over the last thirty years.

- It is clear that change in the international economic order has affected the structured environment in which central government now operates (see Chapter 6). However, much of the discourse on globalization has overstated the extent to which central government has had its powers ameliorated and to which political decisions are now being made beyond the control of government. For example, international fora are not a new phenomenon: it has always been the case that they can be used as much to facilitate the power of national government as to impose constraints on it. The point here is that patterns of dependency and sovereignty have been shifting over the last thirty years between and within British central government and other supranational organizations. But, the process is as much one of positive-sum, as of zero-sum game (see Chapters 6 and 7).

- The arenas of the core executive have changed. Formal Cabinet has become less important, whilst the Prime Minister's Office has become more policy-active. In addition, ministers are operating in different arenas, working in international bodies and with regulatory and private bodies. Their sources of advice have multiplied, and they have become more active in policy-making. However, the key structures and resources of the core executive have remained the same. Departments continue to structure what goes on within central government, and the relationships of dependency are still important (see Chapter 9).

- The Civil Service retains many of its traditional elements. Officials are still the dominant policy advisers within the core executive, and their advice on political operations within Whitehall remains essential to ministers (see Chapter 9). However, their role has changed. The trend has been for senior officials to become more involved in management, pushing the policy-making function further down the Whitehall grades. The arguments that suggest that the Whitehall paradigm has withered (see Campbell and Wilson 1995, Foster and Plowden 1996) are exaggerated. Civil servants remain one of the most important actors in the policy process; in particular, their role as gatekeeper between the minister and civil society continues to provide an important structural source of power.

- The resources of ministers have increased (see also Chapter 9). Since 1979, they have increasingly used alternative sources of advice, in the form of think tanks, consultancy agencies, and special advisers, in order to achieve their goals. The relationship between ministers and officials is still one of dependency based on exchange. The evidence we have presented above suggests that, despite the structural changes that have occurred in the policy arena, the most crucial actors are still those located within departments, i.e. ministers and civil servants. Together, these two groups of actors remain the guardians of the policy process.

Governance and state power

Our study has demonstrated how governance has affected the power of the core executive to control the policy-making arena. As we have seen above, governance has been concerned with both exogenous and endogenous change in the policy-making arena. What we have shown is that these changes have affected the resources, context, and structure of the arena in which the core executive operates. Despite the changing environment, the core executive remains the dominant actor in the policy-making process.

How has it maintained this dominant position? In part, this can be explained by the core executive's desire to preserve the 'British political tradition' (see Chapter 9). Thus, although over the last thirty years change has been driven by the core executive (in the form of privatization, agencies, quangos, EU integration, etc.), in other areas such as Europeanization and globalization it has been externally driven. In both cases, however, the core executive has possessed the capacity to adapt to its changing environment. At the heart of this adaptation has been the shared goal of ministers and civil servants to protect their own status and power. In order to achieve this aim, the core executive has clung on to key characteristics of the Westminster model, including hierarchy, secrecy, and elitism. As Marsh et al. (2001: 233) argue:

The Westminster model still informs the value systems of officials and ministers. Whilst there have been changes in intra- and inter-Whitehall relationships, they have not undermined many of the traditional assumptions that the practitioners have about the workings of the system.

This view seems to suggest that officials and ministers are now only partially aware of the world which they inhabit. They believe that they are free to make decisions, when the reality is that both governance and globalization have reduced the status and power of the core executive to little more than the equivalent of that of a parish council within a diocese. They suggest power can be found elsewhere, in particular at the supranational level and in self-organizing networks. There is nothing novel in this argument. For example, a year after the Thatcher Government was first elected, Rose (1980: 1) observed:

The challenge of governance today is an international challenge. Every major European polity faces problems of paying for the policies that constitute the contemporary welfare state, and maintaining the economy that has made both public and private affluence possible. Moreover, contemporary politicians face problems of controlling government itself. The growth of government has created institutions of such complexity and size that they threaten to assume a direction and a force of their own, notwithstanding the intentions of those elected to direct their activities.

Rose argued that the optimism of the 1960s had evaporated, and that by the end of the 1970s pessimism about the ability of government to deliver had become endemic. His outlook was downbeat, believing that changes in the environment were overwhelming the capacity of government to govern. What Rose failed to account for was the capacity of the state and state actors to adapt to their changing environment.

We are sceptical of the arguments that suggest power in the British polity has shifted away from Westminster/Whitehall to the extent that the core executive has had its powers curtailed. Instead, we would suggest that the core executive has had the capacity to adapt, in particular, because change has occurred more broadly within the context of the British parliamentary state (see Judge 1993). The nature of the parliamentary state confers a high concentration of power on the executive. For example, one can recall the arguments made by Lord Hailsham in 1976, when delivering the BBC Dimbleby Lecture, in which he lamented that Britain in effect had a five-year 'elective dictatorship'. More recently, Peters (2000: 42) has observed:

By appearing to argue that the state, or the centre of government, is largely incapable of ruling, it appears to refuse to consider that indeed there are cases in which the centre may be effective. That variance may be by country, with the state in some countries—Singapore, Iraq, but also the United Kingdom—having a great deal of capacity to achieve compliance from society.

Despite the impact of governance on the British polity, it remains the case that the majority of key decisions are made within the executive—parliamentary sovereignty in reality is executive sovereignty (see Smith 1999: 11). This is reinforced by a deferential political culture, secrecy, and elitism. The core executive thus possesses greater capacity than many other actors in the policy-making process to respond to the changed environment of governance and protect its own status and power. As Saward (1997: 26) observes:

. . . by pursuing strategies designed to cope with state complexity, core executive actors are using the key characteristics of the state—its monopoly of the legitimate use of coercion (or, more pointedly, their legitimate capacity to wield their monopoly)—in a more explicit and directed manner than has been evident for some time (though this is true of Britain more than . . . other countries).

We would therefore suggest that power within the British political system remains asymmetrically distributed in favour of the core executive (see below). Furthermore, despite the changes that have taken place in the last thirty years, the policy process in Britain retains the key elements of being predominantly top-down, closed, secretive, and elitist.

The hollow state vs. the reconstituted state

Our narrative of governance has led us to conclude that despite the changes that have occurred in the policy-making arena during the era of governance, the core executive remains the dominant actor. One issue we must, however, consider in more detail is the notion of the 'hollowed-out state' (see Chapter 2). Clearly, our position leads us to be sceptical about this thesis. Evidence suggests that British central government is still powerful (see Marsh et al. 2000: 240). For example, let us examine one of the key elements of the hollowing-out thesis: that power has shifted 'upwards' to transnational corporations and international financial markets, as a result of the process of globalization, and to Europe, as a consequence of EU membership. First, as we argued in Chapter 6, the extent of globalization is often greatly overestimated. Trade is regionalized, not globalized, and while financial markets are increasingly global, they do not affect all states equally, or in the same way. Consequently, states have considerable autonomy in how they interpret the constraints placed upon them by so-called global forces. Secondly, as we saw in Chapter 7, the EU may constrain British government, but it also offers opportunities. More broadly, we would concur with the argument of Buller (2000), that British governments have used the EU for their own ends. Britain is often seen as an awkward partner in the EU (see George 1998), but, as Buller argues, this is a misleading conceptualization. The Conservative Government's stance in relation to Europe probably had more to do with domestic politics than it did with Britain's relations with Europe. The Conservatives used their opposition to Europe to strengthen their image of governing competence: they argued that they could stand up to powerful forces within Britain, such as the trade unions, and forces outside Britain such as the bureaucrats in Brussels. In this way the EU was an asset to the Conservatives. It may have restricted their autonomy to a limited extent, but it gave them an opponent to define themselves against: they could pose as the defender of Britain against the EU and, as such, as the opponents of Britain's power being transferred to Brussels, or hollowed out. Indeed, Tony Blair (2001) seems to be rethinking the nature of sovereignty:

I see sovereignty as not merely as the ability of a single country to say no, but as the power to maximise our national strength and capacity in business, trade, foreign policy, defence and the fight against crime. Sovereignty has to be employed for national advantage. *When we isolated ourselves in the past, we squandered our sovereignty—leaving us as sole masters of a shrinking sphere.* (Emphasis added.)

If we are circumspect about the extent to which power has shifted upwards to the supranational level, we are also critical of the extent to which power has shifted outwards and downwards in the form of privatization and the contracting-out of functions to non-state and quasi-state institutions during the 1980–90s. For example, while privatization has undoubtedly changed the boundaries of the state, it has not necessarily reduced the role or power of the state or, more particularly, the core executive. As we saw in Chapter 5, the government has continued to control the privatized monopolies through the creation of state regulatory bodies. As Majone (1994: 79; cf. Saward 1997: 22) observes, privatization tends to strengthen rather than weaken the regulatory capacity of the state. As this book has shown, while the boundaries of the state have changed, the core executive has retained many of its powers, and control over the policy process. We therefore conclude that the state has been 'reconstituted', rather than hollowed out (see Saward 1997, Smith 1999, Richards 1999, Richards and Smith 2000, Marsh et al. 2001).

So far we have made three key concluding observations:

- During the era of the governance, both the British state and with it the policy-making arena have undergone some substantial changes.
- However, governance has not led to a hollowed-out but to a reconstituted state.
- Throughout the process of reconstitution, the core executive has had the capacity and resources to adapt, in order to retain its dominant position within the policy process.

These conclusions do, however, lead to a problem: which model provides the most suitable organizing perspective on the British polity?

Competing models of British government

Revisiting the Westminster model and the differentiated polity model

The Westminster model

As we have seen throughout the course of this book, understandings of the policy process in Britain by both academics and policy-makers have been shaped in different ways by the Westminster system of government—or what is known as the Westminster model. As Rhodes (2000: 5–6; see also Chapter 3 above) points out, there are various versions of the Westminster model, but a number of key characteristics are agreed:

- parliamentary sovereignty
- accountability through free and fair elections
- majority party control over the executive
- strong Cabinet government
- central government dominance

- doctrine of ministerial responsibility
- non-political officials

The Westminster model suggests that, while the doctrine of parliamentary sovereignty underpins the institutions and processes of British politics, the way the system operates is based upon two linked characteristics of the British political system. First, a first-past-the-post electoral system which, while it holds the executive accountable at periodic free and fair elections, almost inevitably gives one party an overall majority. Secondly, strong party discipline, which together with the electoral system produces majority government, strong Cabinet government, and executive dominance of the legislature. In addition, sovereignty presumed a unity and territorial integrity to the central British state.

Essentially this was a closed and elitist system of policy-making, but its closed nature was justified through the principle of ministerial responsibility and periodic elections. Moreover, the public-service ethos was a moral framework based on the assumption that officials were working for the public good, not their own personal interests. Therefore, although they were acting in secret, they could be trusted to make the best possible decisions. The decision-making process was indeed based on officials marshalling the facts and warning ministers of the pitfalls of various options, and the minister making the decision that s/he would have to account for, first to Parliament and then to the electorate.

A range of factors undermined the assumptions of this model:

- Ministerial accountability rarely seemed to work the way that it should. Ministers could hide decisions from Parliament and rarely resigned for reasons of accountability.
- The lines of accountability were further blurred by privatization, managerialism, and the creation of agencies.
- The public-service ethos was challenged by managerialism, which presumes that officials should be constrained by market criteria, and by the 'arms to Iraq' and BSE scandals, which revealed officials to be acting in secret to protect their own interests rather than the public good.
- The unity of the state was undermined by growing regionalist feeling and the development of devolution.
- Territorial integrity was undermined by the increasing Europeanization and globalization of a range of policies.
- Cabinet government was hollowed out by departmentalism and increasingly policy-active prime ministers, who institutionalized their policy-making capacity in the Prime Minister's Office and the Cabinet Office.
- The fragmentation of the state through devolution, managerialism, and multi-level governance appears to have undermined the capacity of the central state.

These changes led Rhodes to suggest that the Westminster model no longer provided an adequate organizing perspective on the British political system. Instead, he constructed what he refers to as the 'differentiated polity' (see Chapter 2) in order to account for change.

The differentiated polity model

The main features are:

- an emphasis upon governance, rather than government
- power dependence, and thus exchange relationships
- policy networks
- a segmented executive
- intergovernmental relations
- a hollowed-out state

The differentiated polity model regards power as being dispersed: the once unified state is fragmented and networks have replaced hierarchy. The policy process has become much more complex: rather than being a linear process with decisions being made in the centre, it has become one where a range of actors are involved.

Clearly, Rhodes is correct in identifying situations where policy decisions now involve public-sector and private-sector actors, agencies, privatized industries, regulators, officials, and ministers. The process of policy-making and policy delivery has become more complex. We only have to look at the way in which rail policy was made in 1947 and how it is made now (see Boxes 11.1 and 11.2). Nevertheless, the key issues are not whether the policy process has changed, but how we analyse that change and what it means in terms of the distribution of power.

Box 11.1 Old forms of governance: the nationalized railways

With the 1947 Transport Act, the role of providing an efficient and integrated transport system was given to the British Transport Commission (BTC). It had overall responsibility for rail policy, whilst the railway service was to be delivered by the Railway Executive. Members of both the BTC and the Railway Executive were appointed by the Minister of Transport. In a sense, although there were a number of different actors in the rail network and a division between policy and operational responsibility, a clear hierarchy existed from the Minister through the BTC to the rail executive. Of course, what was crucially important was that the Minister had the authority and power to make decisions on how rail services should be delivered if he chose. Despite a belief that nationalized industries should not be directly controlled by ministers, through patronage, finance and legislation, the Minister could have considerable impact.

(*Source*: Squires 1999)

Box 11.2 New forms of governance: the running of the railways

The complexity of the policy and implementation process is highlighted by the organization of the railways that has developed with their privatisation, fragmentation and the myriad of contract relationships that have been created. As John Ware said on Panorama (BBC 2001a): 'Whatever the failings of British Rail, one thing was certain, at least you knew who was in charge. Now the system has broken into 100 different pieces all held together by legal contracts. Welcome to the most fragmented railway in the world'.

A glance at who is involved in the delivery of the service indicates the degree of fragmentation. There are a large number of individual train companies such as Virgin, Midland Mainline, and GNER which provide the trains that deliver the services to passengers. Often these companies lease rather than own the trains. The tracks, bridges and signals are owned by Railtrack. Railtrack does not carry out maintenance directly; it is done through a myriad of contractors. Then, of course, government has provided significant amounts of public money available through subsidies to rail companies, through the writing off of Railtrack's £1 billion of debt and through the government's investment programme, which promises £26 billion over the next 10 years. Two thirds of Railtrack's income comes from the government (*Guardian*, 21 Nov. 2001).

In addition, there is a rail regulator, who for example has made an 'enforcement order' for Railtrack to improve the operation of the railways. The Strategic Railway Authority is responsible for monitoring the operation of services on behalf of passengers and providing government money for the provision of better passenger services. It is responsible for the management of passenger rail franchises and ensuring integrated service delivery for passengers. HM Inspector of Railways is responsible for ensuring that the railways meet health and safety regulations. The complex network of different service providers, funders, and regulators have failed to provide a more efficient rail service. Prices have risen, investment has fallen, and the financial situation of Railtrack has deteriorated to the extent that it has effectively been renationalized (see Box 5.6). The flaw was the hiving off of Railtrack and the attempt to make it profit-orientated, while at the same time requiring investment in both safety and better services

(*Source*: BBC 2001b)

Governance and postmodernism: a flawed analysis

One suggestion is that the state has now become a postmodern state (see Chapter 2). In other words, the state is no longer using standardized procedures and institutions to achieve social planning and social progress. For example:

- Legal and administrative order has been lost through managerialism, contracts, and devolution which diversify the forms of mechanisms for delivering public goods.
- The growth of transnational organization and cross-border policy processes has undermined territoriality.

- The state has lost its monopoly of 'legitimate violence' through the privatization of prisons and a number of 'security aspects' of policing.
- Greater attention is paid to the demands of the consumer and the role of participation in the implementing of decisions.

Here, we would reject the postmodernist critique of the state and instead aver that the state remains based on the key tenets of modernism—rationalism, foundationalism, and a belief in an improving future. Indeed, our analysis of the two key variables examined throughout this book—welfare provision and the economy—suggests that the death of the modernist state has been greatly exaggerated. First, the central state in 2000 spent £393,700,000 million. This amount is much greater than the financial resources of any non-state organization in Britain, and much greater than the state has ever spent before. The central state alone directly employs half a million people, whilst those employed in the public sector, including people such as teachers, doctors, and the police, run into millions. The state still has distinct plans for social improvement, whether it is through targets on drugs, crime, educational standards, heart operations, or unemployment. Britain also retains an enormous welfare state: nearly everyone in Britain at some point receives state-funded education, health care, social security, and pensions. The parents of all children under 16 receive child benefit. All children receive free dental care, prescriptions and eye tests.

In the last thirty years, there have clearly been important reforms to the welfare state. Internal markets have been introduced into the health care system. In education there is much greater central control, and the patterns of social security benefits have significantly changed. Nevertheless, many of the key elements of the Beveridge welfare state remain in place and are funded directly by the state (see Pierson 1998). In December 2001 the Chancellor, Gordon Brown, committed the Government to improving health care through a tax-based system rather than shifting to some form of insurance system. The Treasury is committed to increasing the percentage of national income that goes into health care. Whilst elements of the delivery have fragmented, for example, in terms of the relationship between GP fund-holders and NHS trusts and for many services such as those for the homeless, voluntary and private elements have been introduced, there are also attempts to tie these fragmented service deliverers together through joined-up government.

Likewise, in the economy, governments since 1979 appear to have abandoned detailed intervention in the economy, and the process of privatization and disengagement from private production has changed the arena of economic policy-making. Nevertheless, there is little doubt that government still has a continual and substantial impact on economic development in Britain. According to the Treasury (2001), its objectives are:

- maintaining a stable macro-economic framework with low inflation;
- improving the quality and the cost effectiveness of public services;

- maintaining sound public finances in accordance with the Code for Fiscal Stability;
- increasing the productivity of the economy;
- expanding economic and employment opportunities for all;
- promoting a fair and efficient tax and benefit system with incentives to work, save, and invest;
- achieving a high standard of regularity, propriety, and accountability in public finance;
- securing an innovative, fair-dealing, competitive, and efficient market in financial services, while striking the right balance with regulation in the public interest;
- promoting UK economic prospects by pursuing increased productivity and efficiency in the EU, international financial stability, and increased global prosperity, including especially protecting the most vulnerable.

These are all clear goals based on a presumption that the government can and does make a difference to the organization of the economy. Moreover, these differences are progressive, in the sense that they are based on a rationalist belief that government can make improvements. Government continues to have a major impact on the operation of the British economy through expenditure, taxation, investment, and monetary policy decisions, despite the importance of external economic factors. The level of fuel duty, the level of income tax, the structure of the training system, and the nature of corporation tax are all factors under the control of government, and each one can have a direct impact on the day-to-day lives of citizens.

Governance and the modern state: new means, same ending?

What is increasingly apparent is that it is not what the state does that is different, but how it does it. The arguments we have presented in this book lead us to conclude that the goals of the modern state have broadly remained intact—a commitment to progress, good government, welfare provision, economic growth, a stable society, and civil order (see Chapters 3 and 4). However, the mechanisms for achieving these modernist goals have changed. In the postwar era, the most dominant means of state intervention were bureaucracy, legislation, financial control, regulation, and force. Whilst all of these mechanisms still exist, the way they are used and the use of different forms of control have changed the way the state operates. Increasingly, public policy is now delivered through:

- publicly regulated, private mechanisms—as we have seen above, what the government does is use the private sector and voluntary sectors to deliver goods, but the delivery of services are highly regulated (see Chapters 8 and 10). This regulation operates either through the establishment of regulators or through the contracts made between the government of the service and the delivery. Often this regulation is reinforced by the fact that the deliverers of services are dependent on the state for finance. Throughout this book we have argued that the state, rather than being hollowed-out in the governance era, has instead been reconstituted (see also Marsh et al. 2001).

- incentivization—increasingly government is using a rational-choice ontology of providing incentives to form the basis of policies aimed at encouraging modified forms of behaviour. They may be crude as in the case of welfare to work, where young people who do not undertake jobs or training lose their benefits. They can also take a more subtle form, for example, where the publication of league tables are used to shame schools or hospitals into better levels of performance. The use of incentivation is often linked to market models of behaviour based on the idea that if people have information, they can make choices, and that if public money follows people's choices, for example in schools, then the poor performers will have to improve or else ultimately be closed down.

- surveillance—incentives are often based on league tables and targets. These tables and targets are constructed on the growing amount of information that public and quasi-public bodies have to provide for government. The growth of information technology has exponentially enhanced the ability of government to collect and analyse all forms of data. This surveillance of activity is an important element in enabling the central state to control the activities of wide-ranging bodies. This surveillance affects every citizen, increasingly through CCTV, the monitoring of the internet, financial transactions, and working patterns, all of which are monitored by a range of public bodies.

It is extremely difficult to think of any human activity that is not in some way regulated by the state. For example, even the most private of acts, that of sexual intercourse between consenting adults, is not a state-free activity. It is based on a legal definition of sexual intercourse, consenting and adult. Nevertheless, as the state's ability to obtain and process more information develops, so too do the mechanisms for subverting the state. Forces such as the Internet, digital television, and relatively cheap international travel all allow a greater and less controlled flow of ideas and people. The events of 11 September 2001 have reminded people of the fragility of modernism and the ease with which a relatively small group of people can threaten the security of the most powerful nation-state in the world. Elsewhere, over fifty years ago, some of the ideals associated with the modern state were seen to be taken to their extreme conclusion in the events surrounding the Holocaust, following the rise of Hitler and the establishment of the Third Reich in Germany (see Arendt 1951, 1958, Bauman 1989). As Lyon (1994: 32) observes:

Writers such as Hannah Arendt and Zygmunt Bauman have shown how the Holocaust, so far from being an aberration from 'rational civilisation', actually expressed it with exquisite cruelty. How else, than by considering Weber's dispassionate official, could we understand the concentration camp commandant who moved naturally between the gas chambers and his own children's play-room?

What the Holocaust and 11 September illustrated are the contradictions and flaws in modernism: the attempt to resolve problems results in new and often greater problems. Unlike the postmodernist vision, however, the remedies to these problems are not usually the end of grand schemes and narratives, but new modernist solutions. The failure of one form of governance is the establishment of a higher level of regulation (Jessop 2002).

In addition, as we have discussed above, there is the issue of the impact of global and European integration. Here, while it is difficult to deny that there have been significant international changes that affect the context and choices of nation-states, we would reject the ideas of the transformationalists that globalization means the end of the nation-state and the creation of new forms of political organization. There is clearly a set of transnational and international organizations such as the WTO and the EU that have a direct effect on the policy of nation-states. There is also a range of policies like environmental policy and defence policy that are now often developed in international arenas. It is also the case that an increasing number of pressure groups see international arenas as the key sites for decision-making. However, these international organizations and international laws do not undermine the nation-state, but change the terrain upon which they act. They affect the arenas of policy-making for the state and affect what the state can do, but usually it is state actors which are operating in and through these international organizations. As we saw in Chapter 7, on Europeanization, the EU is dependent on nation-states more than nation-states are dependent on the EU.

If we are to understand the policy process in the twenty-first century, we need to be aware of the fact that we are examining a process that is not determined by, but subject to, political forces. As we have argued above, change is subtle and gradual; it is not an easily observable linear shift from a hierarchical modern state to a fragmented, hollowed-out, postmodern state. Change in one area may be counteracted by change in another (see Box 11.3).

Governance and power in the British state: an asymmetric model

What does this mean for the power of the British state? Which model of the state now most appropriately characterizes the British polity? Under the Westminster model, the locus of power was relatively clear: it was the executive, whether defined as the Prime Minister, Cabinet, or departmental government. With the internal and external changes that have occurred since the 1980s, the distribution of power appears to have fragmented—a theme captured in the differentiated polity model. Yet we have also argued that, whilst there have clearly been changes in the policy

---

Box 11.3　The complexity of governance: bananas and farmers

Whilst the WTO has forced the EU to open up its banana market, leading to the small banana producers of the Caribbean being forced out of production by the large multi-nationals of Latin America, elsewhere smallholder French farmers have managed to retain the CAP subsidies for agriculture. This, then, is not simply a process of an inexor-able shift to globalization but a more complex and variegated pattern of different state power in an international political arena. The EU gives up its concession to Caribbean bananas because the farmers of the Windward Isles have less power than the French farmers and the French government. At the same time NGOs may be enabling Wind-ward producers to develop fair trade and organic markets as a way of developing a niche, so that they can survive the Latin American combines. This leads to the rather obvious, yet important, observation that the world is complex and may be even more complex now than it was; but states and power remain important. Nevertheless, the context of politics has changed.

---

arena, the state remains the most dominant political actor within the British polit-ical system. It has the most resources in terms of income (taxation), personnel, information, and force. Whilst there are more actors involved in the policy process and the relationships between them have changed, the relationship continues to be asymmetrical in that the central state continues to dominate when it chooses. The case of Railtrack is a useful illustration of how the state can intervene where it so wishes. Neither the Westminster model nor the differentiated polity model reflects a state that despite undergoing substantial change has been able to retain a high concentration of power at the centre. In order to rectify this problem, Marsh et al. (2001) have proposed the 'asymmetric power' model of the British polity. The key characteristics of this model are:

- a society which is marked by continuing patterns of structured inequality;
- a British political tradition that emphasizes the view that 'Government knows best';
- asymmetries of power;
- exchange relationships between actors in the system of governance;
- a strong, if segmented, executive;
- limited external constraints on executive power.

Below, we will briefly examine what is meant by each of these characteristics:

Structured inequality

Actors continue to have unequal access to the political process and political power. The poor, ethnic minorities, and women are systematically discriminated against, in terms of access to power and the economy. The political system may have fragmented, but many groups are still excluded from the policy process.

The British political tradition

Despite the threats to the Westminster model, the institutions and processes of British politics are underpinned by a view of democracy that continues to stress:

- a limited, liberal notion of representation—here the emphasis is upon the holding of periodic, relatively free and fair elections;
- a conservative notion of responsibility—here the emphasis is on the need for strong and decisive, rather than responsive, government.

Of course, both the British political tradition and the Westminster model present a false picture of how the British political system actually works. The key features—parliamentary sovereignty, ministerial responsibility, and collective responsibility—do not function as the model suggests. Unsurprisingly, however, this is the view of democracy shared by the actors in the core executive; it legitimizes their authority and power, and as such, how the political system works. It has shaped the process of constitutional reform and it continues to maintain elite rule. The code that underpins the British political system is still one that emphasizes that the men (*sic*) in Whitehall, and, more broadly, the core executive, 'know best'.

Asymmetric power

There are crucial asymmetries of power in the British political system. Rhodes (1997) rightly observes that resources have, to an extent, shifted away from the core executive to other actors, and that the process of governing has become more complex. Increasingly, the delivery of public goods involves the creation of networks including government, regulators, and private and third sector actors. However, whilst the government is often dependent on these organizations for the delivery of the service, they in turn continue to depend on the government, which has a unique set of resources—force, legitimacy, state bureaucracy, tax-raising powers, and legislation—which are unavailable to other actors. The relationship between the government and most other interests thus remains asymmetrical. The government effectively sanctions membership of networks, and has a number of mechanisms for reasserting control where necessary. Only interests which themselves have crucial resources, such as knowledge, expertise, finance, and access to the media—and we would argue these are invariably economic (e.g. the City, the CBI, or the Institute of Directors) or professional (e.g. ACPO, the NFU or the BMA)—have consistent privileged access to, and influence over, government.

One example of this pattern was evident in the aftermath of the fuel crisis in September 2000 (see Box 8.7). After the crisis, the government created a task force which was essentially a network of the key actors, including government, oil companies, and major hauliers—all powerful economic interests with resources to exchange. However, all these actors signed a 'Memorandum of Understanding' in which they publicly, at least, recognized the Government's dominance and accepted that the government has the authority to prevent future fuel blockades.

A pattern of exchange relationships

Like Rhodes, we accept that power is not zero-sum but involves exchange relation-ships that are based upon patterns of dependence. Private companies, transnational organizations, voluntary organizations, quangos, and agencies are involved in a process of exchange with different levels or sections of government. However, the continued strength of the executive and its control of significant resources means that, whilst the Government sometimes fails to get its way, it still continues to win policy battles much (we would argue most) of the time. Moreover, whilst external and internal changes have affected the process of the delivery of public goods, the central state, directly and indirectly, still has significant influence on how and what services are delivered.

A strong if segmented executive

Despite recent constitutional reforms, Britain retains a strong executive. The core executive is clearly not a unified whole, and Rhodes rightly emphasizes its seg-mented character. However, power continues to be concentrated within the core executive, and the majority of policy decisions are made at departmental level. Indeed, there have been recent moves to (re)assert greater central government authority in policy and organizational terms. To cite one policy example, the last Conservative Administration attempted to assert central control over education policy, and this move has continued under Labour. Following the introduction by the Conservatives of a national curriculum Labour has increased state control, with a growing emphasis on standards and by the creation of procedures to allow direct intervention by central government to improve schools, bypassing the local education authorities (see McCaig 2001). Similarly, in the organiza-tional field the emphasis on joined-up government (see Chapter 10) is in large part an attempt to reimpose central executive control on diverse institutions of governance

A limited pattern of external constraints

We do not deny that the pattern of external constraints on government is chan-ging. It is clearly the case, for example, that government can only have a limited, if any, impact on international financial markets. However, one should be wary of becoming carried away by such arguments for a number of reasons. First, govern-ments have always been constrained. Second, governments can be strategic, whilst markets cannot. Third, markets are dependent on government. Fourth, citizens are still subject to considerable state power. Thus the relationship between global and national forces is contingent and interactive, not determined, and the British gov-ernment still has a considerable range of options. For example, Castells (1998: 330) argues that the EU is successful precisely because: '[it] does not supplant the existing nation states but, on the contrary, is a fundamental instrument for their survival on the condition of conceding shares of sovereignty in exchange for a greater say in world, and domestic affairs'. Like power, state–global relations can-not be conceived in zero-sum terms. Moreover, as we argued with relation to both globalization and the EU, such 'constraints' also provide opportunities for strategically calculating governments.

We would argue that the 'asymmetric model' of Marsh et al. (2001) provides the most convincing organizational perspective on the British system of governance, as it captures the notion of change that has occurred by governance, while also more accurately reflecting the still concentrated nature of power with British politics.

Governance and public policy today

During the last thirty years, policy-making has become much more difficult and complex. As Davis (2000: 242) observes:

... policy coherence becomes a problem as policies and interrelationships become more complex, and as the electorate fractures along multiple fault-lines. Finding the institutional capacity to take a longer view becomes the most difficult challenge for . . . governance.

Since 1997, the Blair Government's attempt at addressing this challenge has broadly been two-pronged. First, it has rejected the 'corporatist solution' adopted by Labour governments of the 1960s and has instead embarked upon a strategy aimed at binding together different elements of society—government, the private sector, the voluntary sector, etc. (see Chapters 8 and 10). Such a strategy is tactically astute, as Government can enjoy the plaudits where such initiatives are successful, and where they fail, responsibility is shared. Second, the Blair Government has pursued a strategy of joined-up government. This is an attempt to resolve one of the perceived problems of the governance era—fragmentation—by wiring the system back up together again (see Chapter 10). The programme of joined-up government (JUG) is still progressing, and it would be wrong to attempt any firm conclusions concerning its potential success or failure. Indeed, JUG is almost certainly not the end point in rectifying the pathology of governance, but only the start of a new phase in the continued reconstitution of the state. As we enter the twenty-first century, the future of public policy-making in Britain appears to be conditioned by the core executive attempting to resolve a dilemma: on the one hand it needs to meet the ever more disparate needs of an increasingly complex and diverse society while at the same time it wishes to maintain its status as the most powerful actor in the policy process. Resolving this dilemma will not be a simple task.

References

ABERBACH, J., PUTNAM, R., and ROCKMAN, B. (1981) *Bureaucrats and Politicians in Western Democracies.* Cambridge, Mass.: Harvard University Press.

ADDISON, P. (1975) *The Road to 1945: British Politics and the Second World War.* London: Cape.

ADONIS, A., and HAMES, M. (1994) *The Thatcher–Reagan Revolution.* Manchester: Manchester University Press.

ALLEN, D. (1981) 'Raynerism: Strengthening Civil Service Management', RIPA Report 2(4).

ALLGIER, T. (1995) Electoral Registration Research Project. University of Brighton: Sussex.

ANDERSON, P. (1963) 'Origins of the Present Crisis', *New Left Review*, 161: 26–53.

APPADURI, A. (2000) 'Disjuncture and Difference in the Global Cultural Economy', *Theory, Culture and Society* 7: 295–310.

ARCHER, C. (2001) *International Organisations*, 3rd edn. London: Routledge.

ARENDT, H. (1951) *The Origins of Totalitarianism.* Cleveland, OH: London: Allen & Unwin.

—— (1958) *The Human Condition.* Chicago: University of Chicago Press.

ARTIS, M. (1998) 'The United Kingdom', in J. Forder and A. Menon (eds.), *The European Union and National Macroeconomic Policy.* London: Routledge.

BACHE, I. (1998) *The Politics of European Regional Policy: Multi-Level Governance or Flexible Gatekeeping?* Sheffield: Sheffield Academic Press.

—— (1999) 'The Extended Gatekeeper: Central Government and the Implementation of EC regional policy in the UK', *Journal of European Public Policy* 6: 28–45.

BACON, R., and ELTIS, W. (1976) *Britain's Economic Problem: Too Few Producers.* Basingstoke: Macmillan.

BAKER, D., and SEAWRIGHT, D. (1996) *Britain: For and Against Europe.* Oxford: Oxford University Press.

BAKER, D., EPSTEIN, G., and POLLIN, R. (1998) *Globalization and Progressive Economic Policy.* Cambridge: Cambridge University Press.

BAKER, K. (1993) *The Turbulent Years: My Life in Politics.* London: Faber & Faber.

BALE, T. (1999) *Sacred Cows and Common Sense.* Aldershot: Ashgate.

BALL, R., HEAFY, M., and KING D. (2001) 'Private Finance Initiative: A Good Deal for the Public Purse or a Drain on Future Generations?', *Policy and Politics* 29: 95–108.

BALOGH, T., OPIE, R., SEERS, D., and THOMAS, H. (1968) *Crisis in the Civil Service.* London: Blond.

BARBERIS, P. (2000) 'Prime Minister and Cabinet', in R. Pyper and L. Robins (eds.), *United Kingdom Governance.* Basingstoke: Macmillan.

BARKER, A. (1998) 'The Labour Government's Policy Reviews and Task Forces: An Initial Listing and Analysis'. *Essex Papers in Politics and Government*, 126. Colchester: University of Essex.

BARNETT, J. (1982) *Inside the Treasury.* London: Deutsch.

BARREL, R., and DURY, K. (2000) 'Choosing the Regime: Macroeconomic Effects of UK Entry into EMU', *Journal of Common Market Studies* 38: 625–44.

BAUMAN, Z. (1989) *Modernity and the Holocaust.* Cambridge: Polity Press.

BAYLIS, J., and SMITH, S. (eds.) (1997). *The Globalization of World Politics*. Oxford: Oxford University Press.

—— —— (eds.) (2001). *The Globalization of World Politics* (2nd edn). Oxford: Oxford University Press.

BBC (1994) *Newsnight*, 13 Sept.

—— (1999) *Analysis*, 3 Apr.

—— (2001a) *Panorama*, 4 Feb.

—— (2001b) *BBC News*, 7 Oct.

—— (2001c) *BBC News*, 15 Oct.

BEATTIE, A. (1995) 'Ministerial Responsibility and the Theory of the Modern State', in R. A. W. Rhodes and P. Dunleavy (eds.), *Prime Minister, Cabinet and Core Executive*. London: Macmillan.

BEER, S. (1982) *Britain Against Itself*. London: Faber & Faber.

BENN, T. (1980) *Arguments for Socialism*. London: Cape.

BERGER, P., and LUCKMAN, T. (1967) *The Social Construction of Reality*. Harmondsworth: Penguin.

BEVERIDGE, W. H. (1942) *Social Insurance and Allied Services*. London: HMSO.

BICHARD, M. (1999) *Modernising the Policy Process*. London: Public Management and Policy Association.

BIRCH, A. H. (1964) *Representative and Responsible Government*. London: Allen & Unwin.

—— (1984) 'Overload, Ungovernability and Delegitimation: The Theories of the British Case', *British Journal of Political Science* 14: 135–60.

BLAIR, T. (1998) 'Modernizing Central Government', speech to the Senior Civil Service Conference, London, 13 Oct.

—— (1999a) Speech at the Lord Mayor's Banquet, 22 Jan.

—— (1999b) 'Doctrine of the International Community', Chicago, 23 Apr.

—— (2001) 'Britain's Role in Europe', speech to the European Research Institute, University of Birmingham, 23 Nov.

BODDY, M., and LAMBERT, C. (1990) 'Corporatist Interest Intermediation: Government-Building Society Relations in the UK', in A. Cawson (ed.), *Organised Interests and the State*. London: Sage.

BOGDANOR, V. (1997) *Power and the People*. London: Gollancz.

BRITTAN, S. (1983) *The Role and Limits of Government*. London: Temple-Smith.

BROWN, G. (1998a) Speech to the News International Conference, Sun Valley, Ida., 17 July.

—— (1998b) Speech to the IMF and World Bank, 6 Oct.

BUDGE, I., CREWE, I., McKAY, D., and NEWTON, K. (2001) *The New British Political System*. Harlow: Longman.

BULLER, J. (2000) *National Statecraft and European Integration: The Conservative Government and the European Union*. London: Pinter.

—— (2001) 'The Advantage of "Tying One's Hands": Rules, Autonomy and the Europeanisation of British Economic Policy' (unpublished paper: University of York).

BULMER, S., and BURCH, M. (1998) 'Organizing for Europe: Whitehall, the British State and the European Union', *Public Administration* 76: 601–28.

BULPITT, J. (1983) *Territory and Power in the United Kingdom*. Manchester: Manchester University Press.

—— (1986) 'The Discipline of the New Democracy: Mrs Thatcher's Domestic Statecraft', *Political Studies* 34: 19–39.

BURCH, M., and HOLLIDAY, I. (1996) *The British Cabinet System*. Hemel Hempstead: Prentice-Hall

—— —— (2000) 'New Labour and the Machinery of Government', in Coates and Lawler (2000).

BUTLER, D., and KAVANAGH, D. (2001) *The British General Election of 2001*. Basingstoke: Palgrave.

CAIRNCROSS, A. (1996) 'The Heath Government and the British Economy', in S. Ball and A. Seldon (eds.), *The Heath Government 1970–74*. London: Longman.

—— (1997) *The Wilson Years: A Treasury Diary 1964–1969*. London: Historians' Press.

CAMPAIGN FOR FREEDOM OF INFORMATION (2001). *Government to Abandon Freedom of Information Timetable?* London: CFI.

CAMPBELL, C., and WILSON, G. (1995) *The End of Whitehall: Death of a Paradigm*. Oxford: Blackwell.

CAMPBELL, J. (1993) *Edward Heath: A Biography*. London: Cape.

CARRINGTON, P. (1988) *Reflect on Things Past: The Memoirs of Lord Carrington*. London: Collins.

CASTELLS, M. (1996) *The Information Age: Economy, Society, and Culture*, i: *The Rise of the Network Society*. Oxford: Blackwell.

—— (1998) *The Information Age*, iii: *The End of the Millennium*. Oxford: Blackwell.

CATTERALL, P., KAISER, W., and WALTON-JORDAN, U. (2000) *Reforming the Constitution: Debates in Twentieth-Century Britain*. London: Cass.

CAWSON, A. (1986) *Corporatism and Political Theory* Oxford: Blackwell.

CERNY, P. G. (1990) *The Changing Architecture of Politics: Structure, Agency and the Future of the State*. London: Sage.

—— (1995) 'Globalisation and the Changing Logic of Collective Action', *International Organization* 49: 595–625.

CHAPMAN, L. (1978) *Your Disobedient Servant*. London: Chatto & Windus.

CHAPMAN, R. A. (1997) *The Treasury in Public Policy-Making*. London: Routledge.

CM. 2764 (1966) *The National Plan*. London: HMSO.

CM. 4262-1 (1999) *The Stephen Lawrence Inquiry: Report of an Inquiry by Sir William Macpherson of Cluny*. London: HMSO.

CMND. 4310 (1999) *Modernising Government*. London: HMSO.

CMND. 4342 (1999) *Teenage Pregnancy*. London: HMSO.

CMND. 4506 (1970) *The Reorganisation of Central Government*. London: HMSO.

CMND. 5291 (2001) *The House of Lords: Completing the Reform*. London: HMSO.

CMND. 8616 (1982) *Efficiency and Effectiveness in the Civil Service: Government Observations on the Third Report from the Treasury and Civil Service Select Committee*. London: HMSO.

COATES, D., and HILLARD, J. (eds.) (1986) *The Economic Decline of Modern Britain*. Brighton: Wheatsheaf.

—— and LAWLER, P. (eds.) (2000) *New Labour in Power*. Manchester: Manchester University Press.

COCKETT, R. (1995) *Thinking the Unthinkable: Think-Tanks and the Economic Counter-Revolution 1931–83*. London: Fontana.

COHEN, N. (1999) *Cruel Britannia*. London: Virago.

COLERAINE, LORD. (1970) *For Conservatives Only*. London: Stacey.

COOGAN, T. (1996) *The IRA*. London: Arrow.

COXALL, B. (2001) *Pressure Groups in British Politics*. Harlow: Longman.

CRAM, L. (1997) *Policy Making in the EU*. London: Routledge.

CRONIN, J. E. (1991) *The Politics of State Expansion*. London: Routledge.

CROZIER, M. (1975) *The Crisis of Democracy*. New York: New York University Press.

DAEDLER, H. (1963a) *Cabinet Reform in Britain 1914–63*. Stanford, Calif.: Stanford University Press.

—— (1963b) 'The Haldane Committee and the Cabinet', *Public Administration* 41: 117–35.

DANIEL, C. (1997) 'May the Taskforce Be With You', *New Statesman*, 1 Aug.

DAVIES, A. (1995) *We, the Nation: The Conservative Party and the Pursuit of Power*. London: Little, Brown.

DAVIS, G. (2000) 'Policy Capacity and the Future of Governance', in Davis and Keating (2000).

—— and KEATING, M. (eds.) (2000) *The Future of Governance*. St Leonards, NSW: Allen & Unwin.

DAY, P., and KLEIN, R. (1992) 'Constitutional and Distributional Conflict in British Medical Politics: The Case of General Practice, 1911–1991', *Political Studies* 50: 462–78.

DEAKIN, N. (1987) *In Search of the Post-War Consensus*. London: Suntory International Centre for Economics and Related Disciplines, LSE.

—— and PARRY, R. (2000) *The Treasury and Social Policy*. Basingstoke: Macmillan:

DEARLOVE, J., and SAUNDERS, P. (2001) *Introduction to British Politics*, 3rd edn. Cambridge: Polity Press.

DENHAM, A., and GARNETT, M. (2001) *Keith Joseph*. Chesham: Acuman.

DIETZ, M. (1992) 'Context is All: Feminism and Theories of Citizenship', in C. Mouffe, (ed.), *Dimensions of Radical Democracy: Pluralism, Citizenship, Community*. London: Verso.

DOLOWITZ, D., MARSH, D., O'NEILL, F., and RICHARDS, D. (1996) 'Thatcherism and the 3 "Rs": Radicalism, Realism and Rhetoric in the Third Term of the Thatcher Government', *Parliamentary Affairs* 49: 455–70.

DOREY, P. (1995) *British Politics since 1945*. Oxford: Blackwell.

DOWDING, K. (1995) *The Civil Service*. London: Routledge.

DOWNS, A. (1957) *An Economic Theory of Democracy*. New York: Harper & Row.

DREWRY, G., and BUTCHER, T. (1991) *The Civil Service Today*, 2nd edn. Oxford: Blackwell.

DUDLEY, G., and RICHARDSON, J. J. (1996) 'Why Does Policy Change over Time? Adversarial Policy Communities, Alternative Policy Arenas and British Trunk Road Policy 1945–1995', *Journal of European Public Policy* 3: 318–38.

DUNLEAVY, P. (1991) *Democracy, Bureaucracy and Public Choice*. Hemel Hempstead: Harvester Wheatsheaf.

—— (1999) 'Electoral Representation and Accountability', in I. Holliday, A. Gamble, and G. Parry (eds.), *Fundamentals in British Politics*. London: Macmillan.

DUTTON, D. (1997) *British Politics since 1945: The Rise, Fall and Rebirth of Consensus*, 2nd edn. Oxford: Blackwell.

DYSON, K. (2000) 'EMU as Europeanization: Convergence, Diversity and Contingency', *Journal of Common Market Studies* 38: 545–66.

ENGLISH, R., and KENNY, M. (2000) *Rethinking British Decline*. Basingstoke: Macmillan.

FABIAN SOCIETY (1964) *The Administrators*. London: Fabian Society.

FAIRBRASS, J., and JORDAN, A. (2001) 'Multi-Level Environmental Governance: A New Political (Dis)Order?', paper presented at Multi-Level Governance Conference, University of Sheffield, 28–30 June.

FEIGENBAUM, H., HENIG, J., and HAMNETT, C. (1998) *Shrinking the State*. Cambridge: Cambridge University Press.

FINER, S. E. (1970) *Comparative Government*. London: Allen Lane.

FLINDERS, M. (2001) *The Politics of Accountability in the Modern State*. Aldershot: Ashgate.

FOLEY, M. (1992) *The Rise of the British Presidency*. Manchester: Manchester University Press.

—— (2000) *The Blair Presidency*. Manchester: Manchester University Press.

FOSTER, C., and PLOWDEN, F. (1996) *The State under Stress*. Buckingham: Open University Press.

FOSTER, C. D. (2001) 'The Civil Service under Stress: The Fall in Civil Service Power and Authority', *Public Administration* 79: 725–49.

FOWLER, N. (1991) *Ministers Decide*. London: Chapman.

FOX, C. J,. and MILLER, H. T. (1995) *Postmodern Public Administration: Towards Public Administration*. London: Sage

FRASER, N., and GORDON, L. (1994) 'Civil Citizenship against Social Citizenship? On the Ideology of Contract-versus-Charity Status', in B. van Steenbergen (ed.), *The Condition of Social Citizenship*. London: Sage.

FREEDEN, M. (1999) 'True Blood or False Genealogy: New Labour and British Social Democratic Thought', *Political Quarterly* 70: 1–16.

FUKUYAMA, F. (1992) *The End of History and the Last Man*. London: Hamish Hamilton.

GAMBLE, A. (1994a) *Britain in Decline*, 4th edn. Basingstoke: Macmillan.

—— (1994b) *The Free Economy and the Strong State*, 2nd edn. London: Macmillan.

—— (1999) 'State, Economy and Society', in I. Holliday, A. Gamble, and G. Parry (eds.), *Fundamentals in British Politics*. Basingstoke: Macmillan.

—— (2000a) 'Theories and Explanations of British Decline', in R. English, and M. Kenny (eds.), *Rethinking British Decline*. Basingstoke: Macmillan.

—— (2000b) *Politics and Fate*. London: Polity.

—— (2000c) 'Economic Governance', in J. Pierre (ed.), *Debating Governance*. Oxford: Oxford University Press.

—— and KELLY, G. (2000) 'The British Labour Party and Monetary Union', *West European Politics* 23: 1–25.

—— and PAYNE, T. (1996) 'Conclusion: The New Regionalism', in A. Gamble and T. Payne (eds.), *Regionalism and World Order*. London: Macmillan.

GEORGE, S. (1998) *An Awkward Partner: Britain in the European Community*, 3rd edn. Oxford: Oxford University Press.

—— and BACHE, I. (2001) *Politics in the European Union*. Oxford: Oxford University Press

GIBBINS, J. R., and REIMER, B. (1999) *The Politics of Post-Modernity*. London: Sage.

GIDDENS, A. (1986) *The Constitution of Society*. Cambridge: Polity Press.

—— (1990) *The Consequences of Modernity*. Cambridge: Polity Press.

—— (1994) *Beyond Left and Right*. Cambridge: Polity Press.

—— (1997) *The Third Way*. Cambridge: Polity Press.

—— (1998) 'The Future of the Welfare State', in M. Novak (ed.), *Is There a Third Way?* London: Institute of Economic Affairs.

—— (2000) *The Third Way and its Critics.* Cambridge: Polity Press.

GILBERT, B. (1970) *British Social Policy 1914–39.* London: Batsford.

GILMOUR, I. (1997) *Whatever Happened to the Tories? The Conservatives since 1945.* London: Fourth Estate.

GOODIN, R. E., and DRYZEK, J. (1995) 'Justice Deferred: Wartime Rationing and Postwar Welfare Policy', *Politics and Society* 23(1): 49–73.

GOUGH, I. (1979) *The Political Economy of the Welfare State.* London: Macmillan.

GRANT, W. (2000) *Pressure Groups and British Politics.* London: Macmillan.

GRAY, J. (1998) *False Dawn.* London: Granta.

GREENLEAF, W. H. (1983) *The British Political Tradition*, i and ii. London: Methuen.

—— (1987) *The British Political Tradition*, iii. London: Methuen.

GREENWOOD, J., PYPER, R., and WILSON, D. (2001) *New Public Administration in Britain*, 3rd edn. London: Routledge.

GRUGEL, J. (1999) 'European NGOs and Democratization in Latin America: Policy Networks and Transnational Ethical Networks', in Grugel (ed.), *Democracy without Borders.* London: Routledge.

GUTTSMANN, W. (1963) *The British Political Elite.* London: MacGibbon & Kee.

HABERMAS, J. (1990) *The Philosophical Discourse of Modernity.* Cambridge: Polity Press.

HALL, J. (ed.) (1995) *Civil Society: Theory, History, Comparison.* Cambridge: Polity Press.

HALL, P. (1999) 'Social Capital in Britain', *British Journal of Political Science* 29: 417–61.

HARDT, M., and NEGRI, A. (2000) *Empire.* Cambridge, Mass.: Harvard University Press.

HARLING, P. (2001) *The Modern British State: An Historical Introduction.* Cambridge: Polity Press.

HARRIS, K. (1982) *Attlee.* London: Weidenfeld & Nicolson.

HART, D. (1972) 'The Genesis of the Northcote–Trevelyan Report', in G. Sutherland (ed.), *Studies in the Growth of Government.* London: Routledge & Kegan Paul.

HAY, C. (1996) *Restating Social and Political Change.* Buckingham: Open University Press.

—— (1999a) *The Political Economy of New Labour: Labouring under False Pretences?* Manchester: Manchester University Press.

—— (1999b) 'Crisis and Political Development in Postwar Britain', in Marsh et al. (1999).

—— (2000) 'Contemporary Capitalism, Globalization, Regionalization and the Persistence of National Variation', *Review of International Studies* 26: 509–31.

—— and RICHARDS, D. (2000) 'The Tangled Webs of Westminster and Whitehall: The Discourse, Strategy and Practice of Networking within the British Core Executive', *Public Administration* 78: 1–28.

—— and WATSON, M. (1998) *Rendering the Contingent: New Labour's Neo-Liberal Conversion and the Discourse of Globalisation.* Cambridge, Mass.: Centre for European Studies, Paper 8.4.

HAYEK, F. (1944) *The Road to Serfdom.* London: Routledge & Kegan Paul.

HAZELL, R., and CORNES, R. (1999) 'Financing Devolution', in R. Hazell (ed.), *Constitutional Futures.* Oxford: Oxford University Press.

—— and MORRIS, B. (1999) 'Machinery of Government: Whitehall', in R. Hazell (ed.), *Constitutional Futures.* Oxford: Oxford University Press.

HAZELL, R., and O'LEARY, B. (1999) 'A Rolling Programme of Devolution: Slippery Slope or Safeguard of the Union?' in R. Hazell (ed.), *Constitutional Futures*. Oxford: Oxford University Press.

HC 232 (2001–2) Report of the Comptroller and Auditor General, *Policy Development: Improving Air Quality*. London: HMSO.

HC 236-1 (1982) *Third Report from the Treasury and Civil Service Committee 1981–82: Efficiency and Effectiveness in the Civil Service*. London: HMSO.

HEADEY, B. (1974) *British Cabinet Ministers*. London: Allen & Unwin.

HEATH, E. (1998) *The Course of my Life: The Autobiography of Edward Heath*. London: Hodder & Stoughton.

HECLO, H., and WILDAVSKY, A. (1981) *The Private Government of Public Money*. London: Macmillan.

HELD, D., and MCGREW, A. (2000) 'The Great Globalization Debate', in Held and McGrew (eds.), *The Global Transformations Reader*. Cambridge: Polity Press.

—— —— GOLDBLATT, D., and PERRATON, J. (1999) *Global Transformations*. Cambridge: Polity Press.

HENNESSY, P. (1989) *Whitehall*. London: Fontana.

—— (1992) *Never Again: Britain 1945–51*. London: Cape.

—— (1998) 'The Blair Style of Government', *Government and Opposition* 33: 3–20.

—— (2001) *The Prime Minister: The Office and its Holders since 1945*. London: Penguin.

HEYWOOD, A. (1997) *Politics*. Basingstoke: Macmillan.

—— (2000) *Key Concepts in Politics*. Basingstoke: Palgrave.

HIGGOTT, R. (1998) 'Review of "Globalisation"', paper prepared for the Economic and Social Research Council, 20 Nov.

HILL, A., and WHICHELOW, A. (1964) *What's Wrong with Parliament?* Harmondsworth: Penguin.

HILL, M. (2001) 'EU Technology Programmes and the British Policy Process'. PhD thesis, University of Sheffield.

HIRST, P., and THOMPSON, G. (1996) *Globalisation in Question*. Cambridge: Polity Press.

HOBSBAWM, E. H. (1993) 'Britain: A Comparative View', in B. Brivati, and H. Jones (eds.), *What Difference Did the War Make?* Leicester: Leicester University Press.

HOGWOOD, B. (1992) *Trends in British Public Policy*. Buckingham: Open University Press.

—— (1997) 'The Machinery of Government', *Political Studies* 45(4) 704–15.

HOLLIDAY, I. (2000) 'Executives and Administrations', in P. Dunleavy, A. Gamble, I. Holliday, and G. Peele (eds.), *Developments in British Politics* 6. London: Macmillan.

—— GAMBLE, A., and PARRY, G. (eds.) (1999) *Fundamentals in British Politics*. Basingstoke: Macmillan.

HOOD, C. (1991) 'A New Public Management for All Seasons', *Public Administration* 69: 3–19.

HOOGE, L., and MARKS, G. (2001) *Multi-Level Governance and European Integration*. Md.: Rowman & Littlefield.

JACKSON, P. (1997) 'The Evolution of International Society', in Bayliss and Smith (1997).

JENKINS, R. (1991) *A Life at the Centre*. London: Macmillan.

JENNINGS, I. (1966) *The British Constitution*. Cambridge: Cambridge University Press.

JESSOP, B. (1994) 'The Transition to Post-Fordist and the Schumpeterian Workfare State', in R. Burrows, and B. Loader (eds.), *Towards a Post-Fordist Welfare State?* London: Routledge.

—— (1999) 'Narrating the Future of the National Economy and the National State? Remarks on Re-mapping Regulation and Re-inventing Governance', in G. Steinmetz (ed.), *State/Culture*. Ithaca, NY: Cornell University Press

—— (2002) 'Multi-level Governance and Meta-Governance', in I. Bache and M. Flinders (eds.), *Multi-level Governance: Interdisciplinary Perspectives*. Oxford: Oxford University Press.

JOHN, P. (1998) *Analysing Public Policy*. London: Pinter

JOHNSTONE, J. (1999) 'Questions of Change and Continuity in Attlee's Britain' in Marsh et al. (1999).

JONES, B., and KEATING, M. (1985) *Labour and the British State*. Oxford: Clarendon Press.

JORDAN, A. (2002) *The Europeanization of Environmental Policy*. Basingstoke: Palgrave.

JORDAN, A. J., and RICHARDSON, J. J. (1987) *Government and Pressure Groups in Britain*. Oxford: Clarendon Press.

JUDGE, D. (1993) *The Parliamentary State*. London: Sage.

—— (1999) *Representation*. London: Routledge.

KANDIAH, D., and SELDON, A. (eds.) (1996a) *Ideas and Think-Tanks in Contemporary Britain*, i. London: Cass.

—— —— (eds.) (1996b) *Ideas and Think-Tanks in Contemporary Britain*, ii. London: Cass.

KAUFMAN, G. (1997) *How to be a Minister*. London: Faber & Faber.

KAVANAGH, D. (ed.) (1985) *The Politics of the Labour Party*. London: Allen & Unwin.

—— (1987) *Thatcherism and British Politics: The End of Consensus?* Oxford: Oxford University Press.

—— (1997) *The Reordering of British Politics*. Oxford: Oxford University Press

—— and MORRIS, P. (1989) *Consensus Politics from Attlee to Thatcher*. Oxford: Blackwell.

—— and RICHARDS, D. (2002) 'Prime Ministers, Ministers and Civil Servants in Britain', *Comparative Sociology* (Apr.): 1–28.

—— and SELDON, A. (2000) *The Powers behind the Prime Minister*. London: HarperCollins.

—— —— (2001) *The Power behind the Prime Minister*. London: HarperCollins.

KEATING, M. (2000) 'The Pressures for Change', in Davis and Keating (2000).

KECK, M., and SIKKINK, K. (1998) *Activists beyond Borders: Advocacy Networks in International Politics*. London: Cornell University Press.

KELLNER, P., and CROWTHER HUNT, N. (1980) *The Civil Service: An Enquiry into Britain's Ruling Class*. London: Macdonald.

KERR, P. (1999) 'The Postwar Consensus: A Woozle that Wasn't', in Marsh et al. (1999).

KILLICK, M., and ROBINSON, J. (2001) 'Conceptualising Europeanisation: Technical and Substantive Europeanisation and the role of Policy Networks and Advocacy Coalitions'. Mimeo, University of Sheffield.

KING, A. (1975) 'Overload: Problems of Governing in the 1970s', *Political Studies* 23 (2–3): 284–96.

KING, A. (1985) (ed.) *The British Prime Minister*. Macmillan: Basingstoke.

KNAPP, M. (1996) 'Are Voluntary Agencies Really More Effective?', in D. Billis and M. Harris (eds.), *Voluntary Agencies*. London: Macmillan.

KOOIMAN, J. (ed.) (1993) *Modern Governance: Government–Society Interactions*. London: Sage.

—— (2000) 'Levels of Governing: Interactions as a Central Concept', in J. Pierre (ed.), *Debating Governance*. Oxford: Oxford University Press.

KRIEGER, J. (1999) *British Politics in the Global Age: Can Social Democracy Survive?* Cambridge: Polity Press.

LACLAU, E. (1990) *New Reflections on the Revolution of our Times.* London: Verso.

LANDRECH, R. (1994) 'Europeanization of Domestic Politics and Institutions: The Case of France', *Journal of Common Market Studies* 32: 69–88.

LAWSON, N., and BRUCE-GARDYNE, J. (1976) *The Power Game.* Basingstoke: Macmillan.

LINDBLOM, C. (1977) *Politics and Markets.* New York: Basic Books.

LINDQUIST, J. (2001) 'The Problems of Proximity and Place: Situating Transnational Advocacy Networks', paper for workshop on Transnational Activism and Problems of Democracy in East and Southeast Asia, Stockholm, 14–15 Sept.

LING, T. (1998) *The British State since 1945.* London: Polity Press.

LIPSEY, D. (2000) *The Secret Treasury: How Britain's Economy is Really Run.* London: Viking.

LOWE, R. (1990) 'The Second World War, Consensus and the Foundation of the Welfare State', *Twentieth Century British History* 1(2): 152–82.

LOWNDES, V., and WILSON, D. (2001) 'Social Capital and Local Governance: Exploring the Institutional Design Variable', *Political Studies* 49: 629–47.

—— PRATCHETT, L. and STOKER, G. (2001) 'Trends in Public Participation, part 2: Citizens' Perspectives', *Public Administration* 79: 445–55.

LUDLAM, S. (1992) 'The Gnomes of Washington: Four Myths of the IMF Crisis of 1976', *Political Studies* 40: 713–27.

—— (2001) 'New Labour and the Unions: The End of the Contentious Alliance?' in S. Ludlam and M. J. Smith (eds.), *New Labour in Government.* Basingstoke: Palgrave.

—— and SMITH, M. J. (1996) *Contemporary British Conservatism.* London: Macmillan.

—— —— (eds.) (2001) *New Labour in Government.* Basingstoke: Palgrave.

LYON, D. (1994) *Postmodernity.* Milton Keynes: Open University Press.

McCAIG, C. (2001) 'New Labour and Education, Education, Education', in Ludlam and Smith (2001).

McCONNELL, A. (2000) 'Issues of Governance in Scotland, Wales and Northern Ireland', in R. Pyper, and L. Robins (eds.), *United Kingdom Governance.* Basingstoke: Macmillan.

MACDONAGH, O. (1958) 'The Nineteenth-Century Revolution in Government: A Reappraisal', *Historical Journal* 1: 52–67.

McEACHERN, D. (1990). *The Expanding State: Class and Economy since 1945.* Hemel Hempstead: Harvester Wheatsheaf

MACKINTOSH, J. P. (1977) *The British Cabinet Government,* 3rd edn. London: Stevens.

McKIBBIN, R. (1974) *The Evolution of the Labour Party 1910–24.* Oxford: Oxford University Press.

MAJONE, G. (1994) 'The Rise of the Regulatory State', *West European Politics* 17: 77–101.

MANDELSON, P., and LIDDELL, R. (1996) *The Blair Revolution: Can New Labour Deliver?* London: Faber & Faber.

MANN, M. (1997) 'Has Globalization Ended the Rise and Rise of the Nation State?', *Review of International Political Economy* 4: 472–96.

MARKS, G., and HOOGE, L. (2001) 'Types of Multi-Level Governance: What, Where, Why?', paper presented to the Multi-level Governance Conference, University of Sheffield, June.

—— —— and BLANK, K. (1995) 'European Integration from the 1980s: State-centric versus Multi-Level Governance', *Journal of Common Market Studies* 34: 341–78.

Marquand, D. (1991) *The Unprincipled Society*. London: Fontana.

—— (1992) 'Half-way to Citizenship? The Labour Party and Constitutional Reform' in M. J. Smith and J. Spear (eds.), *The Changing Labour Party*. London: Routledge.

Marsh, D., et al. (1999) *Postwar British Politics in Perspective*. London: Polity Press.

—— and Rhodes, R. A. W. (1992) *Policy Networks in British Government*. Oxford: Clarendon Press.

—— and Smith, M. J. (2000) 'Understanding Policy Networks: Towards a Dialect Approach', *Political Studies* 48: 4–21.

—— Smith, M. J., and Richards, D. (2000) 'Bureaucrats, Politicians and Reform in Whitehall: Analysing the Bureau-shaping Model', *British Journal of Political Science* 30: 461–82.

—— —— —— (2001) *Changing Patterns of Governance: Reinventing Whitehall*. Basingstoke: Palgrave.

Marshall, T. H. (1950) 'Citizenship and Social Class', in T. H. Marshall and T. Bottomore (eds.), *Citizenship and Social Class*. London: Pluto Press.

Massey, A. (2001) 'Policy, Management and Implementation', in S. Savage and R. Atkinson (eds.), *Public Policy under Blair*. Basingstoke: Palgrave.

Mazey, S., and Richardson, J. J. (1993) 'Interest Groups in the European Community', in J. J. Richardson, (ed.), *Pressure Groups*. Oxford: Oxford University Press.

Menon, A., and Forder, J. (1998) 'Conclusion: States, the European Union and Macroeconomic Policy', in Forder and Menon (eds.), *The European Union and National Macroeconomic Policy*. London: Routledge.

Metcalfe, L. (1993) 'Conviction Politics and Dynamic Conservatism: Mrs Thatcher's Managerial Revolution', *International Political Science Review* 14(4): 212–21.

Middlemas, K. (1979) *Politics in Industrial Society,* London: Deutsch.

—— (1986) *Power, Competition and the State,* i: *Britain in Search of Balance 1940–1961*. London: Macmillan.

Miliband, R. (1972) *Parliamentary Socialism*. London: Merlin.

Mitchell, J. (1999) 'From Unitary State to Union State: Labour's Changing View of the United Kingdom and its Implications', *Regional Policy and Politics* 9: 9–13.

—— (2002) 'Towards the New Constitutional Settlement', in C. Hay (ed.), *British Politics Today*. Cambridge: Polity Press.

Moore, B. (1967) *Social Origins of Dictatorship and Democracy*. Harmondsworth: Penguin.

Moravcsik, A. (1993) 'Preferences and Power in the European Community', *Journal of Common Market Studies* 4: 119–49.

Mueller, H. (1984) *Bureaucracy, Education and Monopoly: Civil Service Reforms in Prussia and England*. Berkeley: University of California Press.

Mulgan, G. (2001) 'Joined-Up Government: Past, Present and Future', paper presented at British Academy Conference on Joined-up Government, 30 Oct.

—— and Wilkinson H. (1995) *Freedom's Children*. London: Demos.

Myers, A. R. (1952) *England in the Late Middle Ages*. London: Penguin.

Naughtie, J. (2001) *The Rivals: The Intimate Story of a Political Marriage*. London: Fourth Estate.

Newman, O. (1981) *The Challenge of Corporatism*. London: Macmillan.

Niskanen, W. (1971) *Bureaucracy and Representative Government*. New York: Aldine Atherton.

NORTHCOTE, S., and TREVELYAN C. (1954) The Northcote–Trevelyan Report. Reprinted in *Public Administration* 32: 1–16.

NORTON, P. (2000) 'Barons in a Shrinking Kingdom: Senior Ministers in British Government', in R. A. W. Rhodes (ed.), *Transforming British Government*, ii: *Changing Roles and Relationships*. Basingstoke: Macmillan.

OFFE, C. (1984) *Contradictions of the Welfare State*. London: Hutchinson.

OHMAE, K. (1995) *The End of the Nation State: The Rise of Regional Economics*. New York: Free Press.

OSBORNE, D., and GAEBLER, T. (1991) *Reinventing Government*. Reading, Mass.: Addison Wesley.

PARRY, G., and MOYSER, G. (1994) 'A Map of Political Participation in Britain', *Government and Opposition* 79: 340–62.

—— —— and DAY, N. (1992) *Political Participation and Democracy in Britain*. Cambridge: Cambridge University Press.

PARSONS, W. (1998) 'Fuzzy in Theory and Getting Fuzzier in Practice: Post-Modern Reflections on Responsibility in Public Administration and Management', in A. Hondeghem (ed.), *Ethics and Accountability in a Context of Governance and New Public Management*. Amsterdam: IOS Press.

PASCALL, G. (1993) 'Citizenship: A Feminist Analysis', in G. Drover and P. Kerans (eds.), *New Approaches to Welfare Theory*. London: Elgar.

PATEMAN, C. (1989) 'The Patriarchal Welfare State', in *The Disorder of Women*. Cambridge: Polity Press.

PAYNE, A. (2000) 'Globalizaton and Modes of Regionalist Governance', in J. Pierre (ed.), *Debating Governance: Authority, Steering, and Democracy*. Oxford: Oxford University Press.

PEACOCK, A. T., and WISEMAN, J. (1967) *The Growth of Public Expenditure in the United Kingdom*. London: Allen & Unwin.

PEDEN, G. C. (1991) *British Economic and Social Policy: Lloyd George to Margaret Thatcher*. London: Phillip & Allen.

PEELE, G. (1999) 'The Growth of the State', in I. Holliday, A. Gamble, and G. Parry (eds.), *Fundamentals in British Politics*. Basingstoke: Macmillan.

PERROW, C. (1970) *Organizational Analysis*. London: Tavistock.

PETERS, B. G. (2000). 'Governance and Comparative Politics', in J. Pierre (ed.), *Debating Governance*. Oxford: Oxford University Press.

PIERRE, J., and STOKER, G. (2000) 'Towards Multi-Level Governance', in P. Dunleavy, A. Gamble, I. Holliday, and G. Peele (eds.), *Developments in British Politics* 6. Basingstoke: Macmillan.

PIERRE, J. (2000) 'Introduction: Understanding Governance', in Pierre (ed.), *Debating Governance*. Oxford: Oxford University Press.

—— and PETERS, B. G. (2000) *Governance, Politics and the State*. Basingstoke: Macmillan.

PIERSON, C. (1991) *Beyond the Welfare State? The New Political Economy of Welfare*, Cambridge: Polity Press.

—— (1998) *Beyond the Welfare State? The New Political Economy of Welfare*, 2nd edn. Cambridge: Polity Press.

PIMLOTT, B. (1988) 'Is Post War Consensus a Myth?' *Contemporary Record* 2: 12–14.

PIRIE, M. (1993) *Blueprint for a Revolution*. London: Adam Smith Institute.

PIU (Performance and Innovation Unit) (2000) *Wiring it up: Whitehall's Management of Cross-Cutting Policies and Services*. London: HMSO.

PLATT, R. (1998) 'So You Want to be a Citizen?' *New Statesman*, 6 Feb.

POLLARD, S. (1992) *The Development of the British Economy, 1914–1990*, 4th edn. London: Arnold.

POLLIN, R. (1998) 'Can Domestic Expansionary Policy Succeed in a Globally Integrated Environment? An Examination of Alternatives', in D. Baker, G. Epstein, and R. Pollin (eds.), *Globalization and Progressive Economic Policy*. Cambridge: Cambridge University Press.

POLLITT, C. (1990) *Managerialism in the Public Services*. Oxford: Blackwell.

PONTING, C. (1986) *Whitehall: Tragedy and Farce*. London: Hamish Hamilton.

PORTER, B. (1994) *Britannia's Burden: The Political Evolution of Modern Britain, 1851–1990*. London: Arnold.

PRABHAKER, R. (2001). 'School's Policy: Three Faces of Labour'. Mimeo, University of Sheffield.

PRODI, R., and KINNOCK, N. (2001) *The Commission and Non-Governmental Organisations: Building a Stronger Partnership*. Brussels: European Commission.

PRYCE, S. (1997) *Presidentializing the Premiership*. London: Macmillan.

PUNNETT, M. (1994) *British Government and Politics in the United Kingdom*. Aldershot: Dartmouth.

PUTNAM, R. (1993) *Making Democracy Work*. Princeton, NJ: Princeton University Press.

—— (1995) 'Bowling Alone: America's Declining Social Capital', *Journal of Democracy* 6: 65–78.

PYPER, R., and ROBINS, L. (eds.) (2000) *United Kingdom Governance*. Basingstoke: Macmillan.

RAWNSLEY, A. (2001) *Servants of the People: The Inside Story of New Labour*. London: Penguin.

REIGER, E., and LEIBFRIED, S. (1998) 'Welfare State Limits to Globalization', *Politics and Society* 26: 363–90.

RHODES, R. A. W. (1988) *Beyond Westminster and Whitehall*. London: Unwin Hyman.

—— (1996) 'The New Governance: Governing without Government', *Political Studies* 44: 652–67.

—— (1997) *Understanding Governance: Policy Networks, Governance, Reflexivity and Accountability*. Buckingham: Open University Press.

—— (2000) 'Governance and Public Administration', in J. Pierre (ed.), *Debating Governance*. Oxford: Oxford University Press.

RICHARDS, D. (1997) *The Civil Service under the Conservatives 1979–1997: Whitehall's Political Poodles?* Brighton: Sussex Academic Press.

—— (1999) 'Central Administration', in P. Catteral (ed.), *Britain in 1998: A Review of the Year*. London: Institute of Contemporary History.

—— and SMITH, M. J. (2000) 'Power, Knowledge and the British Civil Service: The Living Chimera of the Public Service Ethos', *West European Politics* 23: 45–66

—— (2001) 'New Labour, the State and the Constitution', in S. Ludlam and M. J. Smith (eds.), *New Labour in Government*, Basingstoke: Macmillan.

RICHARDSON, J. J. (2000) 'Government, Interest Groups and Policy Change', *Political Studies* 48: 1006–25.

—— and JORDAN, G. (1979) *Governing under Pressure*. Oxford: Martin Robertson.

RIDDELL, P. (1998) *Parliament under Pressure*. London: Gollancz.

RIDDELL, P. (2000) *Parliament under Blair.* London: Politico's.

—— (2001) 'Blair as Prime Minister', in A. Seldon (ed.), *The Blair Effect: The Blair Government 1997–2001.* London: Little, Brown.

RIEGER, E. (2000) 'The Common Agricultural Policy', in H. Wallace and W. Wallace (eds.), *Policy-Making in the European Union.* Oxford: Oxford University Press.

ROBINS, K. (1997) 'What in the World's Going On?', in P. du Gay (ed.), *Production of Culture/ Cultures of Production.* London: Sage.

ROBINSON, W. I. (2001) 'Social Theory and Globalization: The Rise of a Transnational State', *Theory and Society* 30: 157–200.

ROLLINGS, N. (1994) 'Poor Mr. Butskell: A Short Life, Wrecked by Schizophrenia?', *Twentieth Century British History:* 5(2) 183–205.

ROSE, R. (1980) (ed.) *Challenge to Governance: Studies in Overloaded Polities.* London: Sage.

ROSE, M. (1991) *The Post-Modern and the Post-Industrial.* Cambridge: Cambridge University Press.

—— (2000) 'When and Why Does a Prime Minister Change?', in R. Rhodes (ed.), *Transforming British Government,* ii: *Changing Roles and Relationships.* London: Macmillan.

—— (2001) *The Prime Minister in a Shrinking World.* Oxford: Polity Press.

ROSENAU, J. (1992) 'Governance, Order and Change in World Politics', in J. Rosenau and E. O. Czempiel (eds.), *Governance without Government.* Cambridge: Cambridge University Press.

—— (2000) 'Change, Complexity and Governance in a Globalizing Space', in J. Pierre (ed.), *Debating Governance.* Oxford: Oxford University Press.

RUSSELL, L., SCOTT, D., and WILDING, P. (1997) 'The Funding of Local Voluntary Organisations', *Policy and Politics* 24: 395–412.

SAMPSON, A. (1962). *The Anatomy of Britain.* London: Hodder & Stoughton.

SANDERS, D. (1990) *Losing an Empire, Finding a Role: British Foreign Policy since 1945.* London: Macmillan.

SAUNDERS, P. (1985) 'Corporatism and Urban Service Provision', in W. Grant (ed.), *The Political Economy of Corporatism.* London: Macmillan.

SAVAGE, S., and ATKINSON, R. (eds.) (2001) *Public Policy under Blair.* Basingstoke: Palgrave.

SAWARD, M. (1997) 'In Search of the Hollow Crown', in Weller et al. (1997).

SBRAGIA, A. (2000) 'The European Union as Coxswain: Governance by Steering', in J. Pierre (ed.), *Debating Governance.* Oxford: Oxford University Press.

SCHAFFER, B. B. (1957) 'The Idea of a Ministerial Department', *Australian Journal of Politics and History* 3: 59–78.

SCHOLTE, J. (1997) 'The Globalization of World Politics', in Baylis and Smith (1997).

SCHOLTE J. A. (2000) *Globalization: A Critical Introduction.* London: Macmillan.

SCOTT, J. (1994) *Poverty and Wealth.* London: Longman.

SELDON, A. (1981) *Churchill's Indian Summer: The Conservative Government 1951–55.* London: Hodder & Stoughton.

—— (1994) 'The Rise and Fall (and Rise Again?) of the Post-War Consensus', in B. Jones et al. (eds.), *Politics UK.* Hemel Hempstead: Harvester Wheatsheaf.

—— (1997) *Major: A Political Life.* London: Weidenfeld & Nicolson.

SHARPE, L. J. (1985) 'The Labour Party and the Geography of Inequality: A Puzzle', in D. Kavanagh (ed.), *The Politics of the Labour Party.* London: Allen & Unwin.

SKLAIR, L. (1995) *Sociology of the Global System*. Hemel Hempstead: Harvester Wheatsheaf.

—— (1998) 'Transnational Practices and the Analysis of the Global System', paper presented at the London School of Economics, Transnational Communities Programme Seminar Series, May.

—— (2002) *Globalization: Capitalism and Its Alternatives* (3rd edn). Oxford: Oxford University Press.

SMITH, M. J. (1993) *Pressure, Power and Policy: State Autonomy and Policy Networks in Britain and the United States*. Hemel Hempstead: Harvester Wheatsheaf.

—— (1994) 'The Core Executive and the Resignation of Mrs Thatcher', *Public Administration* 69: 235–55.

—— (1995) 'Pluralism', in D. Marsh and G. Stoker (eds.), *Theory and Methods in Political Science*. London: Macmillan.

—— (1999) *The Core Executive in Britain*. Basingstoke: Macmillan.

SPENCE, D. (1992) 'The Role of British Civil Servants in European Lobbying: The British Case', in S. Mazey and J. J. Richardson (eds.), *Lobbying in the European Community*. Oxford: Oxford University Press.

SQUIRES, M. (1999) 'Change and Continuity: An Appraisal of Railway Policy Making in Great Britain'. PhD, University of Sheffield.

STALKER, J. (1988) *Stalker*. London: Harrap.

STEPHENS, P. (1996) *Politics and the Pound: The Conservatives' Struggle with Sterling*. London: Macmillan.

STOKER, G. (1998) 'Governance as Theory: Five Propositions', *International Social Science Journal* 50: 17–28.

STONES, R. (1988) 'The Myth of Betrayal: Structure and Agency in the Labour Government's Policy of Non-Devaluation 1964–70'. PhD, University of Essex.

—— (1992) 'Labour and International Finance', in D. Marsh and R. A. W. Rhodes (eds.), *Policy Networks in British Government*. Oxford: Oxford University Press.

STRANGE, S. (1971) *Sterling and British Policy*. Oxford: Oxford University Press.

—— (1998) *Mad Money*. Manchester: Manchester University Press.

SYMONS, J. (1957) *The General Strike*. London: Readers' Union.

TANT, A. P. (1993) *British Government: The Triumph of Elitism*. Aldershot: Dartmouth.

TAYLOR, M. (1996) 'What are the Key Influences on the Work of Voluntary Agencies?', in D. Billis and M. Harris (eds.), *Voluntary Agencies*. London: Macmillan.

T'HART, P. (1993) 'Symbols, Rituals and Power: the Lost Dimension of Crisis-Management', *Journal of Contingencies and Crisis Management* 1(1): 36–50.

THATCHER, M. (1993) *The Downing Street Years*. London: HarperCollins.

THEAKSTON, K. (1995) *The Civil Service since 1945*. Oxford: Blackwell.

—— (1998) 'New Labour, New Whitehall?', *Public Policy and Administration* 13: 13–34.

THOMPSON, H. (1996) *The British Conservative Government and the European Exchange Rate Mechanism, 1979–1994*. London: Pinter.

TOMLINSON, J. (2001) *The Politics of Decline: Understanding Post-war Britain*. Harlow: Longman.

TOWNSEND, P. (1979). *Poverty in the United Kingdom*. Harmondsworth: Penguin.

TOYNBEE, P., and WALKER, P. (2001) *Did Things Get Better? An Audit of Labour's Success and Failures*. London: Penguin.

Treasury (2001) 'Aims and Objectives', www.hmtreasury.gov.uk/About/about_aimsobject.cfm

Tsoukalis, L. (2000) 'Economic and Monetary Union', in H. Wallace and W. Wallace (eds.), *Policy-Making in the European Union*. Oxford: Oxford University Press.

Walden, G. (2001) *The New Elites*. London: Penguin.

Wallace, H. (2000a) 'The Institutional Setting', in H. Wallace and W. Wallace (eds.), *Policy-Making in the European Union*. Oxford: Oxford University Press.

—— (2000b) 'The Policy Process', in H. Wallace and W. Wallace (eds.), *Policy-Making in the European Union*. Oxford: Oxford University Press.

Walsh, K. (1995) *Public Services and Market Mechanisms*. London: Macmillan.

Ward, H., Grundig, F., and Zorick, E. (2001) 'Marching at the Pace of the Slowest: A Model of International Climate-Change Negotiations', *Political Studies*, 49: 438–61.

Weiss, L. (1998) *The Myth of the Powerless State*. Cambridge: Polity Press.

Weller, P. (2000) 'In Search of Governance', in Davis and Keating (2000).

—— Bakvis, H., and Rhodes, R. (eds.) (1997) *The Hollow Crown: Countervailing Trends in Core Executives*. Basingstoke: Macmillan.

Whiteley, P. (1983) *The Labour Party in Crisis*. London: Methuen.

Wilson, H. (1971) *The Labour Government 1964–1970*. Harmondsworth: Penguin.

—— (1976) *The Governance of Britain*. London: Weidenfeld & Nicolson.

Wilson, R. (1998) 'Modernising Central Government: The Role of the Civil Service', speech at the Civil Service Conference, London, 13 Oct.

Woolcock, S. (2000) 'European Trade Policy', in H. Wallace and W. Wallace (eds.), *Policy-Making in the European Union*. Oxford: Oxford University Press.

World Bank (1992) *Governance and Development*. Washington, DC: World Bank.

Young, H. (1999) 'The Final Triumph of All the Butchers and Whisperers', *Guardian*, 25 May.

INDEX